Let's Have a Talk:
Conversations with Women
on Art and Culture

Let's Have a Talk:
Conversations with Women
on Art and Culture

Lauren O'Neill-Butler

Karma

for Octavia and Inès

Table of Contents

Introduction
Lauren O'Neill-Butler

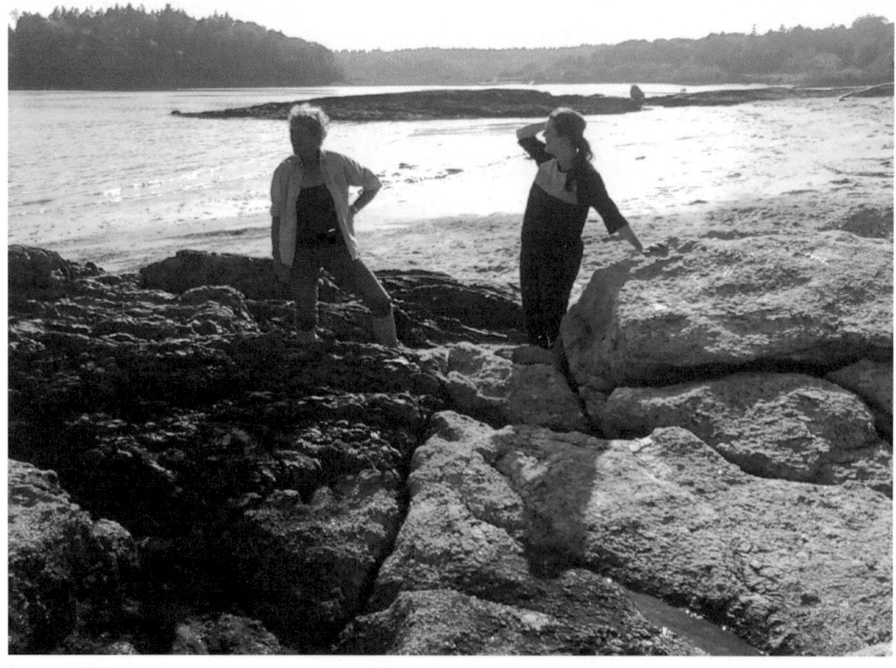

Lucy Lippard and Lauren O'Neill-Butler in Maine, August 2012.

The idea for this book took root in late August 2012, while I was driving from a wedding in Camden, Maine, to Lucy Lippard's home off the state's rugged coast. She had kindly agreed to an interview on her inspiring life and work, in advance of a show opening at the Brooklyn Museum the following month (*Materializing "Six Years": Lucy R. Lippard and the Emergence of Conceptual Art*). Adam Putnam, a friend and artist who also happened to be in Maine, was helping me film the interview—a big relief as I loathe managing a camera and a voice recorder while keeping a conversation lively, although I have been known to do it. The chance to meet with Lucy for an intergenerational dialogue on her life and work was thrilling. I've long respected her integrity as a writer who merges activism with her criticism and the ways in which she has transformed contemporary art history—primarily by speaking directly to artists.

At some point during the ride Adam asked me how I'd arranged this visit. Through email and then a phone call, as usual, I told him—I had just spoken to Lucy and she said she'd heard that I'd interviewed some of her friends, and that it had gone well. It then hit me how much of the interviewing I'd done at that point—Lippard was the eighty-second published piece—worked in that intuitive way: through constellations of meetings and introductions, recollections of past conversations, and sometimes a chance shot in the dark to see if someone was game. I never had a strict agenda and yet, by the end of 2020, I ended up with 150 interviews. I consider these as fragments adding up to a whole, which is, paradoxically and pleasurably, always a work in progress. I'm not sure the project will ever be completed, or why it would ever need to end.

The majority of these interviews were published online in *Artforum*'s interviews column, which I edited for eleven years. In each piece, a subject talks about their work in as-told-to format. These were usually based on a short interview, which was then transcribed and edited into a document. The ease and flow I eventually gained with this method led me to feel as though I could try to speak with anyone and everyone, like a Douglas Huebler–esque conceptual art project. It is an ongoing, seemingly endless form of collaborating. During 2020's pandemic summer, Emmanuel Olunkwa and I cofounded *November* magazine, an online publication that began with interviews with thinkers about art, politics, media, architecture, and philosophy. Alongside coeditors Dawn Chan, Aria Dean, and Alec Mapes-Frances, *November* quickly became one of my most treasured alliances and broadened my thinking about the nature of interviewing.

What is it to interview someone? And what is it to take the transcription of that event and collaboratively edit it into an as-told-to statement? For one thing, it's never the same. For me, it has been all about giving priority to the artists' voices, while attempting to reach a broad range of people. It's also a way of taking oneself out of the conversation just enough to provide a platform for someone else. It's about downsizing ego. It's about listening. This dovetails with my own critical writing on artists and art, and its primary mode of empathetic projection— of not regarding an artist as other. By speaking directly to artists and producing, in their own words, a study of their works and the social conditions underpinning them, I discovered new ways to think about how art is made and what that might mean to both artist and audience. Very often, current art writing is simply news, critical analysis, market reporting, or a journalistic feature. It is my hope to present a corrective and show that the artworks discussed herein are never simply symp-tomatic of an era. The artists were usually ahead of their time, anyway, a true (if well-worn) chestnut.

The incredible variation among the people I've interviewed has required a flexible style of asking questions and editing. Sometimes the edits have felt downright bizarre—a mashing up of language and mean-ing. In other cases, the result has traveled straight from the speaker to the page with barely any work or prodding on my end. In each piece, I strived for naturalness and for a relaxed yet rigorous voice. Since moving to New York City in 2003, I've also felt a need to escape the limitations of an excessively scholarly approach. Even in my art crit-icism, I've attempted to write to an audience both new to *and* well versed in any given subject. Achieving that was never easy, but I always pictured a reader just arriving at a larger cultural conversation about art, and I wanted them to feel invited and included.

Several of the interviews focus on what it was like to be living as an artist in the 1960s and '70s: the intergenerational conflict and political turmoil that marked those years, the vast differences (and sometimes vile similarities) between that world and today's. Building on waves of social and feminist histories, my method of interviewing was meant to address a gap in today's prevailing and dominant narratives of art. In their otherwise divergent pieces, Lynda Benglis, Yoko Ono, Joan Jonas, and Monir Shahroudy Farmanfarmaian each discuss these years—what it was like when they first moved to New York City, what the art scene looked like to them then, which artists they were inspired by, and much more. In a long interview with the trailblazing art dealer Virginia Dwan, she talks about the establishment of her gallery in

Los Angeles in 1959 and the landmark exhibitions she organized in the 1960s of early Minimal, Conceptual, and Land art. Julia Bryan-Wilson's 2011 interview about her book *Art Workers: Radical Practice in the Vietnam War Era* could be looked at as a complement to Dwan's interview, and the ways in which such dematerialized art merged with artistic protest.

I began working at *Artforum* in 2008, a few months before Barack Obama was elected president for the first time, and at the moment the world felt like it was bursting with endless possibility. In various ways, these interviews reflect on subsequent world events—which leavened that political positivity into a "cruel optimism," à la Lauren Berlant—including the global economic crises and recessions from 2008 onward; Occupy Wall Street in 2010; the Arab Spring in 2011; major climate events (such as the 2011 Great East Japan Earthquake); the US announcement of the end of the Iraq War in 2011; the rise of the Islamic State; the emergence of Black Lives Matter in 2013; and the #MeToo movement in 2017.

The eventual arrangement of these pieces into a book after a decade or so became an aspect of my work, and I knew I would have to develop criteria for inclusion—the binding thread. I also anticipated editing myself, which for me is what writing really *is*, in the end. Some of the interviews didn't quite convey the artist's voice, particularly if they were discussing collaborations. Also, the various roundtables I had spearheaded didn't fit the format. The activity of rereading the pieces and thinking about how to present them was consequently also a process of remembering what was happening politically and personally at the time each article was published. That I had interviewed Bryan-Wilson on the Art Workers' Coalition of 1969 and was speaking in 2011 with W.A.G.E. (Working Artists in the Greater Economy), who were coming up with a plan for how to implement artists' fee schedules within cultural institutions, was not lost on me. By having these pieces sit near each other in the book, it's easy to see how history connects to the present, and how that relation becomes, in a way, a "continuous present," to borrow an idea from Gertrude Stein. Such resonances and relations can be found throughout the book and are implicit in the intergenerational approach I discussed earlier.

I chose to present the interviews in alphabetical order because it felt, under the sign of Stein, both formal and random. When I asked the writer Lorrie Moore how she put together her 2018 book of collected essays and criticism, she said: "It certainly was the first time I read them all in chronological order—which I don't recommend." She then proffered "how the book should be read": "in random bits and pieces here and there." It's my hope that the reader will pick this book up from time to time and flip through to something they want to read right then. That's exactly what the process of doing the interviews felt like: while landscaping the cultural fields there was always at least one person doing something in that very instant who I wanted to talk to, and who I knew could add something vital to the larger cultural conversation. Plus, as Moore rightly notes, "one is always writing what one would like to read."

These interviews have kept me in that conversation. What I ultimately wanted to read was something elastic enough to capture the personal and the political, the subjective and the social, simultaneously. I wanted a book that would add up to a "long, spoken essay on the state of contemporary art and culture," as writer Chris Kraus phrased it when I first asked her for initial thoughts on this project. I wanted that spoken quality to emerge, to be palpable, and that's why I conducted most of these interviews in person, face-to-face—at a kitchen table, ideally. As Suzanne Lacy said in her interview: "Now is an interesting time to reconsider the aesthetic and ethical concerns of the '70s because, to put it plainly, the 'horses' mouths' are still around."

Throughout the book you'll notice various ways of reflecting on a changing political moment: consider Judy Chicago telling me in 2007 that "[w]e are about to see ... a global feminist art movement," which "isn't about giving white middle-class career women more rights. It's about a fundamental change on our planet." In her 2011 interview, Mary Kelly echoed this change, and, importantly, a constant need to reinvent: "Quite a while ago, when I had a show at the New Museum in 1990, I began to ask if in fact this moment of feminism and psychoanalysis was really over, or if it had any meaning for people now," she said. "I realized it just keeps reinventing itself in many different ways."

Some of the principal catastrophes of recent years are touched upon in these pages. Observe Rebecca Solnit speaking in 2009 on her book written in the wake of Hurricane Katrina and Sakiko Sugawa talking about the work of Social Kitchen in Kyoto after the 2011 earthquake in Japan. In 2014, Lucy and I spoke on the record again: this time, we focused on climate change, fracking, and oil drilling in the southwestern United States, which she had written about for a new book. In the summer of 2020, I had the honor of speaking with Adrian Piper (again) and Nell Painter about the coronavirus pandemic, the toppling of statues, and racial justice protests.

This charting of attitudes and reactions speaks volumes about the past decade and that's why it felt important to compile and reposition these interviews into a book. There is also an issue of access: my interview with Chicago in 2007 was only published in print (in *Bitch* magazine) and is therefore harder to find than the online-only articles. Moreover, the interview with Lippard from Maine and my interviews with fierce pussy, Andrea Fraser, Eleanor Antin, Joan Semmel, and Carolee Schneemann were all produced originally as videos, and so I have edited the transcripts for this book. More critically, the reason to bring these pieces together is to show how these artists have been in dialogue on particular topics—from identity politics to climate change—and to register their responses to the radical sociopolitical upheavals of our times.

The critical significance of this assembling can be clarified by one of my favorite thinkers, Hannah Arendt, and her fundamental ideas on political action and the power of public speech and conversation. For Arendt, action and speech are closely related, but speech takes priority; it's how we reveal ourselves to the world but it's also how we show our uniqueness, our distinct personalities, our abilities, and our traits. It is vastly different from the privacy of the heart. Without public speech, all action loses its particular and individual agency.

The world is not simply true or false. That's why Arendt emphasizes that to know anything about, well, *anything*, a person needs not just to speak freely but also to listen, freely, in a shared public space where people can "exchange their opinions and perspectives with one another, over against one another" (*The Promise of Politics*, 128). This action promotes an understanding of what links and separates people, how our worldviews diverge. In a shared public space, one can ask how people are listening, what listening changes in oneself, and how, consequently, that can lead to more directly transformative means, such as confrontation and social change.

What does it mean to open up space for another person's voice to be heard? That basic question underpins the interviews collected in these pages. While rereading them, I realized that my approach has always been to edit with the lightest touch possible, and to get out of the way so someone could talk—openly and freely. When I asked for her thoughts on this, art historian Katy Siegel summed it up perfectly and I knew I had to quote her: "Speech, and especially conversation, treats thinking and feeling as material acts, subject to the conditions of the room, of bodies, of the weather, and mood—of response to another person. It's an act of making, and making together, that is alive in the way that the best art and music are as well."

Adrian Piper

Adrian Piper, *Food for the Spirit #7*, 1971, gelatin silver print, 15 × 14 ½ inches (38 × 36.8 cm).

July 5, 2018
The New York Times

Adrian Piper is a conceptual artist and analytic philosopher based in Berlin. She received her doctorate in philosophy from Harvard University in 1981, under the supervision of John Rawls, and went on to publish articles and books principally on metaethics, the history of ethics, and the thought of Immanuel Kant. She has taught at many universities, including Georgetown (where, in 1987, she became the first tenured African American female professor in the field of philosophy), Harvard, Stanford, and at Wellesley, which terminated her full professorship in 2008, after she moved to Berlin and decided not to return to the United States until her name was removed from the Suspicious Travelers' Watch List. A 2018 retrospective of her work, Adrian Piper: A Synthesis of Intuitions, 1965–2016, *at the Museum of Modern Art, was the largest show the museum has ever assembled for a living artist.*

LOB: You arrived at philosophy in the 1960s through your work as an artist. Judging from your retrospective at MoMA, it seems the two fields were never mutually exclusive for you. Is that correct?

AP: Yes, that's definitely true for me. Each field calls on different capacities of the mind—philosophy on intellection, critical reflection, and cognitive discrimination; art on perception, intuition, and visualization—even though bringing a work in either field to completion requires the involvement of all of these capacities. But I would go further and suggest that any two disciplines are never in themselves necessarily mutually exclusive for anyone. Those who are inclined to exercise their abilities in more than one creative discipline (and philosophy is no less a creative discipline than art) are not usually also inclined to the kind of binary, either/or thinking that permits activity in one only at the expense of another.

The pressure to choose between them usually comes from external sources, such as families, colleagues in either or both fields, or administrative officials. I was very fortunate to grow up in a family that encouraged all forms of creative expression. The APRA Foundation Berlin Multi-Disciplinary Fellowship tries to give some of that back, by promoting multidisciplinarity as a counterbalance to socially imposed uniformity and unidimensional creative development. I believe we're going to need to cultivate these multiple inner resources in order to successfully navigate the challenges of globalization and cross-cultural travel.

I never consciously aim for or even think about any particular connection between my work in art and my work in philosophy. But what I notice in retrospect is an exchange of information between them of a sort that informs both, each in its own way. As to how that manifests in each field, that depends on the specifics of the philosophical text or artwork in question. The creative process in art has its own logic, and the creative process in philosophy has a different logic. In both cases, the process tells me what I need to do, and I just do it. Thinking about what it means and how it all relates comes later—much later.

LOB: Could we take an example from the show, to discuss how an artwork works philosophically?

AP: There are several works in the MoMA retrospective that deploy the device of mimicry, of echoing back familiar rationalizations. For example, you'll find that device in *Four Intruders Plus Alarm Systems* (1980) and *Decide Who You Are #15: You Don't Want Me Here* (1992). During the time these works were being produced, my philosophy work was undergoing a couple of processes that I now see as connected. First, I was making my way through the jungle of higher education in philosophy (which I describe in detail in *Escape to Berlin: A Travel Memoir*) and also developing the account of pseudorationality that informs the second half of Volume II of my philosophic work *Rationality and the Structure of the Self*. I believe that my experiences in academia were the source of that account and that the uses of mimicry in these and other artworks were reflections or examples of it. But as to which came first, and what influenced what, these are questions I find impossible to answer.

LOB: What would you say to someone who believes art can't do much in terms of resisting oppression and transforming racist attitudes?

AP: I would ask such individuals what they think *can* do much in resisting oppression and transforming racist attitudes. I would ask them whether they think Rosa Parks's *in*action, of simply sitting there in her seat on the bus and refusing to move, did much in terms of resisting oppression and transforming racist attitudes. If it turns out that the only initiative that, in their view, can do much in terms of resisting oppression and transforming racist attitudes would be a massive and continuing organizing effort funded by the Gates Foundation, which is unlikely to happen, I would infer that this belief conveniently relieves them of the responsibility of resisting oppression and transforming racist attitudes whenever and wherever they encounter them in the course of their daily lives.

For example, do such individuals protest to the policeman who is patting down an African American teenager on the subway platform? Or do they look away? Do they refuse to cooperate with the workplace scapegoating of the lone African American token in the office? Or do they go along with it in order to keep their jobs? Do they seek out and patronize African American–owned places of business? Or are those places of business too far away to be convenient? Do they live in an integrated neighborhood? Or do they feel that would be too unsafe? If emulating what Rosa Parks did on her way home from work is too much for them, then they have no right to complain that art does too little.

LOB: For decades you've written about Kantian theory but you're also trained in Vedic philosophies. In terms of exploring self-consciousness, what connects both for you?

AP: Despite my best efforts, I have been unable to find any concrete evidence that Kant had direct knowledge of Vedic philosophies. But the similarities are so many and so striking that it's hard to believe he didn't. Kant's concept of a detached, observing consciousness that unifies our experience is very similar to the Samkhyan concept of Purusha. His analysis of truly ethical action as justified by its intentions rather than its consequences is very similar to the yogic doctrine of Vairagya in the Bhagavad Gita. And his transcendental idealism shares so much in common with Shankara's Vedantic doctrine of Maya that they could almost be in direct dialogue.

To study both Kant and Vedic philosophy in conjunction is to supply for the Vedic concepts a detailed philosophical analysis in the Western tradition, and to supply for Kant a concrete practical application in the Vedic tradition. Kant provides the road map, Vedic philosophy the destination. Together they bridge the gap between theory and practice that was opened by the self-protective reaction to Socrates's execution on the part of subsequent Greek philosophers.

LOB: Your major philosophical book *Rationality and the Structure of the Self*, Volumes 1 and 2 (http://adrianpiper.com/rss/index.shtml), is self-published and available to read on your personal website. Why did you take that route?

AP: Actually both volumes are published by my foundation, the APRA Foundation Berlin. I made the decision to go this route because, after Cambridge University Press had accepted both volumes for publication, its marketing department then demanded that I cut one hundred pages from each volume in order to make it easier to sell them. Open-access publication has made it as easy as possible to read them, and therefore virtually *impossible* to deliberately misrepresent their content. These benefits are much more important to me than any financial ones.

LOB: Why focus on rationality and anomaly?

AP: Rationality is the permanent and foundational obsession of the field, whether in the foreground or in the background, because it is constitutive of the methodology and content of the discipline. But attention to deviations from rationality is usually confined to mere failures to meet its requirements—for example, failures to reason clearly, to make fine-grained distinctions, to calculate consequences correctly, to apply the right principles to the appropriate cases, etc.

The really interesting deviations—cases that call into question the adequacy of those principles themselves—are systematically ignored, in order to protect the status quo of race and gender homogeneity in the profession. These are the deviations that require the revision or replacement of these principles in order to explain entirely new empirical discoveries—for example, of a mathematical genius who happens to be a woman! Or a "white"-looking person who publicly acknowledges her African ancestry! Or a person who violates both masculine and feminine stereotypes! From the point of view of traditional habits of reasoning and conceptualization, these are human anomalies, analogous to empirical anomalies in the physical sciences.

Human anomalies receive little or no attention in philosophy, because they destabilize those deeply embedded conventions of thought in the field that undergird most of the research that goes on in it. Now, if you happen to *be* one of those anomalies, this stubborn, phlegmatic resistance to your very existence becomes very interesting indeed. You can't help thinking, What is making these smart people suddenly so stupid? And even worse, What is making these nice people suddenly so evil? What are the cognitive mechanisms by which *their* abilities to think clearly, make fine-grained distinctions, apply moral principles consistently, etc., are suddenly deteriorating noticeably in your presence?

Once you start asking these questions, you're in the same ballpark as Thomas Kuhn was when he started asking similar questions about anomalous empirical events as a cause of professional resistance to theory change in the physical sciences. Resistance to anomaly is always about a choice to protect the familiar and convenient against the disruptive effect of difference; and resistance to human anomaly in particular is always about a choice to protect the personal advantages of segregation against the disruptive effect of integration by the Other. Kant's *Critique of Pure Reason* provides the best and most thorough analysis of this phenomenon I've ever seen.

LOB: You also demonstrate how philosophical controversies that lit up the eighteenth century are still burning strong today—as so many protest movements are also showing us, including Black Lives Matter. What strategies, if any, could that movement take away from your writings?

AP: My work in philosophy doesn't presume to tell anyone what to do. It addresses the foundations of ethics—metaethics—rather than normative ethics. So it doesn't prescribe any particular strategies for action to anyone. These can be meaningfully formulated only by those who are directly involved in and therefore maximally well informed about the circumstances under which action is required.

However, perhaps my work can offer a way of understanding what is at stake in the Black Lives Matter movement that may be of use. The basic argument of *Rationality and the Structure of the Self* is organized around the distinction between egocentric and transpersonal rationality. Transpersonal rationality consists in hard-wired cognitive dispositions that define us as human beings: consistency, coherence, impartiality, impersonality, intellectual discrimination, foresight, deliberation, self-reflection, and self-control. Egocentric rationality consists in placing these dispositions in the service of satisfying our personal desires and advancing our self-interest.

It's easy to conceive the Black Lives Matter movement as merely advancing the self-interest of African Americans in surviving and flourishing within a society whose self-interest is systemically opposed to this. This reduces the impetus for protest to a conflict of interests between those who join or support this movement and those who resist it—as though all that were at stake were whether or not police are justified in being so terrified of an African American teenager that shooting him in the back is a defensible preventive measure. To conceive the issue merely in these terms turns it into a contest as to whose interests are to prevail—those who see trigger-happy police as protecting their interests or those who see them as sabotaging theirs. This view of the situation lends itself to the conclusion that the United States is still fighting the same race war it was in 1860.

There's a lot of truth to this view. But it ignores the fact that the Black Lives Matter movement is not fighting merely to protect and advance the interests of African Americans. It is fighting to cultivate a fundamental level of humanity in all Americans. The transpersonally rational dispositions I've listed constitute the ancient foundation of the historically recent idea of a universal human right that extends basic freedoms, responsibilities, rights, and resources to every human being, regardless of their interests—not merely to those whom the police are personally inclined to protect. That African Americans have survived and flourished for four hundred years by resisting an environment devoted to dehumanizing them demonstrates quite conclusively how highly their capacities for transpersonal rationality are developed. The statement that Black Lives Matter is a reminder to those whose perpetuation of that environment has effectively dehumanized *them* to develop those capacities just as highly; i.e., that their own humanity also matters.

LOB: Do you have an ideal reader for these books?

AP: To really read any discursive text, whether a philosophical tract or a legal contract, is a disturbing and cognitively disorienting experience, because it means allowing another person's thoughts to intrude into your own and rearrange your beliefs and assumptions—often not in ways to which you would consent if warned in advance. Even when you deliberately decide to learn something new by reading, you put yourself, your thoughts, and your most cherished suppositions in the hands of the author and trust her or him not to reorganize your mind so thoroughly that you no longer recognize where or who you are. It's very scary; hard, painstaking work of determined concentration under the best of circumstances. So particularly with philosophical texts, the whole point of which is to reorganize your thinking, people often don't really read them at all; they merely take a mental snapshot of the passage that enables them to form a gestalt impression of its content, without scrutinizing it too closely.

This "snapshot" approach to reading protects the reader against the potentially disruptive mental effects of the text, while enabling enough of it to filter through to ensure at least a minimal comprehension of its content. But it also enables misunderstanding and misrepresentation of what the text actually says that can be so profound as to invalidate the gesture of reading it in the first place. In the last forty years, a highly regarded tradition in one part of the field of Kant scholarship has developed that is predicated on deliberately disregarding what Kant actually says. My worst nightmare for *Rationality and the Structure of the Self* is a reader who approaches the text with this "snapshot" habit of reading. I worked hard to make the prose style of this work as clear and accessible as possible, given the complexity of the argument. All I ask of an ideal reader is that they take the time to really read it.

LOB: You've said that an epistemic skepticism drives your work. Could you elaborate?

AP: As an attitude rather than a philosophical position, epistemic skepticism consists in always second-guessing your own judgments—about yourself, other people, and situations; always monitoring those judgments to make sure you're seeing clearly, have the facts right, aren't making any unfounded inferences or deceiving yourself, etc. Women are particularly skilled at this because their judgment, credibility, and authority start to come under attack during puberty, as part of the process of gender socialization. They are made to feel uncertain about themselves, their place in society, and their right to their own opinions. If that socialization doesn't work, they can't be made to obey, to defer and to depend on others to make important decisions for them. Obviously this is a horrible, misogynistic practice, now known as "gaslighting" after the 1944 George Cukor film. But the benefit is precisely this self-critical attitude—of careful review of and reflection on the adequacy of one's own thought processes.

This attitude actually does put into concrete practice the philosophical position of epistemic skepticism that has a very long and honorable history going back to Descartes and even further back to Socrates. It has had a very beneficial effect on my work in philosophy because my judgment, my credibility, and my authority to make philosophical pronouncements started coming under attack from the moment I entered the professional part of the discipline. The challenges, slights, and attempts at intimidation were unremitting. In part, I have the self-confidence my parents gave me to thank for surviving them. But there is no doubt in my mind that this female reflex of self-doubt and self-criticism also had a lot to do with it. I don't deceive myself into believing that all of my philosophical views are right. But thanks to that reflex, they are well grounded.

LOB: What do you consider among your most important achievements?

AP: I can name four off the top of my head:

(1) To have taken care of my mother during the last two years before her death from emphysema.

(2) To have escaped from the United States with my life.

(3) To have successfully treated most of my post-traumatic stress disorder symptoms myself, by writing *Escape to Berlin*.

(4) To have finished *Rationality and the Structure of the Self* at the same standard of quality I apply when I criticize other philosophers' work—thereby demonstrating to my own satisfaction that it's not an unrealistic or impossible standard to meet. Of course you do have to be willing to get kicked out of the field in order to meet it. You'll notice that I haven't included the MoMA retrospective in this list. That's because that was not my achievement, but rather the curators' and MoMA's achievement. My contribution was to refuse to ship the work unless MoMA formally, in writing, respected the curators' final selection of works exactly as they had compiled it. That meant significant budgetary adaptations on MoMA's part; and the fact that everyone involved rose to that challenge in order to serve the best interests of the institution commands my undying gratitude and admiration. It's why MoMA is MoMA.

LOB: What are you working on now? How do you feel it relates to your past?

AP: In philosophy, I'm finishing up my exegetical study "Kant's Metaethics: First Critique Foundations of His Theory of Action." The book has two main aims: first, to demonstrate that it's not possible to make sense of Kant's ethics without a firm basis of reference in the *Critique of Pure Reason*; and second, to show how that interpretation of Kant's ethics can help solve certain long-standing problems in Ramsey-Savage decision theory—while, reciprocally, that standard version of decision theory can help solve certain long-standing problems in Kant's ethics. These two fields have regarded each other as mortal enemies across the purportedly unbridgeable Kant–Hume divide for over a century. It's time to put that animus aside and bring the conceptual resources of each into a project of mutual cooperation.

My conviction that this is the right direction for Kant scholarship to take has been growing steadily ever since I first started reading Kant as an art student at the School of Visual Arts roughly fifty years ago. It received a huge boost when I began studying decision theory with Rawls at Harvard roughly forty-five years ago. Thinking about the relationship between these two bodies of scholarship has been a beacon of light—of reason, reflection, and the pleasure of pure thought for its own sake—that has nourished my love of philosophy and helped me to survive the punishment meted out by the profession. Because actually doing philosophy has always functioned for me as a sanctuary and a solace, there is nothing the profession could do to me that would ever destroy the pleasure I take in it. Looking back, I'm quite proud of having protected my commitment to the discipline in the face of all that.

In art, I'm working on a new piece called *The Pixel Grayscale System of Human Classification*. The title is pretty much self-explanatory. It proposes a constructive, value-neutral alternative to the sick and outmoded system of "racial" classification we've inherited from nineteenth-century pseudoscience. Of course it will be very inconvenient for those whose self-worth or social advantages depend on locating themselves within that outmoded system.

But adaptation is the price of progress. I started researching this topic for a biology term paper in high school when I was fourteen. The findings were quite clear, and the science is now over a century old. So it has always been obvious to me that the fantasy of racial

difference has no foundation in genetic fact. It's merely the last out-
post of segregation, the kind that exists only in the minds of those
who think they need it as a source of status and self-differentiation.
I feel the need to present a concrete alternative that might free us to
jettison that crutch and replace it with a solid and realistic criterion of
self-identification that nevertheless cannot be confused with tangen-
tial issues of self-worth or social status.

Adrian Piper

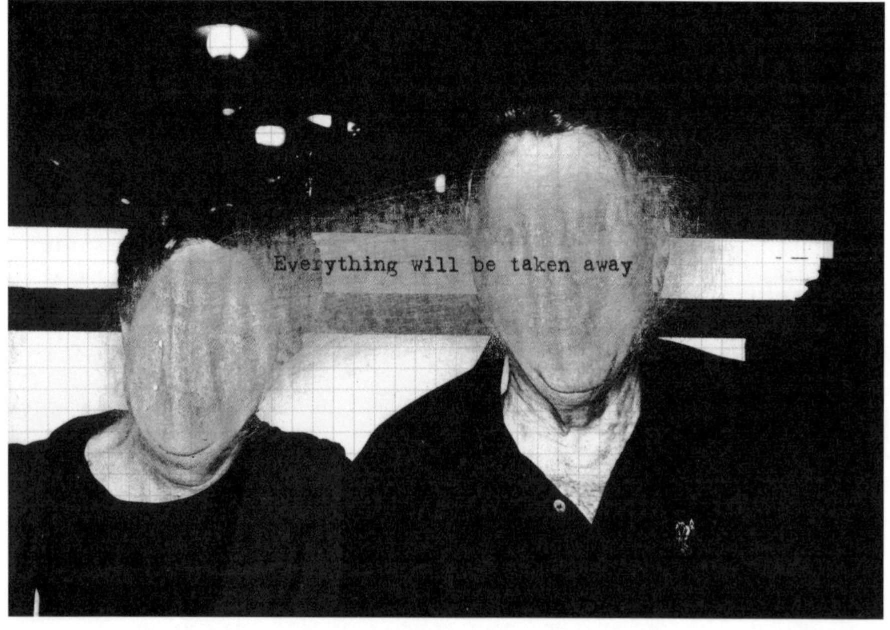

Adrian Piper, *Everything #2.8*, 2003, ink-jet text and sanded photocopy on graph paper, 8 ½ × 11 inches (21.6 × 27.9 cm).

July 17, 2020
November

Adrian Piper is a conceptual artist and analytic philosopher based in Berlin. My first interview with her appeared in the New York Times *in summer 2018, during her retrospective at New York's Museum of Modern Art.* Adrian Piper: A Synthesis of Intuitions, 1965–2016 *was the largest show the museum had ever produced for a living artist. For that piece, I wanted to provide information that other coverage had missed, including key details—in her own words—on her extensive career in philosophy. The interview has remained very dear to me. I often reread it when I'm seeking clarity, guidance, or when I just wonder: What might Adrian say? In 2020, it's been on my mind time and time again. So, I'm grateful to have another opportunity to speak with her, and I am even more proud that she is the first subject to be featured in this new editorial venture.*

LOB: I saw via an update on your website that you reached a personal best with your memorization of the Yoga Sutra in November 2019. How has that been going?

AP: I'm in transition between being able to rattle them off mechanically and absentmindedly from the surface of my mind, and the deeper levels at which I can remain present to absorb their sound and meaning in the moment of chanting them, and allow their full significance to open my mind further. That's a deep dive.

LOB: When you left the United States and academia in the spring of 2005—during an extremely harrowing time in your life, as detailed in your travel memoir *Escape to Berlin* (2018)—you were just beginning to offer philosophy courses based on your lifelong study of yoga and ancient Indian philosophy, including Vedic principles of insight and peace. Could you talk about what that meant prior to parting the ivory tower?

AP: In addition to the protective and supportive function of those courses, which I described in "Philosophy En Route to Reality: A Bumpy Ride," creating them was a way of consolidating and structuring all of the knowledge of the Vedic tradition I had gained through my own practice and studies over the preceding forty years. It was a wonderful, inspiring process just to have to organize all that experience in a transmissible form, and to think long and hard about the best method for communicating the material to American college students in such a way as to make it land in the right place in their minds. Given the ways in which that tradition has been distorted by its American reception (I discuss this in a short essay at the APRA website), the solutions to those challenges weren't obvious. There was a moment in my first semester of teaching Vedanta Ethics and Epistemology when it became necessary to demonstrate Headstand to the class. At that point I knew I was in uncharted territory. It was such a solace and a gift to be able to be totally absorbed in the challenges of this teaching process, given what was going on all around me. My preoccupation with teaching the texts functioned as a kind of spiritual armor that I really needed at that point. I would wish for anyone undergoing similar pressures that they find that place in their mind that can be a sanctuary and refuge from all of it. From that place, the "ivory tower" looks more like a prison.

LOB: On what can one depend on in this time of deluge? What kind of spiritual armor helps?

AP: Here's a simple five-point plan distilled from the principles of nonviolent resistance I learned in the early Civil Rights Movement (a short explanation of its background can be found on my website): (1) Know yourself: Learn to live without self-deception of any kind. Always acknowledge your bad motives up front, never make excuses for your failures, never rationalize your faults. Always look your flaws straight in the face and take responsibility for their consequences, never blame other people when things go wrong for you. Always find out what you did to contribute to that, and don't flinch from owning it. Be compassionate with your failings, but never self-indulgent. Self-deception is the most poisonous obstacle to remaining anchored in reality, and if you can't do that now, you're dead meat. (2) Act honorably: If you practice (1) doggedly, the pain of confronting your imperfections will nudge you toward actions that don't cause you that kind of pain—actions that are honorable even if they're not perfect. Because they're anchored in self-knowledge, they will strengthen your foundation in reality. (3) Honor your mortality: Once you've planted yourself firmly on that path, come to terms with the reality that you are going to die, that your time is limited; and resolve to make the best use of it you can. That means making honorable conduct your top priority and being prepared to sacrifice whatever is necessary, including personal advantage, in order to protect it. You should be prepared to die at any moment without regret, remorse, or self-reproach, knowing that you did your best. (4) Seek its meaning: It also means having, adopting, or developing a metaphysical belief system that enables you to live with and understand the meaning of your mortality. Here there are many options, both religious and nonreligious. The only one that doesn't work at all is materialism, because it can't explain what happens to consciousness after the body dies without violating the law of the conservation of energy. But any metaphysics that can is fine (5) Defend your values: When living and acting honorably becomes more important to you than staying alive at any cost, you are ready to fight effectively for what you believe in, because then you can't be bought, bribed, or bullied into betraying yourself, your cause, or your comrades.

LOB: In a recent op-ed by Tiffanie Drayton, she frames her escape from the United States in terms of being an American refugee. I wondered if that term resonates with you.

AP: It does, yes. Drayton refers to the United Nations definition of refugees as "people who flee their homes because of war, persecution, or violence." The OED defines *persecution* as "A particular course or period of systematic violent oppression; *esp.* one directed against the members of a particular religious or political group, race, etc.; infliction of punishment directed against those holding a particular belief; persistent annoyance or injury; harassment." Incidents of persecution, i.e., the course of systematic punishment, harassment, and violence inflicted over my fifteen years at Wellesley College, are described in overview in *Escape to Berlin: A Travel Memoir*. The formal charges that constituted my lawsuit against the college list and document thirteen of those incidents in detail. The *violent* incidents include the vandalizing of my home; two burglaries within two weeks (on the second break-in, nothing was taken) soon after my release from hospital; the repeated puncturing of my tires before my weekly commute home from the college; and the college's explicit rejection, in writing, of my four doctors' warnings of a "rapid deterioration" in my liver disease should necessary medical accommodations be refused. I fled my home because of these incidents of persecution and violence. So I am a refugee according to the UN definition. But I would want to distinguish sharply between being a refugee and being a victim. The latter term doesn't resonate with me at all. I'm a refugee from American racism, but I'm not a victim of American racism, because my refugee status is the result of my conscious choices; and I accept their consequences without reservation. If I had been willing to pass for "white," if I had accepted and internalized the American caste system, if I hadn't publicly rejected it, ridiculed it, and mocked people whose self-esteem depended on it, I wouldn't have elicited the persecution and violence I experienced there. So I wouldn't have had to leave the United States in order to escape it. I knew at the time that I was defying powerful forces, but I did those things anyway. Had I known in advance the vindictive rage I would call forth, I still would have done them. And had I not left the United States when I did, I would not now be alive to do this interview. But that's fine. It was the price of finding out what really lies behind the smiley-face mask of American "Have-a-nice-day!" civility, in the supposedly cultivated circles in which I was traveling. It's always better to come to terms with the reality, no matter how ugly it is. So I've never had even a moment's regret for any of those choices. I only wish I'd seen the writing on the wall sooner and gotten out sooner. Fifteen years after my escape, I still celebrate it every day, and grieve for those who want to get out but can't. Thanks to the bungled handling of the coronavirus pandemic by your nutcase president, the member states of the European Union have closed all of their borders to American travelers. This is a tragedy in the making, particularly for the vast majority of Americans—of all colors—who have roots in Europe.

LOB: In 2009, you established the APRA Foundation Berlin Multi-Disciplinary Fellowship, which, as you noted in our last interview, promotes "multidisciplinarity as a counterbalance to socially imposed uniformity and unidimensional creative development." Has this fellowship transformed your thinking about multidisciplinary tactics, and if so, how?

AP: It was more the other way around, that realizing how important multidisciplinarity was to my own survival led me to want to nurture it in other people. It's been very satisfying to find out how other such trespassers survive, and to help them flourish. They are the pathfinders for an emerging global culture that demands the flexibility and resources necessary for crossing social boundaries on a daily basis, and contributing productively to whatever subcultures in which they presently find their habitat. Refugees, take note.

LOB: The foundation also supports a dissertation fellowship for philosophy PhD students. Do the two fellowships have to have any connections in theory or practice?

AP: No. They are completely independent. Whereas the Multi-Disciplinary Fellowship furthers the simultaneous development of divergent modes of creative production, the Philosophy Dissertation Fellowship furthers a higher and more comprehensive degree of specialization in one particular field. It requires a prior course of study in philosophy that is not presently offered in full in the vast majority of accredited philosophy departments, because it includes two logic courses plus coursework in Indian, Chinese, Arabic, and Jewish philosophy—in addition to the standard fare. So it may be a while before we can fund any fellows for this one.

LOB: In our previous interview you mentioned you were at work on a piece that offers an "alternative to the sick and outmoded system of 'racial' classification we have inherited from nineteenth-century pseudoscience": *The Pixel Grayscale System of Human Classification*. Might you be able to share any updates on it?

AP: The impact of introducing the idea turned out to be enough for me conceptually. I got bored with the process of actually producing the work, so I've abandoned it.

LOB: What are you working on now?

AP: Only The Shadow knows! ;D For over a year, I've been working on a site-specific piece oriented toward the German context. Unfortunately, it really does have to remain a secret until it opens, for strategic reasons.

LOB: What are your thoughts on two recent developments in Germany: Berlin's new anti-discrimination law and the Green party's call to delete the word *Rasse* from the Constitution?

AP: Of course, there's always a gap between what the law prescribes and what happens in practice. But changes in practice always begin with acts of self-determination, in which we conceptualize what we want the practices to be, formulate and enact principles that encode them, and implement those principles in practice, over an extended period of time, as best we can, given necessarily limited resources, competing priorities, and all-too-human failures of will, nerve, or conscience. The key is always identifying what practices we want to implement badly enough to actually expend the time, energy, and resources necessary to realize them. These recent developments in German jurisprudence show us what transformative principles German society, as mediated by its politicians, is deliberately choosing to actualize and integrate. The project of reformulating Article 3, Paragraph (3) of the Grundgesetz so as to eliminate a concept that everyone knows is a bogus and racist relic of the Nazi era is not only about achieving justice; it's also about bringing the document into closer accord with the facts. Being able to face the facts is part of being a grown-up. Can you imagine this occurring in the context of American politics? Can you imagine either major party in the United States proposing either one of these measures? The very idea of striking the word *race* from the Fifteenth Amendment of the American Constitution would be unthinkable and inappropriate because too much of American history, and the fabric of American identity and character, is woven into this bogus concept. Whereas eliminating the concept of "race" from the German Constitution is a strike against lingering racism in Germany, eliminating it from the American Constitution would be a reinforcement of the racist underpinnings that have structured and corrupted American history since its inception. But since racial discrimination is purportedly a thing of the past in the United States, an anti-discrimination law is unnecessary, right? To me now, it scarcely seems possible that these sick and incoherent fantasies are still part of the deep foundation of American society in the twenty-first century. But they are. By contrast, Germany is right now in the midst of a debate over the feasibility of a scientific study to determine the depth and prevalence of racism in its police forces. But the debate itself is merely a tactical one, as to whether such a study would best serve the aim of reducing racism in Germany. All sides take for granted that racial discrimination is one of Germany's most pressing problems, and all sides are prepared to take the initiative of instituting precautionary measures in order to solve it. They don't deny the existence of the problem, then wait until Germany's major cities explode into riots, violence, mayhem, and murder. That distance, between the American political mindset and the German one, is one of the many reasons I moved here.

LOB: Do you think the great waves of protests worldwide now against police brutality and racism will cause changes in global culture, and if so, how?

AP: No, I'm very sorry to say that I don't see that happening. Just to be clear, the primary targets of these global protests are *American* police brutality and racism. I argue in *Escape to Berlin* that the United States goes through these violent convulsions at least once a generation, but that the structural conditions that cause them are too deeply embedded in American culture to be uprooted. Americans need their racism. Social media may magnify the reach of these events into other countries and cultures and provoke their reactions. But those other countries and cultures already know how America really ticks; and they themselves function differently. There are very few areas of life in which any country in its right mind would take its cue from what's going on in the United States as to how to solve its own problems. At best the United States provides a cautionary tale to other countries as to what not to do. From the outside looking in, its repetitive cycle of incessant police and civilian brutality against African Americans, and the predictable explosions of pain, rage, and rebellion it regularly incites, is a tragic and sickening spectacle. These inevitably recurring events debase America's standing in the world more than any mere diplomatic faux pas ever could. It is precisely because America's status and reputation have been so damaged by these events that it has elicited these global waves of protests against its police brutality and racism. For the global protesters, the opportunities for self-advancement that constituted the "American Dream" are no longer worth the costs.

LOB: Do you think they will cause changes in the art world, and if so, how?

AP: Again, I doubt it, as much as it breaks my heart to say so. These protests move people of conscience to join them, to do what they can to fight the conditions that engender them. But those people are always in the minority, and their best efforts are always necessarily limited. They fight anyway, in order to maintain their self-respect, defend themselves, and help others in whatever ways they can. These are the people for whom the very thought of being seen as complicit is unbearable. But confronted with the choice between actively fighting racism and profiting from its continued existence, most people choose the latter. American racism offers so many blessings to its beneficiaries. Think of all those Americans who believe they would be less than nothing, were they not "white." As Eldridge Cleaver would have put it, they prefer to be part of the problem rather than part of the solution. For those opportunists, the "American Dream" is alive and well.

LOB: I'm sure you're aware of the current US debate around taking down some statues and monuments. What's appropriate: keep them up, put them in a museum, or destroy them?

AP: Erasing the past in order to solve the problems it presents is a very American approach, and it never works. Physical artifacts are the embodiments of the time, energy, and resources invested in creating them, so they express the values of the society that allocated those resources. We must never, ever forget that American society once paraded and celebrated those values—actually not all that long ago. Those statues and monuments are the most concrete reminders we have—of who we once were and who many of us still are. They bring us face-to-face with that repulsive part of ourselves that we all would prefer to forget. But if we forget it, we will repeat it. So we need to preserve these statues and monuments in their original historical contexts, in a manner that makes clear to every viewer how dangerous and destructive those contexts were and how obsolete they now are. Only a museum devoted to educating the public about the long history of American racism, and its reach into the present day, can do that successfully. That's where those statues and monuments belong—all of them.

LOB: What would you say to someone who claims they are "colorblind," that they are unprejudiced, impartial, and therefore nonracist?

AP: The only individuals I have ever heard or heard of who make such claims with a straight face are self-styled "whites." So I'm assuming that the speaker in this instance also falls into that category. I would ask such a person whether or not their claim to be "colorblind" also applies to the way they see themselves. If so, it implies that they don't believe they are "white" after all. Whether or not they accept this implication would be an interesting test of how accurate their self-description as "colorblind" actually is. If, on the other hand, their claim to be "colorblind" does not apply to the way they see themselves, I would ask for their justification for exempting themselves from their self-professed colorblind impartiality. And I would ask them to explain in what sense that self-exemption is consistent with their putative nonracism.

Agnès Varda

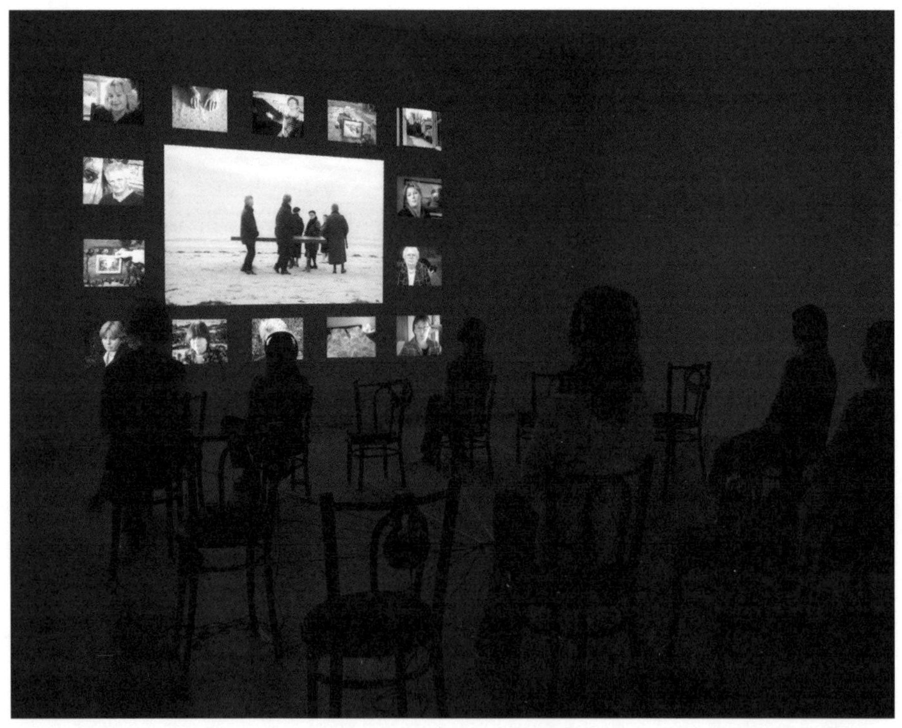

Agnes Varda, *Les Veuves de Noirmoutier*, Cartier Foundation for Contemporary Art, Paris, 2006, installation view.

March 10, 2009
Artforum

The inimitable director Agnès Varda was widely known for her films—the French New Wave classic Cléo from 5 to 7 *(1961) and* The Gleaners and I *(2000) are just two. Here she talks about her exhibition at Harvard's Carpenter Center for the Visual Arts, which opened in spring 2009.*

This is my first installation in the United States, and it makes me very happy. Dominique Bluher, a lecturer in Harvard's Visual and Environmental Studies program, was in France in 2006 for a seminar about my work, and she saw the major solo exhibition I had at the Cartier Foundation for Contemporary Art in Paris, which featured seven or eight installations. She decided to show one of them, my 2004 work *The Widows of Noirmoutier*, at the Carpenter Center, and things began to fall into place.

The exhibition in Paris was titled *L'île et elle* (The Island and She) and was completely inspired by and shot on the island of Noirmoutier, which is located off the west coast of France, not far from Nantes, where my husband, Jacques Demy, shot *Lola* [1961]. We spent a lot of time there near the ocean in a windmill that worked until the 1960s. Jacques passed away in 1990, but I still go there with my children and my grandchildren. Since this is an island with many sailors and fishermen there are, perhaps even more than elsewhere, a lot of widows around, including myself. I started to think about how I could express and share that.

In the middle of the installation, there's a 35 mm film of women on the beach, all dressed in black and moving around a large table. Fourteen monitors surround this film, and there are fourteen seats in front of the installation. On each of the seats there's a set of headphones. You can only listen to one video at a time, and, in each, a widow speaks to you for about three or four minutes.

It's very touching because the widows are all very different from one another. One is an older woman who has been a widow for over twenty years; another one has just lost her man recently and she's still very upset by it. All the women speak about loss and missing their husbands. I filmed their faces and sometimes their beds, or their hands holding an image of their late husband. I wanted to be alone with them while filming to make them feel more confident.

The videos are looped, so perhaps after listening to one widow, you'll take another chair and another set of headphones and listen to another. Viewers tend to pass the headphones and switch chairs frequently; you get the sense you're listening to one woman alone in the room, but you're really in a group of people the entire time. If you don't put on the headphones or sit down, then the fourteen videos just appear to be silent and you don't hear anything but the ocean and a violin from the central film.

For this installation, and in all of my installations, I've tried to create another way for an audience to watch films. I plan to make many more video installations in the future. I'm about to have another exhibition in Séte, a city in the south of France. I'm creating three works for that show. I've been making films for so long, for over fifty years now, but I really think I have two paths of work—cinema and installation. They overlap, of course. My installations use films and, one might say, my recent film—*Les Plages d'Agnès*—is a kind of installation.

Aki Sasamoto

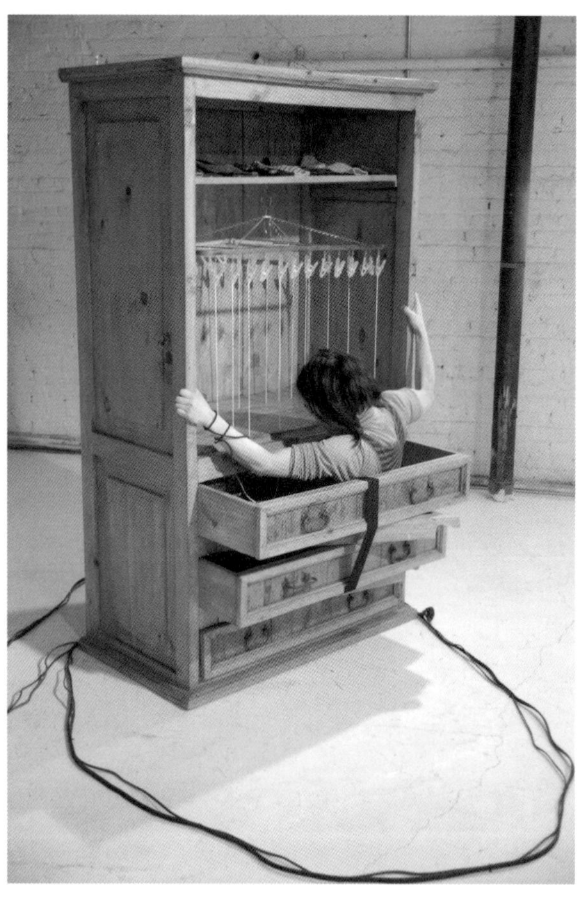

Aki Sasamoto, *Secrets of My Mother's Child*, 2009,
performance view.

July 8, 2009
Artforum

Aki Sasamoto is a Japanese artist who often draws on performance, sculpture, and dance for her works. Here, she describes her sense of dislocation after performing and also talks about her role as a founder of Culture Push, a collaborative artists' group.

Throughout June, I experienced a sense of the unreal and constant self-doubt. A friend pointed out that I always take my time to return to real life after a performance and that I had spent the previous two months performing almost every day in four different shows. I thought I had bored her with my disorientation stories. (Is it like having an easily dislocated shoulder: no longer surprising, though the pain is acute each time?) To some extent, I enjoy the struggle to reconstruct reality after a performance, testing preexisting notions of how the post office and laundry machines operate, or whether people in my address book actually exist. It feels like a type of jet lag, and when I'm in this state, I don't feel like I belong in a single location. The clocks inside and outside me don't match. Jet lag symbolizes the void, the space of disillusion, and the space of re-creation.

There are two ways of being for me. One is *thiis world* (the everyday, banal relationships, and talking). The other is *thaat world* (productions, improvisation, and introspective thinking). There's also a void that occupies the lapse between *thiis* and *thaat*. The void sometimes consumes an entire month, and I find it's interesting enough to pass through many times. In this liminal period I navigate using my smell-like sense, which triggers instant reminders of distant memories and knowledge from other spaces. After enough sniffing of clues, *thiis* and *thaat* start to crystallize and inspire curiosity again.

For instance, cofounding Culture Push separated *thiis* and *thaat* within my art practice. All my egoistic work goes to *thaat world*, and when I work for other creative minds, through this nonprofit art organization, I'm in *thiis world*. Last year, I was interested in running a symposium for Culture Push that brought together a diverse group of people. I wondered what would happen when a mathematician, sculptor, dancer, chef, and doctor spent a day or month in workshops together. I wanted to find the void among expert minds and compartmentalized knowledge. So *Doing* was a one-day event with ten specialists, each sharing an activity that's essential to their personal or professional practice. Culture Push is also running a month-long residency called Genesis Project with different types of artists at Basekamp in Philadelphia this August.

Nonetheless, to organize these events for others is a job that helps me to see the shape of *thaat world*. Learning step-by-step about founding an organization, fundraising, and networking was very different from my self-indulgent artistic productions. However, working for Culture Push frees me to go further in the direction of the solitary, internal self-absorption of my performance and installation work in *thaat world*. In my own art, I use judgments, generalizations, and fictions, all crafted as close as possible to my experiences, to draw out personalized opinions and theories on nothing and everything. I want to create something that seems borderline real or general but simultaneously completely introverted and sealed up in my dreams.

The foremost judgment about my work should always come from me. The reception of the work is secondary. And when I perform, I direct my voice toward the void, pushing *thiis world* off into the distance. But I would be satisfied if I could find one person who connects with what I do. I look forward to meeting that person and talking with them about the void.

Alex Bag

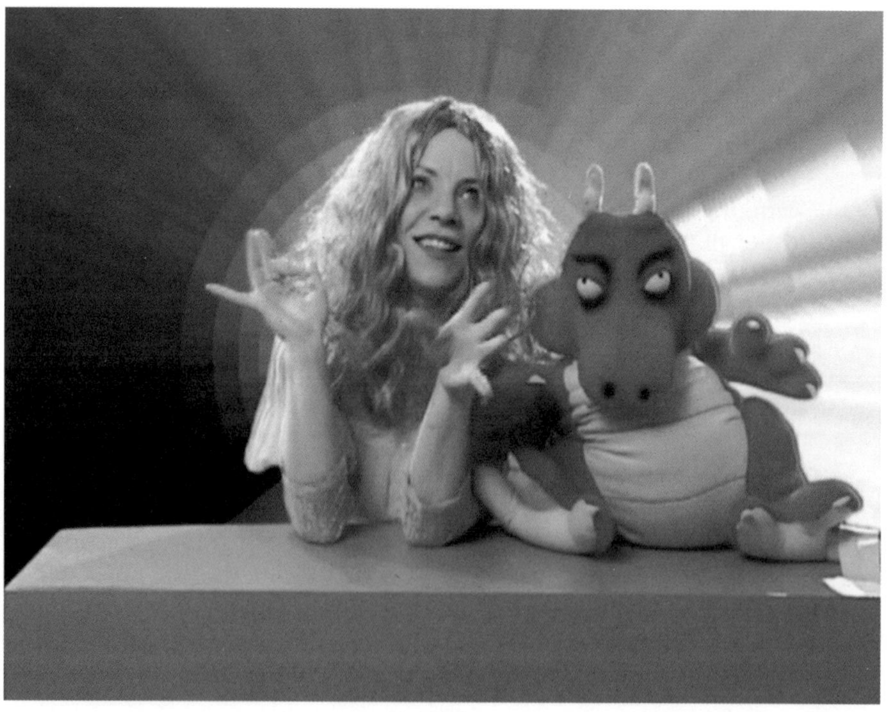

Alex Bag, *Untitled (Project for the Whitney Museum)*, 2009, video (color, sound, 38 minutes).

January 6, 2009
Artforum

Since the mid-1990s, the New York–based artist Alex Bag has created a wide array of acerbic video art—by turns hilarious and horrific—that frequently features Bag herself. Her commissioned exhibition was on view in winter 2009 at the Whitney Museum of American Art.

My mother starred in two children's television programs: in the mid to late '60s she hosted *The Carol Corbett Show* on WPIX in New York City, and in the '70s, in the tri-state area, she had a show on WCBS called *The Patchwork Family*. Each show follows a conventional format: my mother sits behind a desk with a puppet and is joined by various guests. A music guy sings a song with a small studio audience of children, someone paints with the kids, somebody comes on with animals, and another person brings a moon rock, to name a few examples.

My new work is based on preexisting footage of both of these shows. Using Chroma-key technology, I'll be appropriating whole segments. Chroma key is my new best friend. I only recently began to work with it. Nothing is ever high-tech in my work, and I like Chroma key for its DIY aspect. If anyone is inspired by my work, or simply thinks that they could do it better, then that's the greatest thing. In theory, but also in practice, I prefer not to seduce the viewer with technology.

In this new work, instead of being happy, smiley, and full of song, the hostess will be prone to depression, maybe a cutter—I don't know yet. I'm working with actors who are my friends. I give them some direction; in this project, for example, I instructed them to act as though they're writing a suicide note to the youth of today. If they can only tell them about one thing, what will it be? If you're going to have a studio audience full of children, don't think about entertaining them. Instead, think about where you can derive some degree of earnestness. I don't think my work has to be age-appropriate, but it does need to have a sense of urgency.

I'm a writer, and I consider that to be my primary strength. I'm really not an actress. Even though my videos look improvised, much of it is typically scripted. Since no one is a professional actor, we always use cue cards. When you're shooting on video, you can keep doing it until you have it right. The whole thing is planned out, and then I leave room for ... magic!

The Whitney show is new for me in terms of the size and scope of the audience. Anyone can walk in and see the piece in the lobby—you don't even have to pay to see it, which I really like. It's nice to have this kind of challenge. I like being given assignments. It's easier than simply pulling things out of the air. The fact that there are set parameters based on the space and its accessibility produces its own set of complications and joys.

I was a guest on *The Patchwork Family* when I was a child. Once there was a guy from a zoo, and because it was my mother's show, I had a monkey to myself all day. I pushed the monkey around in a doll stroller. It was the greatest day of my life—and it's been all downhill since then! Reruns of my mother's shows were on rotation through the early '90s, and I recall watching them Saturday mornings when I was in college. My clearest memories of the shows are from that period. If I stayed up all night on a Friday, as I was wont to do, there she was in the morning, standing before a psychedelic background sporting a big collar and singing songs to a puppet; it was great footage to fall asleep to. When I was really young, I found the shows disturbing; there was always an audience full of children with whom she'd share stories that she had already told to me, which could get very confusing. It was only in reruns that I really began to enjoy them.

Amy O'Neill

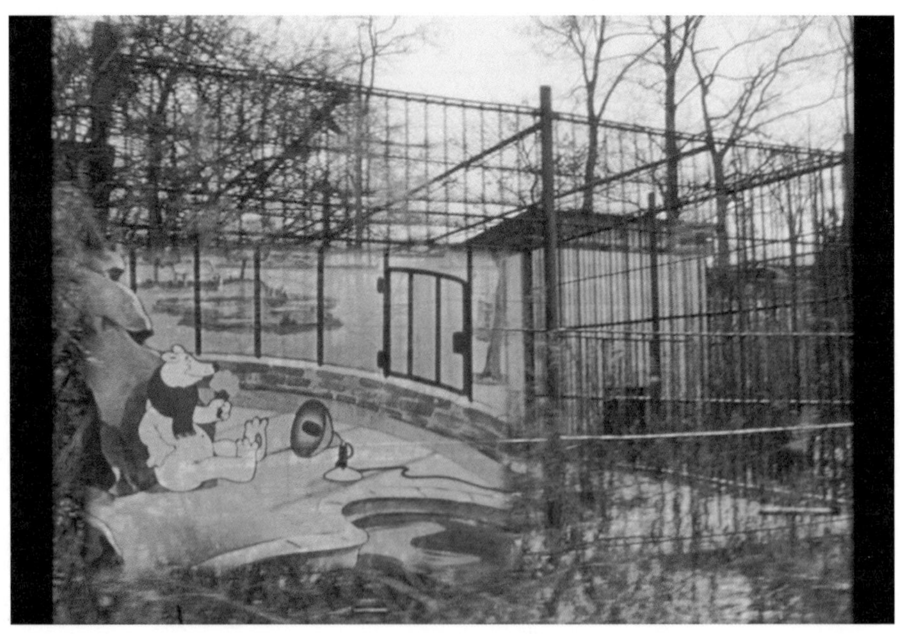

Amy O'Neill, *Zoo Revolution and The Well Fed Wolf*, 2017, 16 mm transfer to HD video (color, sound, 8 minutes 6 seconds).

June 2, 2017
Artforum

Amy O'Neill is a New York–based artist known for her works that sift through the ruins of Americana. Her exhibition Convex Cornea *ran at Kristina Kite Gallery in Los Angeles in summer 2017.*

My father once told me a story about a rumor that spread throughout his high school in Western Pennsylvania. To commemorate the assassinated president, school officials had asked for the face of John F. Kennedy to be grafted onto the head of their mascot, the Indian Chief Monacatootha, which appeared on a giant mural adorning the school's entrance. I was born and raised in that area, where things tend to get muddier than anywhere else in the United States. It's a place to which my work keeps returning.

Zoo Revolution and the Well Fed Wolf is a 16 mm film retrofitted to play in my parents' 1970s television console. Over a death metal soundtrack by the band Orphan, the film brings together an abandoned petting zoo and a storybook forest I visited as a child. Today the original snack bar, rusted cages, and the Old Woman Who Lived in a Shoe house are invaded by wild brambles and on the verge of disappearance. Footage from two children's films—a cartoon and an educational PSA on good eating habits—have been injected throughout the piece. I can't remember precisely when I first saw those shorts, but I like to imagine digesting them during my first grade class's "slow" period, in a cool and darkened classroom after lunch.

A lot of what I do takes many years to evolve. *Deconstructing 13 Stripes and a Rectangle* continues a work I began about a decade ago, around the time I first shot the petting zoo and the storybook forest. I asked a flag manufacturer to sew a batch of US flags minus the stars, and then I proceeded to hollow out the flag, excising the plain blue field and the stripes, leaving only the structural seams. This action was less about desecrating a flag than about physically opening up conversations about the continued casualties of war taking place worlds away, in Afghanistan and Iraq. An ongoing drawing series takes those stripped flags as subjects; for these, I've applied a wax transfer technique to paper, which is a gentler approach for expressing my fears about the tattered condition of the United States' political landscape. I draw like I think: piecemeal, over time. It's kind of like surveying land, a job I assisted my father on—which I liked to think of as stories morphing into horizons, and then into lines.

A similar process occurred for my *Bean-Bag Flats* series. For these, fabric panels from the much-coveted 1970s chairs have been deconstructed at their seams, flattened, and pinned to the wall. Their outlines resemble torsos—in the style of Weebles, egg-shaped toys from my youth. Screen-printed jelly bean patterns run throughout the fabric, which is also littered with T-shirt iron-ons of slogans such as SIT ON IT!, all from the '70s and pressed onto the flats.

I'm not nostalgic for a past that I only remember tangentially. These works aim at questioning how childhood souvenirs bring us to our current Trumpian juggernaut of telling tales. Or, as the cognitive psychologist Ulric Neisser once said about memory: "Out of a few stored bone chips we remember a dinosaur."

Andrea Fraser

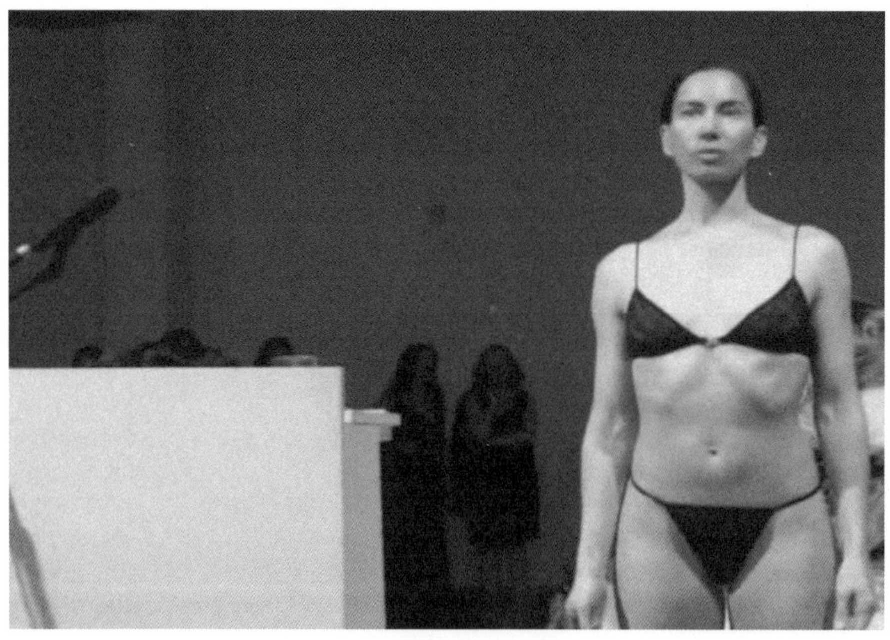

Andrea Fraser, *Official Welcome*, 2001/2003, video (still), monitor or projection (color and sound, 30 minutes).

February 26, 2016
Artforum

I spoke with the Los Angeles–based artist Andrea Fraser about her life, her influential work, and her sound installation Down the River, *2016, which was part of the Whitney Museum's "Open Plan" exhibition series in the spring of 2016. An extension of her longtime investigation of institutions, the audio work brought recordings from Sing Sing correctional facility, located up the Hudson River from the Whitney Museum, to the freshly empty space of the museum to comment on increasing inequality in the United States.*

LOB: When did you move to New York?

AF: I moved to New York in 1981 from Berkeley, California. I dropped out of high school after two years and two weeks, slightly before my sixteenth birthday. I felt pretty uncertain about my future. And then I decided that I wanted to move to New York. I had a brother and a sister here who had moved before me. I first landed on East 4th Street with them, and then we moved into a three-bedroom apartment on Avenue B and 10th Street, on Tompkins Square Park, where I lived for about a year and a half before we lost the lease and they left town. And then I was really on my own. Then I applied to a couple of art schools, and I was accepted at the School of Visual Arts (SVA). So I started studying there midyear, in January 1982. After two years there, I dropped out to go to the Whitney Independent Study Program (ISP), where I started in January 1984.

LOB: Why did you want to become an artist after landing in New York?

AF: My mother studied painting with people like George Grosz at the Art Students League in New York in the '50s. She was from Puerto

Rico. She continued to paint during my early childhood, and then stopped painting and wrote poetry, made Super 8 films, and then went on to get a PhD in psychology. So I had a vision of what it might be to be an artist. And that's one of the reasons I knew I had to come to New York. But when I arrived there I didn't know what I was going to do. There was also the sense of educational failure that came along with having dropped out of high school. During my first few months in New York, I went to museums all the time. I was at the Metropolitan Museum probably four times a week. I knew that place like the back of my hand. It was in that period that I desperately tried to take in what I could from the great cultural institutions of New York.

On the one hand, that triggered tremendous investment and aspirations. And on the other hand, there was a deep anxiety about whether I would ever be good enough, whether I'd ever be adequate, whether I would ever be legitimate enough in relationship to those institutions, which represented a culture that was very different from the culture I grew up with. So when I got wind of some critical perspectives on institutions, particularly from Craig Owens at SVA, they really resonated for me.

LOB: Who were your other influences at that time?

AF: Well, it was an amazing time to land in New York. It was a transitional period—when it was pretty expensive, but it was still possible to find cheap enough places to live. A lot of people taught at SVA. There weren't that many places to teach. I had the opportunity to study with some extraordinary people at SVA. I took a performance class with Simone Forti. I took video with Dara Birnbaum. I took drawing with Thomas Lawson, who then hired me as his assistant, while he was publishing *Real Life* magazine. He introduced me to some of the artists of the Pictures Generation. I studied with May Stevens, who was very active in the Women's Art Movement in New York from the '70s and who brought in Adrienne Rich to do a poetry reading.

And then, sort of by accident, I ended up in the class taught by Craig. I had never heard of *October* magazine. I had never heard of Craig, but I ended up in his class together with Gregg Bordowitz, Mark Dion, Tom Burr, and Collier Schorr, among others. It was an amazing group of young artists that I discovered in that class, and I became friends with. Craig was a tremendously important person to me and he introduced me to a critical thinking about art and about art institutions. I remember his first class: he did a kind of Foucauldian analysis of his power in the classroom. From that moment on I was totally smitten and ready to buy whatever he had to offer. And it was Craig who guided me to the Whitney ISP.

Through Craig, I met Barbara Kruger, Martha Rosler, and Jane Weinstock. Through Tom, I met Allan McCollum, and through Allan, I met Louise Lawler, whose work just blew me away. Craig invited me to write an article about her work, which was published in *Art in America* in 1985. I encountered Yvonne Rainer; I first saw her films at the Whitney program in the mid-1980s, and they had a big influence on me. Her film *Journeys from Berlin/1971* made a huge impression, primarily for her capacity to maintain the personal, the explicitly political, the subjective, and the social all together in a way that was different from the examples of Californian feminist art that I grew up seeing. And then later her film *The Man Who Envied Women* premiered while I was at the ISP. I was also extraordinarily lucky to hear Hans Haacke and Vito Acconci give seminars, as well as historians like Benjamin Buchloh. I was also studying Michael Asher's important work—I could go on and on about this. Mary Kelly's *Post-Partum Document* was also very important to my development. After writing about Louise Lawler's work in 1985, one of the next things I wrote was a review of the book of *Post-Partum Document* when it was published in the United States. Her work was an extraordinary model for artistic research as a kind of psychoanalytic research through feminist analysis. Martha Rosler was also a model for me in that way, offering an artistic practice that's not only about the making of artworks, but which also involves a serious writing and research practice.

LOB: Incredible. Do you remember anything specific Owens said in his Foucauldian analysis?

AF: Oh god, I should dig up my notes at some point. I think it was a fairly straightforward reflection on the arrangement of the classroom and his position up at the front—his authorization by the school to take this position of power. I grew up a hippy kid in a lesbian-feminist household in Berkeley. The women's movement and the women's art movement were the contexts of my childhood. There was a general hostility toward institutions and authority. So of course I felt a great deal of affinity with his critical analysis.

LOB: How did that feminist context inform your work?

AF: How I understand institutions and how my own practice developed had as much to do with the feminism as with the research-based and political aspects of Conceptualism that are more often seen as the roots of institutional critique. So when I arrived in New York, with a native hostility to institutions and authority, the politically engaged aspects of Conceptual art definitely resonated for me. But the feminist investigations of subjectivity, sexuality, identity, and gender coming out of the '70s were also very important.

I tried to bring those two methodologies, if you will, together. One was the deep archival research and fieldwork of Conceptual art, which Hans Haacke and Michael Asher had developed in such important ways to investigate institutions, with an approach to site-specificity that took it beyond architectural places and spaces into the social and economic contexts and the social histories of sites.

But from feminism, what was important to me was another kind of research, an inward research, an investigation of the self, of the personal as political, and introspection as research—not only introspection in terms of an investigation of the self as an individual, but an investigation of the relational psychological and social structures that define us and also motivate our participation in those relations and social structures. So the work that I developed really came out of an intersection between those two arenas of practice, and their strategies, and their concerns.

LOB: Can we talk about your first work of institutional critique, *Woman 1/Madonna and Child 1506–1967*, from 1984?

AF: Yes, that's an artist's book in the form of an exhibition brochure. I think it's about thirty-four pages long. The images were made by rephotographing superimposed slides of works by de Kooning and Raphael. The rephotographed images collapse these extremes of representations of women in art history. The images are juxtaposed with quotations from art historical texts. I wanted to examine how art history constructs the artist as a transhistorical subject and, in particular, how that construction is articulated in relation to representations of women. And then it was under the influence of Louise Lawler's work, to a large extent, and also feminist performance, that I had the idea of appropriating positions and functions within museums. And that's what led me to my first performances in the form of museum tours in 1986. I had also started to read Pierre Bourdieu, who became incredibly important to me and was a big influence on the way I started to think about and understand art institutions and the art field.

LOB: Can we talk about *Museum Highlights* from 1989?

AF: Yes, that was a live performance in the form of a docent-led museum tour that I created for the Philadelphia Museum of Art. It exists in three different forms, a live performance, which not that many people saw, a video that I was able to shoot in the museum, and then a text that was published with tons of footnotes in the journal *October*. So in the form of the video and the texts, that work was able to continue to live and circulate.

In terms of my own development, it's probably the most significant piece still because the research for that project led me to think about not only the history of museums in the United States, but also the context for how museums developed, and how we arrived at the private nonprofit museum in the United States from the model of the European public museum. And that led me to think about public policy in the United States going back to the nineteenth century, which led me to think about the development of philanthropy and of the nonprofit sector in the United States. And through that research, I learned about the deep-seated hostility to government, to the public sector, and to any redistributive forms of taxation that are so central to the politics of America going back to the nineteenth century. We were seeing those economic ideologies from the nineteenth century return in the 1980s under Ronald Reagan, with cutbacks to public welfare programs that had developed with the New Deal and in the '60s under President Johnson.

I saw the volunteer docent as a figure for the museum's ideal visitor, someone who enters into this intimate relationship with the museum—internalizing the discourses of the museum, and then embodying it and representing the museum to its public, and, in a sense, performing the museum.

Then, relatedly, in 1991 I did a piece called *May I Help You* where I hired performers to be in a gallery during open hours for the run of a show, and wrote a script for them to perform for everybody who came in. That piece was important for me because it was a different way of thinking about performance. It was the first multivoiced performance that I did, with about seven different voices, and it was structured as a class pyramid, from what might be the most legitimate voice in that context to the voice of someone who feels excluded and illegitimate in that context.

LOB: Let's fast-forward and talk about the Whitney show you're installing right now.

AF: The Whitney Museum offered me eighteen thousand square feet for two weeks, which was a challenging invitation for an artist who doesn't make things. The project I developed is called *Down the River* and it's an audio installation. The space will be completely empty. The title is meant to evoke the phrase "going up the river," or going to prison, namely, to Sing Sing, which is a huge maximum security prison that is thirty-two miles up the Hudson from the museum in New York. And so we went up the river to Sing Sing and recorded ambient sound in cellblock A, which is reportedly one of the largest prison housing units in the world. I'm bringing the sounds to the Whitney's fifth floor to link art museums and prisons, which I see as two sides of the coin of inequality in our increasingly polarized society.

Museums and prisons have experienced a parallel boom since the mid-1970s. During this period, the US prison population ballooned by 700 percent, making the United States the world's largest jailer. Museums and prisons are two institutions that we tend not to think about together since they're divided geographically, where museums are created by starchitects as the showpiece buildings of urban redevelopment projects while prisons are moved out of urban centers, further and further away from the families of prisoners and the worlds of urban elites. Museums represent freedoms and our tolerance for diversity, for experimentation, and also for transgression—the challenging of social norms and conventions—whereas prisons revoke those freedoms and punish transgression. So the project attempts to relink these institutions.

I also think they're structurally linked because their twin expansion has everything to do with inequality, produced by the massive upward transfer of wealth that we've seen since the 1970s and the enormous fortunes that exist at the top of our economic pyramid. Some of that money has come into museums and supports artists like me. But with that massive upward transfer of wealth, there's been less and less money at the bottom. Poverty has increased. Social mobility has decreased. The upward transfer of wealth has been enabled by the reversal of progressive taxation policies, which created revenues that could be put into social programs and into a safety net. So the safety net was replaced with a dragnet. The project attempts to relink these institutions across this social and geographical divide, and to challenge the Whitney's audience to think about what this beautiful, wealthy museum is not and what is defining of our society right now in America, which is the mass incarceration of people, most of whom are poor people and people of color.

Anohni

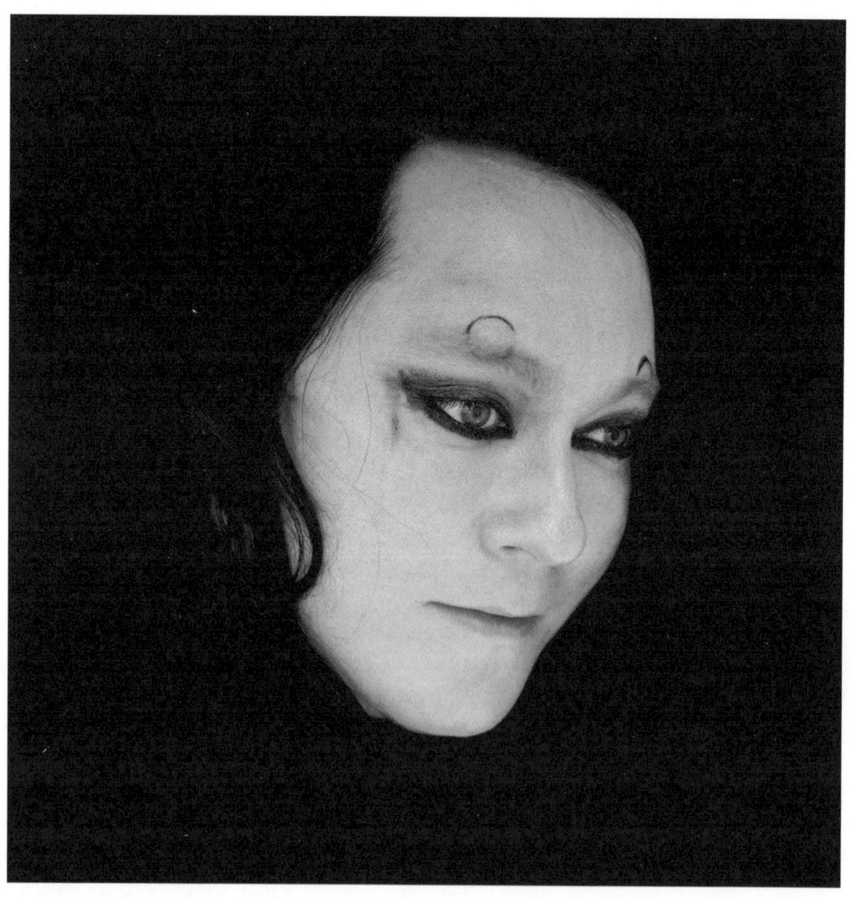

Anohni, photo by Colin Whitaker.

July 11, 2016
Artforum

Feelings aren't facts in Anohni's debut solo album HOPELESSNESS *(2016)—but that doesn't mean they're useless. The eleven songs therein speak frankly from the heart and lay a rhythm for direct action. Creating friction with upbeat electronic tempos and chilling lyrics about downbeat issues,* Hopelessness *has been called a protest album.*

LOB: *HOPELESSNESS* seems to suggest that violence shouldn't be understood or theorized as an abstraction but rather as something increasingly commonplace, a lived reality with an extensive history. How were you trying to frame violence in this work?

A: I collaborated with a group of women in New York City a couple of years ago and we developed this system of tenets that we called "Future Feminism" because we were all concerned about the future, basically. The first tenet was "The subjugation of women and the earth is one and the same." The time-honored enslavement of the feminine now climaxes in the virulent decimation of the biosphere. Our propensity for warfare, violence, and hierarchy—born innocently enough out of some survival instinct—now ushers us along the path to ecocide. Judeo-Christian religious texts have been rooting for an apocalypse for thousands of years. But these patriarchal death cults had to wait until the twentieth century to find the technology and capitalism that could finally make their dreams come true.

LOB: While acknowledging histories of violence, the album offers what might seem like love songs, flirting with the NSA or a drone bomb. Could you describe some of your processes for writing lyrics?

A: When I was a kid, one of my means of self-defense was to disarm perpetrators with a confounding display of vulnerability. I guess some of these songs come out of that impulse. People used to say that if you were being raped you should act crazy and scream and gnash your teeth, hopefully jolting the aggressor out of his stupor and scaring him into a fresh moment of perspective, or at least giving him a moment's pause in which you could escape. The lyrics for this album were an attempt on my part to be more vigorous in the ways that I used my influence. Honestly, I was sick of writing pastoral songs. It felt too passive in the face of what's happening. I wanted to try to model another approach and see how far I could push it in terms of content. Once I dove into the idea of singing harder lyrics against euphoric dance tracks and got past the phase of self-censorship, the first draft of the work came pretty quickly. It was easy to write lyrics about these subjects, which have preoccupied me for such a long time. In that respect it's actually a very personal record.

LOB: Did you feel like pop songs might speak more powerfully about drones, for instance, than news reports or even protests?

A: Music is a different way of communicating, using our voices expansively to communicate a depth of feeling, or an impassioned belief. It reaches a different part of the psyche, and so it can be useful.

LOB: Listening to the album I was reminded of Eugene Thacker's writings about our increasing indifference to the planet (which he calls "the world for us") and the planet's increasing indifference to us ("the world in itself"), as well as "the world without us," a horrific endgame. Do you think, at this point, the world would be better off without us?

A: I experience hope and hopelessness both as feelings rather than facts. It's important to be honest about how I feel. But it will be our immediate actions and not our feelings that determine the future of life on earth. The case for the necessity for hope or the need to deny feelings of hopelessness sometimes feels like a red herring. Plenty of destructive people feel bountiful hope. And a lot of really effective organizers and activists feel, at times, a terrible sense of hopelessness. But that doesn't stop them from continuing to take action.

LOB: The album gives us a dark image of our era; it also has mystical moments (lyrics about wanting to be born into the past, seemingly directed to a higher power, for example). Is there room for mysticism these days, given our grave, real, and nonabstract problems?

A: I don't think of spirituality as something abstract. I see it as inseparable from the world/universe in all its most tangible aspects. I think the separation of our ideas about spirituality from the practical face of nature and life is one of the ways we've been hoodwinked into behaving virulently, believing that true spiritual value lies elsewhere, on another faraway plane, perhaps in the heavens.

LOB: Do you think identity politics is back (or if it ever left)? What might this term mean now?

A: I sometimes feel that I have been manipulated in the United States into thinking that the pursuit of my own identity politics is the final road to global justice and wellness. There is a reason why monied interests keep all the hate plates spinning, year after year, sniping at us and keeping us all stuck in triage, while behind the scenes the big guns go in for another round of wealth extraction. In the '80s, I remember watching as half of America voted for Reagan out of fear that gay men would otherwise be tainting the water supply with AIDS. But Reagan's actual legacy was neoliberal capitalism and the dismantling of legislation that had long protected the working class. Now we have a vastly poorer general population, with significantly diminished access to education, advocacy, financial security, healthcare, or truth in media. Here comes Trump, a billionaire, still harnessing working-class people across the country who fantasize that he shares their often-bigoted points of view, when really he's just another mogul trying to pull the wool over their eyes. It will take stoicism to root out the carcinogenic individuals and institutions that manipulate us into compliance with easy-to-digest morsels of fear and pedestrian bigotry. My teacher Vito Russo used to say the three phases of a plague were denial, blame, and then, finally, fear.

Aura Rosenberg

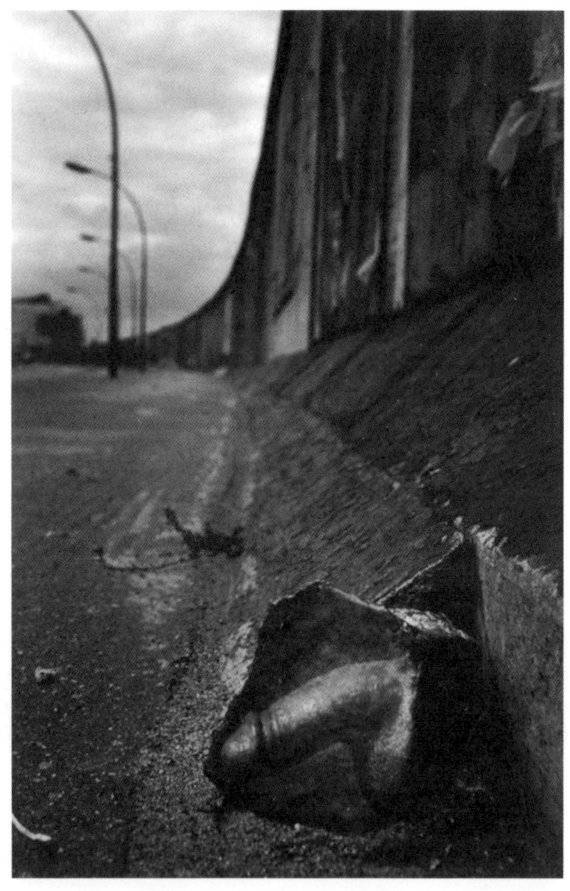

Aura Rosenberg, *The Dialectical Porn Rock*, 1989–93,
C-print, 40 × 30 inches (101.6 × 76.2 cm).

July 20, 2012
Artforum

The New York–based artist Aura Rosenberg here discusses four group shows happening during summer 2012, which presented works made over the past twenty-five years, from her investigations into pornography to her photographs with children.

Some of my work has been inspired by a curiously dated source: "The Afronomical Ways," a black-light poster from 1972, which features fluorescent silhouettes of men and women posed in various sexual positions. Each position is supposed to represent a different sign of the zodiac, and each figure has an Afro. In the late 1980s, I made several body imprint paintings referencing that poster. I've recently returned to this work, but instead of using my own body, I've asked couples to make the imprints. Last spring, during the opening of my show at Sassa Trülzsch Gallery in Berlin, two dancers made one of these paintings that became part of the installation. This summer, Seth Kelly has included *Sagittarius*, a new work from the series, in *These Transitional Spaces*, the show he curated at Franklin Street Works in Stamford, Connecticut.

In 1988 I began to work primarily with photography and sculpture. I was sharing a summer house in the Catskills with some friends, and, with the woods nearby, I wanted to make something overtly fetishistic from the natural materials at hand. My friend Mike Ballou was dividing his time between making his own work—sculptures with porn images—and fishing for trout in a stream on the property. One day I noticed the way light hitting the rocks in this stream brought images to mind. So as a practical joke, I glued his porn clippings onto the rocks, covered them in resin, and put them back in the water for him to find. Struck by the contrast between the altered rocks and their natural setting, I started to photograph them. Robert Smithson's essay "The Dialectical Landscape" inspired the title of this series: *The Dialectical Porn Rock*. Back in Manhattan, I started to see the rocks as things in themselves and arranged them indoors in a variety of configurations. When I moved to Berlin in 1991, this city—filled with monuments to its sometimes troubled past—became a new context for my rock works. The connection of sexuality and nature, however mediated, gave way to a sense of opposition vis-à-vis the body and its control by the state. This summer, I'll be showing outdoor installations of *The Dialectical Porn Rock* for the first time, in *Creature from the Blue Lagoon*, the show that Bob Nickas curated at Martos Gallery in Bridgehampton, New York.

In 1989 my daughter Carmen was born, and two long-term projects involving childhood overtook my work with porn. I titled the first *Berlin Childhood*, after Walter Benjamin's allegorical memoir of the same name, a collection of forty-two texts written when he was in exile from the Third Reich. For this work, I shot photos of contemporary Berlin to match Benjamin's entries from half a century earlier. The subtext to this work was my own family's flight from Germany and my return to raise my daughter there. The second project, *Who Am I? What Am I? Where Am I?* is a series of photo portraits of children. As a gift, I had brought face paints for Carmen's kindergarten in Berlin. Her teacher, Marie Schmitz, and the class had a lot of fun with them. For an exhibition at the Kunstlerhaus Bethanien, I chose to collaborate with Marie on portraits of the painted children. Back in New York, I wondered what it would look like if I asked artists to make these paintings, which I would again photograph. Of course, the artists I invited often approached portraiture via their own practices. The children, however, weren't merely blank slates. Together, the artist, the child, and I shaped images that reflected us all. The series to date includes over eighty collaborations. Because this work questioned normative relations between adults and children, it was regarded as more transgressive than my porn work. For example, some saw Mike Kelley's stylization of my daughter as a goth, or Laurie Simmons's portrayal of her daughter Lena as a marionette, as abusive. Ironically, in the latter case, the idea was Lena's. Three of these portraits will be included in *Too Old for Toys, Too Young for Boys*, a show at LA's OHWOW gallery this summer, curated by Alex Gartenfeld.

With Carmen now grown up, I've gone back to working with pornography, to renegotiate aspects of this work that weren't fully explored. The terms, however, have changed. Just as my work with childhood spans a period of changing attitudes toward images of children, so too is my focus on pornography tied to a period shift. When I googled some of the actors whose images I used before, a website called The Golden Age of Porn came up. My old source material has become a relic. Nevertheless, the sense of lost time intrigues me, and I titled a new series of paintings, drawn from the same material, *The Golden Age*.

This summer I'm also presenting a corner installation of porn rocks in *Buy My Bananas*, Julia Trotta's selection of women artists working with sex and comedy, at Kate Werble Gallery's Annex Space in New York. Together these various shows offer a sampling of my oeuvre in different contexts. Hopefully, the connections will register how my work has grown organically out of lived experience and how it mirrors changes in our culture at large concerning the intersection of childhood and sexuality. At the very least, they're encouraging me to reflect on these questions.

Beryl Korot

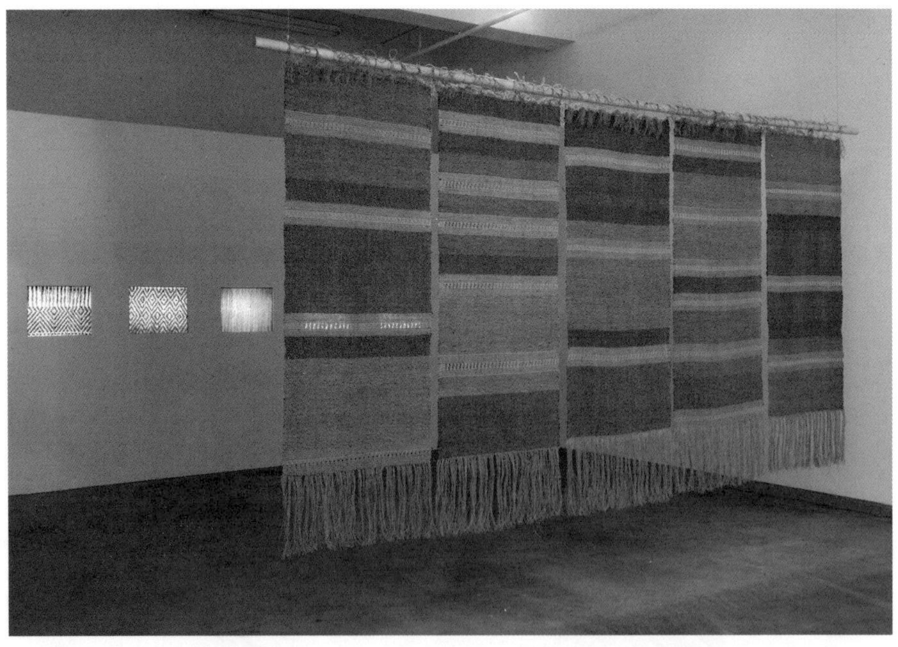

Beryl Korot, *Text and Commentary* (detail), 1976–77, weavings, drawings, 5-channel
video (black and white, sound, 30 minutes), installation view.

November 14, 2017
Artforum

Beryl Korot's groundbreaking video installation Text and Commentary, *1976–77, inspired by the Jacquard loom and how it impacted engineer Charles Babbage's invention of the punch card, was originally exhibited at Leo Castelli Gallery in 1977. The piece was included in* Thinking Machines: Art and Design in the Computer Age, 1959–1989 *at the Museum of Modern Art, New York, in 2017–18.*

Nineteen seventy-four was a pivotal year for me. I found myself working in three communications media at the same time: in print (as an editor of the publication *Radical Software*), in video, and at the loom. It was a revelation to me that all three encode and decode information in lines. I was also drawn to the multichannel genre developing at that time because it most clearly challenged the traditional viewer–broadcaster relationship. The viewer had to leave the living room and go to a public space to view the work. And the loom—which was actually the first computer on the face of the earth, in that it programs patterns according to a numerical structure—was the most sophisticated technology I could find to understand the programming of multiples.

Conceiving of each monitor as a thread, I constructed the multichannel installation *Dachau 1974* according to basic thread structures for binding a cloth, with channels one and three and channels two and four juxtaposing pairs of images as the work proceeded in time. In essence, I created a nonverbal narrative structure based on a visual, and not a literary, source. This distinction was very important to me. The visual structure of woven cloth, based on the buildup of lines, precedes human writing by thousands of years and holds a key to the organization of visual and textual information. The words *text* and *weave* share the same Latin root.

Text and Commentary is a handmade work created for the camera. Five weavings hang from a dowel facing five video monitors built into a free-standing wall. As I wove at the loom, I hung a camera from the ceiling to record the process at varying distances. The images became quite abstract. I edited the piece by drawing all the images I shot on three-by-five cards and spreading them out on the floor to come up with a sequence of images. The work produces a dialogue between an ancient technology and the then-new medium of video. When it's exhibited, there's also a pictographic score for the five channels of video as well as five weavers' notations. All elements of the work coexist and provide varying perspectives of virtually the same information, but within the limitations of each medium.

Currently I'm working on *Curves*, which is a series of abstract drawings on paper, made with ink, pencil, and thread, that reference the human torso. As these works develop, threads are sewn on the surface of the paper with a digital sewing machine. The relationship between the handmade and the machine-made is basic to this work. Instead of oil or watercolor, here the programmed structure of the threads allows the original drawn markings to be seen in a new way and adds texture, color, and depth to the surface of the work. The sewing machine is programmed to sew on the surface of the paper in predesignated areas. The kind of stitching, with its shape and degrees of being open or closed to the surface beneath, is another example of the impact of the computer on something as basic as the sewing machine.

Beverly Semmes

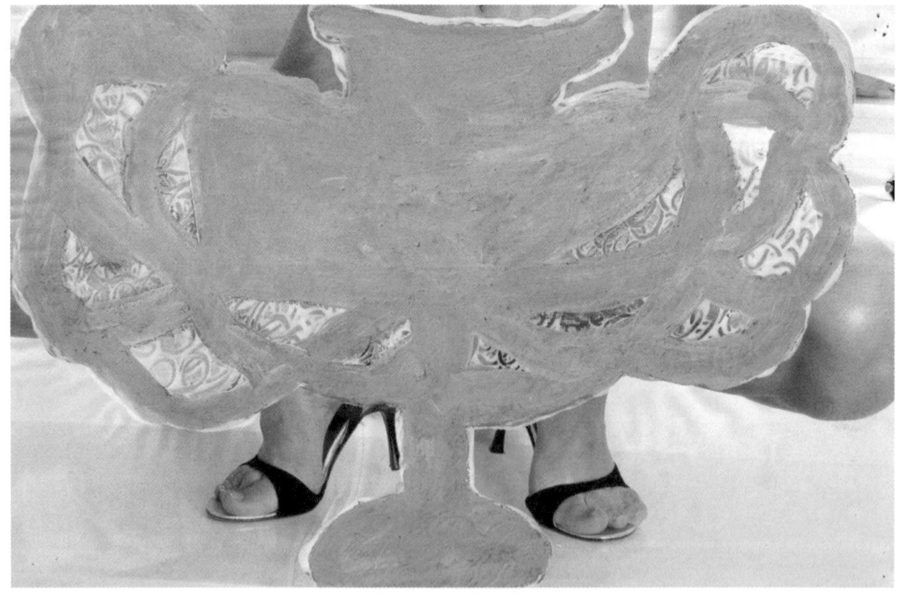

Beverly Semmes, *Pink Pot*, 2008, paint on magazine page, 7 ½ × 10 ¾ inches (19.1 × 26 cm).

February 5, 2014
Artforum

Beverly Semmes is a New York–based artist who has exhibited internationally since the late 1980s. In 2014, Los Angeles's Shoshana Wayne Gallery presented two of Semmes's large-scale dress works, produced in 1992 and 1994, while in New York, Semmes showed selections from her ongoing Feminist Responsibility Project, *as well as ceramics, at Susan Inglett Gallery.*

In the early 2000s, I inherited a stack of 1990s-era porn magazines. It's a long story in itself, but basically I was helping a friend in upstate New York who wanted to get rid of them but was too embarrassed to take them to the town's recycling center. I took them home. Not long after, I was working in my studio and I thought: I need these. As I was cracking them open, I had the idea to get some paint out. The first pieces were essentially cover-ups—fluorescent censorships. This is how the *Feminist Responsibility Project* began. I wanted the *FRP* works to have a protective aspect: protective to the viewer, protective to the subject. The covering up is nurturing—in a grandmotherish way—and it's complicated. The redactor is spending a lot of time with the imagery, censoring to keep you from getting/ having to see the original material. The images break out of the control: there are rules, but these codes keep getting broken and content slips forward.

I'm often putting this body of work to the side while I focus on another project, but then I end up returning to it. At this point it's been more than ten years, and I've made hundreds. They've taken on a painterly surface; they're structured in response to the absurdly concocted magazine scenarios. I make these drawings at the kitchen table.

There's a lot of editing afterward. I'm rethinking and reworking them all the time. There will be pieces in the "not working" category that later become my favorites. It evolves.

I recently installed my show at Shoshana Wayne in Santa Monica—the main gallery is an expansive rectangular space—and the 1994 piece I'm showing there, *Buried Treasure*, fills the room. Reseeing this work after many years, I was struck by how much of a drawing it is. There's one long sleeve and it drapes around the floor. The black crushed velvet is very light-absorbing; it has an oily burnt wood quality, a superblack, like vine charcoal. Many of my sculptures from the '90s were designed to take up space. The viewer is pushed way to the side; you can't really walk into the room. Like the *FRP*, there's a graphic sensibility to my sculptural work of this time. The *Feminist Responsibility Project* is more intimately aggressive.

As the Susan Inglett Gallery show in New York approaches, I continue to ask myself about the relationship of the drawings to my ceramics. The question has been hanging over my head for at least five of the ten-plus years I've been doing the *FRP* drawings. Ceramics has been my most consistent medium—the one I continue to return to. I began working in clay right after I finished school. The pieces are hand-built. I begin with a lot of very wet clay and then build them up over time, adding handles. They're heavy and off-kilter, and there's no goal of perfection or lightness as with traditional craft. The glaze has a skin-like aspect; the works are extremely tactile. The ceramics enter into the gallery space as outsiders, as "anti-," and on some level I've always thought of the *FRP* drawings as doing the same.

Carol Bove

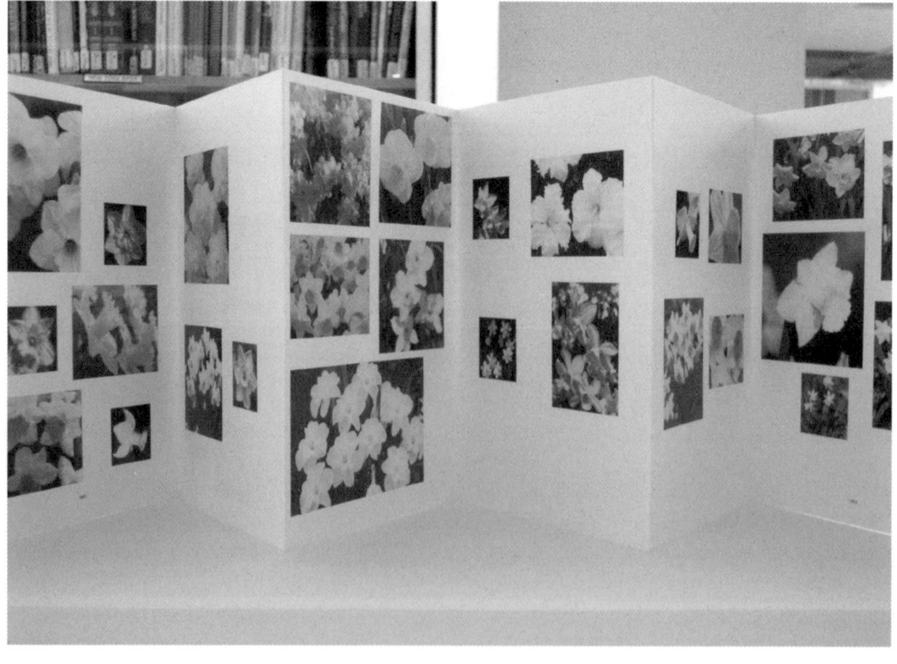

Carol Bove and Janine Lariviere, *Twentieth-Century Narcissus* (details), 2009, installation view.

April 13, 2009
Artforum

Carol Bove is a Brooklyn-based artist known for incorporating made and found objects, primarily from the 1960s, into her works. Her solo exhibition at the Horticultural Society of New York opened in spring 2009 and featured an accordion-fold book, which she discusses here.

Twentieth-Century Narcissus is a project that Janine Lariviere began in 2002 through her research on flower bulbs and their hybridization and registration. It's essentially a collection of daffodils (cut from catalogs) that are arranged on a timeline according to their registration dates. It's about twelve feet long, and each page represents one year. Although Janinc finished the book in 2005, she never published it. When I learned that I had the opportunity to have an exhibition at the Horticultural Society of New York this spring, I wanted to include it since it had introduced an important set of ideas into my thinking about "period eye," a term that refers to what seems to look good at a particular moment in time. The book will be shown alongside my new abstract sculptures and a collage.

A fair amount of research went into making the book. Janine investigated the hybridization and registration processes for daffodils (i.e., *Narcissus*), as well as the system for their classification. The appendix to her book contains a clear introduction to a lot of this material.

On the one hand, the book is a response to the catalogs that arrived at Janine's door, which offered a view of commercially available and popular bulbs. But on the other hand, it's a reflection of commerce itself, which plays a decisive role in the creation, distribution, and persistence of particular flowers.

Janine was working on the book during my 2003 exhibition at Team Gallery in New York. Around that time, she got me thinking about bulb flowers as beautiful but dismissible objects that act as a richly encoded index of culture. In that show, I focused on the late 1960s and '70s, and I invited Janine to exhibit flowers that were registered during those years, to investigate the ways that taste could be perceptible through flowers, or whether period eye manifested through these flowers. Janine planned it so that the flowers would continuously bloom throughout the run of the show, which was a real feat since it was six weeks long. The weather cooperated, thankfully, and we were able to bring flowers to the show nearly every day. If all goes well, the flowers will be at this exhibition, too. There are flowers that look, to my eyes, very '60s or '70s. For the 2003 show, Janine grew a daffodil called Beige Beauty, which is a sweet little mini with a flattened profile and creamy beige color—so '60s looking. We wanted to get Suede—a brown daffodil from the early '70s—but she didn't find it until the ground froze and it was too late to plant. A brown daffodil from 1973 in this timeline really seems like evidence of the history of taste! One feature of the book is that it shows not just which flowers were registered or popular during the century but which ones were continually grown. Daffodils are all clones of one another; each cultivar (or variety) is genetically identical, so you can't renew a variety once it's faltered. Flowers need to be continually in circulation and nurtured to persist, which always strikes me as such a clear metaphor for the history of ideas.

Carolee Schneemann

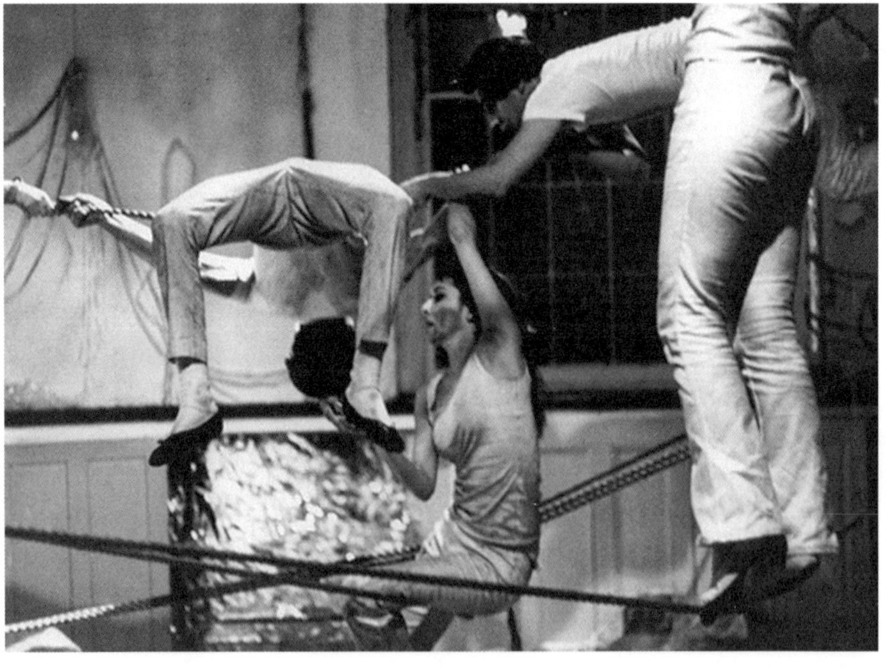

Carolee Schneemann, *Water Light/Water Needle (St. Mark's Church) II*, 1966, gelatin silver print, 20 × 25 inches (50.8 × 63.5 cm).

July 16, 2012
Artforum

The singular American artist Carolee Schneemann was perhaps best known for her expressive paintings, installations, films, and videos from the past five decades and their unwavering focus on identity, subjectivity, and sexuality. Born in 1939 in Fox Chase, Pennsylvania, she received her BA from Bard College and an MFA from the University of Illinois. After moving to New York in 1961 with James Tenney, who was then a composer-in-residence at Bell Telephone Labs in New Jersey, Schneemann was introduced (via composers Philip Corner and Malcolm Goldstein) to the cofounders of the Judson Dance Theater. In the mid-1960s she produced some of her earliest performances with the group at Judson Church, including Newspaper Event, *1962;* Lateral Splay, *1963;* Chromelodeon, *1963; and* Meat Joy, *1964, and played Manet's Olympia in Robert Morris's* Site, *1964. As part of* Artforum*'s 2012 online interview series to commemorate the fiftieth anniversary of the first concerts at Judson, I talked with Schneemann about her "love affair" with her collaborators and "the startling erotic ritual" that was* Meat Joy.

LOB: How did you get involved in Judson?

CS: Judson, before it was Judson, was a love affair for me in looking at new and extended materials. I met these amazing dancers and conceived of them as a kind of collage material that was fully dimensional. I met them through my partner, James Tenney, who was friends with Malcolm Goldstein and Philip Corner. Through Philip, I came to meet Yvonne Rainer, Elaine Summers, and a few of the other Judson participants. Philip told me that there were a bunch of dancers who had studied with James Waring and Anna Halprin, and that they were taking completely new directions for movement and relational aspects of dance. So I went to early rehearsals and it was perfect for me—this potentiality of extending my materials. I was moving from painting to extended media and I saw the dancers as extended media.

LOB: Where would you first meet with the dancers?

CS: I began to work with the group of dancers before we became Judson. We were just a loose affiliation and I was the first visual artist that wanted to choreograph with this group. I think we first met in James Waring's studio and then we were given the basement in Judson Church for rehearsing. Of course we didn't know we were going to move up from the basement into the main parish hall, and into the church itself, and into the culture of New York City.

LOB: Could you say a little more about how you saw the dancers as extended media?

CS: I saw each dancer as a vibrant, physicalized potentiality of a collage dynamic that I could conceive of by moving them and recombining them through space, through the juxtaposition of their aspects and energy. My first performative works for Judson were based on kinetic drawings that I would bring into our rehearsals. I would then ask the dancers to climb a ladder holding cans of paint and leap off the ladder in a way that would spill the paint, thus taking painting into this extended dynamic. Unfortunately, I discovered that dancers are very worried about their wrists and ankles. They were quite unwilling to jump off the ladder, which is how I began to create physicalizing exercises and contact improvisation out of my own drawings and physicality and then pass it on.

LOB: How collaborative was this work in the end?

CS: For the early movement pieces, I would bring in the drawings that had a set of interactions I wanted them to explore. It became highly collaborative though. It's just wonderful to think back how flexible we were together and how available we were to each other. My very first performative work in New York, right out of college, was at the Living Theatre on a dark night. I built an environment out of shards of broken glass. Yvonne participated in that, as well as Malcolm and Philip and a trombonist I had just met—because he was making disturbing sounds on 28th Street. So there was an early moment when we were investigating each other's ideas very freely, before more particularized principles established themselves and then not everybody would collaborate with each other to the extent they had initially.

Deborah Hay, for instance, was so splendid. Before I ever stood up and moved in any of my works, she was my alter ego. I would create actions and fractured narratives for Deborah's movement that were the closest to my own sense of physiology. So Judson was like falling in love. The people who worked there just recognized us as being a part of a cultural affinity: there was no caution, no resistance, there was no insurance; we could do whatever we wanted, if something happened to the audience, it happened to the audience. And if any of us fell off a balcony we would have to regain composure. There was no legal involvement. Judson was so amazingly generous and helpful. It was completely open. After I did *Meat Joy*—the startling erotic ritual that it was—the church was reeking from the old chickens and the old sausages, and the Reverend Howard Moody, in all his generosity, gave the Sunday lecture to the congregation in that stinky space.

LOB: Where were you living at the time? What kind of work were you making outside of Judson?

CS: I have the odd creative habit of always doing several things at once. I wake in the morning and I feel that something should be written or pulled from the subtle place between dreaming and waking, where there will be synergy and where something from the unconscious is still creatively present. So that could be drawing and writing. In the early Judson years, I was doing big constructions with motorized parts. I was working in upstate New York and in the city. I found these abandoned cutting boards in my loft on 29th Street, which had previously been a fur cutter's loft. I built constructions with these that include photographic elements and motorized materials: lights, umbrellas. So the work in kinetic sculpture extended into the live actions of the dancers. It was a direct connection for me.

LOB: Is there a particular memory that you have of Judson that seems the most vivid?

CS: The performance group was always so intense, so focused, collaborative, and very sweet as I remember it. We didn't push each other around and we didn't fight over position, or the program, or who had precedence. Certainly Yvonne began to be the most dominant shaping figure of programs. Elaine Summers also did amazing early works with projection systems that were really unique at the time.

But no one got paid! No one got a penny. I don't know how we had cab fare or even money for stamps. Remarkably, I was told that if I went at midnight to a print studio on Seventh Avenue near 13th Street, a woman who worked there—Virginia Admiral, who was married to Robert De Niro Sr.—would let me use her presses. So we also made beautiful flyers for our events. She let me paint her presses and mix blue, red, and white to have a multicolored print.

LOB: Did you ever think of your works as dances?

CS: I never thought I was making dances, because the dancers never accepted me as a dancer, although movement was always strongly in my aesthetic vocabulary. I established my own form—kinetic theater—and developed certain structures, parameters. I had to be in control of the lights and the sounds. *Meat Joy* was the first major performative work I did at Judson Church, but I don't think there are any Judson dancers as such in it. Certainly Phoebe Neville stayed with me, and Meredith Monk was a wonderful performer in *Water Light/Water Needle.*

LOB: What were the audiences like for these works at Judson?

CS: We had quite an ardent audience—we had sociologists, poets, Happenings people, Fluxus. It was very rich. But the audiences could also be diabolical as we moved into more conceptual movement principles. There was great hatred toward me, particularly by the critic Jill Johnston. She felt my work was "brainless." George Maciunas despised the work as being too personal, too sensual. Still, *Meat Joy* was on the front page of every New York newspaper, and for several months everyone's work was called "meat-" something or other. And then the most recent and nice development is my affinity with Lady Gaga, her meat dress.

LOB: Could you talk about the dominant masculine aesthetics that you were up against?

CS: It was still okay to be a dancer in traditions of masculine aesthetics: the dancer was not any competition for major historic importance. She or he was feminized, and belonged to a realm of sensuousness that was not in competition for the macho positions in the art world. But once you were painting or breaking traditions of dance, then there was a great deal of resistance. Part of my aesthetic determination was against Pop art's vitiation of the female—she was turned into an obsessive icon, as always, but this time a spray-painted formulation as if she were a kind of machinery, an idealized sharp-edged machinery that had no real viscera, no vulvic sexual energy. It was all through some phobic idealization. So when the Judson dancers were stripping and tearing things apart and moving through space it was shocking, it was startling, and it took a very activated, de-conventionalized masculine aesthetic to receive it and appreciate it, and that was happening. But we were still marginal.

LOB: Did women in the group talk about their status?

CS: Judson was pre-feminist. Women in the group talked about all the prohibitions around us. But most of us had partners who wanted to be supportive and share the energy. It was only toward the middle of the 1970s that suddenly we began to see that the masculine hierarchies were immovable—namely, restructuring aspects of exclusionary aesthetics, particularly in terms of painting and sculpture. So consciousness raising happened and a sense of separatism had to take place because male friends were saying, We want to discuss feminism with you, we want know what's going on ... but once they discussed it with us it was their ballgame all over again. There was a moment in the '70s where women painters, sculptors, musicians, and theoreticians—we all had to break away from our male colleagues, and sit down and say, What the crap is going on? Women had a marginalized position and it was a tremendous struggle and fight for everything through the 1970s, for work, for salary, for acknowledgment, for critical regard, and to change the pronouns so that not everything was: Man and His Images, the Artist and His Materials.

Catherine Christer Hennix

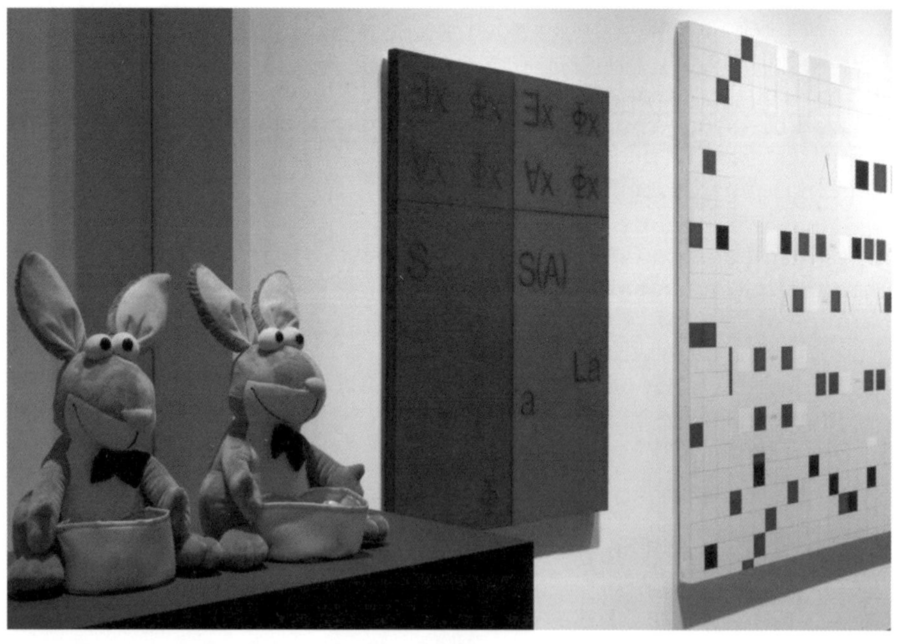

Catherine Christer Hennix: Traversée du Fantasme, Stedelijk Museum Amsterdam, 2018, installation view.

March 14, 2018
Artforum

Polymath artist Catherine Christer Hennix is known for her ground-breaking compositions, including The Electric Harpsichord, *1976, and* Central Palace Music, *1976. A retrospective of Hennix's visual work ran at the Stedelijk Museum Amsterdam in spring 2018. Here, Hennix discusses the exhibition and a performance (on February 16 and 17, 2018) that melded her mathematical interests with traditional practices of sustained pitches in just intonation.*

For the performance of *Blue(s) in Green to the 31 Limit*, I had Benjamin Duboc and Rozemarie Heggen on double bass, Hilary Jeffery on live sound, and my student Marcus Pal, in large part, did the computer parts. The latter was done actually back in September and October, when we began to work on a commission for the recent Lucio Fontana show *Ambienti/Environments* at Pirelli HangarBicocca in Milan. I was commissioned by curator Pedro Rocha to conceive of long-form compositions, or sonic counterparts, to Fontana's monochrome light environments. I titled them "Three Monochromatisms (Composition for the Computer)." The one we performed in Amsterdam drew on distinct computer-generated broken chords derived from "Monochromatism (Green)," which was played in the big green and blue room of the Fontana show. The title is also a reference to Bill Evans's ballad "Blue in Green," for which Miles Davis took credit.

Jazz has always been important to me. A key early experience for me was attending John Coltrane's performances in Stockholm—first with Miles and later with his quintet and quartet. At that time I was learning from Idrees Sulieman, who played with Coltrane back in the 1950s and who introduced me to the many great jazz musicians who passed through Stockholm. In 1970 La Monte Young introduced me to Pandit Pran Nath of the Kirana Gharana tradition, who became my Nada Guru. Studying under him altered my understanding of music altogether. It may not be uninteresting to mention that both the blues and Northern Indian raga arc influcnccd by Islamic musical traditions ... So, there's actually a line from Coltrane to the exponents of Kirana (and Dhrupad) via their roots in African/Eastern devotional music. I have lately tried to make more explicit my appreciation of this connection.

Getting back to the work, *Blue(s) in Green to the 31 Limit* is the first instance in which I used a formation involving two amplified double basses. The musicians joining me were all experienced jazz players, who knew how to accompany my subtle drone. It's still a work in progress.

I work in a system called "just intonation," which means that I have integer ratios between all the recurring frequencies. In this piece there was a correspondence between the frequencies of light and the frequencies of sound that we were putting out in the Fontana light environment, which were dependent on the acoustics. Of course, light and sound are two different media—one is electromagnetic, and the other is acoustic. To me, it's as if I'm adding sound to the light and the body of the light changes. I always liked Fontana's work. But I never knew him, personally. Pedro was aware of my work from a residency I did at the Museu de Arte Contemporânea de Serralves in Porto, Portugal, where I was also working with monochrome spaces and the just intonation of the standing, composite sound wave.

The performance was a success, but it was hard to pull off because I never show my work and I hardly ever perform, so I unfortunately don't have much contact with my audience. My shows are always sold out, but, still, I only have about one gig per year. You just can't do much with that type of schedule. And we're also underfunded, so the preparations aren't well done; the whole thing has to be done on a much more solid basis, and I can't find that foundation. The material support for this work is, simply, totally absent. And it can't be done without that support, so that's why you never see it, that's why you never hear it.

The exhibition opened the same day as the first performance, and so we also had a slightly stressful situation here in getting everything to work. But it's great to see the paintings that I made for *Parler Femme*, a 1991 group show at the Museum Fodor, exhibited again. One of these works is a re-creation of Jacques Lacan's formalization of sexual difference. For this show, I was actually planning to make a big part of it be about Lacan's term "urinary segregation," which seemed quite timely given the North Carolina bathroom bills that were defining access to public restrooms. But then these bills were repealed by the legislator and rephrased, while the Supreme Court declined to hear the original deposition, and it became a non-topic, so to speak, for the time being. Maybe this year or next year it'll come back. My intention was to draw attention to urinary segregation in order to demonstrate a work I had done a long time ago, while still retaining some timeliness. I also added works that illustrate some of the ramifications of segregation. Most of this two-room installation is dominated by an additional set of signifiers, some more iconic than others, which illustrate distinct stages of the phantasm and its singular logic. This logic ranges from the sense it extracts from the unreadable to the sense it extracts from the unthinkable and unimaginable. It strains our abilities to think that commonplace bathroom protocol is part of the origin of what is, in the end, unspeakable. To think that through to its logical end yields an important connection between aesthetics and ethics.

Claudia Rankine

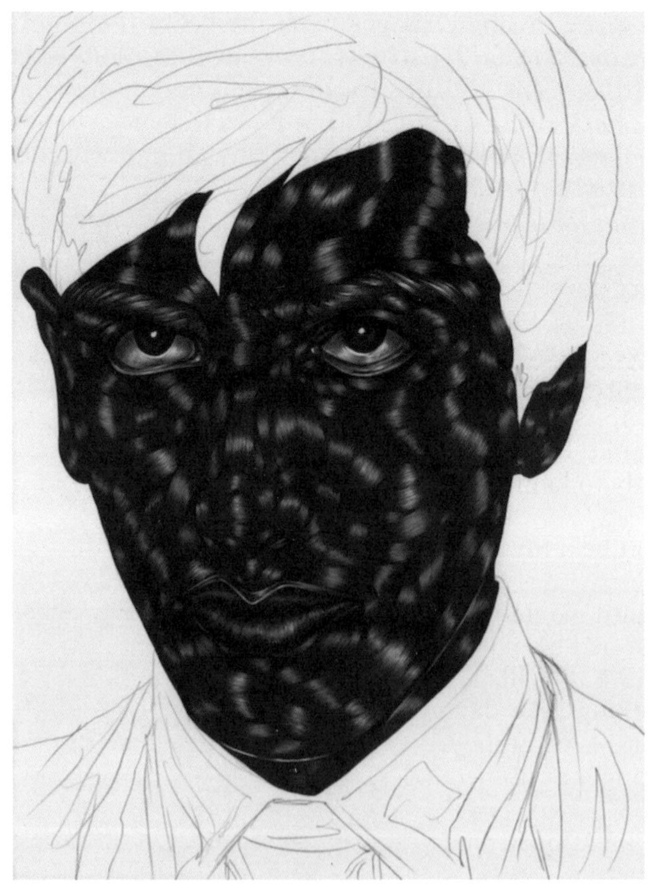

Toyin Ojih Odutola, *The Treatment I*, 2015, pen ink, gel ink, and pencil on paper, 12 × 9 inches (30.5 × 22.9 cm).

March 21, 2017
Artforum

The New York–based Racial Imaginary Institute examines the idea that race is a construct for all of us. Spearheaded by the poet, essayist, playwright, and 2016 MacArthur fellow Claudia Rankine, the institute plans to host exhibitions, performances, lectures, and talks. It is an antidote but not a rejoinder to the new administration in Washington, DC, because, as Rankine notes below, "Trump is not the beginning of this; he's just a blatant manifestation of it. It was in the air for a long time."

LOB: Where does the institute currently stand?

CR: We have a curatorial team, which seemed to make sense since what we want to do is curate events. This team includes Casey Llewellyn, Beth Loffreda, Monica Youn, LeRonn Brooks, Meg Onli, Margo Okazawa-Rey, and Sara'o Bery. And we have an advisory board. Right now, we're getting ready to launch our website, which will be our online home.

LOB: Will it be a roving, mobile space before you set down roots?

CR: Yes, until we find the space. We've had a number of people offer space to us—it's been lovely, actually. Tilton Gallery and Howl Gallery down in the East Village; the Brooklyn Historical Society as well, for talks, and things like that. We're also partnering with the Institute of Contemporary Art at the University of Pennsylvania. The rush to find a site is no longer as immediate because we've had people come forward.

LOB: You mentioned that you want the institute to be among the galleries in Chelsea.

CR: Yes, it's still what we're looking forward to doing, but it's an expensive endeavor, so it's a step at a time.

LOB: Is there an intention to appeal to people in the New York art world specifically?

CR: It's not a question of location but it is a question of being in dialogue. Culture drives a lot of things, including our understanding of who we are. It's certainly the gestalt that tilts our perceptions of self and other. I think it's important that we not be missed, and placement is important to me. It would have been easier for me to bring it to an academic space. I would have had more access and things would have moved much more quickly, but then we would have been inside an elite and closed space, and it would be harder to enter the mainstream, which is basically where we want to be. I mean, what would be lovely is if one of these galleries just had an extra space they would let us use as an extension of their own programming ...

LOB: I'm imagining a visitor looking at Robert Ryman paintings, at Dia, for instance, and then maybe stepping into the institute to hear a dialogue on whiteness that could affect their perception of the whiteness of those works.

CR: Exactly, so that you could have a framing. One of the things I love about Toyin Ojih Odutola's paintings is that she's asking us to think about what it means to color a colored person or a Black person or a white person. I went to her recent show at Jack Shainman and there was Prince Charles, in black pen and pencil, but still presented as white as you remember him. How that whiteness traveled through this black surface was interesting to me. We're bombarded with images of whiteness all the time, but they're not framed as whiteness. Instead they're framed as normality, as American life, as suburban life, as extreme wealth, but never as this thing called *whiteness*. What does it mean to make work that has that conversation as part of its making?

LOB: You've talked about going into an art bookstore and asking to see the books on whiteness, and no one could find them for you.

CR: The person working there looked at me like I was *crazy*. He was like, "What are you talking about?"

LOB: But if you had said Blackness he might have pulled out several books.

CR: Exactly. That white thing: white people aren't considered "white artists." And that means that what they do is *transcendent*. This is art of the highest order. Yet, there are many books on whiteness—by Richard Dyer, Nell Painter, and more.

LOB: Whiteness is also being manipulated by the so-called alt-right as well.

CR: The way American culture has made terms like *white supremacy*, *white dominance*, and *whiteness* such a non-thing contributes to why there's so much surprise about our new administration. Because now you actually have people in the administration who are white nationalists and no one knows what to do with that. The campaign to keep all of this silent and to transform it into a state of normalcy, rather than the state of whiteness, has worked.

LOB: What would you say to someone who thinks this is intrinsic to capitalism?

CR: It would make me feel better if I could think that this was really about the economy, or capitalism writ large. But I don't think so. The KKK was real. It was formed immediately after the Civil War— *immediately*. The Black codes were real, and they were formed with the intent of keeping people of color out of the economy and destabilizing their ability to have any kind of normalcy in terms of education, housing, and other aspects of their lives. So while I would like to believe the rhetoric around capitalism and the economy driving all of this, I just don't. A good example is the people who are on the Affordable Care Act who say they want to keep it but who also want to get rid of Obamacare. They understand that the ACA is useful to them, but they don't want anything that is proximate to Blackness near them. That's not about the economy.

LOB: When did the institute begin for you?

CR: Basically, when it occurred to me that we as a culture have no practice talking about race. The minute race comes up, everybody is armed and defensive, and all social graces disappear, the camps are formed. So at that moment, instead of responding to what was coming at me, I just thought, Why don't we take a minute and talk about why we don't know how to do this? I put out a call for people to write about why they do or won't write about race. And those essays became the book I then edited with Beth Loffreda and the artist Max King Cap in 2014,

The Racial Imaginary: Writers on Race in the Life of the Mind. The idea that Beth and I had at the time was that we would go on. We weren't calling it an institute, but we were asking, "Why don't we have a kind of online collection of art and response and dialogue around this?" We were thinking it would be like Siskel and Ebert or something where we'd be like, "So such and such a film just came out, and how does it address race?" Or, "I saw this show, and she was doing this with race."Around that time, I published *Citizen*. I had no idea that it would become such a public book. It meant that many things I was moving ahead with got put aside. And that lasted longer than I anticipated—suddenly 2014 was 2016. But then things started to quiet down, relatively speaking. And then I thought, wait, this might be the time for us to start this again. It didn't happen in response to Trump. Because Trump is not the beginning of this; he's just a blatant manifestation of it. It was in the air for a long time.

LOB: Is there a mission statement?

CR: Yes, here goes: *Race is one of the prime ways history lives in us*. Our name "racial imaginary" is meant to capture the enduring truth of race: it's an invented concept that nevertheless operates with extraordinary force in our daily lives, limiting our movements and imaginations. We understand that perceptions, resources, rights, and lives themselves flow along racial lines that confront some of us with restrictions and give others uninterrogated power. These lines are drawn and maintained by white dominance even as individuals and communities alike continually challenge them. Because no sphere of life is untouched by race, the institute gathers under its aegis an interdisciplinary range of artists, writers, knowledge-producers, and activists. It convenes a cultural laboratory in which the racial imaginaries of our time and place are engaged, read, countered, contextualized, and demystified.

LOB: What kind of shows are you envisioning?

CR: We're depending on the kindness of strangers. People are loaning work to us for the shows. At this point, we're asking artists to make pieces for us with the considerations I just outlined in mind. We've also had many people come to us and say, "This is my work, it might be of interest to you." Some of us are artists too so we're making work thinking about it. I can show you a piece that I'm working on. I've been trying to think of a thing in our culture that we all partake in, and yet which always lands in the same place. For me, blondeness is one of these things. The minute you think blonde, you're going to think white.

Even if you see it as freedom, if you see it as beauty, if you see it as youth, it creates its own lexicon around whiteness—so whiteness is freedom, whiteness is beauty, whiteness is youth, whiteness is desirability. I'm also fascinated by blondeness as something that's used in white supremacy as a signal of purity, but now it's been taken up by everyone, and in a way that doesn't even pretend to suggest that I was born this way. And so I made these stamps. We're going to start mailing them out. And I hope this is what artists will do—think about extending their practice in a way that's in dialogue with how whiteness functions in the culture.

LOB: The institute's audience is everyone.

CR: Yes, and if that weren't the case then I could have stayed in academia. It was the academic institutions that created the false histories, language, and science around whiteness, race, and Blackness. That allowed the justification of dehumanizing and killing populations. Even when it was then debunked as fabricated, it didn't matter. It was already in the water. And that was that. Sometimes people ask me, "Why aren't you angry with white people?" But I think it's not individuals. It's the culture itself. People are born into this. I also think that people believe in their goodness and they think they're good people. They don't identify as a community of whiteness because that's part of how whiteness is constructed. White people are individuals. They don't belong to the community of whiteness. So to speak about a community of whiteness is appalling to them because they're individuals, they're good people. There's a fantastic critic named Robin DiAngelo. She's responsible for the phrase "white fragility," which is the sense that people are so sensitive to being called out that their responses will go everywhere from tears to murder. She says that what white people should do is begin from the place where they know they're racist. That is, if white people could just accept the fact that they're racist because they're part of a racist culture, and that they belong to a group that has been bred on *internalized dominance*—that's her phrase—then we could start to have actual discussions about what's going on.

Constance DeJong

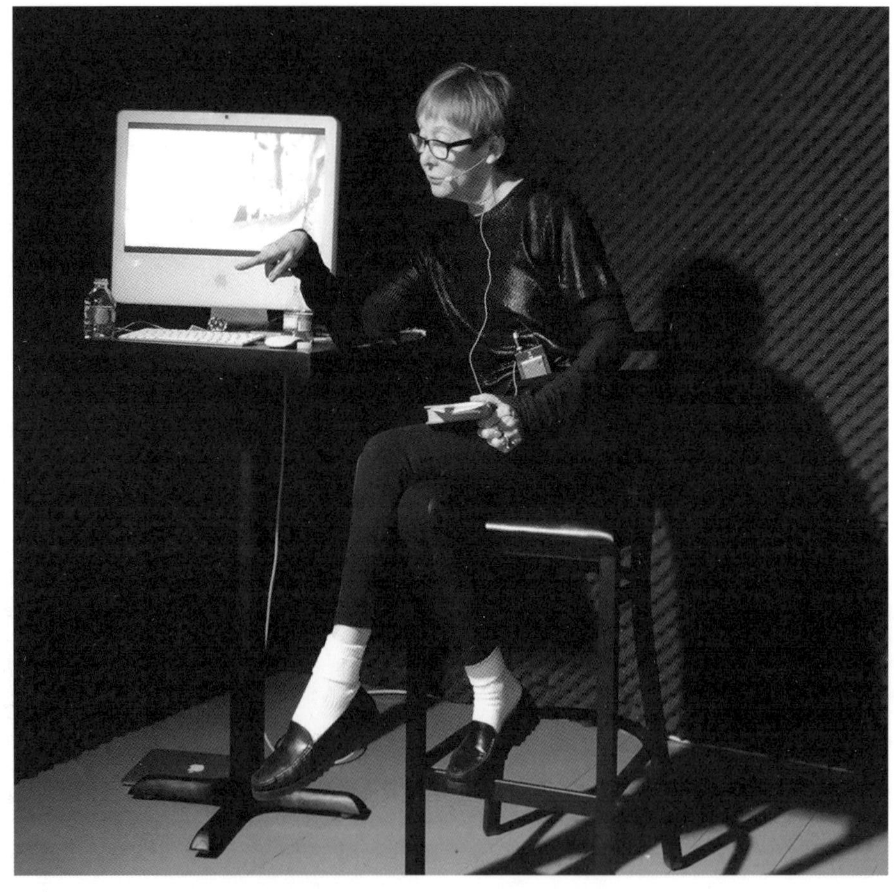

Constance DeJong, *SPEAKCHAMBER*, 2013, duet with an iMac, spoken text with video and audio, 57 minutes.

December 26, 2018
Artforum

Constance DeJong has long demonstrated what language is capable of—how it can be more than just a delivery system for the conventions of novels and short stories. Her scrupulous writings, recordings, and performances are typically suffused with sensitivity and humor, confessions and criticisms. Below she discusses how "the movement of thought" across the mind is a source of structuring language for her and her works in Let me consider it from here, *a four-artist show on intimacy which ran at the Renaissance Society in Chicago in winter 2018–19.*

This is the first time I've exhibited audio works that aren't embedded in an object, such as a chair or a bench that emits sound when a person sits down. Here, the sound is disembodied and installed in a tall-ceilinged, large room with four alcoves inside a Gothic-style building. In two of the niches, and in two places in the room's open space, I've placed umbrella speakers that guide the sound down, though there's a softness to all this, and it sometimes rises back up, given the acoustics of the building. I was hoping the installation would provide intimacy, as I'm interested in the experience of something that's both there and not there. The disembodied voice has been a concern of mine since I was a child, when I would glue my head to a transistor radio under my pillow every night. I was able to achieve a bit of that by using these speakers, which satisfied me. You step into each zone and experience the work by just standing there and listening.

The narratives are made of candles, night, insomnia, and a skylight. Those elements, in their particular ways, initiate content-in-motion remote from clock time, from quotidian activities. An ordinary candle flame conjures a Wells Fargo banker making off with his millions in the anxious view of the insomniac in *Bedside*, "with your tiny circumference of food clothing shelter cinched up tight in bed at this hour, going on four in the morning ..." I've been exploring the second person, you, as a subject. The audio narratives range from about four to seven minutes each. One was a text I had used before in another context, in a radio work, but I reedited, rerecorded, and reengineered it for this show, while the others were written in 2018 with the idea that they were audio works for me to perform. Recently, I've started performing with just spoken language and aural material onstage. Numbers of people have seen me perform over the years with video, but I've derived this new interest so there's no visual.

My fascination with sound came about rather slowly. In maybe 1978, I was sitting in my kitchen on Ninth Street getting ready for the first reading of my book *Modern Love*. I noticed I wasn't looking at the pages anymore, and that I was just speaking. It was a micro-epiphany about real time and sonics for me. It was also an initiation of confronting what I always knew silently, as someone putting language on the page: the time-based nature of language, the changing velocities, the speed, the sequence, and so on. All of that is now central to my work—whether in performance, on a page or a screen, in objects and installations. But it was a slow dawning to involve myself so directly in the way I do now, and it was my good luck to discover that about myself because I find straightforward readings quite difficult—it's not a fit, to be reading from a piece of paper as a live event.

Now when I read, during a performance, it's because within the narrative there's a moment of text: a letter, a paragraph from a book, or something like that—something that is, within the narrative, a written text. When I perform, there's a distinction between the read language and the spoken language. That difference is important to me. For instance, I performed one of the texts during the opening of the show in Chicago. That one features a character that has a bunch of friends near their bed on the floor—i.e., books. During an insomniac moment, after a bad dream, the character remembers a quote from Elizabeth Bisland's *Dreams and Their Mysteries*, written in 1896, and through the character I read this text:

> ... night after night, with calm incuriousness we open the door onto that ghostly underworld, and hold insane revels with fantastic spectres, weep burning tears for empty griefs, babble with foolish laughter at witless jests, stain our souls with useless crime, or fly

with freezing blood from the grasp of an unnamed dread; and with morning, saunter serenely back from these wild adventures into the warm precincts of the cheerful day, unmoved, unstartled, and forgetting.

I have an ongoing interest in dreaming, unlike most of today's neuroscientists. It's a topic that's been pushed off to the side in the United States, though there are a bunch of events related to it. You can go to a dream fair in Las Vegas, and somebody will tell you what it all means. Since Freud, it's as if we've drawn a line in the sand, and we've not progressed, and that baffles me because, of course, if we're fortunate, we sleep and dream every day, for a considerable portion of our twenty-four, diurnal cycle.

As a young person I discarded chronological and alphabetical order, in addition to various other systems we force language into when composing fiction and narrative. At first, this was with a not very clear awareness in response to writing conventions. But as time went on, I became increasingly aware of the movement of thought. It's something we're all familiar with: for example, you're waiting for the bus, but you're thinking about ten years ago, and also, did you turn off the gas? It goes on and on—we're always in many different time frames, for *a lot* of waking life. I suppose I've paid attention to that, and it's a source of structuring. I don't have to use language as a delivery system for any manipulative, controlling binaries or chronological clock time. Rather, I use associative thinking as a basis for how I put language together in my work, and it eliminates whole subjects that don't interest me. It focuses me. It's true that I work with ideas of narrative structure and that process, in part, is about recognizing a space of introspection. If you think about narrative work—be it cinema, performance, opera, novels, you name it—it's very outward. For me, introspection is an ineffable and ephemeral thing, definitely not navel-gazing, and it has crept into the very substance and form of my present work.

Dianna Molzan

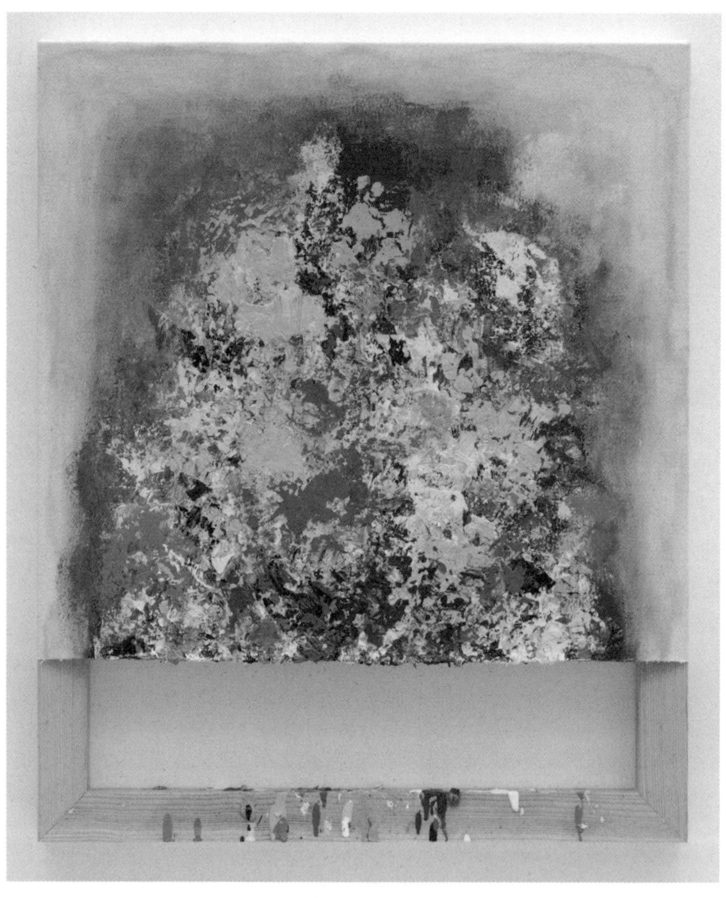

Dianna Molzan, *Untitled*, 2009, oil on canvas, 24 × 20 inches
(60.9 × 50.8 cm).

April 6, 2011
Artforum

Dianna Molzan here talks about Bologna Meissen, *her first solo show in New York as well as her first museum exhibition. The exhibition ran at the Whitney Museum of American Art in spring 2011.*

Like many people, I spend a lot of time visiting art museums. I especially like to visit the big museums and explore the seemingly endless rows of vitrines that contain artisan objects and old bits of stuff from cultures long gone. I think that all of this perusing and my curiosity about these objects, which aren't necessarily given much context in the galleries, have affected my approach to making paintings.

In museums, objects are nearly equalized; that is, there seems to be this process that brings culturally and historically varied works into the present moment for the viewer. For example, in a single afternoon, and under one roof, you can see a pre-Columbian clay pot, a panel of Victorian lace, an El Greco painting, and a Claes Oldenburg soft sculpture—so it doesn't seem that odd to me to kind of re-create that viewing experience within a group of paintings.

Painting has a wonderful ability to conjure up so many diverse qualities using unchanging materials (paint, canvas, frame support)—one work can look sumptuous while another looks coarse, and it all depends on how the materials are applied. Even though it can be said that I'm revealing the structure of painting in my work, illusionism is still very present.

There's no sense of hierarchy from one painting to the next in my work, but instead there's a path of idiosyncratic influence that changes from day to day. This is a conversation about a fascination with objects. In my studio, I'm responding to objects and I'm making other objects that I want people to have a sensory response to, that spark an internal and independent engagement. This is why I don't title my works. When you're moving through the world and come upon something compelling and random, it often doesn't come with a caption and a title, and you must rely on your own wits and deductive reasoning to make sense of it.

In my mind I'm not deconstructing painting; instead I'm exploring and maximizing everything up for grabs inherent to it. More than anything else, I feel like an enthusiast.

Donna J. Haraway

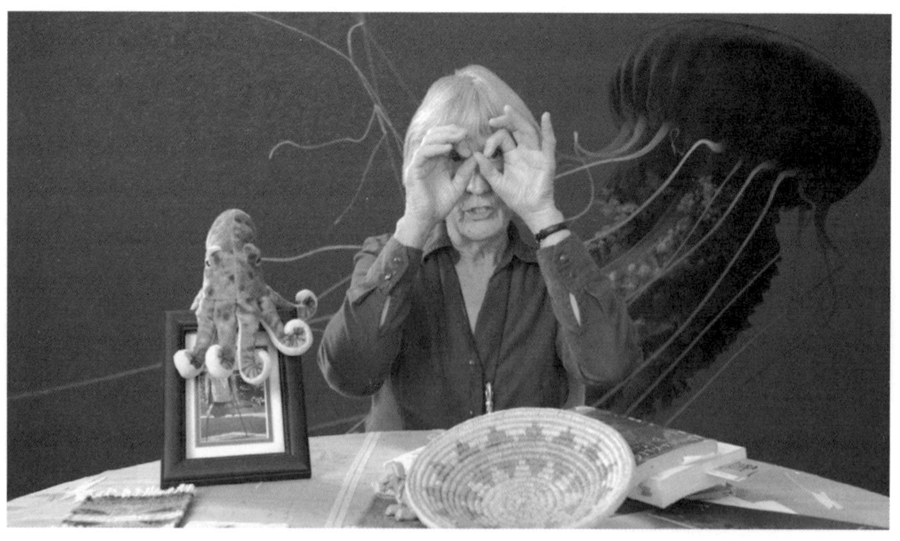

Still from *Donna Haraway: Story Telling for Earthly Survival*, 2016, directed by Fabrizio Terranova.

September 6, 2016
Artforum

From her classic "Cyborg Manifesto," first published three decades ago, to her arguments about the "Chthulucene," multispecies feminist theorist Donna J. Haraway is one of our most daring thinkers. Haraway's book Staying with the Trouble: Making Kin in the Chthulucene *(Duke University Press, 2016) urgently argues for a nonanthropocentric view of climate change and is driven metaphorically and theoretically by the signifier SF—for string figures, science fact, science fiction, speculative feminism, and speculative fabulation—as she discusses here.*

It's not like I have a vendetta against the word *anthropocene*—I understand the intentions of the scientists who initially proposed it in 2000 and the important work it does. But as with other big terms, it's both too big and too small, and it proposes itself as a kind of universal in several senses, as if it's humanity or man that did this thing, as opposed to situated human beings in complicated histories. Many people now—for example, the Inuit of the circumpolar north—are acutely aware of deep and troubling changes in the world they live in. But calling it anthropocene doesn't gather them together, nor does it set up alliances that might be necessary. I have an allergy to the particular etymology of the anthropic: the one who looks up, the one who is not of the earth, the one whose feet are in the mud but his eyes are in the sky; the retelling, once again, of the stories that I think have done us dirt in Western cultures.

That all made me think: if we can only have one word, let's use *capitalocene*. But of course the fact is that we need more than one word. *Capitalocene* is a term I thought I had invented, but it turns out I most certainly did not. (Andreas Malm first used it in 2009 and then Jason Moore picked it up.) Capitalocene refers to the complex networks that have transformed lives for everybody on this planet. Not in the same ways, but deeply still. Capitalism is obviously based on growth—but not just any kind of growth: the growth that depends on resourcing the earth for the kind of expansion and extraction that result in profit, which is, in turn, distributed unequally. This unleashing of the motors of endless growth, extraction, and the production of ever-new forms of inequality is intrinsic to capitalism. It's a vastly destructive process, whether you're talking about social systems or natural systems. Capitalocene at least captures that this is a few-hundred-year-old process of building wealth through exterminationist extraction. In comparison, *anthropocene* implies that this is somehow a species act; that it's the separation of whatever it is that makes us human from all else, and that it's another human exceptionalist move. But that's just wrong. It's empirically, morally, ethically, and emotionally wrong.

This book is about staying with all this trouble. It's about a becoming-with-each-other in another new term: what I'm calling the chthulucene. This can't be done in the mode of critique, which is never enough. In the chthulucene, critique is one of many practices tempered by others that lead to an opening of what's still possible. Chthulu comes from *chthonic*—the earthly powers and processes—human too, but much more than human. But this isn't some sort of ancient, destroyed-by-modernity story. It's an ongoing and present story. These chthonic powers, forces, and entities are coupled with the suffix *–cene*, drawn from *kainos*, or the thick now, the present, which is not instantaneous but extends into many kinds of time, into presence. Into cultivating response-ability.

Nearly every page of the book grows out of connections among art, science, and activism. Artists who are engaging in this overlap especially drew me. For example, the cover is an untitled print by Geraldine Javier. Rooted in a bony pelvis that mimes the shape of a butterfly, the image rises through a skeletal vertebral column made with vibrant filaments that ends in a butterfly with delicate coloration, constructed from dry leaves. The image has human feet—*sort of*—and a human pelvis—*sort of*. The whole thing is living and dying, insectoid and humanoid, fibrous and bony, plant and animal. It's a transformationally metamorphic piece, both disturbing and reassuring. It's also an invitation to stay with the trouble. Fiber arts recur in the book repeatedly—from the crochet coral reef project of Margaret and Christine Wertheim to old and contemporary Navajo weaving, and from cat's cradling to string figuring. The latter is a theoretical apparatus for visual, verbal, and theoretical metaphors I use throughout the book. String figuring, one of the many "SF"s in the book, involves making patterns with others. The various partners engaging in string figuring are active and passive; in their relaying patterns to each other, threads get dropped and things become unraveled or a new pattern emerges that's a source of possibility and joy. String figuring is also akin to the way I write. Perhaps the first things that folks like me think of when they see the signifier SF are science fiction and science fantasy. But quickly come more terms: science fact, speculative fabulation, speculative feminism, so far ... SF keeps ramifying into many terms that are pulled together in this signifier.

One of the most urgent tasks that we mortal critters have is making kin, not babies. This making kin, both with and among other humans and not humans, should happen in an enduring fashion that can sustain through generations. I propose making kin nongenealogically, which will be an absolute need for the eleven-plus billion humans by the end of this century—and is already terribly important. I'm interested in taking care of the earth in a way that makes multispecies environmental justice the means and not just the goal. So I think of making kin as a way of being really, truly prochild—making babies rare and precious—as opposed to the crazy pronatalist but actually antichild world in which we live. It's making present the powers of mortal critters on earth in resistance to the anthropocene and capitalocene. That's really what the book is about.

Dorothea Rockburne

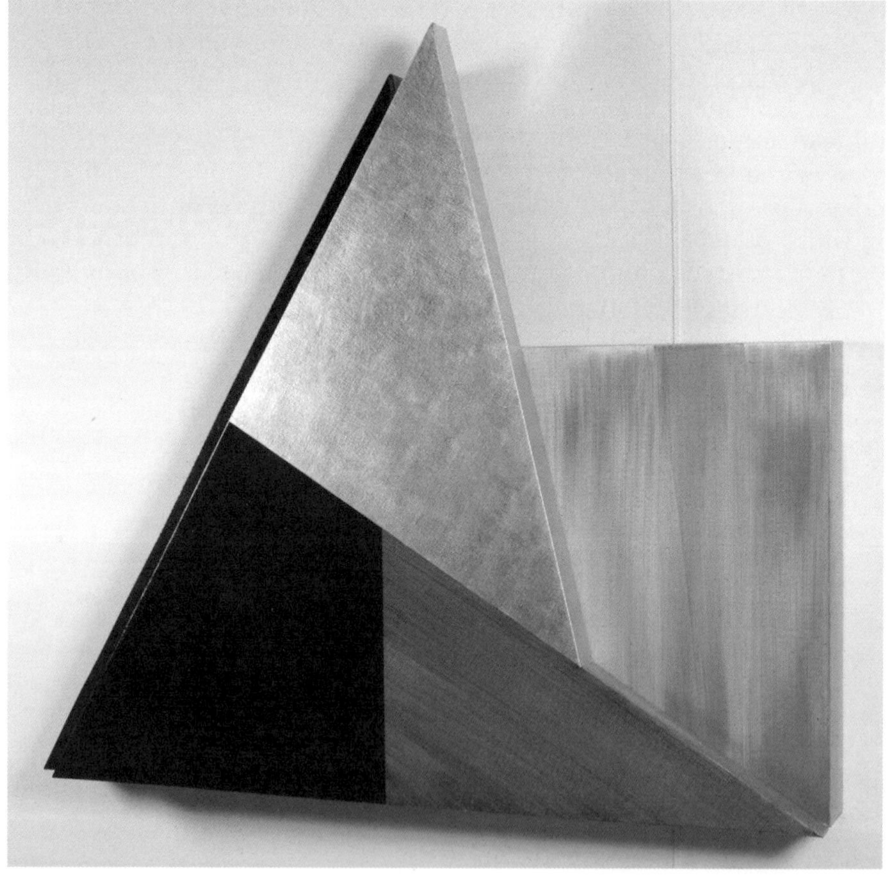

Dorothea Rockburne, *Light shines in the darkness, and the darkness has not understood it,* 1987–88, oil and gold leaf on gessoed linen, 59 × 70 inches (150 × 178 cm).

July 6, 2011
Artforum

Dorothea Rockburne's first retrospective was at the Parrish Art Museum in Southampton, New York, in summer 2011. Rockburne is well known for her commitment to painting, which has carried her career from her intricate geometric studies of the late 1960s to more recent abstractions that explore the solar system. The exhibition also tracked her lifelong interests in ancient knowledge, topology, and astronomy.

Viewers shouldn't have to know a lot about math and science to understand what's going on in my work. Art communicates on an emotional level. While a novice might not understand that Matisse, for instance, was dealing with Byzantine space and not with Cubism, they can still stand in front of a Matisse and fall in love with the work and know nothing about art. However, I think if one understands the basis for an artist's work then it just makes it that much fuller. I can't be responsible for other people's responses; all I can do is paint my heart out and hope that it reaches them, which I think it does.

It's wonderful to have many works in the retrospective that I haven't seen since they were made. For instance, there's a painting from the *Pascal* series, *The Light Shines in the Darkness and the Darkness Is Not Understood*, and it belongs to a museum in Texas. I haven't seen it since it was shown in 1967. All of the works look very alive and have the same presence as when they were made, and it's revealing to me to see the constant thread through it all. I don't have a master plan for my art or life, but as I went through the work and my diaries, I realized that besides having a geometric base for the work, there's also a philosophical base that's continuous.

Usually, when I begin to see work in my mind's eye, I envision the kind of material that it needs. The thought, emotion, and material aren't separate. I'm always following this vision I have, and it has a lot to do with understanding nature, but from the point of view of topology. One of the quotes I use in the retrospective's catalogue is from Max Dehn, my math teacher at Black Mountain College. He said, "Nature is written in numbers." It's important to understand those numbers.

Max was so completely seductive in the way he taught. He had to talk me into taking his class. He must have been in his early eighties. I thought I wasn't trained properly, since people were coming from all over just to study with him. I didn't have much of a math background, but he taught me so much about the mathematics of nature, and it all just sank in and made everything understandable in a way that it hadn't been before.

My work has been based on the golden mean for a long time now. This ratio is something that, when you use it, just lends itself to rhythms and vibrations and magic—force, form, divisions, and so on. It's more obscure in my recent work, but I still begin with that proportion. It's there in the ten latest pieces in the retrospective, which are all from the *Stardust* series. With these, I'm using some pretty complex geometry, but of course I'm trying to simplify it. They're based on topological premises, which I learned from Max, who was also a topologist. Topology is a form of geometry I'm really interested in, and I like that it lends itself to astronomy. I had wanted to make these works for the past twenty years, but more recently some understanding of how to do it developed. When utilizing topology, it's always a matter of trying to put a four-dimensional construct on a two-dimensional surface, and that's very hard to do.

I began to become interested in stardust after someone sent me a photograph of a perfect hexagon over Saturn in 2007. I began to think about how the hexagon got there, and I realized that there must have been an explosion that released particles, and that some electromagnetic current in space pushed on those particles and turned it into this shape. But how that happened remains so mysterious. Of course, when stars explode there are particles, and right now we're really seeing these things through sophisticated telescopes. I'm looking forward to our being able to see further into the earlier universe as time goes on. Perhaps we'll discover not only how but also *why* this all happened.

Ebony G. Patterson

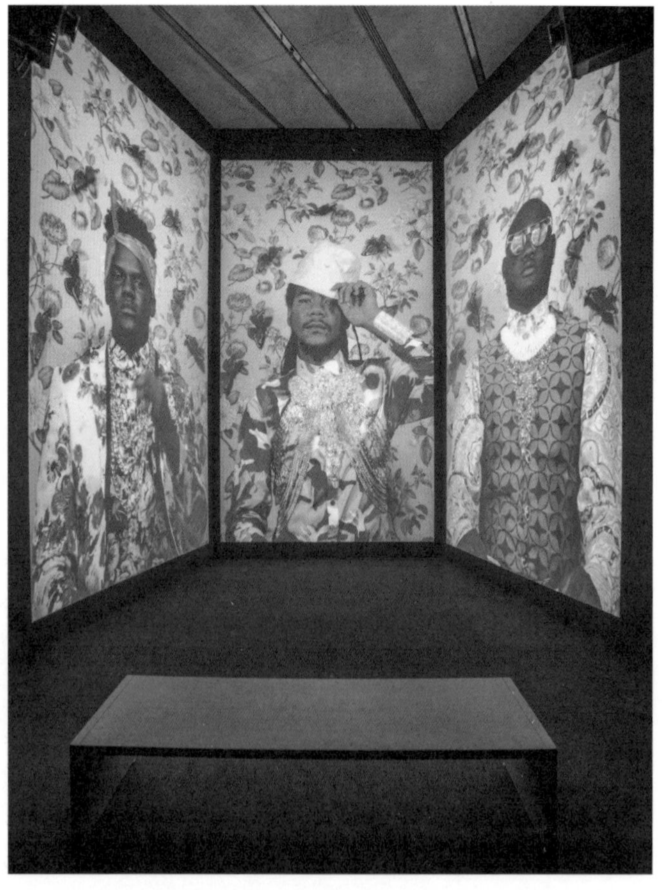

Ebony G. Patterson, … *three kings weep* …, 2018, 3-channel
digital video (color, sound, 8 minutes 34 seconds).

October 4, 2019
Artforum

Ebony G. Patterson's slow and monumental video installation on dress and dignity, ... three kings weep ..., debuted in her solo exhibition at Pérez Art Museum Miami in 2018 and traveled to the Speed Art Museum in Louisville, Kentucky, and then the Nasher Museum of Art in Durham, North Carolina. Below, she discusses the work.

This work comes out of my ongoing research and thoughts around dress as a way of performing dignity. It's the second video I've made, and was prompted, in part, by an article I read in 2015 about doctors at the University of Virginia who believed that Black people experience little to no pain. I thought that was such a tragedy: to be in the field of care and to have such predetermined ideas about something that all of humanity experiences—no matter the color of skin. I began to wonder what would it mean for someone to force an audience to witness their humanity—to strip away this surface that's somehow not seen so that one was forced to look. I also wondered what it would mean to demand that someone sees that person through a stripping or a removal.

"See me" is a phrase I've used in other projects. I consider it a demand, not a request. As I continued to think through the problems of this piece, I wondered: Why would these bodies surrender to anyone? The work is certainly about the value of their bodies! So instead of showing stripping, as I had originally thought, I decided to present these young men getting dressed, and their gaze never leaves you. You see them weep—not bawl. It's not a moment for pity. It's almost as if their tears are cleansing them. The very last thing they do is literally crown themselves. We think of crowning as something bestowed upon a person, but I wanted to show what it means to not wait for that, and rather to sit in one's sense of dignity: to crown oneself.

I have tried to use my work as a way of confronting the viewer through scale, and that's part of the reason why this video is projected so large. I want the audience to be immersed physically, emotionally, and psychologically within the work so they become aware of their own bodies. The video is shown in a place that feels like a chapel. There's an expectation of reverence that happens as you're sitting at the feet of these three young men. They become deities.

The viewer hears lines from Claude McKay's poem "If We Must Die," and the words come forth like needles in utter silence. The poem was written in 1919 and it's extremely relevant today. It's read aloud by a teenage boy, and his voice hadn't quite cracked yet when we recorded. The idea is that a child is leading these men and galvanizing them for their deaths. I wanted to present these bodies in a way that allowed space to demonstrate the full sense of the potential of their vulnerability. I was also thinking about the way the Black male body is weaponized in public space and seen as highly charged. And for Black children, the potential for innocence in public space is in question.

What does it mean for people who have been seen as systematically powerless to employ the tool of dress as a way to perform their value? There's long been a critique of poor people spending too much money on material things, and we've always lived in a world that places value on "things"—and not the person. My work acknowledges that, if I live in a space that says I'm not worthy, what does it mean to use those same tools to throw the question of value right back at you? Like a call-and-response.

I've talked about this a few times before, but it still applies: I once read a blog article written by a woman who describes her mother dressing up to go to a social security office to help an elderly neighbor out. She asked her mother about this and her mom said that she dressed up so that people would just take her seriously. She's negotiating these systems that says bodies like hers are not allowed dignity, but she uses the signifiers of dress as a way to say "I am here and you will take me seriously." But it also goes back to the Civil Rights Movement: MLK talked about the suit as armor.

I would like to think that my audience comes to look, that they don't come to simply see. To look involves analysis, and with looking comes query. It's an active engagement from the start. We take in so much information so quickly all the time. But we've lost a sense of what it means to just stop and look. In that stopping, the viewer might take away something, but that's entirely up to them. All I ask is that they be present.

Elaine Reichek

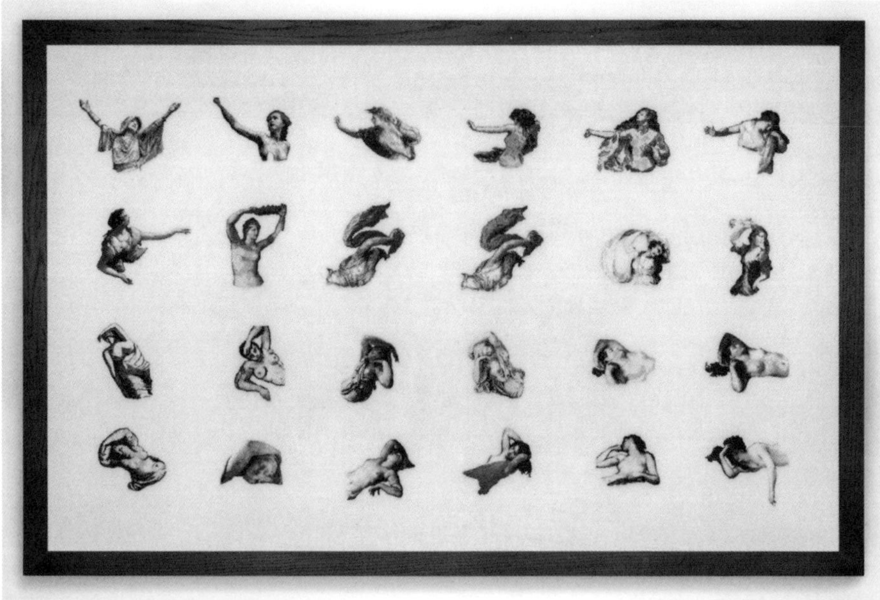

Elaine Reichek, *Toutes les filles* (All the Girls), 2016–17, hand embroidery on linen, 50 ½ × 79 inches (128.3 × 200.7 cm).

April 10, 2018
Artforum

Everything old is new again, and vice versa. Elaine Reichek is a New York–born and –bred artist who has long engaged with some of the women of ancient Greek myths in her works, often via hand embroidery and digital sewing. Her exhibition Now If I Had Been Writing This Story, *which took its title from a poem by Stevie Smith, featured ten works from the past eleven years and was on view at the Secession in Vienna in spring 2018.*

For this show, I wanted to spotlight part of a long ongoing body of work. It consists of two series: *Ariadne's Thread* and *Minoan Girls*. They're really the same project. Because the Secession is historically a particularly rich place, I've chosen works that I felt would both comment on and amplify the site. Gustav Klimt's *Beethoven Frieze* is in the building, and most visitors to the museum go to see that. And if they wander into the contemporary art shows, well, good.

This work deals with the telling, retelling, and deconstructing of rather primal narratives of desire and betrayal, but also of rape, incest, and bestiality. And now it's sited in this unique building, in which classical motifs are married to a modern slab structure. The Vienna Secessionists' Latin motto, "*Ver Sacrum*," refers to classical art as an eternal and unending source of inspiration. So, for me, this presents a nice opportunity to go back and forth between the old and the new—which I always toggle between. There's also a long tradition, of course, of the decorative arts in Vienna. One of the Secession's main ideas was to level the field, on the one hand, between traditional painting and sculpture and, on the other hand, bookmaking, design, textile production, and the "applied arts."

The kind of modernism that it introduced, which itself shuttles back and forth between high art and craft, is still a topic of conversation in the art world.

I was trained as a painter—I'm not trained in craft. But craft was an avenue for me to investigate and has a truly interesting and engaging alternative history, which I felt carried its own meaning. It also allowed me to develop a language that wasn't as reliant on the dominant language of high modernism. So, after going to grad school at Yale in 1964 and getting out of an all-male, mostly painting tradition, I began to use thread. It suited my purposes.

Ariadne's Thread is named after the clue of thread that Ariadne gives Theseus in order to navigate his way in and out of the labyrinth and slay the Minotaur. Of course, the thanks she gets—after plotting the murder of her half brother—is that Theseus abandons her! They sail off together to the island of Crete, she goes to sleep—you snooze you lose—and when she gets up, he's sailing away. The stories of the Minoan girls are about their unbridled desires and transgressions. Of course, the original myths attribute agency only to the gods, but in my retelling, each woman is conscious of her role in the story.

The piece that will introduce the show as you go up the staircase is an appropriated Eugène Atget photograph of a statue at Versailles, a copy of a Roman copy of a Greek statue of Ariadne. Under it, I've quoted lines from Giorgio de Chirico's poem "The Statue's Desire." Inside the main gallery, one wall will be covered with an eighteenth-century neo-classical wallpaper taken from the Hamilton House in Maine. I wanted this backdrop to function like a framing device. There's a lot of framing and reframing in my work, which act metaphorically. I also wanted to highlight how neoclassicism in America is different from neoclassicism in Europe, and how in this young country we never really had a large artisanal class.

I felt I needed to represent all four of the Minoan girls: Europa, the grand matriarch; her daughter-in-law Pasiphaë; and her granddaughters Ariadne and Phaedra. So, I took an image of Klimt's famous *Tree of Life* and turned it into the Minoan girls' genealogy sampler. Because the gods produced a variety of offspring with numerous partners, it's hard to keep track of who begat whom.

Pattern and repetition, both textual and visual, are other things I wanted to emphasize. Bulls appear repeatedly in these myths, the two sisters hook up with the very same Theseus, and you can barely keep track of the suicides. Visual patterns appear both in the wallpaper and in the textile pattern of *You Coasts (Ocher)*, which features Europa perched on Zeus who is in disguise as a bull. I found this pattern on the Victoria and Albert Museum's website and had it silkscreened on linen, and then I added embroidery and stitched a quote from the ancient Greek poet Nonnus, in which Europa assigns Zeus three different roles: "You coasts, pray tell my loving father that Europa has left her native land seated on a bull, my *kidnapper*, my *captain*, and, I think, my *husband*."

Then there's *I Wonder Sometimes*, featuring a rather rapey image of Pasiphaë, with her own bull—a real one!—which I've taken from André Masson's painting and paired with my own cobbled-together translation from *Pasiphaë: Chant de Minos* by the reactionary poet Henry de Montherlant. The show has both hand-embroidered work and embroideries made by a digital sewing machine. One of these digital embroideries, *I Wonder Why*, includes photographs of Sarah Bernhardt playing Phaedra, first as a young woman and later on a farewell tour. Another piece is a riff on Jasper Johns's work, with embroidered text highlighting the words *desire*, *dread*, and *despair* in the repeated names Ariadne, Theseus, and Phaedra. *Ariadne in Crete* remakes a poster created by John Currin for a production of the Richard Strauss opera *Ariadne auf Naxos*. In my rendition Ariadne is even more exaggerated than as he painted her, and the text by Seneca reads, "No daughter of Minos has ever got off lightly in love—sin is always attached!" Another embroidery on canvas mesh, *You Were the Heroine*, allows you to see the stretcher bars behind the surface, part of the backstory.

The newest and largest embroidery, *Toutes les filles*, trades language for gesture. Because the myths began as performances enacted by wandering poets, long before they were written down, gesture is an essential part of each narrative. *Toutes les filles* has twenty-four images representing Europa and her daughters, which I fished out of the sea of Google Images I trawl through regularly. I stitched each image on pink linen in four rows of six. Ariadne is well represented, in her coded pose—hand behind head—that was so well known to the moderns. Henri Matisse used it in *Blue Nude*, which appears here and in my nine-part *Swatch* piece that's lined up on shelves in a cabinet outside of the gallery space. Back to *Toutes les filles*—Pasiphaë appears, as do Phaedra, with arms thrown up in her iconic gesture of grief, and Europa, looking over her shoulder toward the shore as she's being abducted. These women convey their stories not only within the texts, but also through their bodies.

Eleanor Antin

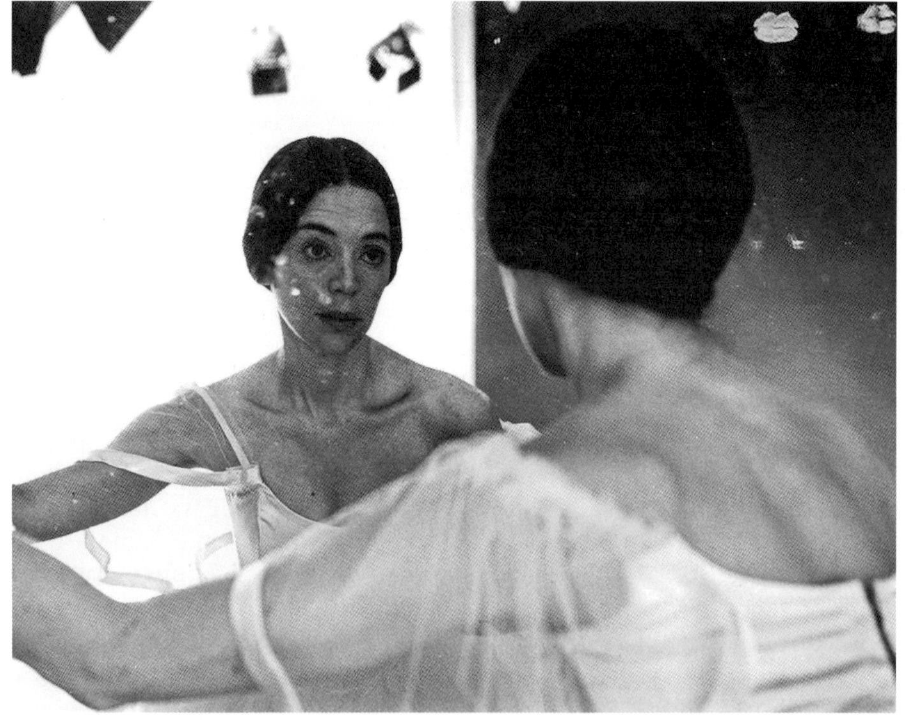

Eleanor Antin, *Portrait of Eleanora Antinova*, 1970s, black-and-white photograph.

November 16, 2013
Artforum

Throughout her nearly fifty-year career, Eleanor Antin has played many roles, from artist to filmmaker to author and beyond. Antin was born in the Bronx in 1935 and moved in June 1968 to Southern California, where she embarked on her early conceptual works and fictional personas, including the King of Solana Beach, Eleanor Nightingale, and Eleanora Antinova. Multiple Occupancy: Eleanor Antin's "Selves," *a survey exhibition of her videos, photographs, performances, and films, was on view at Columbia University's Miriam and Ira D. Wallach Art Gallery in fall 2013, and it highlighted these and other roles that Antin produced between 1972 and 1991. The show traveled to the Institute of Contemporary Art, Boston, in spring 2014. After retiring from twenty-seven years of teaching at the University of California at San Diego (UCSD), Antin worked on her large-scale allegorical photographic series* The Last Days of Pompeii, *2001;* Roman Allegories, *2004; and* Helen's Odyssey, *2007. Her paperback coming-of-age memoir,* Conversations with Stalin, *was published in September 2013 by Green Integer.*

LOB: What was it like to move to California in 1968?

EA: Southern California was a rather shocking experience. It wasn't like going to LA or San Francisco. San Diego was a very sleepy town. My husband and I had just gotten jobs at UCSD.

LOB: Do you consider yourself a Californian artist?

EA: I do. When we first moved there, it was the summer after the Summer of Love. But it didn't feel that way; that spring Martin Luther

King Jr. was killed. The day that we arrived in California was the day that Robert F. Kennedy had won the presidential primary and he was assassinated that night. We didn't know that, we were still cheering because Kennedy was against the war, even if he came to this position very late.

LOB: What was the art community like in San Diego?

EA: Actually I was teaching at UC Irvine first and then I taught at UCSD, but even before that I started to make connections with all sorts of people. UCSD eventually became the most avant-garde department in the country. I believe we were the first department to have photography, video, film, performance, painting, sculpture—though not too many people wanted to do painting and sculpture—and art history all together. We used to have a Festival of the Avant-Garde and that's where I did my first *King* performance. And it became a tighter group, Pauline Oliveros was teaching in the music department and Linda Montano was living with her at the time. I started getting close with a number of feminists from LA, which was really a lively scene and it was very performance-oriented from the beginning. I didn't know Judy Chicago and Mimi Shapiro; I think they started working as painters, but very soon it all branched out and the more conceptually oriented and performance people took over my interest. I became very close with Arlene Raven, who was running the Women's Building; I was very friendly with Suzanne Lacy. Rachel Rosenthal was starting her wonderful performances. There's a whole bunch of people who were hanging around the Women's Building and also the Los Angeles Institute of Contemporary Art, which didn't last for too long. But remember, I live in San Diego, about one hundred miles away, and in those days you could maybe drive up to LA in two hours, but now it's a disaster with all the cars. So between the group in San Diego and my friends in LA, by the 1970s I had a rather wide circle, even though my galleries and my work weren't like anyone else's. When the gallery that I was with on Madison Avenue closed, I went with Ron Feldman in 1976 and I have been with him ever since.

LOB: Were any of the artists from the UC San Diego art community in your work at the time?

EA: I started including people in my productions in 1977 with *The Angel of Mercy*, which is about the Crimean War, the first war that was photographed. I took pictures of friends and colleagues in Victorian costumes. Martha Rosler was a grad student at UCSD at the time and she was in this work. She and I both had a kid about the same age and I remember we'd go to the rather poor imitations of the New York anti-war marches. We used to go together, holding our little kids, thinking they'd like the parade. The first nurse works I did were with paper dolls and they were also done with my friends. Anyone who came and visited me became a nurse: I drew them in their underwear, and they became paper dolls. When I later drew the paper clothes to cover them with, they were transformed into actors in my theater. So some friendly amiable people might become murderers, which meant that some had to become victims. But maybe later, they disavowed their old lives. Maybe they became saintly and saved others from themselves. Maybe they didn't. Lots of high drama in my theater.

LOB: It's interesting to me that you were working with theatricality, which wasn't in fashion in some art circles.

EA: Yes, the early Conceptualists despised theatricality. The establishment didn't approve of me. But I can't help it—that's my nature. I see the world as a theater and all of us as actors. I guess I'm Elizabethan when you think about it. All the world's a stage, so act. I remember I was asked by a magazine to write about my work and I wrote that I was a post-Conceptual artist because of my theatricalism. I thought no one would understand where I was coming from. And then later on, when everyone was referring to post-Conceptualism, I was laughing to myself. A lot of the stuff I was interested in became widely popular: using different media, using theatricality, using one's autobiography—whether invented or real—and using the camera in all sorts of fictitious ways.

LOB: It's very difficult to categorize your work since you use so many different formats, too. We haven't even talked about your large-scale projects on the ancients yet. What prompted those?

EA: I've completed three different photographic series: the *Roman Allegories*, *The Last Days of Pompeii*, and *Helen's Odyssey*. And I've worked with tons of actors. Ancient Greece and Rome had been passions of mine ever since I was a kid. At some point I realized that our empire—the American empire—is quite similar to the Roman Empire. I don't know if life was any good back then for people, but it was certainly a rich and sensual time. For instance, Pompeii was a wealthy town, though it was living on the edge of a disaster. That's how I see the whole world now, especially the United States Empire. Basically I was working for almost a decade on these projects with lots of people. I love working with the creative energy of other people. The work begins with sketches so I know who is going to be who. I choose people who are creative and who can understand me and who I can get together with in that understanding. They end up adding all sorts of things, and that's one of the pleasures of this work. But I do consider it all my vision and, even though people are partaking, I insist upon what I want.

LOB: So it's not exactly collaborating, in other words?

EA: Well, remember I was a teacher for thirty years, so I'm used to bringing creative possibilities out of people. And sometimes someone's suggestion might alter what I have in my mind, make it more plausible or enticing, or sexy. So sure, I'll take that idea, and in that sense we're working together. But I do consider it my passion for the ancient world and its relationship to contemporary time that brought those works into being. I couldn't have done it by myself. But some of my other work I've done completely by myself. I have alternated between those modes. I ended up stopping the ancient series. As much as I love my actors, I wanted to work by myself. And that's when I started my memoir.

LOB: Tell us more about writing the memoir. Do you think you'll keep writing?

EA: I majored in writing in college. I think if I hadn't been so fortunate to come into the art world when it was opening up to possibilities, I wouldn't have become an artist. I probably would have become a writer. But I'm so glad that wasn't what happened, and that I was able to be an artist who makes use of all of these different things.

LOB: Wasn't writing central to everything you've made?

EA: Of course. There was a very nice review of my book recently in the *San Francisco Humanities Review*, which kept comparing me to Philip Roth, which made my publisher who publishes avant-garde works frantic! How dare one of his artists be compared to Roth—the establishment! I like Roth, but anyway, I loved that the writer [George J. Leonard] said my book was a novel.

Ellie Ga

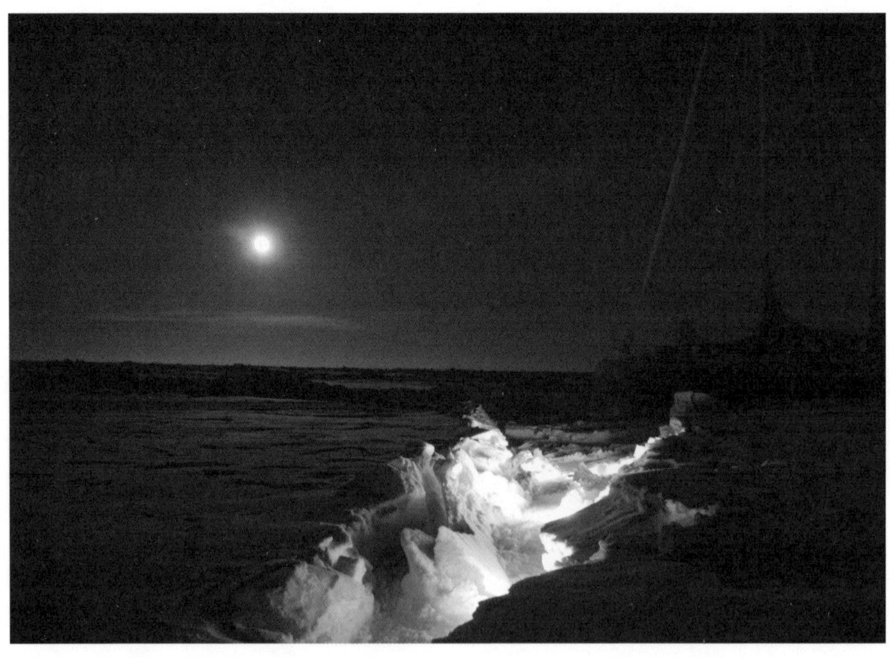

Ellie Ga, *Fissure 5: 83ºN, 2ºE*, 2008–11, digital C-print, 25 × 36 inches (63.5 × 91.4 cm).

March 13, 2010
Artforum

After an eighteen-month residency in the archives of the Explorers Club in New York, Ellie Ga became the sole artist-in-residence from 2007 to 2008 aboard the Tara—*a research vessel lodged in the ice of the Arctic Ocean— and sent occasional reports to her New York gallery, Dispatch. Here she discusses three of the* Arctic Booklets, *which were made as the boat was drifting and during the continuous polar night.*

When I arrived on the boat, a handful of people were already there. Two had been there for more than a year, five had been there for six months, and three of us were going on as new crew. Before I left for the expedition, I was told I should prepare to be aboard for at least six months. On arrival, predictions were that we would drift so fast that we would only be out on the ice for little more than a month. It felt like I was getting to the party too late. Everyone already had a memory and a relationship with the ice. So the first thing I decided to do was to become the ship's archivist.

In individual meetings, I asked the crew to draw a map of our "world"; this project eventually became *Ten Till Two (10:10)*. They had given these strange names to the locations outside the boat because they needed to agree, through language, how to get to particular destinations, to collect data, to check equipment, and so on. They would say to one another, "We're going to Helsinki today, and you go to Tartu, and you go to Charles de Gaulle Airport." But it was really all just snow and ice. These places had no meaning to me back then.

I recorded my crewmates speaking while they drew their maps. Sometimes they would just describe what they were charting, and in other cases they would make up a narrative. For example, the mechanic was also a diver. He and the chief would dive under the boat to check the propellers. He drew an ice floe in the shape of a mushroom and called it *le champignon*. No one had seen it but him. Another person wrote *silence* on his map near the area he labeled *south*. I often thought of the south as silence, too, because the south was the future and therefore the unknown: mystery made it silent. One day, though, the captain saw this map and said, "No, that's completely wrong, the south is not silent." He said that the south is a return to chaos, to civilization, and he crossed out the word *silence* on the area I had labeled *south*.

The most poignant parts of this series are the last entries, where it all actually did become chaos. Toward the end of the journey, everything had changed so much that no one knew where we were anymore. At some point, the boat had turned around in the middle of the night and what used to be east was west and vice versa. We lost all our reference points. Helsinki disappeared; Charles de Gaulle Airport broke up and drifted away.

The *Drift Drawings* began as an attempt to document where we were going. We were never able to see our boat moving, but we could chart our movements through the GPS. As you can imagine, in the old days explorers spent most of their energy just figuring out where they were. We knew where we were every moment, so that wasn't our obsession; instead, we were most concerned with where we were going to be next.

This feeling permeated every aspect of life on the boat, because we organized our life based on weather predictions. Having no control over our course, all we could do was react to those predictions. Every morning we would wake up, go down to the office, look at the GPS, and then chart the course of our drift. This was our morning newspaper. I would trace the little drift based on the computer screen, because I wanted to have a record since our path was constantly changing. So in the drawings you can see where we were—here's September 24, October 1, October 22—and you see how we're going up and down and back and forth. We would have a storm that would push us north and then a storm that would push us south again. In a way, the drawings are fractals of meanderings.

The *Log of Limits (Snow Walks)* is based on hikes I took around the boat, since we were essentially lodged in a giant ice block most of the time. But slowly, as we moved more and more south, we began to see small fractures in the ice and then we would have these major breaks and everything would completely change. Some weeks we could walk completely around the boat, other days only a few footsteps, sometimes not at all. Our world expanded and contracted, and like the *Drift Drawings*, this expansion and contraction of space over time wasn't a straight line. The lines are going back and forth, up and down, east and west, like a yo-yo. Even so, we were beginning to see the limits of our little "world."

fierce pussy

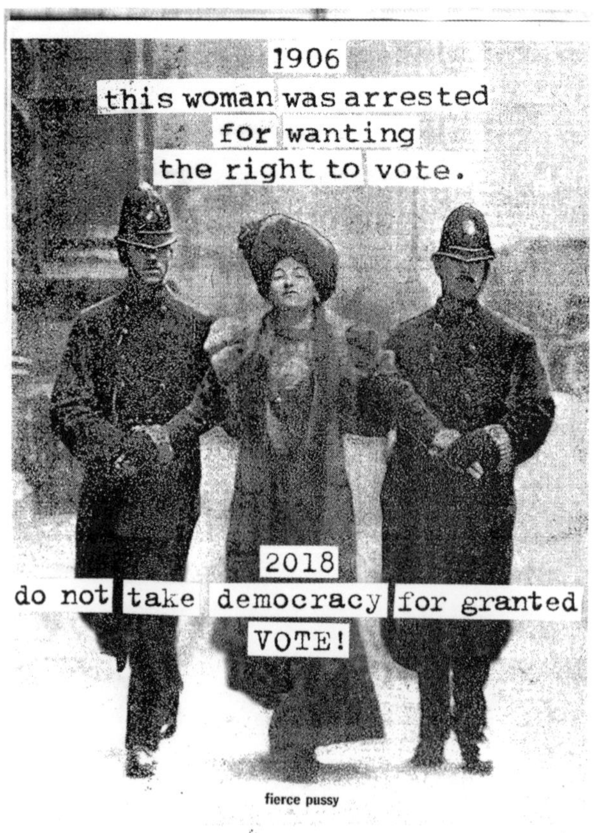

fierce pussy, *Vote*, 2018, poster, 17 × 11 inches (43.2 × 27.9 cm).

September 29, 2018
Artforum

I talked with artists Nancy Brooks Brody, Carrie Yamaoka, Zoe Leonard, and Joy Episalla—the four core members of the New York–based lesbian collective fierce pussy—about their art and activism on the occasion of a feature I wrote about the group for the February 2019 issue of Artforum.

LOB: How did fierce pussy begin?

FP: There was an open call put on the floor of an ACT UP meeting in 1991 for the women to come together. The announcement was stated on the floor that we would be meeting at Zoe's house on such and such a night, and "come one, come all." The backstory is that Zoe had been talking to Suzanne Wright about starting a collective of women because it was one of the things that felt missing in ACT UP. Even though there were a lot of dykes in it, there was such a focus on the male body. The disease was more prevalent among men. A lot of us were doing work in ACT UP about women's issues and there was a desire to do something that was about lesbian visibility, desire, and pleasure—something that wasn't only about illness. We wanted to represent another aspect of our lives and our work. There was so much homophobia at the time. The number of AIDS deaths that occurred unnecessarily was directly due to our government's homophobia and racism. And so some of this was around looking at and responding to homophobia.

At the very first meeting, of about twelve people, we came up with the idea to do the first list poster on a typewriter of primarily derogatory terms that were used against us. It began, "I AM A … ," which was then followed with the list. We saw this work as a way of taking back those terms, so it was actually something positive for us and powerful to turn it on its head that way.

In the early '90s, there was this incredible urgency that we felt, based on our friends getting sick and dying. And in organizing within ACT UP, we learned from that. Also we didn't want to spend hours discussing the idea for a poster. That was one of our first rules: we would make a poster at each meeting and during the next meeting we would go out and wheat-paste it out on the streets.

Not everyone who came to the fp meetings was from ACT UP and not everyone was an artist. We put the word out in a lot of different ways. But because we were putting so much energy into our activism, our art practices were kind of getting pushed to the sideline. Part of the call was to create an art collective. We didn't pitch it as doing direct action—it was more cultural action. And we wanted to make art in this really fast and dirty way, in an activist spirit.

As artists, we used our intuitive feel for the material, like using the typewriter. We used a typewriter because that was how you wrote let-ters, if they weren't handwritten. But we didn't just type it out. We typed it out and maybe backspaced—we changed the weight and height of the letters and moved the words around. The layout was very con-sidered. We liked to have some visual noise. We found a voice that's not any one of our voices, but a kind of synthesis of our four different aesthetics. And it was much more tactile and *messier*. We invited the accident. We didn't try and do a perfect paste-up. So that's the artistic process of some of those lists. Joy and Carrie were working at Condé Nast and they xeroxed them in the offices.

LOB: Can you talk about the wheat-pasting process a little bit?

FP: We would get on the subway and we would, ideally, locate some-body's house in the neighborhood of where we wanted to wheat-paste and use their water and take our buckets. We'd fill up gallon water jugs as well, so we could replenish and remix on the street as we were going. We'd target a particular neighborhood and we'd kind of graffi-ti-style—we called it "bombing"—wheat-paste a bunch of posters up. We'd look at them too. We'd step back and go, "Yeah, that looks good enough," or, "Put another one there." These were really shout-outs for other lesbians. Our posters weren't really about trying to teach anyone. They were to make you feel less lonely and safer on the street, because maybe you saw somebody you recognized.

The funny part of that, or the irony, in a sense, is that so many years later, when we did a small retrospective at Printed Matter, people who came to it said, "Oh my god, I didn't know you guys were part of that. I ripped one of those off the street. I had it on my refrigerator forever."

When we did that Printed Matter show, we sent out a call to everyone who had been in the group that we could remember, something like forty people. We emailed everyone saying, We're going to do this show, come join us. And somehow we were the only four people that showed up. So we figured we're the four that still want to be doing this. And from there we realized we still had a lot to talk about, including new ideas for work. And that's when we started making new projects as fp again, after a long hiatus, and just having it be the four of us.

We also realized how relevant this work still was, especially when we did a remix of our original three posters. We made a new list poster of derogatory names and then added "and so are you," rather than saying "and proud" at the bottom, and people responded negatively.

Our writing sessions became editing sessions, refining sessions, expanding sessions. We'll often go back into earlier works and, if it suits the moment, retool something. Because sometimes the same piece years later means something entirely different. And you can kind of exploit or make the most of that difference, of how the words ring differently now. For example, changing "and proud" to "and so are you" was also reflecting how words have a really different life in daily language right now. For instance, the word *queer* has a really different life. So how do you recognize its contemporary life?

LOB: It seems like you also still wanted to work as "we," or as "she," as one artist? How did the long-term friendship sustain this?

FP: fierce pussy is her own artist. She's got a lot of opinions. There's the collective of fierce pussy and there are all of our different configurations of friendship, over so many years now. There's an organic crossover that happens the way that conversations happen, and you share ideas.

LOB: Does the collective work inform your individual work, as artists?
FP: Each of us has our own studio practices, with strong individual questions and procedures and things that we've been independently investigating. There's also an enormous amount of respect and curiosity in the group for that. We work in different media and have pursued

aspects of the materiality of our work in different ways. But it's interesting that the fp voice is not closest to any one of us. The work we make as fp is nothing like the work we make on our own. It's more like something that comes out of a conversation over dinner, where you're like, "Yeah, we should do something about that!" And our whole way of going about doing the work, there's a balance and tension between these four really strong opinions and aesthetics. But when we hit it, we always know that's that voice. And it's been really interesting that it's been able to maintain an independent voice separate from any of ours. Moreover, collectively, we've developed an intuition.

LOB: That makes sense, since the collective work has such an independent spirit.

FP: We learned from ACT UP that the government's not going to do it for you. You had to be the expert. Don't call the expert to come give you a lecture. And so some of that ethos of taking responsibility is to find out what it is you want to know—and to make what you want to see. We weren't seeing enough images of ourselves on the street. And it did feel scary sometimes. There was a lot of gay bashing at that time. It was directly related to people dying of AIDS and the fear that people had around that, and their misplaced fear and anger. It often didn't feel safe on the street if you looked obviously queer. And so it wasn't about following a model that existed. It was more about remaking the world as we'd like it to be.

LOB: That comes through in the *Transmission* text-based posters you began in 2016, which are written as open letters from the unearthly "descendants in the free state of Transplendency" in the squared-off font that, in the '80s, was used to suggest advanced technology ...

FP: *Transmission* is about how we can apply the brakes: How do we change things? We see something coming down the pike, like fascism, and we think, Let's go around the corner here. How do we change this? Something that's very formally interesting about the *Transmission* is that the language it's written in is not against something. It's actually about locating an entirely different attitude that seems so obvious to all of us, which is more like, "Well, what are you guys doing? Like seriously, are you guys killing each other? Is that true?" And so instead of topically responding to a specific issue and being against that issue, we've found ways to invent. Here's a whole other path we can be taking. Let's name that, or let's speak from that place. If you're coming from the position of marginalized outsider, on a certain level it gives you the freedom to position yourself on the outside, instead of always coming from the inside. The work also relates a little bit to the baby pictures posters we did, in a sense, because there's almost a childlike naïveté to them. Like how do you explain war? How do you explain pollution? What's up with your garbage? What is rape?

We actually talked a lot, while we were writing that work and honing it, about if it's from the future or if it's from another place. And maybe it's both or either. It's more just from a different state of mind. And that sometimes, for instance, in our current political situation, you can get so worn out following what's happening. To respond, respond, respond ... it can just wear you out. So it's an attempt at optimism and an attempt at solidarity. It honors those people, friends, and musicians who have lifted us, as well.

The space of culture is what gives people strength, voice, and presence, and a platform, a place to come together. That can sustain you in a way that electoral politics can't. There's something else going on with that work. It's intergenerational or transgenerational. You can listen to music from six generations ago and maybe it becomes a source of strength and understanding and communication across time and space—to swim the time stream.

LOB: There's a concern with working in the present tense, which comes up in other pieces too, as in *For the Record* from 2013.

FP: We felt like there was a cap being put on the AIDS crisis—that now that some drugs are available to some people, it's all over. But of course, the drugs are still not available to all people. So we needed to work in the present tense, to show that the loss of lives from the AIDS crisis is still in the present tense with us. It's very much speaking from the now. We attended a symposium at Harvard in 2009, and there was a lot of looking back, revisiting. We were all struck by how much mourning was still left inside of us that we didn't deal with at that time because we were so busy. We were on the streets. It's like we were in shock, I think. It was traumatic. And it formed. It's part of who we are today.

Sometimes there's just this chasm where either someone has no idea or they have a very romanticized idea of what it was to be an activist during the AIDS crisis. They've seen some footage but they don't understand why we were that angry or that desperate. *For the Record* is an attempt to bridge that gap of wanting to connect. You can't always do that from a pedagogical position. So for us it was more about saying, You don't even know what you're missing. Which is why the text says things like, You would've really liked him or her or them. We've always felt a responsibility to go forward and do the things that everyone we lost couldn't do. So some of that present voice is an echo of that energy. It's about wanting things to change, wanting a future. It's about both trying to survive and showing a possibility of a way to survive.

Frances Stark

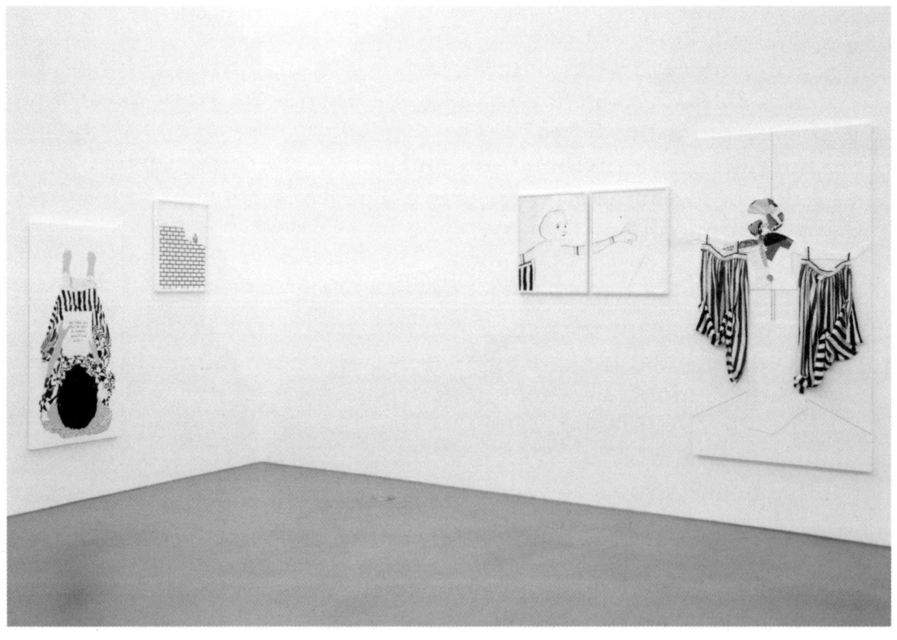

Frances Stark, *The New Vision*, 2008, Portikus, Frankfurt, installation view.

November 21, 2008
Artforum

Los Angeles–based artist Frances Stark is widely known for combining text, image, and literary sources in her collages, which often include thoughtful though tenuous self-referential links to her roles as artist, mother, woman, and professor. The New Vision, an exhibition of her work, was on view in fall 2008 at Portikus in Frankfurt.

This exhibition was quite a surprise. Although I had been planning to do it for at least a year, before I was able to start on my original plans an opportunity arose for another show, which took up a tremendous amount of energy. That large-scale exhibition, at the Secession [*A Torment of Follies*, April 26–June 22, 2008], was organized around an excerpt from a novel that I was "putting to music," so to speak. There I used text in a rhythmic way and choreographed graphic figures around the room almost as if they were performing the text. This show is nearly the opposite of that one.

I had a conversation with a curator from the Hammer Museum, which has an extensive print collection, about the form of "the folly" and more specifically about Goya's follies, or *Caprichos* [caprices]. I began to look at these more, and one image in particular really hit me, a print titled *They Already Have a Seat* [1799]. It depicts two women with chairs on their heads and skirts pulled up to their faces. This particularly ridiculous image struck me.

There were a few other *Caprichos* that inspired some of the pieces in this new body of work. I did a version of the most famous, *The Sleep of Reason Produces Monsters* [1797], with the flurry of bats and monsters behind the figure, as an exhibition poster for a gigantic summer group show I was in, *Pretty Ugly*, at Gavin Brown and Maccarone. Instead of Goya's slumping, somewhat gentle figure, mine is more exasperated. Each of these *Caprichos* has a text that Goya has written, a little snippet or a comment that isn't part of the title but is somehow associated with that particular print. I liked how this text exists in a no-man's-land. About the image of the women and chairs, Goya writes, "If conceited girls want to show they have a seat, the best thing is for them to put it on their head." That really egged me on.

I really felt, when I started to make this show, that it would end up being an exhibition of paintings—despite the fact that I really don't make paintings per se. I hate that I keep having to offer this caveat, but honestly, one could actually call this a figurative painting show—but not entirely, of course.

In a way, the work has more of a "trashy collage" aesthetic. But the images are also more solid and singular and depict bodies in subtly ridiculous, exhausted, or slightly compromising positions, and there is a lot of play with black and white versus color. One of my favorites is a foreshortened figure seen from above with a kind of giant head weighing down the image, and her feet kind of just floating at the top of the canvas. In her hands is a sheet of paper, which reads, "Why should you not be able to assemble yourself and write?" This text comes from a letter I received from a very smart and sympathetic friend, who, in asking me for a contribution to a publication, lamented the fact that I have been writing less and less to focus on making "work." It asks a lot of difficult questions about appropriating text in artworks versus producing original texts for publication. An abridged version of this letter appears in the exhibition in one of the few nonfigurative works, on a painted music stand, next to another letter received from an artist friend who strikes a completely different tone. The juxtaposition becomes a kind of score for the possibility of what I can or will perform.

Georgia Sagri

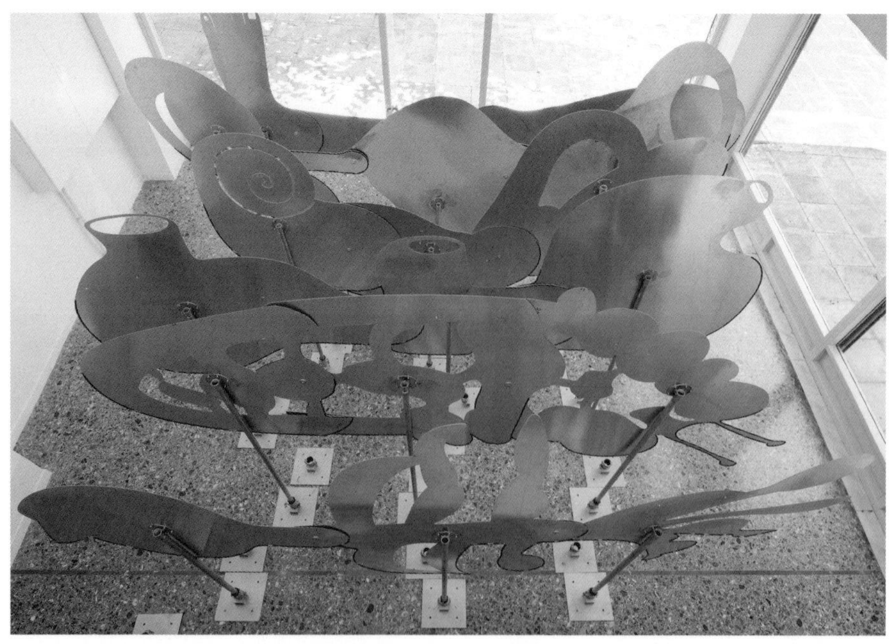

Georgia Sagri, *Soma in orgasm; as leg, as hand, as brain, as ear, as heart, as breast, as sex*, 2017, aluminum, acrylic spray paint, various metallic parts, plastic, and fabric, dimensions variable.

June 5, 2017
Artforum

Georgia Sagri is an artist based in Athens and New York. Here, she discusses Dynamis, *2017, her piece for Documenta 14, which entangled twenty-eight sculptures of organs, ten breathing scores, and six days of "demonstration / performance simultaneously and in continuum" with a chorus.*

My works are declarations, claims, and announcements. They are ghosts—appearances that eventually take shape materially and then disappear. My *Dynamis / Invitation* was emailed to a lot of people—friends, friends of friends. I sent it to so many people because I hope thcy will in turn send it to their friends and make the invitation open up even more. In that sense, materiality isn't simply what's made and finalized. I'm more interested in the tactics that the piece proposes, in terms of how it defines and claims the time and how it's produced.

The invitation is a call for something to take place and a confirmation that it will try to make its declaration possible. It's a text, it has a design, it's distributed in many different ways and it can be utilized by everyone—like a poster on the wall, a message on a flyer that's handed out to passersby—my works could happen if the realm, the moment, factors and agents allow it to be received and make its reason exist.

Production is defined not only by an already existing frame—such as institutions, language, and the specific decisions I've made about the work materially—but by the moment when the work is able to autonomously shift its fate as a piece of art, as something that makes everyone feel responsible to have a claim in its production. My work hinges on this. That's why the up-front language in the invitation—"We need to continue to stay in trouble"—is written the way it is: I want the receivers to respond and to create a purpose, the ground of the work. The invitation itself is not the piece. The piece is made when the text is read, when the message is received, and when curiosity and excitement come. The receivers are all different; I thought it was really beautiful that you wrote to me to ask what is this all about and you wanted to know more about it. The invitation is also, symbolically, a return of Documenta's institutional invitation back to where it belongs— to everyone.

Clearly over the past decade we have been experiencing the decisive development of fascism through the dictating assumption that capitalism is the only way for all of us to organize our lives and deaths. Creative producers under such economic and social pressure can turn into unquestioning automatons of production, working just for the sake of acquiring the authorship stamp *made in art.**

The piece *Δύναμη / Dynamis* is taking place at the same time in two cities, and it acts as a reminder that the social exists. The orgasm is the work's structural methodology. Sexual encounter for all living creatures demands four stages: excitement, plateau, peak (orgasm), and resolution. The sculptures involved in the work evoke organs, and when they go out in public, on the streets, that's the moment of the orgasm, and that's why the sculptures are called *Soma in orgasm; as leg, as hand, as brain, as ear, as heart, as breast, as sex.* The excitement in the piece is the emotional shaping, and the shape of the training, the breathing patterns, and the shape of the sculptures, the shape of the work. The plateau is the moment when this shape makes a trajectory with other trainings, with different forms and others, and of course when this takes place the orgasm happens and the organs go out. The resolution is when, after six days of demonstration and performance, we will all gather to talk and to recall.

Performance—an exhausted term—has the capacity to return an invitation, to distribute power and to let go of representation. It allows for the manipulation of an existing framework. The very fact that its core is nongraspable but at the same time so common accounts for its impossibility as a medium and makes it uncontrolled. One of the dynamic elements of performance is time. Everyone talks about the here and now of performance, the presence of the artist, and performance being ephemeral. For me, what takes place in performance has already been formed before, meaning that it was already. As the material has taken place before, it's a heritage of shadows you carry. Performance is crystal-image. It's projection. It's visual affect. And it has the materiality of a dream.

made in art © Georgia Sagri.

Hong-Kai Wang

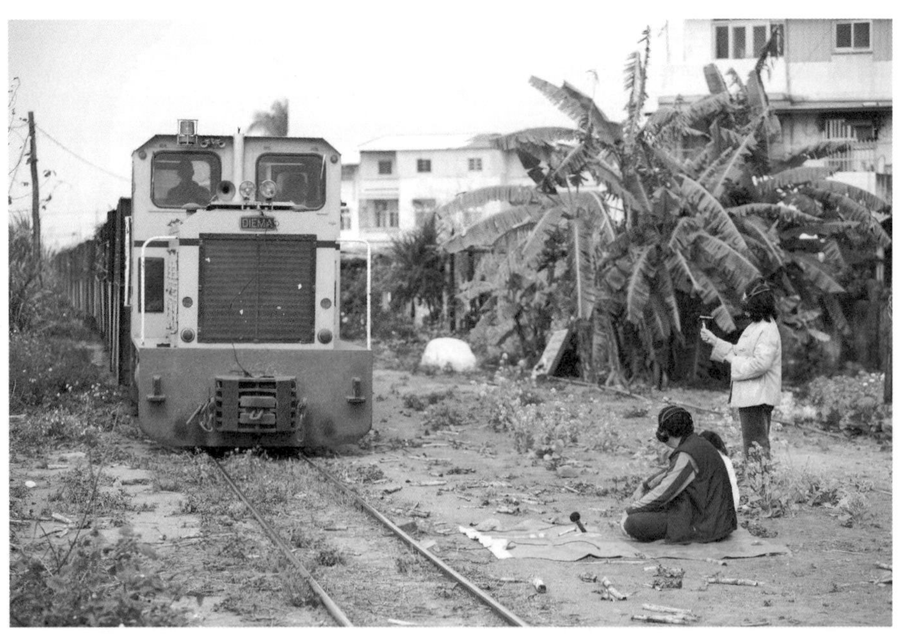

Hong-Kai Wang, *Music While We Work*, 2011, multichannel sound and 2-channel video installation.

August 6, 2013
Artforum

Hong-Kai Wang is a Taiwanese artist primarily working with sound. For Soundings: A Contemporary Score, *MoMA's first major exhibition of sound art, she presented* Music While We Work, *2011, a two-channel video and multichannel audio installation. For* The String and the Mirror, *a group show organized by Justin Luke and Lawrence Kumpf at Lisa Cooley Gallery in New York, Wang contributed the performance* The Musical Condition of Reasonable Conspiracy.

For *Music While We Work*, I invited five couples—retired men who had worked in a sugar factory and their wives—to return to the century-old plant where they were once employed and make audio recordings. The factory is in Huwei, a small town in central Taiwan, where I was born. My parents still live there and my father's former colleague introduced me to this particular group of people. The factory played a key role in my life: we lived a few minutes away from it; I went to the schools associated with it; I even had my first tooth pulled at a dental clinic managed by it. Sugar used to be one of Taiwan's most important exports—there were fifty factories, but now there are only two, and the goods Huwei produces are only for local supply.

Before making the recordings, I organized a series of workshops where the group discussed how they understood and related to the sounds in the factory, while Bo-Wei Chen, a Taiwanese activist and composer, moderated and coached them on how to use the microphones and recorders. They listened to the industrial sounds in so many ways that were different from what I would or could access myself; for instance, they knew what a particular sound meant, whereas I needed a visual reference to identify it. They said they could close their eyes but never shut their ears. The factory seemed to encompass so much sonic information, or so many codes, that these workers knew by heart. It helped me further understand how sound can dictate or inform our relationships and vice versa, and how specific social, political, and even economic meanings are inscribed in our listening.

The piece debuted in Venice and has traveled to Canada, Japan, and Taiwan. It means a lot to me that it's going to New York now, since it's the city where I established my creative identity. *Music While We Work* was also one of my first attempts at collaborating and investigating how listening can be shared, and how people listen together. It helped me think more critically about nonlinguistic sound, and how language can provide a different form of agency and be a tool to explore the process and conditions of how we listen. This, in turn, prompted me to develop a series of performances that largely use speech as a medium.

From our two-year-long conversation about sound and art, Justin Luke invited me to do a performance at Lisa Cooley, which is actually a restaging of a project I produced last year in Rome. *The Musical Condition of Reasonable Conspiracy* began with a phone interview I conducted with my mentor, Chris Mann. He's an Australian composer and poet based in New York, and our conversation focused on what it means to be a composer—culturally, politically, and even ideologically. In the performance, two seated actors reenact the transcription while local composers intervene and contribute. For this specific performance, Jim Fletcher and Rosie Goldensohn will dialogue in real time, while Marina Rosenfeld and C. Spencer Yeh will pretty much have to fill in the gaps. They will listen to the two actors performing the transcription and wait for a moment to intervene, while the two actors have to try to respond to all the unexpected inputs.

My academic training was in political science. I think my interest in sound actually stems from my own social alienation in New York as a foreigner, while trying to learn English. To try to understand, or even speculate about, all of the confusing sound and information around me became very important to me. It became a form of agency, a daily existence. This is why the idea of listening as a form of organization is pivotal to me. We all understand that listening is a very private and personal thing, but I'm actually interested in how it can be shared, and how we relate to one another and negotiate understandings and misunderstandings—and also how we don't.

Howardena Pindell

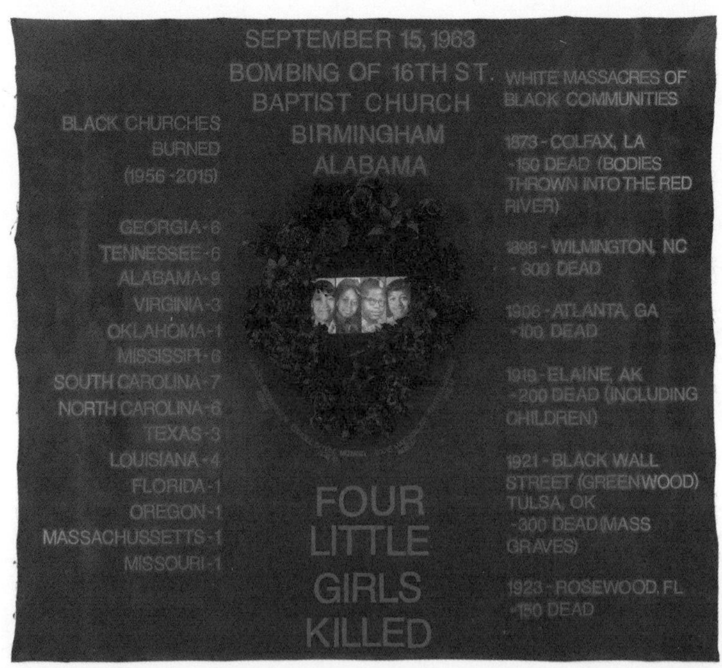

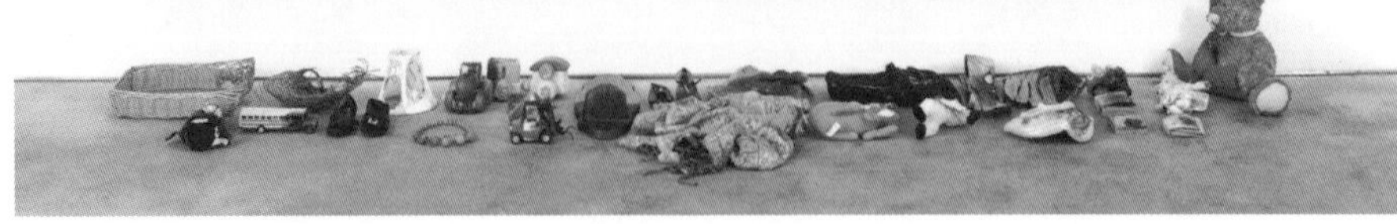

Howardena Pindell, *Four Little Girls*, 2020, mixed media, dimensions variable,
commissioned by The Shed, installation view.

November 30, 2020
November

Howardena Pindell studied painting at Boston University and Yale University in the 1960s and then worked a variety of curatorial jobs at the Museum of Modern Art, where she remained for twelve years. In 1972, Pindell cofounded A.I.R. Gallery, the first artist-run space for women in the United States. In 1979, she began teaching at the State University of New York, Stony Brook, where she is a full professor. Throughout her long career, Pindell has exhibited extensively. I have also long admired her work as an author, activist, and researcher. Her reflective 2020–21 solo exhibition, Howardena Pindell: Rope/Fire/Water, *at The Shed in New York, featured several new pieces that we discuss below. The interview was conducted in November 2020.*

LOB: Have you been making art during the pandemic? I know some of the works in your exhibition at The Shed are new commissions but I'm not sure if they were finished before March ...

HP: Yes, I was working on The Shed exhibition during the pandemic and refused to stop. I have two assistants who help me a lot. They share the labor of making the paintings by punching dots and ovals, sewing, gessoing, and so on. A few paintings weren't finished before March 2020. The film/video *Rope/Fire/Water* was finished in 2019 and updated in 2020 as a result of George Floyd's death, as well as the passing of Congressman John Lewis. I dedicated the film to John Lewis.

LOB: Could you talk about the process of making *Rope/Fire/Water*? It sounds like it had a long gestation period. What did it feel like to return to video after twenty-five years?

HP: *Rope/Fire/Water* grew from the small seed of an idea I had when I was a child of about eleven or twelve years old. (I'm not sure how old I was, but I was very young.) It was a childhood memory of seeing a photograph of a lynching in *Life* magazine. I was visiting a friend, Denise Thompson, in Philadelphia. Her mother was cooking meat. I opened *Life* and saw a gruesome photo of a partially dismembered African American man lying on his back on what may have been a log. He was burning from the inside out. White men were smiling as their picture was taken around the smoldering, charred body. It was as if they were at a picnic. The smell of meat being cooked for dinner and the sight of the brutalized burning body made me ill and I couldn't eat meat for a year. The smell of the cooking fused with the horrific image. I felt helpless. There was nothing I could do. This was during Jim Crow and segregation.

A family friend's father had been lynched for being a prosperous Black businessman. Her eyes still held the gaze of terror she experienced when she lost her father to racist murderers.

I feel the project, or painting, intuitively selects the medium I will work in. I chose to work in film for *Rope/Fire/Water*. In the 1970s I submitted a proposal about what I saw in *Life* to a women's cooperative, A.I.R. Gallery. It was a performance piece. They turned it down. I was the only nonwhite member. The final format, thanks to The Shed, is a film. I feel it's the best way to express the ideas, and I didn't want the piece to be seen only by those who could attend a performance. It's also longer now and filled more with historical facts, which I couldn't easily do as a performance piece. The film/video has legs and increases the size of the audience who can see it. As a performance it would have been very limited.

LOB: You were a founding member of A.I.R., and so I'm wondering how the other members of the group could reject your work? How did that happen?

HP: They had no empathy for issues of race. One of the founding members has been saying for years that she didn't recognize me as Black. Her comment got back to me.

LOB: When you say the film has "legs," it sounds like you might want it to travel outside of the art world, beyond The Shed. Do you have any ambitions for that?

HP: My 1980 video *Free, White and 21* had legs. I'm not sure what to do with *Rope/Fire/Water*. Part of my worry has to do with safety issues, seeing how volatile this election and the past four years have been. I may want to restrict it to the show at The Shed. I need to think about it.

LOB: How long had you been accumulating the data related to lynchings and racist attacks in the United States that you recount in the video? How did you choose what to include?

HP: I have some of the images in my memory of photos I have seen over the years. One of my assistants helped me to locate images. I had also written different accounts of lynching for the appendix of a book published by Midmarch Arts Press in 1997. The book was about an African American woman artist who used negative racial stereotypes of African Americans in a derisive way as well as mocking the civil rights movement. I had noticed that, at the time, African American artists who used images of negative stereotypes of African Americans were welcomed into the white art world. Work critical of negative stereotypes would be rejected. I was also aware of a work, *Accused/Blowtorch/Padlock*, 1986, by African American artist Pat Ward Williams. It shows the image of a lynched African American man with written text. I decided to include the same image of the lynched man in the film.

LOB: Your new painting *Four Little Girls* refers not only to a specific episode of racist violence—the murder of Addie Mae Collins, Carol Denise McNair, Cynthia Wesley, and Carole Rosamond Robertson at the 16th Street Baptist Church in Birmingham in September 1963—but also to the long history of Black churches being burned. While viewing the show, I was reminded of something Adrian Piper said in our interview for this publication regarding that long history: "Americans need their racism." What are your thoughts on that?

HP: I agree with Adrian Piper. I have noticed that racial violence flares up in a poor economy. I would like to refer you to the website of a First Nation educator, Asiba Tupahache of the Matinecoc Nation on Long Island. Her web publication is called spiritofjanuary. com. She deals with issues of oppression. My clearest understanding of oppression and racism came from reading her publications. She's working on a book that I feel everyone should read; she deals with stereotypes and the depth and breadth of racist behavior and beliefs and their sources.

LOB: Thank you for that. What would you say to someone who claims they are "colorblind," that they are unprejudiced, impartial, and therefore nonracist?

HP: I don't believe that one can be colorblind. One who has privileges is often unaware of the suffering of others. Part of privilege is looking down on someone in order to pull oneself above them. It's the privilege of finding employment, rather than being turned away. It means the privilege of property and wealth and passing that along to your family members. It's the accumulation of stable wealth. Racism blocks many access routes to accumulated wealth. That means your workplace may be free of people of color who don't have these privileges, and who would be turned away when you would be hired. It means not wanting anyone who looks different moving into your neighborhood. I'm always careful when white people use the words *colorblind*, *impartial*, and *nonracist*.

LOB: Are the abstract paintings on view in the show political to you or do they elude politics? To me, they felt political; I'm thinking about the new *Plankton Lace* series and how it relates to climate change.

HP: Yes, I would say *Plankton Lace* is more political. According to a friend of mine who is a docent at the Museum of Natural History, plankton provides 50 percent of the planet's oxygen and without plankton the oceans would die. Sea life lives on it. Human activity, like the runoff of fertilizer in the ocean, creates toxic bloom. Florida, for example, has many problems with this bloom, or toxic plankton. Climate change is making it worse.

A beautiful side of plankton is bioluminescence. At night along the shore and in the waves, it creates a luminous hue of blue as the waves roll in. If you google "plankton bioluminescence" you will see very beautiful images of luminous plankton. Much of the sea life in the ocean lives on plankton, including whales.

LOB: I'm curious to hear more about your use of perfume in your paintings, beginning in the 1960s.

HP: Putting perfume on the paintings was just play. However, I wondered recently if it was a way to reverse the negative experience that I had of my friend's mother cooking meat and of seeing the gruesome image of a lynched man and the smell of burning flesh.

LOB: As one of the Museum of Modern Art's first Black curators and as a founding member of A.I.R. Gallery in the 1970s, could you speak to the most important differences between US art institutions then and now? Are things changing for the better at all?

HP: Some museums are changing for the better. The curators at the Museum of Modern Art have totally changed the collection on view to the public recently by integrating men and women of color ... for example, Mel Edwards, an African American sculptor, has a number of sculptures in the same gallery as Jackie Winsor, a white woman artist. When I first came to New York, the art world was white and male, and the only women artists showing were usually the child, the spouse, or the girlfriend of a white male artist.

LOB: I've admired your role as an activist for many years. What makes for effective activism, in your experience? Was there an event or protest that stands out to you as particularly successful?

HP: I feel that the protests that grew as a result of the killing of George Floyd were a total surprise as they were diverse and insistent. Something has fundamentally changed. First Nation people came out to protest Floyd's death, but it wasn't covered in the media. A First Nation friend sent me a video of the protest. Sometimes I protest anonymously.

Sometimes I use my name. Years ago, in the 1970s, I would protest the art world by sending letters in the mail about racism to institutions and individuals that were signed "The Black Hornet." I think activism is different for everyone. My writings reach more people. Although I'm not a filmmaker, I also feel that film and video formats have legs and reach more people than my paintings. An exhibition of paintings has time and place limitations.

I was stunned and thrilled to see my statistical report from 1987—"Statistics, Testimony, and Supporting Documentation," about racism in the art world—resurrected for the 2017 exhibition catalogue for *We Wanted a Revolution: Black Radical Women, 1965–85* at the Brooklyn Museum. I thought it was lost forever.

LOB: Do you think the great waves of protests worldwide against police brutality and racism will cause changes in global culture, and if so, how?

HP: I feel they will create changes in various cultures around the world. Some people seem to be more mindful about the disparities of privilege within their own segments of society. There are also some cultures that are authoritarian that don't tolerate any form of dissent. Those cultures will be hard to change.

LOB: Do you think they will cause changes in the art world, and if so, how?

HP: There will be gradual changes in the art world, but the arts are often the last to change. I recently met with a person who ran the diversity departments in a number of universities. She said that the art departments were the most resistant to change.

LOB: What are you working on now?

HP: I'm currently working on a new plankton painting. In total, I'm working on three new paintings, all abstract.

LOB: On what can one depend on in this time of deluge? What kind of spiritual or nonspiritual armor helps?

HP: I try to think about things rationally through critical thinking. For me, spirituality is magical thinking. Spiritual experiences can be good or bad, but I prefer science and facts over magical thinking. I just try to keep busy doing my own work and try to keep day pages and artist's diaries. I can recommend a book by Julia Cameron, *The Artist's Way*. It was originally written to help writers with writers' block. It turns out that it also helps visual artists. You can read it if you are or aren't spiritual, although she has a positive spiritual aspect. When I read the book, I was flooded with ideas. It's a very positive publication.

Iman Issa

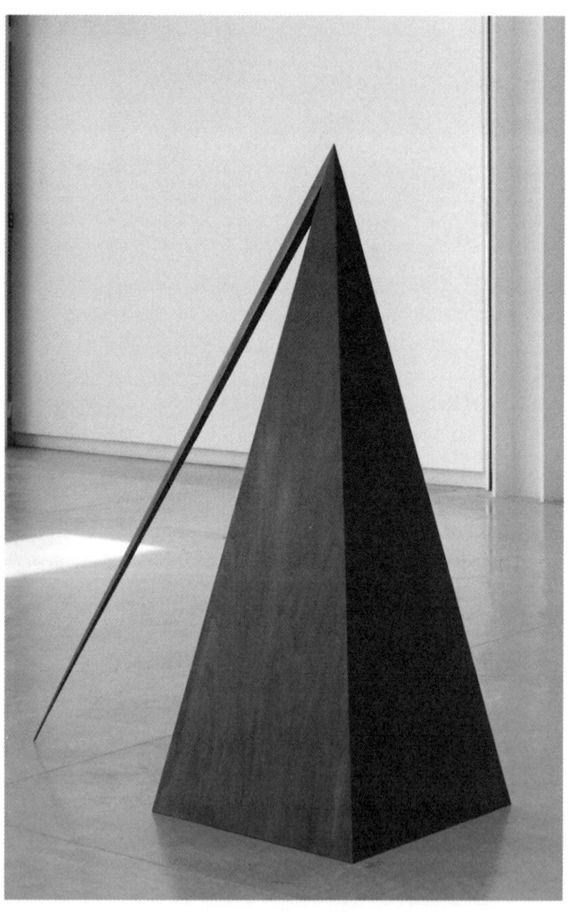

Iman Issa, *Heritage Studies #1*, 2015, blackened wood, vinyl text, dimensions variable, Sharjah Biennial 12, Sharjah, installation view.

March 4, 2014
Artforum

Iman Issa is an artist based in Berlin and New York. Her sculptural series Heritage Studies, *2015–, which revisits forms drawn from history, was featured in the twelfth Sharjah Biennial in 2015.*

This series started from the feeling that I was coming across elements from the past that resonated with subjects on which I was working at the time. It emerged specifically out of a project I completed in 2013 titled *Common Elements*, for which I produced a large amount of material based on existing museum objects and displays. It was interesting to me that I found such material appropriate for illustrating what I deemed as familiar in the personal narratives of four public figures on which I was working at the time, even though these elements had nothing to do with those texts and, in some cases, were separated from them by thousands of years.

And it was while working on that project that I started to wonder why any artist would feel the need to revisit forms from the past, and if this need is identified, how does one go about it without succumbing to an oppressive political project or social agenda? It seemed to me that whenever one looks back, a line is drawn to the present and possibly the future; whether it's one of progression or decline or mere continuity, it didn't matter.

A project emerged from all of those questions and concerns. I had a feeling that it was indeed essential to revisit these elements and forms from the past, that they would have something relevant to say to the present. Thus came the idea of titling the series *Heritage Studies*.

Unlike history, whose study might appear self-evidently constructive, heritage studies seemed to be framed with a practical relevance to the present. As a field it's presented as serving a function, and in many cases that function is clearly articulated. I was drawn to this. In a way, I preferred the essentialist claims of a clearly instrumental field to other ones that might have less apparent agendas when revisiting the past. I was also interested in the idea that these studies I was undertaking would serve a clear need in the present—that they too would have a function.

I was slightly unnerved, though, by the actual forms I ended up producing. I like to think that I go for the most compact way to adequately present my ideas. But for this project, it was clear that the forms had to be large-scale sculptures made out of specific materials, whether from steel, wood, plaster, copper, bronze, aluminum, or other. And even though I've made many three-dimensional objects in recent years, I've always imagined them to function more like images, whereas it was clear that these elements would function differently. I was enticed to place them in the middle of the room and not against the wall as I had done before. I imagined them to occupy and account for their space as well as the potential movement of the viewers who encounter them in a more aggressive manner. I imagined that they would beg for a different sort of interaction from other recent works.

I also wouldn't be comfortable in calling them copies or remakes since most look significantly different from the objects on which they're based—which brings me to the question of, What do these new elements share with their sources if it's not the material, color, appearance, or shape? The answer that I've been able to come up with, thus far, is that they share a speech act. They are addressing or saying something similar to each other, and it's perhaps through doing that that they become the "same." It's an ambitious claim to make but one I'm eager to propose. And having said that, it's important to stress their status as studies, since in no way am I able to posit these as final or conclusive forms, regardless of how finished or precious their presentation may be. You can think of them as propositions waiting for the one who will come by and say, "No, they should actually look different than this. They should be smaller, bigger, a different color, material, or shape."

The captions are also an essential part of the work. I rarely think of myself as someone who produces objects, films, or photographs. Rather, I view these works as displays with various elements that interact with and rely on each other as well as on the time, space, and various conditions in which they exist and are presented. Even though the sources sometimes appear hidden in much of my work, I'm not interested in hiding things or in having the viewer engage in some sort of guessing game. On the contrary, my ideal imagined viewer is the one who would interact with what's present in the space and only what's present. If I can get someone to look, to truly look and perhaps engage in the conversation I believe I'm starting, then I think I'm off to a good start.

Jeanine Oleson

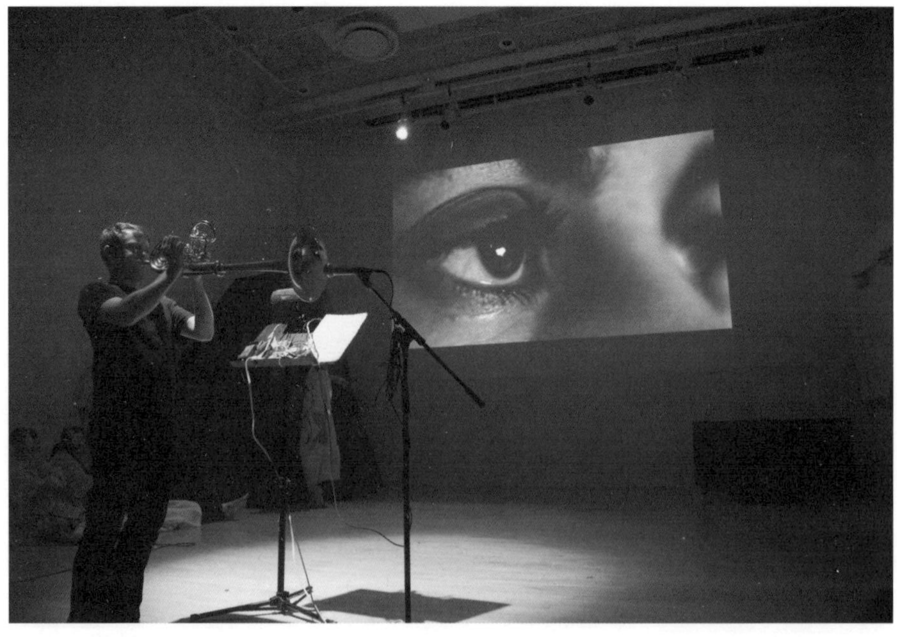

Jeanine Oleson, *Hear, Here*, 2014, performance view, New Museum, New York, June 13, 2014.

April 23, 2014
Artforum

Jeanine Oleson is an interdisciplinary artist based in New York. In spring 2014, the New Museum hosted the first museum presentation of her work, which resulted from her four-month residency at the institution and included an experimental opera, an exhibition, and a series of public programs and workshops.

I've been thinking about the importance of the audience, and more specifically about what constitutes an engaged audience member. Fran Lebowitz once made a comment about the loss of artists, cultural producers, and audiences of people with specific knowledge during the AIDS crisis, and that left a mark on my mind—this idea of a caring engagement that's nonprofessionalized and more like a nineteenth-century connoisseur (as opposed to the ways in which late capitalism has made us all completely dependent on professionalism to drive, well, our drives). So I started to interview opera buffs, because I love people who hold such a vast and fascinating knowledge on this subject and I'm interested in how it is driven by a personal set of concerns. You can't buy the knowledge of opera or of dance; you actually have to invest in it. That's something that's fascinating to me: there's the accumulating information but then there's also a bodily love that's not about the information—it's more of a passion. What drives people to love ideas?

Around the same time, I began to work on *Photo Requests from Solitary*, a project in which we asked people held in solitary confinement to request an image of something they wanted to see, since they are blocked from seeing most images, and in some ways it felt like a polar opposite to the kind of work I've been planning for the New Museum. But in the end, I think that both of these projects are mostly about access, and how one cares for another or for the external, and also how one does something that isn't necessarily connected to them directly or doesn't benefit them, as well as the need for connection or outlet.

I've also been thinking about how to hold two incompatible ideas and produce something new from them, and so in the show and its public performances there will be objects that grapple with this—for instance, there's a brass instrument based on the shape of the inner ear, and there's a light that's based on an eyeball, but instead of collecting light it actually emits light. We'll have a series of nine public programs as a part of the exhibition, including talks, protest karaoke, séances, letters from solitary, and performances with objects in the show like Kelly Pratt playing the horn.

Everything I make ends up filtered through humor and absurdity. For instance, we had a two-act program at the museum in the beginning of March—*The Rocky Horror Opera Show*—which was based on a traditional opera performance situation, where singers performed a normal repertoire of beloved arias. For the audience, we invited opera aficionados—because they have a set relationship to performance—as well as a wider art crowd. It turned out to be really funny, and a two-channel video of the event will be in the exhibition, along with the eighty-plus costumes we made for it. I also asked the museum to bring in Cori Ellison, a dramaturge, as the music curator for the season and as a collaborator on the *Rocky Horror Opera Show*. It's been so inspiring to see her passion for opera and the voice, and that's something I really hope to share. With all the public programs and events, there will be a multitude of voices. There will probably be no dream of a common language—apologies to Adrienne Rich.

Jennifer West

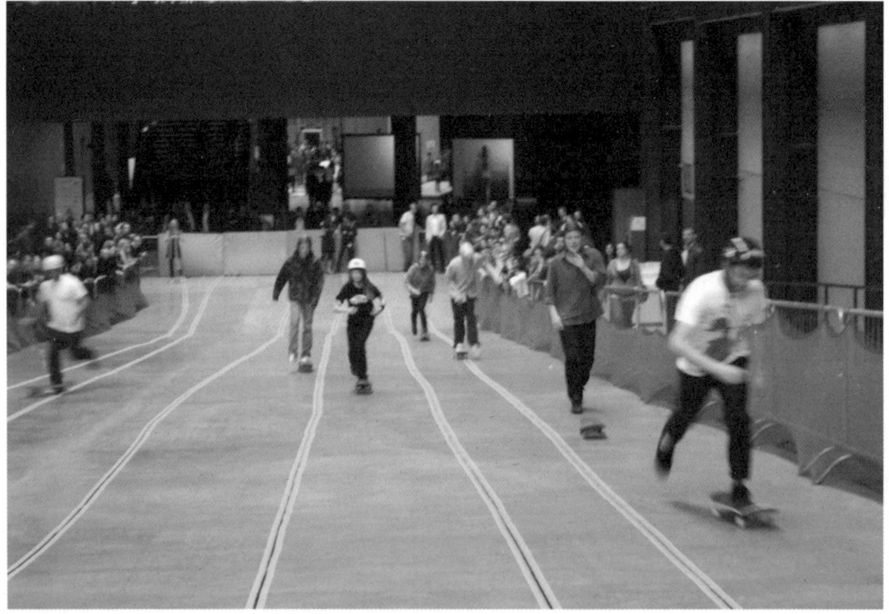

Jennifer West, *Skate the Sky Film (Performance Still, 35 mm film print of clouds in the sky covered with ink, Ho-Ho's, and Melon juice – filmstrips taped to Tate Turbine Hall ramp and skateboarded over using ollie, kick flip, pop shove-it, acid drop, melon grab, crooked grind, bunny hop, tic tacs, sex change, disco flip – skateboarding performed live for Long Weekend by Thomas Lock, Louis Henderson, Charlotte Brennan, Dion Penman, Sam Griffin, Jak Tonge, Evin Goode and Quantin Paris, clouds shot by Peter West)*, 2009.

May 15, 2009
Artforum

In May 2009, the Los Angeles–based artist Jennifer West premiered a new piece, Skate the Sky Film, *at Tate London. Here she talks about her practice of subjecting 16 mm, 35 mm, and 70 mm film to a wide array of substances.*

This project is different for me because I'm working within a twenty-four-hour period in London, and part of it will involve a live audience. I'm also going to show a 35 mm print on a 35 mm projector (on a built platform), which is an exhibition format I haven't used before. I have twelve hundred feet of film of wispy clouds in the LA sky that has been doused with inks and will be taped onto the ramp in the Turbine Hall. Local skateboarders from the London skate scene, many of whom frequent the Undercroft, a skate spot just across the river from the Tate and a byproduct of LA skate culture's migration to England in the 1970s, will be invited to skate directly over the filmstrips, their wheels marking the film.

One of my ideas for this piece was to bring these skaters the LA sky, since skating is all about catching air anyway. Serendipitously, the assistant projectionist for the screening, the artist and filmmaker Tom Lock, is a longtime skater, so he can both skate and project the film while assisting the main projectionist (and artist), Steve Farrer.

Stuart Comer, one of the curators of The Long Weekend, invited me to participate because he saw a relationship between my work and this year's theme, "Do It Yourself." The event was inspired by the Arte Povera and Post-Minimalist artworks in the Tate's *Energy and Process* collections exhibition, and Stuart was interested in my use of everyday materials and experiences, and the way I put a pop angle on them. He saw a connection between my work and aspects of Arte Povera, as well as links between Arte Povera and the alchemical approach of filmmakers like Stan Brakhage and Tony Conrad.

After Stuart sent me photographs of the ramp, which is steep and about 140 feet long, I immediately thought of it as a piece of architecture that would be great to have skateboarders on. I've made other films about trespassing in public space—around the Hollywood sign and in front of David Geffen's beach house in Malibu. I'm interested in the ways in which culture utilizes public spaces, and particularly how skaters will find any place to use, from park benches to step railings to private pools. I wanted to allow them in to this environment, which will be very different for them. I recently saw Gus Van Sant's *Paranoid Park* (2007) and was reminded of the pleasure of watching skating and its gracefulness. So much of that film is just about documenting the skaters and the satisfaction of seeing that experience.

Usually, viewers can infer the process behind my works via their literal titles, which list the substances I've used to treat the film—like someone riding a motorcycle over the material. The narrative of the process has to be put together like reading a book. For this project, I've been thinking about that slippage, as well as the dimension of spectacle. I'm allowing my audience to see how the work has been made, and the very next day they'll be able to see the film. I'll also make a zine that will accompany the project.

As for the title of this work, skateboarders have the greatest, most irreverent names for their tricks, such as disco flip, acid drop, tic tac, bunny hop, melon grab, and sex change. My titles invoke the kinds of substances that are associated with the subject of the work; for example, my film that references the band Nirvana is all about expelling abject elements, and there's another about riot grrrl music that's covered with sweet things and candy. For this piece, I'll treat the film with melons and Ho Hos before they skate on it; only the melon will really affect the film because of its organic acidity.

The performance will exist the way everything exists in the art world (and the skate world); there will be documentation and people will hear about it. I was thinking about this while watching Yves Klein's *Anthropometries of the Blue Period* and *Fire Paintings: Two Performances* and the spectacle of naked women applying paint to their bodies in front of a group of men wearing suits. Also, while looking at the exhibition *WACK!* I noticed photographs of Carolee Schneemann's *Interior Scroll* that I'd never seen before (not to mention the actual scroll!). Looking at them made me feel as though the scope of the work was larger than what I knew of it. I was also inspired while looking at Dan Graham's current exhibition at MOCA. I had the opportunity to see firsthand his two-channel film pieces, such as *Body Press*, which I've known for so long and have taught over and over. It struck me that we know artworks in a very specific way—mostly through documents and photographs.

These works, along with Tate making it possible to skate the Turbine ramp, and my attempts to make that performance just as engaging as the film itself, motivated me to make *Skate the Sky Film* and to try something very new to my practice.

Jessamyn Fiore

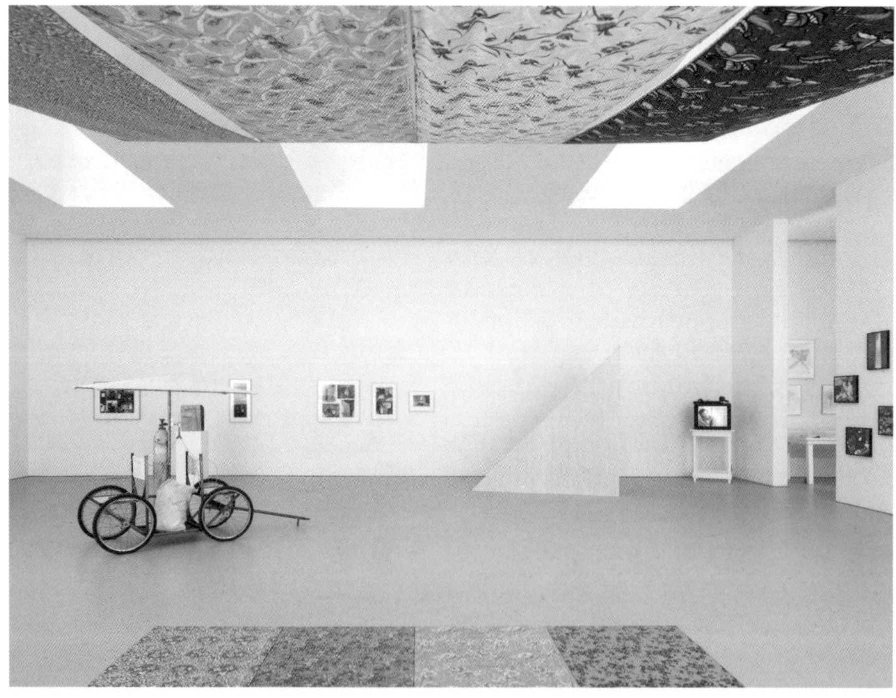

Jessamyn Fiore, *112 Greene Street: The Early Years (1970–1974)*, at David Zwirner, New York, 2011, installation view.

June 26, 2012
Artforum

Curator and writer Jessamyn Fiore organized the exhibition 112 Greene Street: The Early Years (1970–1974) *at David Zwirner Gallery, New York, in 2012, which brought together many of the key works shown in the landmark noncommercial venue. A book copublished by Zwirner and Radius Books shares the title of that exhibition and features extensive interviews with many of the participating artists. Below, Fiore discusses her research for both projects.*

After running Thisisnotashop, a small alternative art space in Ireland, I found myself yearning for a few historic examples of similar independent exhibition venues for inspiration, and that's when I began investigating 112 Greene Street. I was already quite familiar with one of its founders, Gordon Matta-Clark; my mother, Jane Crawford, is his widow, and I basically grew up with his estate. But I was surprised to discover a scarcity of published articles about the history of the venue. There's one lovely book by Robyn Brentano, which she compiled between 1978 and 1980, when the organization left Greene Street and became White Columns. Unfortunately today that text is out of print. I ended up writing my master's thesis at the National College of Art and Design in Dublin on 112 Greene Street, and in doing so I discovered a treasure trove of fascinating stories from interviews with the original artists, which made me I realize how important these primary resources are. It only made sense to have this book take the form of an oral history.

Today 112 Greene Street exists mainly as legend, since so much of the art that was shown there was ephemeral or destroyed. There are some incredible documentary images, but the bulk of the information about the space really comes from the recollections of the vibrant artistic community who worked, lived, ate, and partied there. They used the building as their own creative laboratory, as a site to experiment with multidisciplinary forms of practice. It's really their stories that capture the essence of that moment. It was important for me to make a primary resource of those narratives for future curators and researchers to take from and use for their own projects. But this book is really just scratching the surface. It would be exciting to see it inspire more exploration about not only 112 Greene Street but other spaces like it, particularly in connection to those that exist now, since they play an essential role in supporting artists and deserve recognition.

The amount and diversity of work that happened at 112 Greene Street in such a short time is truly humbling, and that's one reason I wanted to include the time line in the book. In the four years I focus on—its earliest years—you can see that hundreds of artists passed through the space. So many of the great stories in the book about these artists are centered around Jeffrey Lew. He was like the ringleader of a circus there, making it a place where really interesting things could happen. For instance, he didn't care about having a pristine space; he left it rough so you could dig holes in the basement and carve holes in the walls. George Trakas did a piece in 1970 where he actually had a sculpture come up through the floor from the basement to the first floor. Though Jeffrey was irked at first, he grew to love that work, and many said that piece was a key moment in the venue's history.

Another important point is that 112 Greene Street was just one in a constellation of alternative venues. Nearby, at Chatham Square, Tina Girouard, Mary Heilmann, and Richard Landry were renting a building where they hosted large dinner parties with music and dance performances. Simultaneously, Carol Goodden, Matta-Clark, and Girouard were organizing the restaurant Food. The latter became a gathering place for the community while also giving employment to those who needed it and providing a venue for food performance. When it came to art making and exhibitions, they would help each other out and critique each other's work. It becomes clear in the book how essential that networking and peer review was to some of the artists in strengthening their practice and helping them pursue successful careers.

Another aspect that stood out to me during my research was the important role that women played at 112 Greene Street, not only in producing so many shows there but also contributing greatly to the running of the space. Rachel Wood was Jeffrey's wife and she was involved in the day-to-day operations, as was the artist Suzanne Harris, who also lived in the building with her husband, Paul. I think her work is some of the most exciting from that era, but sadly it has been largely ignored by art history. I tried to push Girouard's and Harris's art to the forefront in the show at David Zwirner, and I hope that through this book art historians will become more interested in their output. One of my most sincere wishes is that these two artists get a second look. They're both among the great, but unfortunately often forgotten, artists of that generation.

Jesse Jones

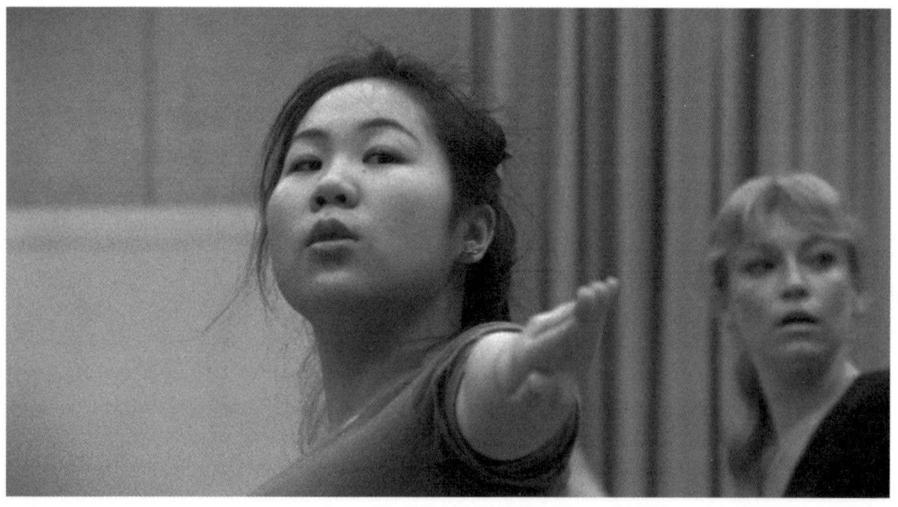

Jesse Jones, *The Struggle Against Ourselves*, 2011, color film in Super 16 mm transferred to video, 21 minutes.

June 29, 2011
Artforum

Jesse Jones is a Dublin-based artist. In tandem with the premiere of her 16 mm film Against the Realm of the Absolute *at the Collective Gallery in Edinburgh, Jones's US debut took place at REDCAT in Los Angeles in summer 2011.*

The REDCAT show brings together two films: *The Spectre and the Sphere*, and a newly commissioned work, *The Struggle Against Ourselves*. The latter film is based on a collaborative project I made this past April with a group of CalArts students. When I was invited to exhibit in LA, I really wanted to host a workshop in the theatrical idea of biomechanics and the series of theatrical études created by Vsevolod Meyerhold in the 1920s. These blend Taylorism with the historic, theatrical devices of commedia dell'arte and Kabuki. The études have an incredibly fascinating history and formally resemble the mass spectacles found in Busby Berkeley's films. But the études have a very different ideological intention, of course. They emerged from a postrevolutionary Russian period in which the idea of the mass still held some idea of historical agency.

Meyerhold's workshops were very influential during the postrevolutionary period and featured participants such as Igor Ilinsky and Sergei Eisenstein. Konstantin Stanislavski was also a big fan of Meyerhold, and he believed that they were going to create the theater of the twentieth century. But because Meyerhold became persona non grata under Stalin, none of his ideas were exported to America. He fell out of history; in America, he's virtually unknown. Rather than stage a reenactment of the workshops, I'm instead attempting to stage this kind of event that was historically impossible; it's presenting a possibility for a different version of mass culture. The performance I made with the students is based on a series of photographs of the Meyerhold workshops that were taken in the late 1930s by Alexander Grinberg. While looking at Grinberg's images it's impossible not to draw comparisons to the high Hollywood spectacles of the '20s and '30s.

Chi-wang Yang of the Cloud Eye Control theater company facilitated the workshops at CalArts. He brought a huge amount of experience to the project and built the performance with the students during three initial workshops to prepare for the film, which was made over a weekend at CalArts. The film appears at first as an observational documentary, but then it shifts into a dream sequence that echoes the Hollywood style of the Berkeley films. In this way, *The Struggle Against Ourselves* is a scramble between two vastly different historical impulses—communism and capitalism—and it questions the ways in which that narrative can be played out through the body.

The other film in the show, *The Spectre and the Sphere*, was made in 2008 in Dublin and Ghent. Both take something from the culture of early-1920s Russia as a starting point—the études for *The Struggle Against Ourselves*, and the theremin in *The Spectre and the Sphere*. There's an attempt within both of these works to excavate these things, which came out of the ether of the postrevolutionary period and at the time operated as a form of popular culture. The theremin itself has these incredibly interesting origins. It was invented in 1919 by Leon Theremin, who, upon its creation, brought it to Lenin. I learned that Lenin was very impressed with the instrument and had wanted to learn how to play "The Internationale" on it, although for various historical reasons that didn't happen. I asked Theremin's great-niece, Lydia Kavina, to play the song for *The Spectre and the Sphere*.

The two films are installed so that there's a dialogue created between them; they're projected on opposing walls and sequenced to play at intervals with a specially designed computer program. I'm also showing a new light installation, which plays two sound tracks at interval points within the sequence, so the audience's vantage point is shifted constantly through the duration of the two works. It's my hope that this light installation draws attention to our spectatorial role within the space of cinema.

Jo Baer

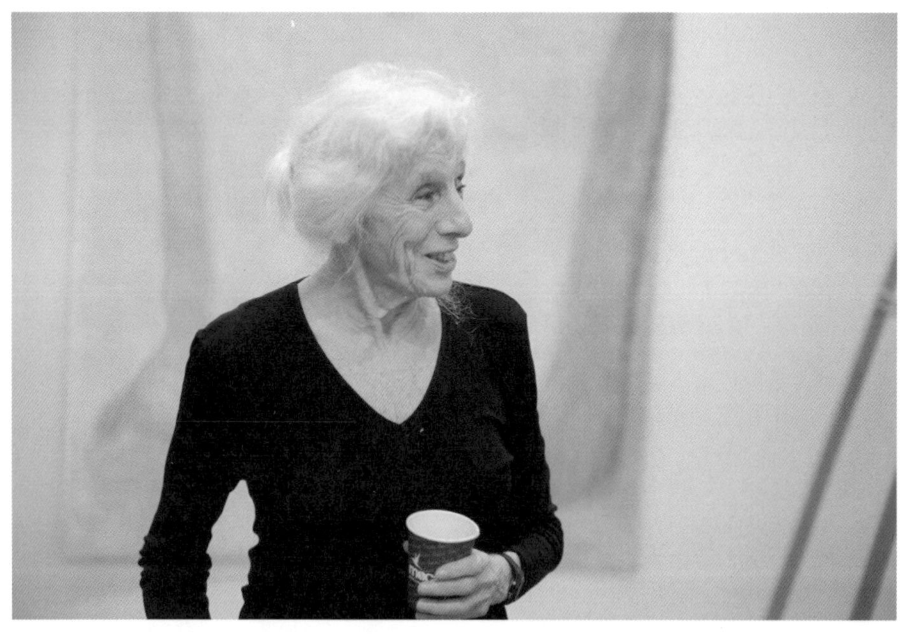

Jo Baer, photo by Ralph Goertz © IKS-Medienarchiv.

July 3, 2010
Artforum

Jo Baer has been painting since the early 1960s and is known for her inimitable hard-edge abstractions as well as figurative works. Her book Broadsides & Belles Lettres: Selected Writings and Interviews 1965–2010 *was published by Roma Publications in summer 2010.*

I wrote these essays when I had something to say. But it was always clear that I'm a much better painter. I never thought of myself as a *writer*. When the opportunity for this book came along a few years ago, I knew exactly what I wanted in it. After everything was xeroxed and digitized, I worked with Roel Arkesteijn, whom Roma brought on as the editor, to refine it. In the process, I realized that one of the most important things to include was the "dialogues" I made with other artists from 1966–67, especially since these pieces had never been published before.

In 1967, Carl Andre gave me a poem, and I created a graphic analysis of it, which he in turn commented on; Mel Bochner wrote out the entries for *existence* and *nonexistence* from *Roget's Thesaurus*; Sol LeWitt gave me a plan for his exhibition at Gallery in April of 1967; and so on. These are works I own and, of course, they're very valuable to me. Most of them began with just sitting around at Max's Kansas City and having drinks at night. I knew many of the Minimalists, and the Pop artists as well. At the time, I was also taking dance classes. I really admired Trisha Brown; also Yvonne Rainer, whose classes I took because I needed exercise. The picture in the book of me in Yvonne's *Trio A* performance is funny: I have this pimp walk, one shoulder down, very aggressive! While all of this was happening, I was trying to work in the studio and also tending house, taking care of my child, getting the groceries, and such. I remember it was a very busy time. In 1975, when my son went off to college, I moved to Ireland. But after six months there I realized what a truly strange person I am—I don't do whimsical things, I didn't intend to live in a castle, but that's what I found, with fireplaces, no heat, one plug and light socket in every room, and I adored it. I felt very much at home. I still owe the coal man three hundred pounds.

This is my first hardcover book, and after living in Amsterdam for twenty-two years, I've noticed that I've had to struggle to remain a painter and not try to become a graphic artist. Collaborating on the layout was very interesting. The Dutch are the best graphic designers in the world. My work on the cover, *Untitled (White Star)*, looks totally different; the designer took all the painterly stuff out of it. Happily, it still would never have occurred to me to do something like that. It looks very forceful, nearly sinister. When I was painting it in 1961, I was trying to do something subtle and ambiguous, but this cover is like, *BAM!*

The book and the process of doing it has made me think a lot about control, which I've realized is very central to my work. I've always asked questions about control and who is controlling whom and so forth. I don't see how you can be a woman and not have to think about control. I think it's a very natural subject if you have your wits about you. Some of my drawings allude to brown rats displacing the black rats, or depict horse bridles and saddles. *Revisioning the Parthenon*, which will be produced as a booklet with the selected writings and interviews, is also about control.

Jo Baer

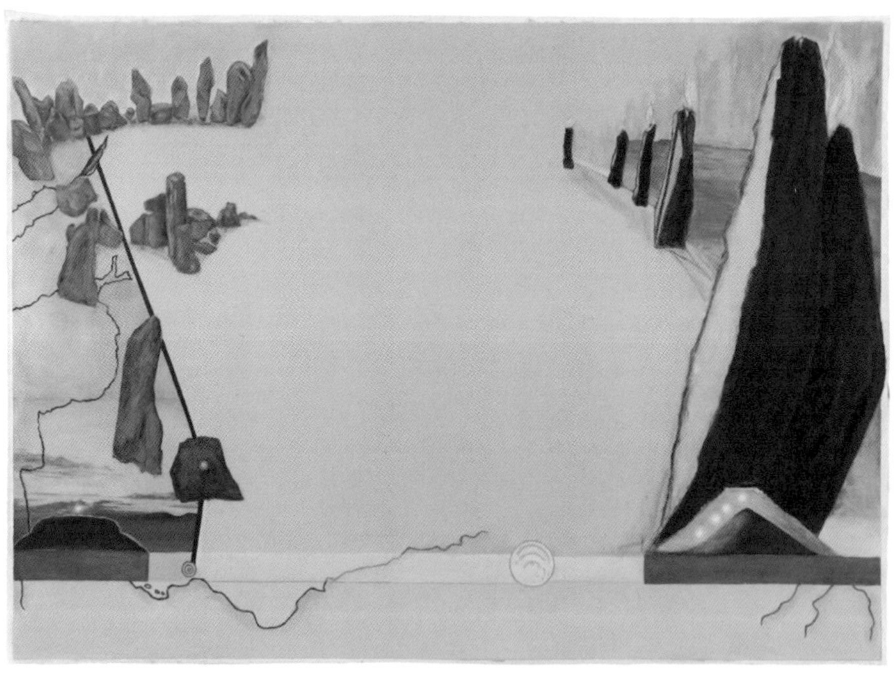

Jo Baer, *Dusk (Bands and End-Points)*, 2012, oil on canvas, 87 × 118 inches
(220.9 × 299.7 cm).

September 1, 2014
Artforum

For the 31st São Paulo Bienal, Jo Baer presented In the Land of the Giants, *2009–13, a series that debuted at the Stedelijk Museum Amsterdam in 2013. Born in Seattle in 1929, Baer became associated with Minimalism in New York in the 1960s. In 1975—"due to Nixon" she moved to the greener pastures of the Irish countryside, where she encountered the primary subjects of these works: ancient burial sites and Neolithic stones.*

These paintings are inspired by my remembering of the Hurlstone, a large megalith set at a diagonal in a field in County Louth, Ireland, which was interesting to me for the enormous aperture set in it—a hole that, when I first looked south through it, seemed to suggest a path extending over the mountains all the way down to the huge earth-mound cemeteries of New Grange and Knowth. At the time, it made me wonder: What have I stumbled on? Is this one of an ancient highway's crossroads—sight through, and turn here? Only much later, in urban Amsterdam, after recalling and then thinking on this, did I put the hard edge down—set the ruler to the page—and that's how these paintings began.

The Irish rural landscape had always struck me as odd. The castle I lived in from 1975 to 1982 was built in the twelfth century, and the ruins of a fifteenth-century church as well as part of a school for scribes sat at the top of one of my fields. In my neighborhood, you would also find standing megaliths and tractors in the same field, or a cottage next to a graveyard from 3000 BC—or 4000 BC even, with a horse there, chomping on grass—all of it just blatantly lying around with nobody noticing. I remember a farmer once bragging about one of the fields,

"Oh yes, there used to be an earth mound here, but I plowed it away."
I told him that its ghosts must have been causing him a lot of bad luck.

In all, it was pretty remarkable to someone from the outside; in fact,
it hit me as close to surreal. Here were immense records of time, and
as a history junkie, one of my evening pastimes was tracing ley lines
on my local ordinance maps, which mark every megalith, ford, graveyard, and tomb. When I really began researching these old stones, I
discovered that the Neolithic, mound-building North Atlantic mari-
time peoples who erected them were unique because they were the first
farmers there, and landed in Ireland around 4500 BC. Their forebears
had left Göbekli Tepe around 7000 BC, colonizing as they sailed along
the coasts of Iberia and Brittany and on to the British Isles. Two of
the earliest court tombs in Ireland are still at their western landing
point, sited on either side at the end of the aforementioned path—a
ritual track. One finds other epic menhirs and lost henges clasping
this line, and they surprised me into a full commitment to the entire
Neolithic project.

These paintings aren't about memories—mine or time's—they're more
about a variety of temporalities and their related forms. They're really
abstract paintings made with images, as I believe that a painting ideally doesn't represent or illustrate a concept, but, rather—as it's always
been—is about its own very deep structure. I think it's important that
people are able to "read" these paintings like a map with lines that go
from here to there.

The viewer will come to understand that I'm a magpie: for decades,
I've collected photographs of odd things, pictures that seem to go
together for me to make a subject. I used to look in secondhand book-
stores for images I could use, and then I would trace them on a grid for
my paintings. But as soon as I could use computers to grid up—circa
1995—I did. Typically, I compose some images on a field, print it all
out in black and white, and then take colored pencils and change things
around. I then scan the image back and play with it some more until I
get what I think will look and be right. When it goes up onto the much
larger surface of the canvas, more changes must be made. In these
particular paintings, the process results in a sense of the compression
of time and memory and imagery that's obvious: the paintings speak a
digital language but the coding isn't difficult to discern.

Right now I'm turning this series of six paintings into replicas—
smaller pigment prints using oversize ink-jet printers and this beautiful

Fabriano watercolor paper. The prints will have the feel and a sense of the paintings, if not the impact. Made for smaller exhibition spaces, they will be large enough to stand on their own in a room along with some of their smaller working drawings. Picasso got around an awful lot that way, didn't he? I think I'm going to do this with all of my image output, at least with those of the past few years. I don't see why paintings should just sit around in warehouses, never shown. Still, it took me nearly fifty years to get my so-called Minimalist work into the canon, and as this work is pretty much on the edge also, I'm not expecting an immediate popular response. However, perhaps prints traveling about to today's many available nonmuseum spaces might go some way toward abbreviating the process.

Revisioning the Parthenon is still a work very much in progress. It's now about eighty pages long and explores and illustrates how Athens used the Parthenon as a propaganda machine. It was partially inspired by the first time I saw the Elgin Marbles in London at the British Museum. I was afraid to say this out loud, but I thought they were really fussy and funky, and I didn't like them. It wasn't until ten years later that I began to read about what was going on in Athens at the time, and the fact that they were the first institutional slave society in the world—not to mention how they disdained and treated women. It was no wonder I hated those marbles!

Joan Jonas

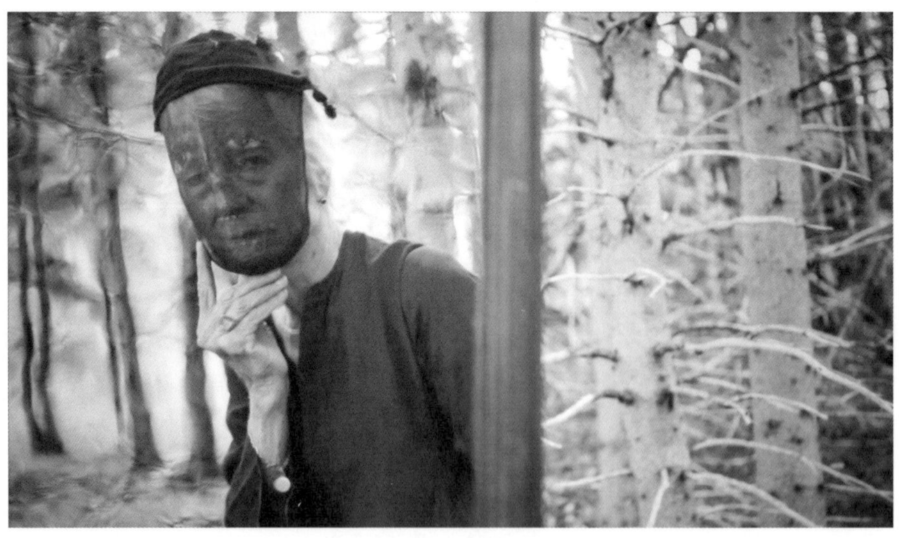

Joan Jonas, *They Come to Us without a Word*, 2015, HD video projection (color, sound, 2 minutes 11 seconds).

April 22, 2015
Artforum

Born in New York in 1936, Joan Jonas is a pioneer of video and performance art, known for her continuous and seamless merging of cutting-edge technology with historic, ancient, and often ineffable source material. They Come to Us without a Word, 2015, debuted at the US pavilion in the 2015 Venice Biennale. The piece, which Jonas discusses here, incorporates videos, drawings, objects, and sound, and extends her investigation into the writings of Halldór Laxness.

I moved back to New York in the mid-1960s to pursue an MFA in sculpture from Columbia University. I was married at the time, and we had an apartment on the Upper East Side. My ex-husband was a friend of Henry Geldzahler's, so we were connected in an indirect way to all the downtown events. For instance, I first heard La Monte Young in those years, which had a deep impression on me. Not long after, I decided to switch from sculpture to performance, having been inspired by works I'd seen by the Living Theatre, Lucinda Childs, and Claes Oldenburg, among others. I also began taking workshops from dancers—Trisha Brown, Yvonne Rainer, and Steve Paxton—because I wanted to learn how to become a performer and to move in front of an audience. The switch didn't seem like a big change because, like other artists in that era, I became interested in combining different aspects of the time-based arts—for me, dance and film—to create my own language. It was also important to me to reference literature and poetry. It still is.

I wanted to have my performances last, and that's why I started making videos. From the beginning I worked with video and I thought of the medium in terms of what's peculiar to it, as compared with film. My early work had an immediate and positive response. Although the audiences were small, word spread very quickly.

Frankly, I never liked the term *performance art*, as it limits people. It's like a lot of women don't want to say their work is "feminist" even though it might be—my first few works were certainly affected by the women's movement. I think that one's work continues to be affected and one continues to be concerned with such issues. You don't fo get them and you don't leave them out; it's just that they're no longer focused on in a particular way.

At certain times I recycle some of my early videos. For instance, in *Reanimation*, 2014, I use *Disturbances*, 1974, which was shot in a swimming pool, though in *Reanimation* it's more about representing a watery world. While working on my new piece for Venice, which deals with ghost stories that come out of Cape Breton, Nova Scotia—an area I've visited and lived in since the '70s—I suddenly saw that I've made visual references to ghostlike images for years without thinking of them as ghosts.

From the beginning I was interested in the people and landscape of Nova Scotia. I've always been attracted to mythology and folktales, and when we first went there I loved that the older people still believed in ghosts and told stories about magical things that happened in nature. I was very drawn to that culture. Also the fiddle music from there is beautiful. For the Venice piece, nearly all the background footage is from Cape Breton, which I shot over various years. It interests me to mix different video technologies, to compare the way things looked then with how they might look now.

I made a video last summer with my dog wearing a GoPro in Cape Breton and mixed it with footage from two other video cameras that I had. It interested me to see that footage against the other format. In the '90s I shot videos that I never used, of young women performing in the landscape of Nova Scotia. I do a lot of that kind of work when I'm there, and I don't necessarily use it. But in a strange way it fit perfectly into this current project, and so I like very much seeing this square format all of a sudden appear in the present rectangular format. I find it very interesting to see those technologies intercut with one another. I think it's part of the process.

I'll go to Canada again in August. It will be the first summer in which I won't have an immediate deadline of new work. I've gone through many stages of processing for this Venice project—doubting, being excited when it was accepted, and then being scared that I couldn't more or less come up to the task of being in that spotlight, which is what it is. It's quite complex to be representing a nation. It's the most focused-upon show in my experience. But now that my work is almost ready in the pavilion, I'm simply happy to be here, without thinking on what it means to represent the United States. Of course, I'm excited to be selected; it's a great privilege, and I made the piece with this place in the back of my mind. It's wonderful to be in the context of the Biennale with so many good artists past and present. I most enjoy seeing new work by others, being able to do a new piece myself, and to have people see it all.

Joan Semmel

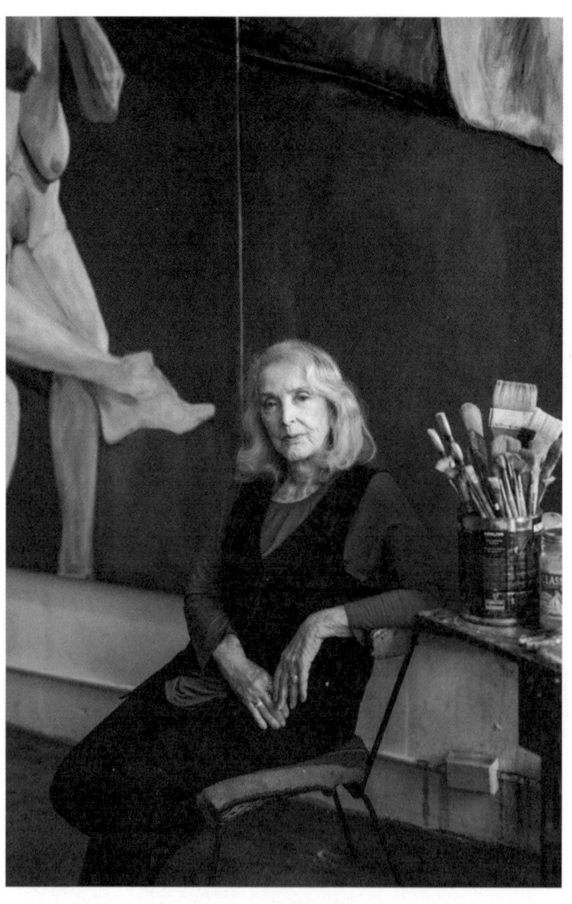

Joan Semmel, 2019, photo by Taylor Miller.

January 15, 2013
Artforum

From her feted Technicolor paintings of copulating couples to more recent canvases of her aging nude body, the feminist critique in Joan Semmel's five-decade career of self-exposure has always been blunt and unwavering. Born in 1932 in the Bronx, Semmel moved to Madrid in the 1960s and then back to New York in the 1970s, where she turned from abstraction to figuration—specifically to a non-idealized, nonnarrative self-portraiture based on pictures taken from her own perspective. Now a professor emeritus of painting at Rutgers University, Semmel has shown her work in numerous solo and group exhibitions. Semmel's retrospective, A Lucid Eye, *ran at the Bronx Museum from January 24 to June 9, 2013. Curated by Antonio Sergio Bessa, the show included twenty-seven of Semmel's self-portraits from the past six years. Simultaneously, she had a solo exhibition of new work at Alexander Gray Associates in New York from April 17 to May 25, 2013. Here, she discusses showing her paintings in her home borough as well as what it has meant to be an "outsider" for so many years.*

JS: In general, my work with the body was about contesting the whole history of the nude in art and the way the woman is seen in art and in the popular culture. So these paintings are an extension of that whole attitude.

LOB: But it was also about showing yourself aging over time, and a non-idealized kind of self, right?

JS: Absolutely. Art had always dealt with idealization: the idealization of the individual in portraiture, the idealization of the body, the idealization of the sexual image. One of the reasons I decided to use myself was because I wanted it to be a specific body, a specific person who is not idealized, so that the culture absorbs people as they are, not as they would like them to be. I was also a convenient model. I was the closest person at hand and also I hate having other people in the studio with me. So I could be alone.

LOB: Have you worked with assistants?

JS: I do now, just because I need a little help. But usually I never had assistance [before]. I don't like having people in the studio with me. I've done just about everything myself.

LOB: Is the idea of the present central to your work? You seem to be always dealing with something that's happening right now.

JS: I haven't really thought of it in terms of the present, but I think that what I have done is tried to capture the actuality of how one sees and experiences oneself. And one can only experience oneself moment by moment. Some of my really new work deals with the idea of motion, blur, how we see ourselves in movement, not static. We even see other people the same way. We have, for instance, a still life. A still life is still—it's an object—but a person is never still. A person is always in motion. And that's part of my reason for starting to explore that whole idea of the person in motion. The person is constantly changing and is never the same, moment by moment. The body is the same way. It's constantly changing. So that moves me into the idea of aging, because the constant motion gradually moves you into the changes that take place in your face and body as you get older. For me, it's important to explore some of that, given the demographics of society today. I have always been interested in the work having a relationship to social problems but not in a pedantic way, and not in an agitprop way, but to the connections that are there in the world—to some of the things I would like to see change in the culture. And some of the things I would like to see change have to do with beauty, ideal images (what they are and how they affect people), and with aging, which—at this point—is a major change with the whole demographic: the number of people who are old and ignored as if they don't exist in terms of all the cultural images, in terms of marketing. All those things I find compelling in terms of my own life and my own life is always very much in my paintings. I started to do this work as a feminist. I saw how constricted women were and I was trying to help—to do what I could to liberate people. I don't like to use the language of revolution if it comes to the extreme, but it is really what motivated me. The 1970s were a wonderful time—just the sense of hope that we could change the world. We did change it some, and we have to change it more. I think my work as an artist was my way of trying to change it.

LOB: Were you active with any of the feminist art groups in the 1970s?

JS: I was active with all of them: the Ad Hoc Committee of Women Artists, the Art Workers' Coalition, Women in the Arts, and more. Each person has their own narrow memories, but my memory of feminism in the 1970s was that it was a wonderful time where women came together. We visited each other's studios and groups, talked about work with each other. Most of us were unable to get shows at that time, and some very big names now were in those groups. That's why it's quite wonderful when I hear that someone is finally receiving recognition. We were all there pushing so hard just to get ourselves seen, and we couldn't, so we went to each other's studios. That was a radicalizing process. For me, that memory is important and then during the years when we still couldn't get out after the backlash to feminism, and the guys came back in—the whole macho guy thing—we supported each other, all of us. I think without that support we might not have been able to hold on all these years, to keep working, to have the kind of affirmation that we gave each other. That was one of the most important parts of that whole movement, I think.

LOB: Did you feel that you were an outsider as a woman *and* as a painter, when painting wasn't hot?

JS: Yes, I was also an outsider because I was a painter, and I still find myself very defensive: "Yes, I'm a painter. I'm a feminist and I'm a painter." How can one do that? Well, I do it. I don't like restrictions of any kind, and I don't like people to tell me what I can and can't do. And that goes whether they're my parents or feminists or the critics, whatever. I've tried to follow my own needs in the work, and I assume I'm talking about other people's needs also.

LOB: Can you talk about why you've remained a painter?

JS: Painting for me is very natural, and it engages you on all levels. It engages you physically, which I like, and it engages you mentally. People think that it doesn't deal with reasoning or the intellect, but it's not true. In order to be a good painter, you need also to have a kind of intellectual understanding of how you frame your picture, why you're doing it, what you're looking for, how it relates to other work. All of those things come into play when you're making a painting—but not all at the same time. Sometimes you work and you let the work carry you. Then you step back, and when you step back you make certain decisions about what you have or what you see. So it's that back-and-forth process which I find very engaging also: the physical aspect of making the work, of allowing it to happen, and then stepping back and deciding on what it is that you're about. The painting will often tell you what you're about rather than you always telling it what you're about. I like that process because it's more intuitive, but it's still very intellectual because of the decision-making process that goes with it.

LOB: It has that quality of self-reflection you mentioned earlier ...

JS: Exactly. But I think also painting is a contemplative art. For a photo, you snap a picture, but a painting builds over time. There's an element of time and touch, and both of those things for me are essential. That's what I like about it. One of the reasons that painting is less in favor now is because of how the attention spans of people have shortened so much that they don't have the time to stand and look at a painting; they want to move. To really to see a painting you have to look a little bit. So that's just a change in the way people absorb information. Painting is not information; it's something else. It's an aesthetic experience that encompasses all of the things that I spoke about.

LOB: Are there approaches or tactics you use in your paintings to try to have the viewer stay longer?

JS: When I'm working I try not to think about the viewer, frankly. In a certain way, you do target an audience. My early work was directed at women. I want everyone to look at it; I don't care if men look at it too, but really I was speaking to women. And that was shifting the audience because if I was painting for the men I think it would have been a very different physical approach. But at this stage my audience is whoever comes, and I don't really think about the audience anymore. I can't paint to the audience. The audience has to come to me.

LOB: Let's talk about the Bronx Museum show.

JS: So the Bronx Museum came to me. I don't think there's such a thing as a universal art, but we do have to speak to each other, not only to people who are the same as us. So I think that the work the curator chose is work that can speak to anyone and the issues that are involved there are issues for all of us.

LOB: When did Sergio Bessa approach you for the show? How long did the process take and were you involved in the installation?

JS: Sergio approached me several years ago. At that time, I was inviting all the museum curators to come to the studio. I was interested obviously in having the work seen in institutional environments, not just in galleries. So that was my reason to invite these curators, and he came up with Holly Block, who was the director of the Bronx Museum. I'd known Holly for many years. So they came together and I showed them everything—well, almost everything. I showed them a lot of work, and he came back last year and told me he was interested in the small portraits and in doing a show of them. I said fine, I thought that would be very nice. And he wrote to me and said, "Hey, I've decided to enlarge the show," and then picked out some of the other paintings to go along with the small portraits and that would be shown in the larger gallery. And that's how it worked. At first I went into the installation, but they weren't very happy with what I had done. He had a really good idea of what he wanted to do, and I thought, let the curator be the curator. So he did it and it was great. I think it's a really good installation in terms of the architecture of the building.

LOB: How does it feel to be back in the Bronx?

JS: I hadn't been there since I was nineteen years old. That's when I left the Bronx, and my great dream at that point was always Manhattan. At this point, to go back to the Bronx is very fun, because I remember walking down the Grand Concourse where the museum is. I grew up just six blocks away from the museum, and I used to walk on the concourse with my mother and my brother. So it was very interesting to go back to that environment and to see my work there. It's exhilarating in a way: that this is where I came from and this is where I've gone.

LOB: And when did you live in Spain?

JS: I lived in Spain for seven and a half years. My ex-husband at that time was working there and we lived there and separated there and I stayed on by myself. My son was born there. I became very much a part of the world of art there. I met all the artists. At the time, I was an Abstract Expressionist, believe it or not, and I showed extensively. It was cosmopolitan in a lot of ways, and I met all kinds of people I would never have had access to here in New York. Also, I think it's very interesting to live for an extended period in another country, because you get a better understanding of the things you take for granted. And you also get to understand how each place thinks of itself as the center of the world. Each place is sure that it's the center of the world and the most important, so the experience informs you of so many things. I found it to be a great experience.

LOB: What was it like to be a woman painting in Spain?

JS: The whole idea of a woman painting was very radical there. After I invited an artist to my studio, he told me, "Well, we came, and we thought we were going to see flowers." When I came back to New York, I was already a feminist without calling it feminism, because I understood at that point how the whole society was structured in a way that made it impossible for women to move out and be themselves. I mean, a woman back then in Spain … it was hard! One of my friends came alone and my husband had to sign a lease for her because they wouldn't take a woman's signature. If you had a bank account, your husband could go and take your money. You couldn't go to his but he could go to yours. You couldn't get a divorce there—there was no way. So there were all of these things that were still extremely archaic in my mind, and when I came back I was primed to walk right into the whole feminist situation.

LOB: I wanted to talk about the title of the show: *A Lucid Eye.* Where did it originate?

JS: Sergio is interested in how I use the camera in the paintings, how I show it. For me, that was just natural because I use the camera to take the picture and then I paint from that. I first started doing that when I was working with a group of paintings that were of women in a locker room at a gym, in the late 1980s. When I took the pictures there, I didn't want the women around to start posing for me. I wanted it to be natural. So I took pictures in a mirror, because most of those places just have mirrors all around. It's just mirrors and more mirrors. And when I took the picture in the mirror, I also got myself holding the camera in the mirror. But then I really liked the whole idea of me pointing the camera out at the audience, because the picture of me in the mirror with the camera destabilized who was looking at whom. So that was another way for me to take the point of view that I used in earlier self-body images into the more third-person pictures of the locker room. Those were the first pictures with the camera. Later, I just used myself with the camera. The artist doing the self-portrait always had the person standing with the easel and brush in their hand, looking out at the audience—so there was always that projection of how a self-portrait should be made. I wanted it to be sure that you could see that this is the artist—female artist—making these pictures, that it was the point of view of this female artist. So with me holding the camera there, it was clear that I was the one who took the image.

Judy Chicago

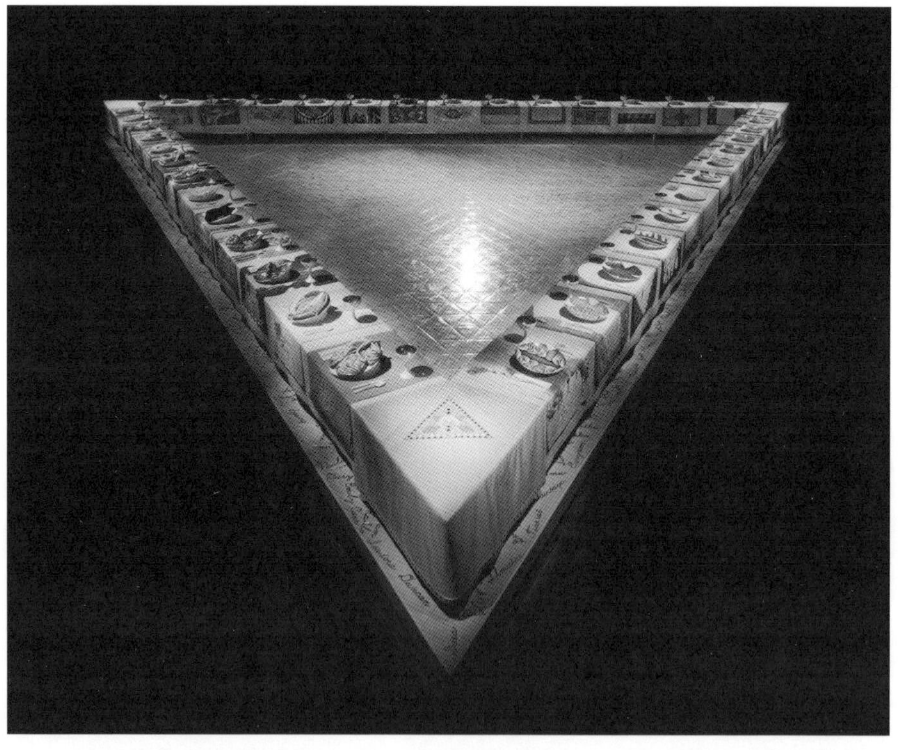

Judy Chicago, *The Dinner Party*, 1974–79, ceramic, porcelain, and textile,
576 × 576 inches (1463 × 1463 cm). Brooklyn Museum, New York, installation view.

Spring 2007
Bitch magazine

In the early 1970s, Judy Chicago created the Program for Feminist Art at California State University-Fresno and at California Institute of the Arts; in 1973, she cofounded the Women's Building in Los Angeles with art historian Arlene Raven and designer Shelia de Bretteville. Shortly after, she began her best-known collaborative work: The Dinner Party, *a massive, triangular table set with thirty-nine place settings, each representing a historic female figure—from Sappho to Artemisia Gentileschi to Sojourner Truth—was a multimedia monument that employed numerous techniques (ceramics, needlework, china painting, gilding) and was more than five years in the making.* The Dinner Party *debuted at the San Francisco Museum of Modern Art in 1979, and though the exhibition was profitable for the museum ("the bookstore made so much money they bought a computerized cash register they called 'Judy,'" notes Chicago), it inspired heated arguments everywhere, from the feminist community to the halls of Congress. As an explicit comment on women's erasure from the annals of history, the piece was both more political and—with its famously vulvic painted plates—more sexual than much modern art of the time, and its coverage by mainstream news and art publications was, though widespread, largely derisive.*

LOB: Did you have any idea, in 1974, that *The Dinner Party* would become such a feminist landmark?

JC: I set out to try and teach women's history through a monumental work of art, and from the beginning my goal was for it to be permanently housed. I just was very naive about how that happens. I just thought that then it would be toured around the world and it would end up permanently housed. After it premiered, I was starting to work on a porcelain room for it; I moved up to Northern California with the intention to do testing on ceramics. I had no idea how I'd pay for it, but that had never stopped me. So it was a complete shock when instead of my dream coming true, the museum system shut down and *The Dinner Party* became the piece that nobody wanted to show.

I've had a really long struggle to get here and to fight for the recognition of feminist art, because there's been a real resistance to both the word and to acknowledging the importance of the feminist art movement. There were all these decades of people doing grassroots organizing and women petitioning their museum and trying to find permanent housing [for the piece], and finally it was achieved because of Elizabeth Sackler, Arnold Lehman (the director of the Brooklyn Museum), and the trustees of the Brooklyn Museum. I never dreamed how long it would take; I never imagined the level of controversy that erupted. But it's sort of live and learn, and I think out of that I have learned quite a lot.

LOB: What kept you going through these tumultuous years? When art critics called the work "kitsch" and conservatives called it "porn," and when Congress proposed to cut funding to the University of the District of Columbia in 1990 if you donated the work to the school.

JC: That was a sustained effort to silence me and to pretend I didn't exist, and to try and pretend *The Dinner Party* hadn't been seen by a million people. But there are two things that sustained me. One, my knowledge of women's history: I knew the stories of women who had gone before me and I knew what they had encountered. When Elizabeth Blackwell went to medical school, she was the first woman doctor—she was only accepted into the school as a joke. She was spit at on the street and no one spoke to her for two years. Sojourner Truth was humiliated when she lectured; a man said to her, "You must be a man, you can't be a woman." Susan B. Anthony was ridiculed. I think knowing what women before me had been able to overcome in order to make the changes upon which we stand was really important to me.

The other thing is that I've been very fortunate to have a number of people who have supported me, because without support you just can't do anything. I'm sure it wasn't easy for them; in some cases they were ridiculed publicly by critics and writers who said, "Oh, they're Judy Chicago groupies, what do they know?" Even if they were museum people, or collectors—or, in the case of *The Holocaust Project*, holocaust scholars—that didn't stop writers from accusing them of bad judgment for believing that my work was important. It wasn't just me who had to stand up to it.

LOB: But within the feminist community there was also some controversy. *The Dinner Party* opened up many discourses on feminism—on feminism and race, for example, since Truth was the only Black woman represented in the piece. Meanwhile, feminist art critics hadn't developed a language of their own, so it was difficult for the work to receive their input, and easy for critics to bash it. All in all, though, it seems like *The Dinner Party* was instrumental in the way that it challenged feminists during this time. Is that right?

JC: Well, I think that's true. Although one of the things that was exceedingly disappointing, and I agree with you about learning from it, was the degree to which feminist critics picked up the language of [*New York Times* art critic] Hilton Kramer, and is an indication of the degree to which women are still in thrall to patriarchal authority. You know, when *The Dinner Party* was shown in 1996 as part of the *Sexual Politics* exhibition at UCLA's Hammer Museum that was curated by Amelia Jones, the women's studies department at UCLA threatened to picket the show! I remember Through the Flower's board hearing this and the discussion was, "How could hundreds of thousands of perfectly ordinary women recognize that *The Dinner Party* celebrated women, but so-called feminist theorists didn't get it?"

LOB: It seemed like the reviews of the show were negative because it was openly feminist, and this was a significant move for Amelia Jones. Christopher Knight, of the *Los Angeles Times*, in his review of the show, wrote: "*Sexual Politics: Judy Chicago's* Dinner Party *in Feminist Art History* is the worst exhibition I've seen in a Los Angeles museum in many a moon ... Now the work has been foolishly trotted out at the UCLA/Armand Hammer Museum of Art as the catalyst for a look at feminist issues from the last quarter-century."

JC: As much as Amelia Jones had studied what happened to me, she was unprepared for what happened to her. She was attacked in very much the same way I had been attacked. At that point there wasn't that much critics could do about *The Dinner Party* since it was already such a part of our history. People were studying it, and like you said, people were also beginning to look at the discourse around it. But for Amelia, she became the target of some pretty brutal criticism.

LOB: But there have been some revelatory reviews as well, though most have been in the last decade. *New York Times* art critic Roberta Smith's 2002 review of *The Dinner Party* at the Brooklyn Museum is definitely important to mention.

JC: It was fantastic. The way the *Times* works is that once somebody tenders an opinion, nobody can challenge it within the paper; all the other articles have to be consistent. And so, with that review, Roberta Smith basically reversed the twenty years of the *New York Times*'s attitude. I called [former SFMOMA and Hammer Museum director] Henry Hopkins after the review and said, "Henry, am I a different person than I was yesterday? Is *The Dinner Party* a different piece?" Because once the *Times* changed its opinion, everyone changed their minds. It was incredible, [but] disappointing too. I mean, I was very glad to receive the review, don't get me wrong, but people should think for themselves.

LOB: I want to go back to the feminist art movement of the late 1970s, particularly critics like Lucy Lippard and Arlene Raven who were standing up and taking controversial risks by trying to expose your art and other feminist art to the public. Despite their efforts, which now have to be sought out since this subject is barely taught, it seems to me that the history of the feminist art movement is commonly misunderstood. It's not enough to say that the optimism of the era is gone and that the complexities surrounding sexual politics and contemporary art have surpassed the ideas in your work.

JC: The mainstream art world's attitude toward the 1970s feminist art movement—that it was something minor, and that it's now passé— gets transmitted into their writings on it. So one of the things I'm looking forward to in 2007 is that the real story is going to emerge through these exhibitions.

You know, feminist art has spread all over the world. But it is a long way from being recognized, and that's one of the reasons Arlene and I came up with the Feminist Art Project. I went back to teaching in 1999, and over the last seven years I've taught at six different institutions. One of the reasons I went back was to see what was happening in university art education. Well, I was horrified! Young women are not learning about feminist art, still not learning women artists, and are still not encouraged to work out of their experience as women—and if they do there's no comprehension of what they're doing, so that they're not [getting] guidance and support from their professors. That's where a lot of my thinking has been focused, on how to change that.

LOB: You present feminism as heroic and expressive: there's frequently a unified symbol of female imagery (a triangle or flower, for example) and you use embroidery, ceramics, and china painting—forms that have been called "feminine," but raise craft to "high" art. Why did you choose these materials?

JC: I've always chosen particular techniques for their expressive purpose. And I often work, even before I veered away from modernism and Minimalism, in fringe techniques. I've worked with fireworks, I went to auto-body school, and I've worked in plastics. I've worked in techniques that were not so rooted in the Eurocentric tradition because it allowed an opening of expressive possibilities. This is fairly significant in the history of women artists—you go back to the seventeenth century, when women had to use the prevailing forms (biblical painting, for example) and insert their content into that. I tried that with Minimalism, and even when I got some personal content in there it wasn't perceived. So when I started *The Dinner Party*, I looked to medieval art, which taught Christian religion through religious imagery. I was looking for new forms to represent content, I had done this series called *The Great Ladies* with sprayed acrylic, but I wanted something more specific in terms of technique, which is how I stumbled on china painting.

There's been a lot of misunderstanding of my choice of techniques for *The Dinner Party* and even later work, as if I made a feminist proclamation, like, "I'm going to use china painting and needlework because it's always been associated with women." No. Both had unexplored aesthetic potential, [and] that probably was because they were associated with women and weren't taken seriously by the mainstream. Nevertheless, had they not had that [potential], I would never have chosen them. But once having chosen them, of course, I realized there was an irony in using these degraded techniques, since I was using them to express a degraded, diminished history. So the techniques fit the content.

LOB: Most of your work is concerned with teaching women's history, and your nonprofit, Through the Flower, practices feminist art pedagogy, and takes its name from your first book. Can you touch on your contributions to feminist art education?

JC: The original idea was to build on the success of *The Dinner Party* and to make Through the Flower an independent institution—it just took twenty-five years! Now, Through the Flower, which is a feminist art organization, is turning its attention more to education and long-term planning. One of the things we're working on is the development of a *Dinner Party*-related curriculum for grade school, middle school, and high school.

LOB: I'm sure there will be school tours going through the Sackler Center, so these will be important in developing young feminists. But you know, I read *Through the Flower* for the first time while preparing for this interview and I wish I'd read it much earlier—like when I was first learning about women artists ten years ago!

JC: Well, we brought it back on iUniverse. I could say I'm flattered, but it also speaks to the fact that there has not been as much change as I would have hoped for in those thirty years since it was published. If *Through the Flower*, which was the outpouring of a young woman struggling to find her own voice, is still relevant, that means there hasn't been enough change.

LOB: It does, unfortunately, still apply to the current situation, even when something like 60 percent of people in art school are women. As you say, this history is treated as totally passé, as if gender in art is no longer an issue.

JC: I've had to work outside of the art market because the market wasn't interested in distributing what I had produced and wanted to produce. Now that's starting to change, but it's very interesting to see what work is becoming marketable. Of course, it's the work that's the least disruptive.

One of the issues that I hope will become the subject of some discourse is: Can feminist art be absorbed by the mainstream, or will it be cut off from its radical roots? Because feminist art, at least as I conceived of it, was intended to create change, to reach a broad audience, and not to be consumed by a small elitist audience, one of the biggest problems for women has been sustaining our institutions, our magazines, and our schools. And that's a place where work by women like Elizabeth Sackler, who have the means to be philanthropists, could act as a tremendous model. Still, there has been a lack of understanding of the importance of financial support or a lack of willingness on the part of women to take risks and support those vehicles, organizations, forms, and institutions that give us a voice. Until that happens, we're going to stay on the margins.

LOB: That leads into my final questions: What are your suggestions for feminist art and your thoughts on the future of feminism? And what's some advice you might give to emerging feminist artists?

JC: This goes back to your earlier question about how I've sustained myself—I've done so by understanding where I am and where we are in history. This isn't about giving white middle-class career women more rights. This is about a fundamental change on our planet. And art is part of this larger struggle. We are about to see, as I mentioned, that what has happened is a global feminist art movement. For young women who live in countries where it's literally dangerous to make feminist art, many leave their country of origin and they go to New York or they go to London and they begin to work for a Western audience. Even though it's understandable that they do that, we have to be willing to take the risk to challenge the structures of society that both imprison and silence us. I hope that *The Dinner Party* will act as a model because of its story. There I was—a young woman without any of the trappings that artists usually have in order to get their work [out]. I didn't have a major curator, or a collector, or a critic; in fact, they were all aligned against me. All I had was the power of the art. [What] we are taught in school is that there are a small number of people who care about art, and that you have to work for that audience. Well, I didn't. And what I learned from what happened with *The Dinner Party* is that the power of art can be enormous.

Julia Bryan-Wilson

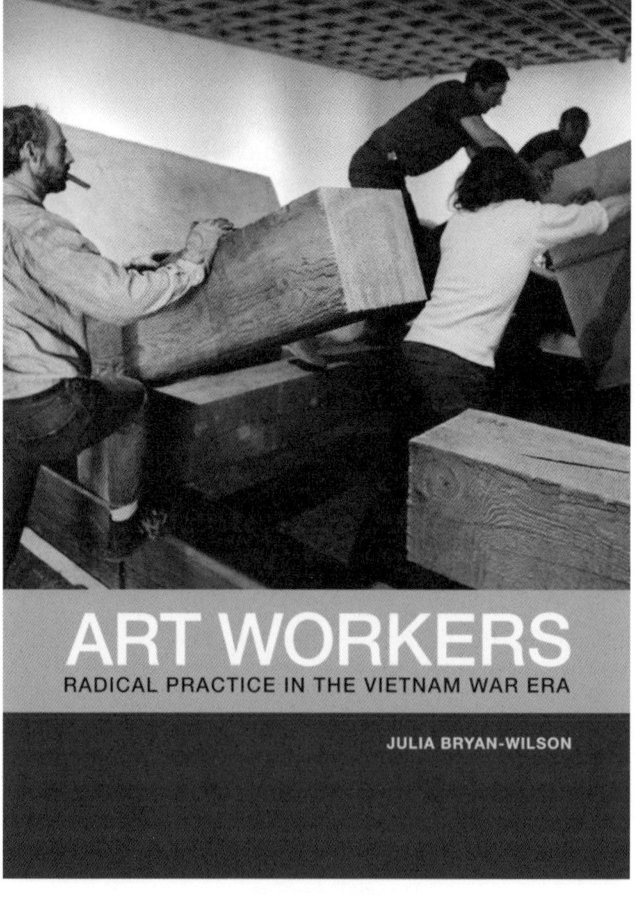

Cover of Julia Bryan-Wilson's *Art Workers: Radical Practice in the Vietnam War Era* (2009).

October 19, 2009
Artforum

In her book Art Workers: Radical Practice in the Vietnam War Era *(University of California Press, 2009), Julia Bryan-Wilson examines artistic labor in New York in the 1960s and '70s. Here she talks about her research and the questions that energized the project.*

The more interested I became in the legacies of the Art Workers' Coalition and the New York Art Strike, the more I became concerned with how artistic labor registers—or doesn't—within a wider field. It was both inspiring and somewhat vexing to consider how artists and critics attempted to organize as workers and label themselves as such, particularly during the Vietnam War, when debates about the value of artistic production were raging within culture and within protest politics. How does art *work*? This question challenged me and pushed the project forward.

In my preliminary writings on this subject, I investigated how the eruption of anti-war protests within New York museums was central to institutional critique in the United States. That assertion is still very much alive in *Art Workers* and informs much of the book. But I also ask larger questions about the flexibility of ideas of artistic labor at this time and how such labor was mobilized or altered by specific artists and groups.

A single book can't say everything about this moment, and mine certainly doesn't aim to be comprehensive. People around the globe were thinking about artistic labor, including Fred Lonidier in California and the Rosario Group in Argentina, to name just two. Yet I began to concentrate on influential figures (artists Carl Andre, Hans Haacke, and Robert Morris, and writer Lucy Lippard) to think through how their work and their participation in movements like the AWC might tell a new story about the political and artistic milieu of the era around the Vietnam War—which also, crucially, saw the flowering of Minimalism and Conceptualism.

Early on, I received some useful feedback from a reader who asked whether it might be a contradiction to organize the book as a series of case studies of canonical figures, since one somewhat contested aspect of this collective organizing sought to break down such hierarchies. While the book does include more marginal players, I intentionally focus on underexplored aspects of well-known art workers to expand our traditional understanding of this period and to consider the ways in which histories themselves are written.

In addition, I wanted to retain and amplify the contradictions, because in fact the attempt to redefine artists as workers circa 1969 was shot through with ambivalence, uncertainty, and paradox. For instance, a few of the figures I research viewed their activism and their art as constituting completely separate practices. Then there are others, like Lippard, who merged their political work with their art-world involvements. Lippard moved into an advocacy role as a feminist critic through her sense of herself as an art worker because she was interested in reevaluating women's labor. And from the start, feminist imperatives motivated my project; feminism helped me theorize the uneven valuation of different kinds of work and how different kinds of workers—across lines of gender, race, and class—are compensated.

The word *practice* in my title is vital; the phrase *radical practice* is a direct citation of Herbert Marcuse. He, of course, was a major intellectual player in that time, and his theories informed many of these art workers. I know *practice* has become slightly overused, but it's a very period-specific term. It also indicates that artists and writers were rehearsing or refining various modes of aesthetics and politics. It's a brief time span that I'm looking at—just a handful of years. But the incredible amount of organizational energy that was generated—especially how artists came together to effect change within the museum system—is still relevant. And it has been interesting to witness the activities of recently formed groups like Working Artists and the Greater Economy and the "State of the Arts" poster project about contemporary artists' political and occupational power—or lack thereof. Much has shifted in the intervening decades, but some of the issues that obsessed the art workers of the late 1960s (then, as now, a time of war and economic upheaval) remain pertinent today.

Karla Black

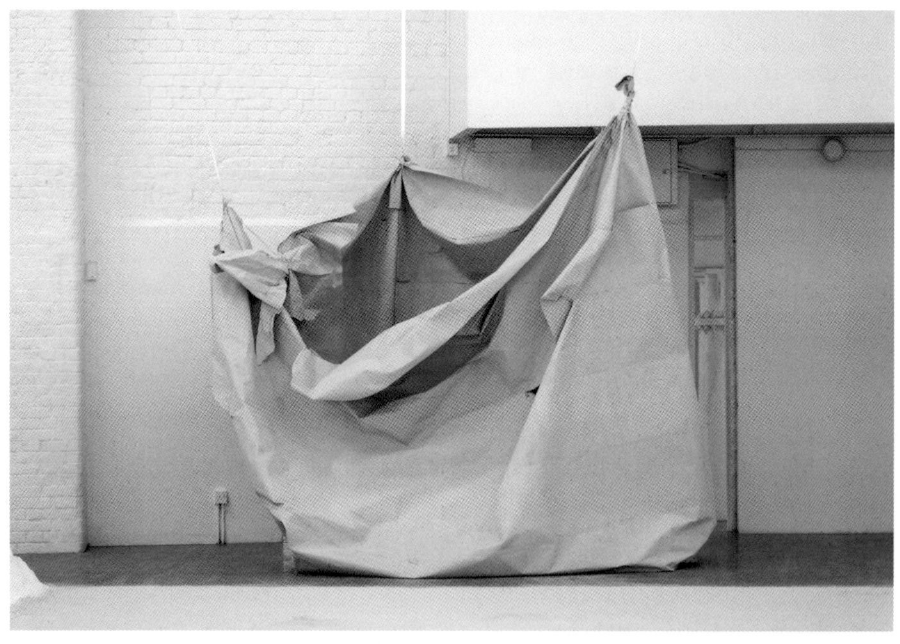

Nothing Is a Must, 2009, sugar paper, chalk, ribbon, lipstick, and glitter hairspray, 122 ⅛ × 118 ⅛ × 71 ⅝ inches (312 × 300 × 182 cm).

October 13, 2009
Artforum

The Glasgow-based artist Karla Black is known for her sprawling floor-based and hanging sculptures that comprise diverse materials such as plaster, Vaseline, acrylic paint, lipstick, nail polish, and body lotion. Here she talks about her fall 2009 show at Modern Art Oxford.

When I'm nearly finished making a work, I ask myself, If this was a painting, would it be a good painting? If I decide that the answer is yes, then I'm done. I use impermanent and raw materials like paper, polythene, plaster powder, and cosmetic products in my sculptures not because they easily change and decay but because I want the energy, life, and movement that they give. I would much rather have the sculptures stay exactly as they are the moment I finish making them. But I also know that if my first priority were to preserve the work forever, or for as long as possible, then I'd use stone, metal, or wood. But those materials don't have the qualities I want. It's a double bind.

My work needs to occupy the kind of large rooms that Modern Art Oxford has to offer, and it needs to enter into the institutional realm in order to become what it really is. The work is both a protest and a compromise at the same time. While it tries to dismantle the demands of being permanent, transferable, and stable, as required by most art institutions, it also physically and sculpturally negotiates within those conditions and reaches compromises that allow it to exist in those places.

I prioritize material experience over language as a way of learning and understanding. The physical human experience that comes from the inside out precedes language and is most absorbent for us, most unselfconscious, when we are fully in it and therefore completely unaware of any image of ourselves, of how we think we might look to others. The moment we become aware of ourselves from the outside in, as an image that others can see, or as a subject that holds a particular meaning, symbolic or otherwise, then we split from that primary experience of the physical world and must think. Traditionally, painting offered an optical escape from this world by providing a window onto another. Sculpture can offer some sort of escape, too, through an actual engulfment in the physical.

In art-school critiques, my classmates sometimes said my work looked "feminine" and "domestic." I could see what they meant, but that was never my intention and still isn't. I like pink, and if someone wants to say that's because I'm a woman, then perhaps it is. I'm interested in those kinds of cultural judgments that come from the outside. In the end, I decided to just do what I want to do, to use the materials and colors I want to use, because I want to enjoy making the work as much as I can. It's hard enough to make something that's any good, so you may as well start with some sort of self-indulgence.

I felt that judgments of femininity or domesticity were derogatory and that they meant, perhaps, that the work wasn't very good or not serious. (I still wonder why I thought and, to a certain extent, still think that. Is it because of some residual misogyny in myself?) There are a lot of men who use pink—Franz West, for instance. But who says that his work looks feminine or domestic? Why is it only women's art that is gendered? I was recently asked, "How do you think your work would differ if you were a man?" Would anyone ever ask a man, "What would your work look like if you were a woman?"

Kathryn Andrews

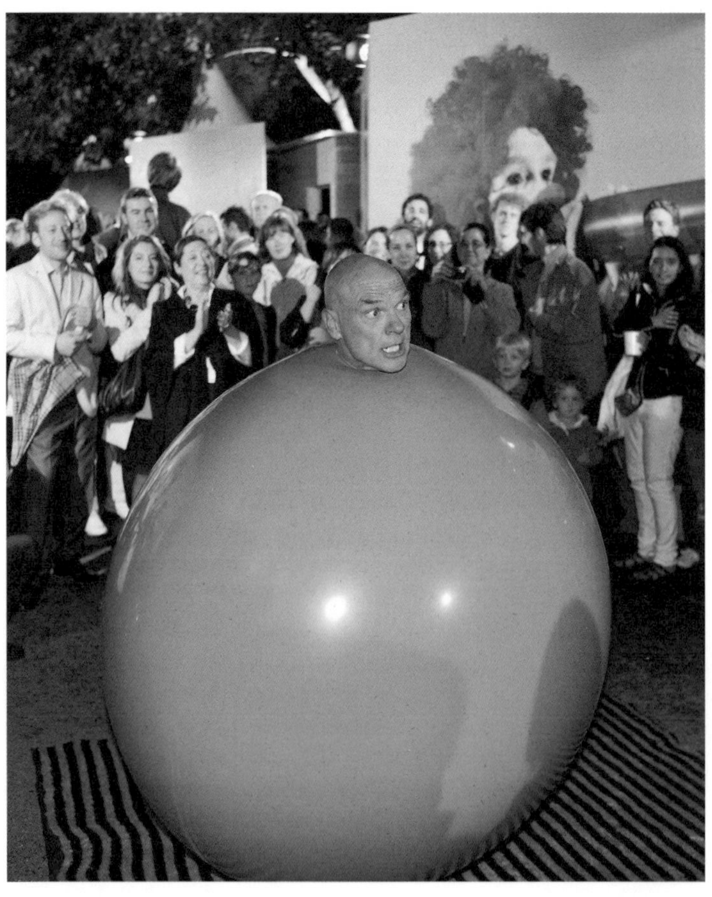

Kathryn Andrews, *Voix de Ville*, 2012, performance at Art 43 Basel, Art Parcours, Basel, Switzerland.

June 1, 2012
Artforum

The Los Angeles–based artist Kathryn Andrews here talks about work she was presenting at Art Basel and at the Institute of Contemporary Art, Philadelphia, in summer 2012.

The piece I'm making for Art Parcours is a spectacle-type event with a series of five stage sets that each have different images: they're all stock pictures of idyllic landscapes or people interacting with odd objects—a clown with a large balloon, a drunken man with a beer glass, a polished-chrome viewfinder overlooking an Italian city, a Swiss chalet. Within this architectural framework, which will be installed in a sort of zigzag, there'll be a series of vaudevillian performances. My intention is to create a situation that questions how we locate the subject of the work and the viewer. The performers will do their routines, one will begin just as another ends, and their acts will be seductive, courting the viewer's attention. The viewers will get drawn into the stage sets and caught there, framed by the acts. They may start to feel like both tourists and performers—constantly in motion, pursuing the next attraction, yet unable to move freely due to the spatial constraints of the sets. I'm excited about this, because most of my previous works deal with how we perceive a sculpture or painting as a static scenario rather than as an active event. I suppose I'm trying to take that question to performance and go another way with it: To what degree do we perceive something as seemingly lively as performance as image? And what happens when the viewer is involved in breaking its traditional frame?

The floor and wall sculptures I'm showing in *Made in L.A.* are among those active works of mine that have a theatrical quality; they function as props or sets. But the viewer is invited to consider himself or herself as their subject, as a performer. Complicating that, components in each sculpture—a clown suit, for instance—are rented, so each work exists in a temporal exchange that's ongoing. It implies a history of the bodies that once inhabited that costume, or the bodies that will inhabit it.

The piece I'm showing at the ICA, *Serial Killer*, is something of a bridge between these two shows. The work consists of a mobile fence on wheels. Once a month, a performer—a human statue—enters the space, grabs the fence, and moves it unusually close to another work within the show. The statue subsequently stands still next to the fence for two hours and then leaves. But the fence stays there for a month, when another human statue comes in and moves it to a new location. Over the course of the exhibition, this fence is constantly reframing the works. It creates a series of triangulations between the viewer, the performer, and the other artists' pieces. It asks us how we construct notions of autonomy, and what it means to view an artist's work as a contained situation. It pokes at the impossibility of that.

This work doesn't require agreement from the participating artists in the show. When museums curate group shows they don't call up every artist and ask them where to place everything: "Who should we put next to you, and how many inches away?" Art institutions rarely do this; they wouldn't be able to function. The curators asked me if they should ask each artist's permission for my piece to be in proximity to theirs. I didn't respond, leaving the problem of agency with the museum. I was later told that all the artists were "informed" that this piece would be moving throughout the exhibition, so everyone is at least aware of it.

Often in my work I'm trying to address the relationship of popular desire to specific materials and forms and what happens when that desire goes unchecked. We're all seduced by ... whatever. There are millions of things out there that suck us in and it's easy to be critical of their mechanisms and our willingness to embrace them. Instead of saying, "Hey, all that shit over there is bad, it dupes us," I hope my work says something more like, "No, actually we suck ourselves in because we really enjoy having a mediated experience." It's sort of a rabbit-hole problem. When we see our own attachment to these illusions, we can laugh at ourselves.

Katy Siegel

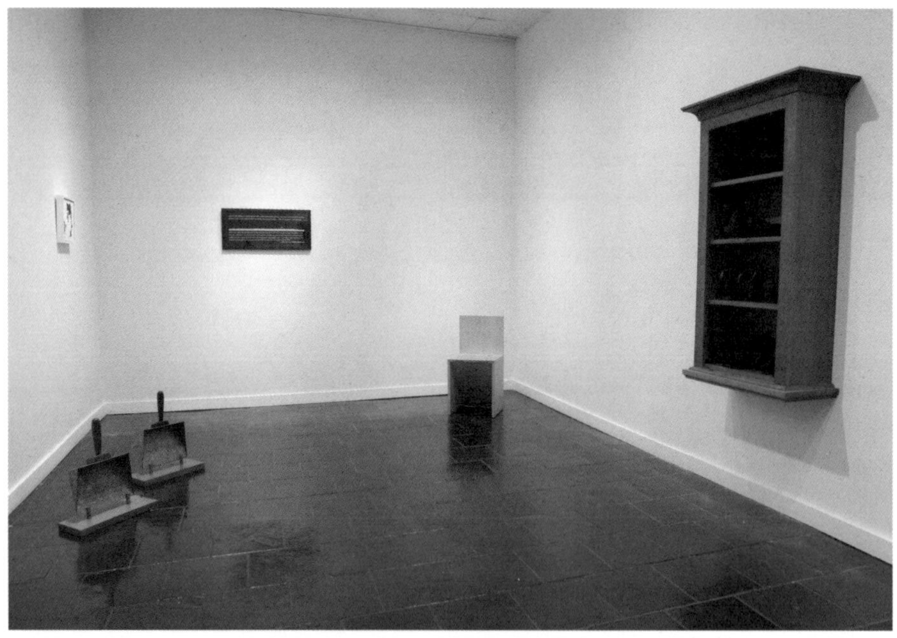

View of *Americanana*, 2010. From left: H.C. Westermann, *Dustpan – Amaranth*, 1972; H.C. Westermann, *Dustpan – Douglas Fir*, 1972; Kara Walker, *Jockey*, 1995; Elaine Reichek, *Sampler (Above the Fields)*, 1999; Donald Judd, *Chair*, 1991/2002; James Turrell, Nicholas Mosse, and Bill Burke, *Lapsed Quaker Ware*, 1998.

October 11, 2010
Artforum

Katy Siegel organized Americanana *for the Bertha and Karl Leubsdorf Art Gallery at New York City's Hunter College, where she was an associate professor of art history. London-based Reaktion Books published her book* Since '45: America and the Making of Contemporary Art *in fall 2010.*

Americana*na*. Everyone leaves off the last "na." They think it's a typo. But I wanted it to evoke the absurdity of European settlers using Indian words to name soccer clubs and suburban streets, or the new urban woodsmen butchering pigs in Brooklyn, or the countless other attempts in our culture to recover a lost past. The title also echoes *Indianana*, a not very well-known work by Mike Kelley, and so it's a little tribute to him.

The artists in the exhibition aren't reproducing Americana in a straightforward way. Instead they're self-consciously coming out of it and reiterating or reworking it in some new fashion—whether for some social or political purpose or just with the consciousness that this is something they're recovering. You can see it in Robert Gober's butter churn covered in barnacles. It's like something old that has drifted away and then returned crusted with time.

The idea for the show came out of research for my new book. I realized that there's a strain of American contemporary art that's focused on American history, production, and social values. That's not as emphasized in the book itself—it's a minor motif. Yet among all the social histories I covered, this was the most vibrant in terms of visual material, and it deserved an exhibition.

Americanana doesn't go off on a lot of tangents. And we're not talking about folk art—there have already been good shows about *that* old weird America. This is an exhibition featuring artists who are interested in common American objects—painted signs, quilts, butter churns, rubber stamps, and copper kettles—and particularly in the way they're made. These are things anyone could make without being a professional artist or going to a fancy school; though they require skill, they're not fussy, labored, or self-conscious. This is a tradition Donald Judd, for instance, wrote quite a bit about, and it's very evident in his work. No one has really studied this subject, but Judd's library contained many catalogues of Shaker objects and furniture, available because these things were undergoing a revival in the US as part of American taste-making in the 1960s.

Part of what drew me to this subject is that postmodernist theory was bad at addressing the fact that American history is a history of revivals, and also its traditional anti-capitalism. Today we see—correctly—America as one of the chief countries imposing capitalism on the world. But in the nineteenth century, capitalism was seen as European and as something that was being imposed on America, at the cost of the traditional independent man, the artisan and farmer, and on communities like the Shakers. It's this pre-superpower America that comes back again and again in contemporary history and culture.

I think today's resurgence is sparked by the feeling that capitalism is collapsing. The global business culture that seemed so permanent to people ten years ago now offers limited rewards. There's also the decline of America as it becomes one nation among many, which allows us to see more clearly the particularities of America and American history. Just as Japanese artists have attended to what's Japanese, or as Korean artists have considered Korea, American artists are now looking at their country through local lenses.

Lisa Tan

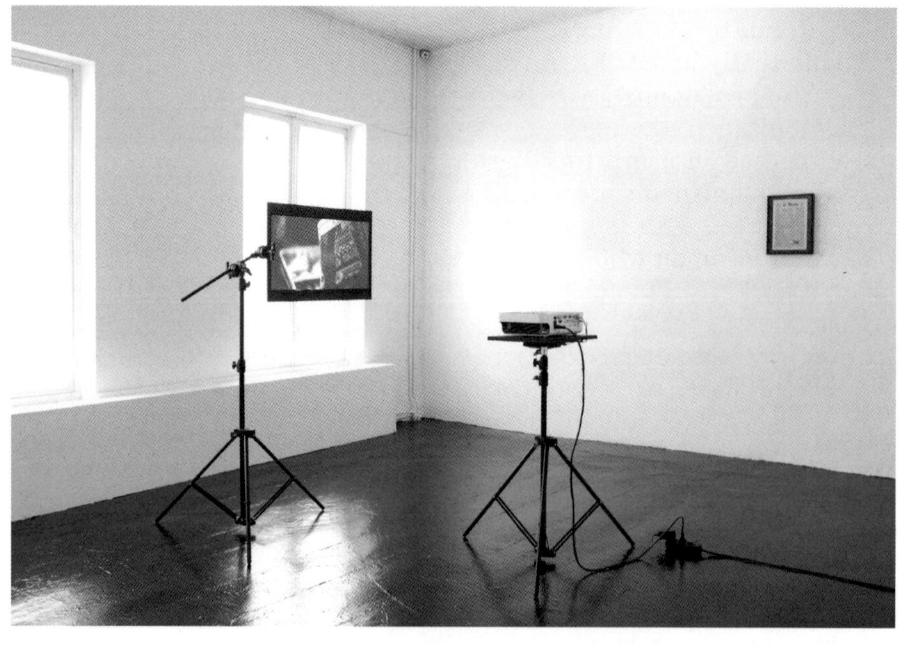

Lisa Tan, *Les Samouraïs*, 2010, digital video, light stands, painted wood, projector, and text, 3 minutes 36 seconds.

April 19, 2010
Artforum

For her exhibition at FDC Satellite in Brussels, Lisa Tan presented Les Samouraïs, *a work based on Jean-Pierre Melville's classic 1967 film. Exploring themes of isolation, history, relationships, and the everyday, which are all central to the artist's work, the show was on view in spring 2010.*

I was attracted to the restrained qualities of Melville's *Le Samouraï*: the color palette is really narrow and nearly monochromatic and there's hardly any dialogue. He was very resistant to making his films in color, but by 1967 black and white wasn't marketable. You can tell Melville really hated the transition to color. Even the small bird, the pet of the protagonist, was chosen for its drabness. It's a gray-brown female bullfinch; the males have pink-orange feathers. I learned that the bird died in a fire that burned down Melville's studio when he was almost finished shooting *Le Samouraï*. It's a minor thing, but the thought stayed with me as I began to research the fire with the help of a young woman who lived in the Thirteenth, where the studio was located, in Paris.

In our correspondence, I learned that this person had moved from the United States to France to be with her lover. At the time, she was spending her days alone waiting for him to return from work each day—which reminded me of the bird in Melville's film. In return for taking photographs of different sites in Paris, I mailed her items she requested. For taking pictures of where Studios Jenner once stood, I sent her a couple of jars of peanut butter; for pictures of Marché aux Oiseaux, the bird and flower market that has taken place every Sunday for the past two hundred years near Notre Dame, she asked for Neutrogena face wash and Lipton French onion soup. We became pen pals over the next year and are still good friends.

I was thinking about this project as a memorial for the bird this insignificant creature—and I was also interested in a theme of bonding, foreshadowed by death. So after a while I thought, Why notjust add another bird? Melville's *Samouraï* is built around ideas of solitude, isolation, and detachment, so it's a very simple gesture to foil the film. By adding a bird, it not only alters the film but also modifies an occurrence in history, albeit fictitiously. It's messing with the master's work and is a bit mischievous in that way.

The installation of the show turned out black and white, which I like. Also, the gallery is the size of a bedroom, so it mimics the intimacy of the film. The room has two windows, which are very similar to those in the opening scene of the assassin's apartment. The armature that the video is projected upon comprises standard light stands that reference Melville's studio and also keep the proportions of the bird's cage. There's a photograph of the front and back pages of *Le Monde* from the day the studio burned down. These are hung on either side of the space, which might imply the pages in between.

I grappled with the story of my relationship with the young woman for a long time and decided not to include it in the final work. I reconciled the fact that as a story it's nice for me, but it probably doesn't have any interest for a wider public. Many of my works have this element: a narrative that speaks to some lived resonance in my life, but I need to edit the work so that it transcends my own experience. I consider it a process of distillation. To some degree, I tend toward a spare visual presentation and create a veneer in the finished work to mediate the overly sentimental content. The hope is that this creates more entry points for the viewer.

Lisi Raskin

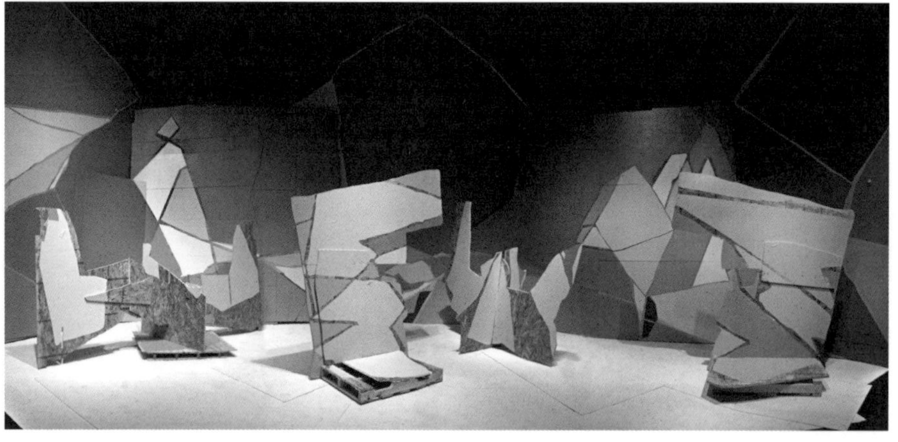

Lisi Raskin, *Armada*, 2009, wood, paint. Installation view, Blanton Museum of Art, Austin, Texas.

March 24, 2009
Artforum

The Brooklyn-based artist Lisi Raskin has explored fear, Cold War tensions, and sites that rely on nuclear power in her works. Here she discusses the process of making Armada, *an installation that went on view in spring 2009 at the Blanton Museum of Art at the University of Texas, Austin.*

The *Mobile Observation* series began over a year ago. The first part of the project, *Command and Control*, was commissioned by Bard College and was exhibited at the Park Avenue Armory for the ADAA fair in 2008. Following that, I was commissioned by Bard to take a road trip to expand the series, and I traveled to several sites near Tucson: the Titan Missile Museum, the White Sands Missile Range in New Mexico—which is the site of the 1945 Trinity nuclear test— and a large empty lot of airplane carcasses, called the Bone Yard, whose proper name is the Aerospace Maintenance and Regeneration Group. *Armada*, my work at the Blanton, is based on the Bone Yard. I wanted to use my road trip as source material as the *Mobile Observation* projects unfolded. Normally, I make site-specific works within institutions and galleries, but this project also includes an element of working with the landscape and a question of how to engage space in a more direct way. When Risa Puleo, a curator at the Blanton, approached me, I was beginning to think about the landscape of the Bone Yard. The project emerged pretty organically and intuitively once I visited Austin and decided to use her backyard as a production site and to make the work with a team of local assistants there. I knew I wanted to create a telephone line from my inspiration in Risa's suburban yard in 2009 to my initial inspiration in a backyard in 1984 in Coral Gables, Florida, when I first became aware of the possibility of war, nuclear annihilation, and these kinds of test spaces.

There were several experiences I tried to conjure when I was working on the installation. For instance, I remembered sitting in my van in the Bone Yard: I looked toward Davis-Monthan Air Force Base, and there was a huge plume of gray and black smoke that fighter jets were flying into; they were basically running an intense drill. Another day, I parked the van next to a chain-link fence, and it turned out that I was directly under the flight path of the pilots who were out for the day's exercise. After lunch that day, I parked my van, serendipitously, again under the path as they were coming back.

I connected these memories to other, very specific visceral moments. When I was a kid, I used to sit on the hood of my mother's Chevrolet Malibu Classic and look up at the sky and watch the planes go by. I would imagine what it would be like if I were to witness a bomb falling from one of the planes. Because a backyard, or a suburban site, was the first location that served as a backdrop while these fears and desires developed within me, it was motivation to use Risa's backyard as a kind of memory space.

Working in her backyard, however, created an interesting duality regarding site-specificity and project identity within the actual museum itself, which is not like a kunstverein, or PS1, where I've previously had installations. There are nineteenth-century landscape paintings in the Blanton that we had to be very careful around. Although I wanted to take over the project-space room completely, there were things I had to be cognizant of, like fire codes. This was new for me. Using the backyard as the space of production allowed me to leap over the rules of the institution so my creative process went unhindered.

While I had memories, drawings, and notes with which to work, once I began on *Armada* I realized that I didn't really want to control or deal with any of the preconditioned ideas I had about what the project might look like. Instead, I wanted to try to abstract it and forget about the idea that abstraction always references something. I thought about the wings and nose of the airplanes and how to make shapes that might communicate those elements, but I was able to dispense with this tendency pretty early on. I was also playing with how I could tweak the scale of such massive planes by using cheap materials. I made two 12-by-12-foot paintings, which is something I've never done before.

I rejected all my impulses that might have made me treat the work as though it were precious. The construction was direct, improvised, and intentionally precarious so that if there were accidents on the way to the museum—we transported it in an open truck—I could incorporate them. I think this element added another layer to the project, and in a way it was also an avenue to explore and utilize failure.

Liz Deschenes

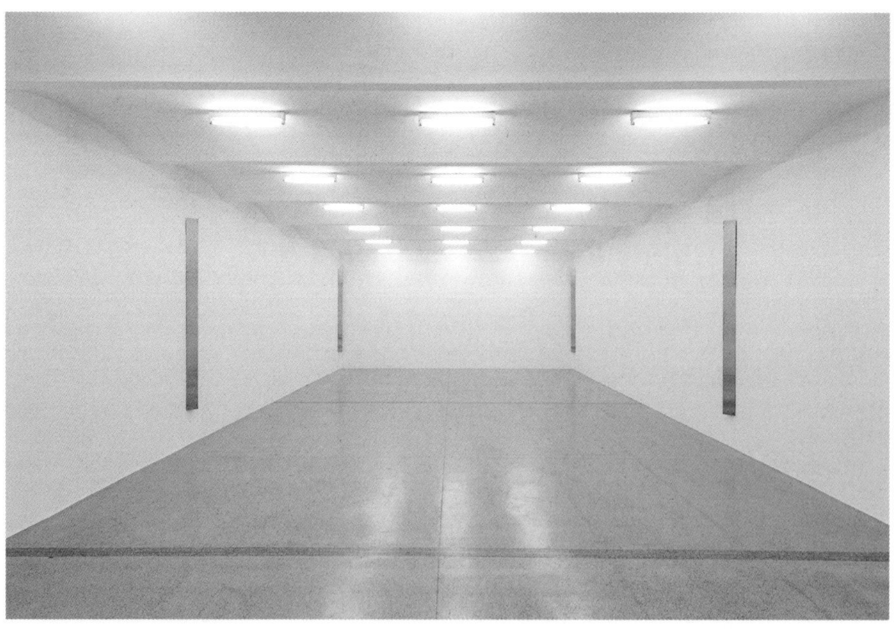

Installation view of *Liz Deschenes*, Secession, Vienna, 2012.

January 22, 2013
The Paris Review Daily

For many years Liz Deschenes's work has articulated a materialist stance; rather than taking pictures of things in the world, she usually works sans camera, turning to the inner life of photography and proposing discursive questions about its philosophical, scientific, and experimental possibilities. Deschenes has recently called her approach "stereographic," a term originally coined in the 1850s for two nearly identical prints that are paired and viewed through a stereoscope to produce a 3-D illusion of a single image. Deschenes employs this operation of doubling and dividing to give the viewer a chance to actively participate in her work, and it also places an emphasis on the constantly changing nature of her recent photographs.

LOB: These photograms began in Vermont, by being exposed by the night sky. Do you prefer to work nocturnally?

LD: I worked at night for purely practical reasons. Simply put, the paper I used for these pieces is light sensitive, so working during the day—no matter how sunny or cloudy—would overexpose the paper.

LOB: What was it like to install in the Secession? Take us through a little bit of the process of putting the show together in the space.

LD: Secession, as you mentioned, has a rather esteemed history. In response to the building, I wanted to reframe the spaces and the entry point. By doing so, the order of the spaces was thus altered. Bettina Spörr, the curator, was instrumental to this project—among other significant contributions, she managed to convey, in only a twenty-four-hour site visit, the dynamism and unique artistic opportunity that sums up Vienna's Secession. I always make scale models for the projects too, and lately, I've made models of the photographs at a one-to-one scale, so that I can get a better sense of the final works in space.

LOB: You have some upcoming shows, in London at Campoli Presti and in New York at Miguel Abreu Gallery. Will *Stereograph 1–16* be presented again soon elsewhere? Will the installation change, or be "finished," if so?

LD: I've decided not to reconfigure these works in new venues. As for the works being finished, I'm reminded of the title of Johanna Burton's essay for Secession's catalogue, which was drawn from something I said in an interview recently. I was asked about my relation to Henri Cartier-Bresson's notion of the decisive moment and in response I said that, in my work, "There is no decisive moment." But actually, there are so many decisive moments, and their effect is cumulative. Sometimes decisions are altered or changed entirely—for instance, I thought this work could travel to London, but it won't. Instead, I'll make new pieces that will respond to that site in more specific ways that are yet to be determined.

LOB: Stereographic vision activates the viewer, making one more aware of the constantly changing work in the gallery. It seems like this perception could also extend outside of the gallery, too. Is that something you aim for?

LD: Yes—and I'd like to take on other venues too, not just galleries and museums. I don't have an ideal site, though I like the idea of the work being installed at unexpected places, like when On Kawara's work was installed in an elementary school classroom.

LOB: You're deeply engaged with photography, but there's also a painterly and sculptural aspect to your work. Still, I wonder if light is really your medium. Do these works represent light, or is it more that they are light?

LD: The work reflects or absorbs light, certainly. I'm hoping that they simultaneously suggest other ways of viewing, even if the shift is barely perceptible in the moments of viewing.

Lorraine O'Grady

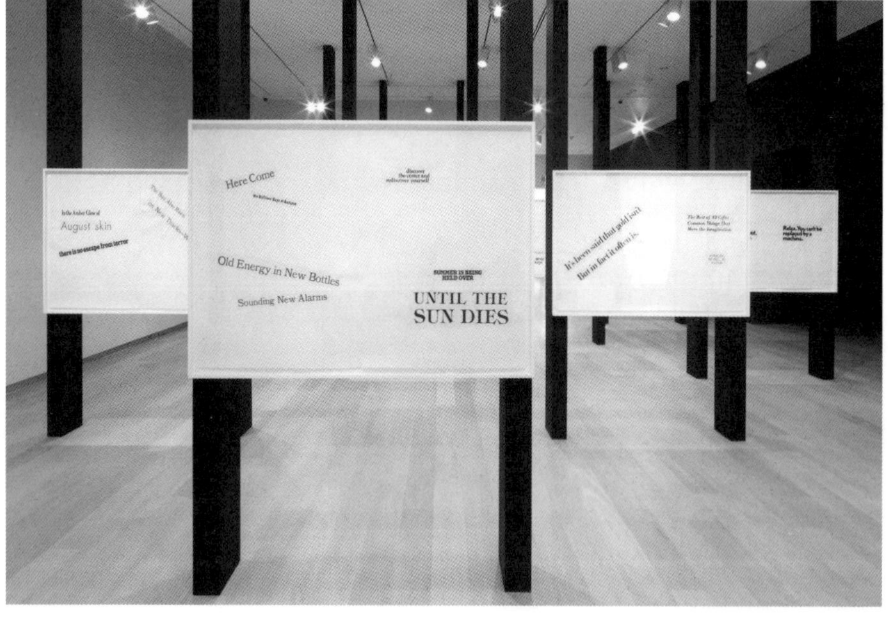

Lorraine O'Grady, *From Me to Them to Me Again*, SCAD Museum of Art, Savannah, GA, September 20, 2018–January 13, 2019, installation view.

November 19, 2018
Artforum

Lorraine O'Grady's longtime engagement with the diptych, as seen in her collage series Cutting Out CONYT, *1977/2017, was highlighted in two solo exhibitions in fall 2018: at Alexander Gray Associates in New York and at the SCAD Museum of Art in Savannah, Georgia. The series is a radical selection from her earliest artwork,* Cutting Out the New York Times (CONYT), *1977, reworked and distilled, as she discusses below.*

The form of my work has proven to me to be more important than the content. If you had told me when I started forty years ago that I would be saying that, I would probably have laughed. But the diptych has always been, in a sense, my primary form, even in the performances. For me, the diptych can only be both/and. When you put two things that are related and yet totally dissimilar in a position of equality on the wall, for example, they set up a conversation that is never-ending. It's a totally unresolvable, circular conversation. And I think that the "both/and" lack of resolution—the acceptance and embrace of it, as opposed to the Western "either/or" binary, which is always exclusive and hierarchical—needs to become the cultural goal. The diptych, which is actually anti-dualistic, has served me to make the point against "either one, or the other."

I taught a course in Futurism, Dada, and Surrealism at the School of Visual Arts for twenty years. I admired those artists that dodged the draft in World War I and went off to Zurich. But I also felt they'd suffered an acute shock: their teachers and parents, formed in the nineteenth century, had led them to believe that European culture was built on the mind, on rationality. And then, of course, they'd had to face the irrationality of European culture with the outbreak of a war that even today makes no real sense. Their response to that was to willingly surrender to the irrationality they'd witnessed, and to create from the language of the subconscious a *sur-realité*, an above-reality. While I understood their need to surrender to the random, that could never ever interest me as a goal, since I'd always felt the culture I was immersed in was completely irrational. My trajectory instead was not to surrender but to try to conquer the random, to wrest some rationality from the irrationality that so many "others" to the normative culture have to live with.

When I hit the New York art world in the early 1980s, it was a shock to my system. Not only was it segregated between races—it was also segregated along lines that were so subjective there was no logical countering of them. Everywhere I'd been in the world up to that point there had at least been objective measurements of my accomplishments, from SATs to exams for federal service. The year I graduated from college, out of twenty thousand who took the Management Intern Exam I was one of two hundred, and the first girl from Wellesley, to pass. I didn't have to *prove* myself. And later, when I became a translator, I mean, either you could translate accurately or you couldn't. So when you come into the art world and you see a totalized worldview that's quite provincial, because it's isolated everything but itself, and *that's* what's telling you that you're derivative—that you're not interesting—well, it seemed a little out of line with reality. But now I think it was more like a dislocation from reality, an exaggeration of the irrationality that, as a woman of color, I had experienced all along.

What I found in Surrealist language was the obverse of what the Surrealists had found: it enabled me not to surrender to the random but to control it. That's why I did *Cutting Out the New York Times (CONYT)* in 1977. During the 1960s Cuban Missile Crisis I'd been a contract analyst at the Department of State and had to read like ten newspapers and three transcripts of Cuban radio a day, so language had just melted away at that point. I wanted to see if I could take the public language of the *New York Times* and make it personal. And unlike the confessional poets of the time who confessed from the inside out, I wanted to see if I could create a "counter-confessional" poetry that would "confess" from the outside in.

In 2017, forty years later, I felt an urgent need to reconnect to the voice of that 1977 piece, which I'd begun as a writer but finished more as a visual artist. The shock of entering the art world in 1980 had caused

a distortion in what I produced, it seemed, away from the more expe-
riential and toward the more argumentative. I wanted to go back to
that earlier voice so as to get on with new work. *Cutting Out the New
York Times (CONYT)* had succeeded in its first goal to make public language private, but it had failed, I believed, in its second goal—to create
counter-confessional poetry. Too many rules of cutout composition
had overwhelmed those poems of ten and twelve or even more panels
each. But I thought forty years of experience might correct the failure.
And they did.

At first, I felt simple relief. I called the show at the Savannah College
of Art and Design *From Me to Them to Me Again* to signal a return.
But now I think that was the wrong title. I should have called it *From
Me to Them to We Again*. Because creating these totally new haiku-like
objects in *Cutting Out CONYT* had not only illuminated the role of
the diptych in my personal work, it had given me a glimpse into what
might be my contribution to culture as a whole.

Lorrie Moore

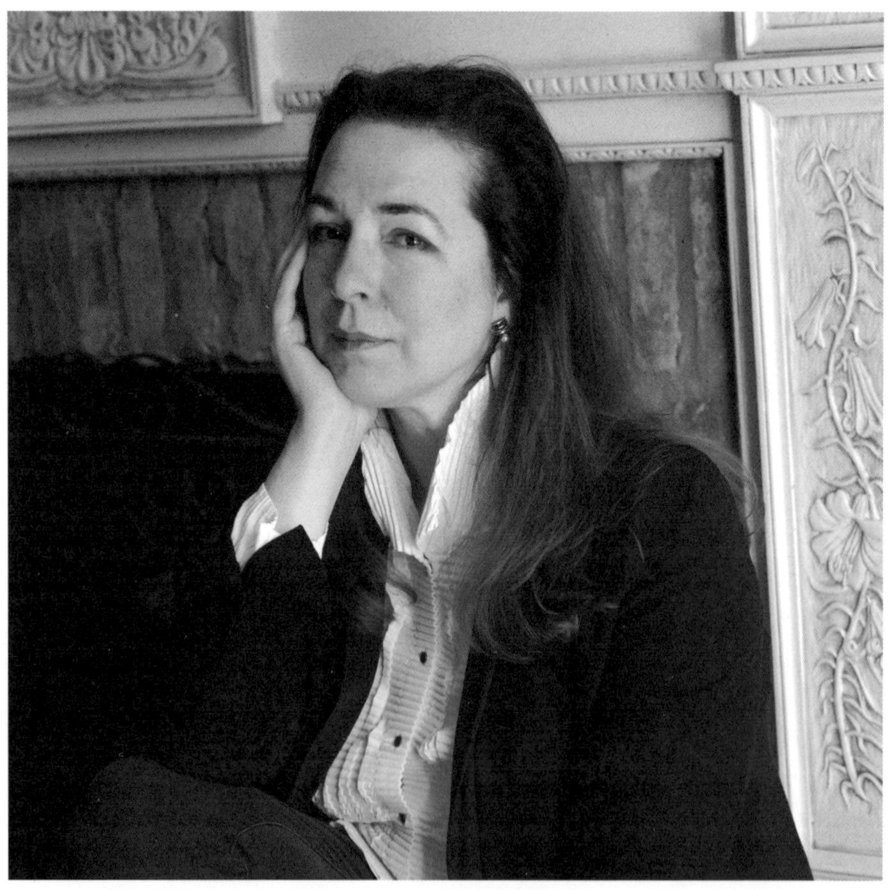

Lorrie Moore, photo by Christopher Berkey.

April 6, 2018
Artforum

Written over a period of thirty-four years, mostly on the spur of assign-ments from various magazines, Lorrie Moore's new book of col-lected nonfiction, See What Can Be Done: Essays, Criticism, and Commentary *(Knopf, 2018), gathers together sixty-six articles that all sparkle with the same inimitable intellect one finds in her best-selling fic-tion. Below, we talk about the factors motivating her to write about books, politics, and prestige television, and what was gleaned from republishing her ideas.*

LOB: In your latest book, you tackle such an expansive constel-lation of figures and topics (from President Obama to Stephen Stills to Lena Dunham). How did you conceptualize congregating these texts? Did it ever feel like there was a single thread holding them together? Or a few threads?

LM: They were all written separately and are freestanding responses to a variety of things. When reading the proofs, I noticed ideas of resilience, improvisation, and mother-love did recur, but this wasn't deliberate—it's just an accident of having written about different topics over a thirty-five-year period. And having all these pieces be by me. These are clearly themes I return to. Who knew? Proofreading reveals all.

LOB: It's pretty great how your interests in TV and the law come through in the book, and of course how you end up putting them together in a few different essays.

LM: Thank you for noticing! Again, since each is an individual response written at different times, any overlap is serendipitous—but also a little inevitable.

LOB: Another theme, if we can call it that, might be that you've written about so many great women. Was that intentional? You note, "It is sometimes, as a feminist in the world, difficult to stay pleased." I wondered how that might have factored into some of these pieces. Was there a desire perhaps to see women acknowledged more for their work?

LM: I didn't have to make writing about women a conscious or purposeful or artificial thing since I gravitated to all my subjects naturally and for various reasons. I wasn't choosing women because they were women. I was choosing them because they were great.

LOB: The essays "On Writing" and "Memoirs" pull back and survey the land more generally, but they also have many first-person assessments and personal anecdotes. What specifically has led you to avoid, as you've noted, the "authoritative third-person voice of God"?

LM: As a writer I'm not inclined to the personal essay. But I like them as a reader. So when discussing a film or a book I would often let snippets of personal essay emerge. It allows for the review to become more personal and for the reader to understand how a cultural event fits into the everyday life of the reader, viewer, voter, or bystander.

LOB: Is there a particular essay you love, or—better yet—hate? You mention not everything is in the book. Was there a particular topic or era you wanted to avoid?

LM: I think I like best the essays on Alice Munro, Miranda July, Peter Cameron, *True Detective*, and O. J. Simpson. I don't think I deliberately avoided anything—but again, these topics were largely assigned ones.

LOB: Before the assignment, there was the request. You mention the late, legendary editor Robert Silvers sending you books with a note asking you to "see what can be done." What was it like working with him for nearly twenty years?

LM: I started working for Barbara Epstein initially and she assigned me Joyce Carol Oates, Alice Munro, and John Updike, whom she referred to as the Big U. After she died, Bob began to be in touch and he could be adventurous and unexpected in his assignments. And he was the one who allowed me to write about screen narrative. I hadn't seen anyone doing that before in the *New York Review of Books*.

LOB: Have you written about contemporary artists at all? Or thought about it? Just curious if there's something or someone you're drawn to from the art world, or art history ...

LM: The book contains pieces on music, biography, theater, film, literary fiction, and television. But the visual arts are missing—I'm not sure why. (I do pay attention to the painterly aspects of cinematography, however; might that count?) I once wrote a small piece on a Rubens painting (not included here) and wanted to write about a Van Dyke painting that I loved and which the Frick has moved into storage. And ostensibly I'm a first cousin (many times removed) of Whistler, on the boring, religious, maternal McNeill side, but the art world *is* rather missing from the book, isn't it? I've been close friends with several visual artists so maybe that caused me to step back and be quiet on the subject. I do have a mention of Alex Katz in the Beattie piece and de Chirico is mentioned in conjunction with Clarice Lispector (he painted her portrait).

LOB: Well, I know of one magazine that would love to have you. Was this the first time for you to reread some of these essays? I was curious about the decision to put them in chronological order, too.

LM: It certainly was the first time I read them all in chronological order—which I don't recommend. But the order allows a reader to skip around more easily, which is how the book should be read: in random bits and pieces here and there.

LOB: I definitely skipped around, and I kept thinking of your citation of Aristotle in the book's introduction, "Those who are to be judges must also be performers," and how you turn that on its head to say, "Those who are performers must also be judges—once in a while." Which, you also say, is "a difficult but obligatory citizenship," like jury duty. Can you talk a little more about what was activated for you in writing these essays? Was being part of the cultural conversation the main motivating factor?

LM: To be part of the cultural conversation—yes. Also, one is always writing what one would like to read, whether it's fiction or nonfiction.

Often I couldn't find sufficient discussion of something—*The Wire*, for instance, or *Friday Night Lights*—and so I decided to contribute something.

LOB: So nothing was written because of FOMO ...

LM: I just had to look up FOMO. I never write anything out of fear. And certainly not fear of missing out. Does FOMO stand for something else? Feelings of malaise offset?

Lucy Dodd

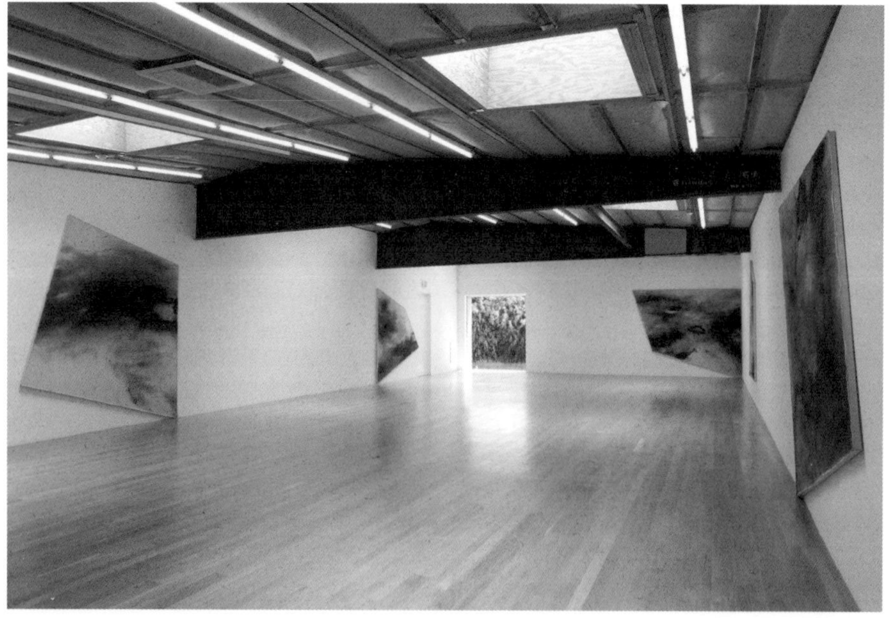

Lucy Dodd, installation view of *Foss*, 2013. Blum & Poe, New York.

July 17, 2013
Artforum

Lucy Dodd is an artist based in New York. Her exhibition Foss *opened at Blum & Poe in summer 2013. Below, Dodd discusses the origins of the eight paintings on view in the show, as well as a tale she cowrote in 2004—a chief source of inspiration for this project.*

In 2004, Jason Rhoades, Paul Theriault, and I began a project in LA called the *Foss*. It's hard to explain how the project started or what it was because none of us knew at the time. *Foss* was the word to describe this dilemma and in the beginning it was also the acronym for our secret studio. But *Foss* became a word for many things, and it became many things, because all of us needed different things. Paul was the mastermind behind the *Foss*. His collages were brilliant and deserved a venue. These works inspired JRho. I had just finished my undergraduate degree at Art Center, and had no idea what I was in for.

Things are not as they were in 2004. We bought CDs at Tower Records—we listened to Alicia Keys on repeat. I took strange adventures into empty buildings while location scouting for the *Foss* around LA. The weirdest was at 1100 Wilshire, an empty triangular skyscraper on the edge of downtown; *Fear Factor* once shot there. Paul wanted a gallery. Jason wanted a garden. We ended up working in a storefront. There were a lot of towels and hot glue involved, plus a huge copper tube with a crystal skirt, a floss container with the L scraped off, rolls of elastic, and precious stones, among other things. But it became too much and we closed shop. When the physical *Foss* was taken away, it was replaced by the characters of the fable—the catfish who wanted velvet whiskers, the butterfly who wanted to fly in the rain, and a dove

with a broken wing—as well as a water plant that was found in the trash
and that managed to revive, which became the *Foss* plant. Some of this
was eventually taken out to Wonder Valley, California, where it was left
to bake in the sun and disintegrate into the Mojave Desert floor in a
corral on Jason's property.

Jason described the *Foss* as a rebirth, and he ended up writing the fable.
The *Foss* is my lost placenta, the perpetual generating force of the
water plant, the cycles of my work. I don't know if Paul ever believed
in the *Foss* in the first place even though he was the one who made it all
up. He moved to Chicago and started playing Ping-Pong with R. Kelly.
I had no idea what the *Foss* was at the time, and they kept telling me,
"The *Foss* is yours," and I kept thinking, What the *Foss* is going on … ?

This year, as I began to work on this exhibition, I discovered the letter
I wrote to Blum & Poe from back then asking if they'd like to discuss
the possibility of showing the *Foss*. Then I came across a weirdly precise commercial from Tide that played during the halftime show of
the Super Bowl. It set up a scenario that began to ripple inside me:
salsa spills and falls miraculously in the shape of Joe Montana on a
fan's football jersey; next there's a nationwide frenzy to see the "miracle stain"; and at the end of the commercial, the fan's wife—a Ravens
fan—washes the stain out and pronounces: "No stain is sacred."

With the vanishing *Foss* and Tide on my mind, I stretched and primed
seven shaped canvases on the floor of my studio. Their sizes and
shapes were determined by the studio's unique architecture and by an
equilateral triangle painting that holds them together as a unit. This
painting is called the key; there are eight paintings, including the key.
The lines of the floorboards determined the horizon lines on the wall.
I kept going in and looking at them all stretched and taut and white
and clean. They were the crispy ship sails you see on the horizon, but
I had to take them through the storm. One day, I went into the studio
and the first stain was there: my dog, Bubs, had peed. She had broken
the seal for me, and with the odor remover Nature's Miracle, I could
begin again.

Lucy R. Lippard

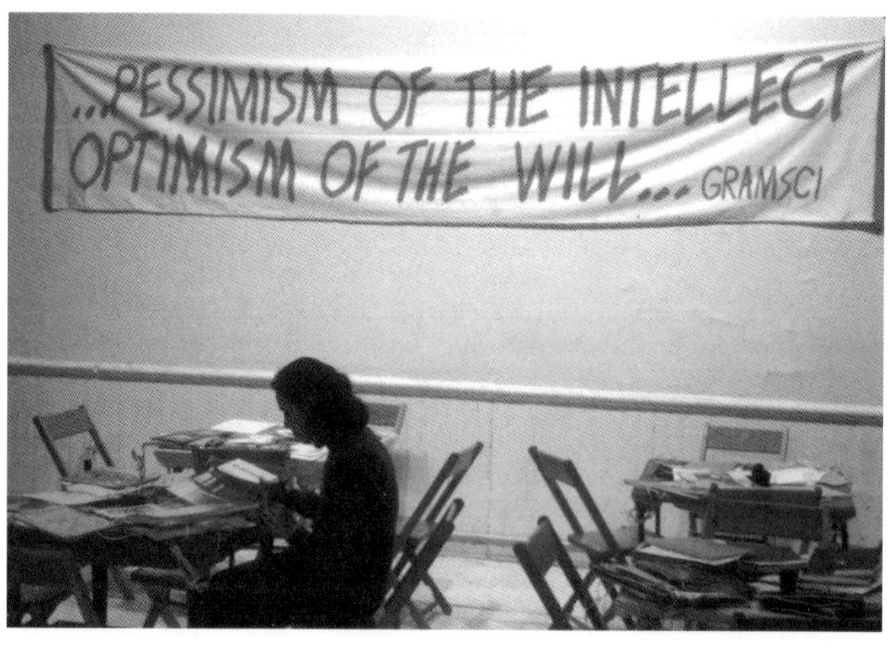

View of *Vigilance: An Exhibition of Artists Books Exploring Strategies for Social Concern*, Franklin Furnace, New York, 1980. Banner by Mike Glier.

September 11, 2012
Artforum

Celebrated for her deeply influential and interwoven work—as author, activist, and curator—Lucy R. Lippard is recognized as one of contemporary art's most significant critics. Born in New York in 1937, Lippard began her career as a writer in 1962 and subsequently produced numerous groundbreaking exhibitions and books throughout the 1960s and '70s; she was involved early on with the Art Workers' Coalition, Printed Matter, and the Heresies *journal, among other influential organizations and publications. Over the decades she has received several awards and fellowships, in addition to an honorary doctorate from the Nova Scotia College of Art and Design.*

Plucked from her twenty one published books, her significant tome Six Years: The Dematerialization of the Art Object from 1966 to 1972, *an annotated record of Conceptualism's rapid international growth, was the subject of an exhibition at the Brooklyn Museum's Sackler Center for Feminist Art. Organized by Catherine Morris and Vincent Bonin, the show was on view from September 14, 2012, to February 3, 2013, and surveyed the impact of Lippard's work alongside the rise of the women's rights, civil rights, and anti-war movements. I visited Lippard at her summer home in Maine right before the show opened. Below, she reflects on her life then and now, the Brooklyn Museum show, and her recent work about Galisteo, New Mexico—a small town where she has lived for nearly twenty years.*

LOB: What was your initial reaction to the Brooklyn Museum show, when it was proposed to you?

LL: I just said that I'm not interested in spending my life dwelling on the past, but go ahead and do it. I trusted Catherine. She calls me about things to approve, such as the title of the show, which I objected to.

LOB: Why?

LL: Well, the first title that was proposed was my name and then something, and I didn't want my name to be the first thing. And then there's the mug. They're making a mug with a quote with something like, "art doesn't have a sex but artists do." Catherine called and said, "Lucy, you're not going to like this, but the gift shop wants to do a mug." Overall, they've done a terrific job with the show. Though the cover of the catalogue is not quite what I had in mind; I didn't win that one. MIT Press did its own thing.

It's going to be strange because it's not like I was responsible for Conceptualism. The show is making it look like I played a bigger role than I did. All I did was hang out with artists. That's how you find out what's going on, in the studios, obviously. My son was reading *Six Years* recently or thumbing through it and he said, "You guys had a lot of fun!" And I said, "Yeah, we did!"

LOB: It seems like it was a lot of hard work, and not as glamorous or full of international travel as people might think?

LL: I didn't travel that much because I was a single mother, basically, and I didn't have any money. It's funny because early on I made more than my artist friends because I got like twenty-five bucks for a review. I think the first reviews I did paid eight dollars each. The artists weren't selling anything. Then, suddenly, they start selling—and selling and selling!

LOB: And you kept writing, and writing.

LL: I love to write. I'm lucky enough to have freelanced all my life.

LOB: Did you have any idea that *Six Years* would be so influential?

LL: It was just something that I was dying to do. I could have written theories about what was going on and stuff, but I wasn't into that. I just wanted to show people what was madly exciting and nutty—and at the time it was. You could just do anything and call it art. Dada was my art historical field, if I had one. I have a master's in art history. I liked Dada and it sort of played into Conceptual art, in a way.

LOB: Where did you study art history?

LL: At NYU's Institute of Fine Arts.

LOB: Did you write a thesis there?

LL: A master's thesis, yes. It wasn't on Dada; it was on Max Ernst. I wanted to do something on fantastic landscapes, but they said that was too big for a master's thesis. I was working at the Museum of Modern Art, and I was helping out on a Max Ernst show—interpreting and translation and stuff—so they said, do Ernst!

LOB: You mentioned in a preface to the catalogue that the "imaginative richness and freedom of the era is still with you."

LL: I always say that Conceptualism and feminism were the two things that really changed my life. Though now people wouldn't think it has anything to do with it—it's definitely the bedrock.

LOB: The freedom part is what got me ...

LL: Duchamp said, if an artist calls it art, it's art. I'm paraphrasing but that was a Surrealist and Dada idea. I had always been interested in word and image, and one reason why I liked writing about art was that you could never get it. You were always somewhere between the word and the image, and you knew perfectly well that you were never going to be able to hop all the way over. I tried all kinds of silly experiments to look at photographs and words as photographs *as* words and stuff like that.

Art turned out to be a really good place for me. I thought I was going to be a great novelist—but I was not a great novelist. There's an artist in Spain now who's doing an art project on my one and only novel, *I See You Mean*, and she's using all the written texts about photographs in the book and now she's taking the actual pictures. For me, criticism was a really wonderful place where I could play and use my own imagination a little and so forth, and the artists were playing too.

LOB: Do you think the artists saw you as a peer, and vice versa?

LL: We were all peers, yeah. We were all starting out together. It was a lot of fun. I collaborated with various people on their work. In fact, my next book, which is going to be the second part of this history of

New Mexico, is going to be funded by a piece that Bob Barry and I did together in 1970 or something. I had totally forgotten about it. The idea is that I would review his piece—I can't remember if his piece existed, or whether it was just talk, or one of those things we did. Then he showed some version of it at Galerie Lelong about five or ten years ago. He said, if it sells, you can have your cut. I said, "Ooh! That'd be nice." Then I forgot about it, and it did sell, for more money than I thought those things would ever sell for. The dealer got half and we split the other half, and that will support me for a year to do this book. I live modestly.

LOB: Those times just seem much more fluid than now; we don't really have writers and artists collaborating so much.

LL: It was very fluid, and it was really nice for me. I wasn't an artist. I didn't want to be an artist. I wanted to be a writer, but I didn't want to be an art critic, which was so dull. I always figured: Why take it out on the artists? It was much more fun to write about something that I liked. So I took it out on society. I figured I'd save my critical faculties to bitch and whine about politics.

LOB: Looking back at *Six Years* now, does the political aspect feel strong, or weaker?

LL: If anything, it feels much weaker, because I became much more of an activist, politically. Of course we picketed the Modern, and we picketed the Met, and so forth. We were all against the war. We'd go to those demonstrations, but we didn't do activist art. I did that in the 1980s but not in the '60s.

In the '60s it was a different kind of politics. We had this dream that artist books would be in drugstores and airports, and then we realized that the content wasn't there. The form was there because we had these little cheap books and that could be nice, but nobody would have cared while in a drugstore to pick one of these things up. The content was the form—where it went in the art world, how it was handled, how it was distributed, and so forth. That's why Seth Siegelaub was so important. He really knew how to bypass the powers that be. That was very inspiring to me. I had some similar ideas, but he was really doing it. Seth had a real business mind. Not that he ever made any money—I don't think anyone did in those days—but he did have a clear notion of how things moved through systems or structures. I was more intuitive.

LOB: But there are many parallels between you and Seth.

LL: Yeah, well, we lived together on and off for a couple of years, and we're still good friends.

LOB: And you both left New York ...

LL: Yeah. He left New York long before I did. He left in '71, I think, and was distributing and printing Marxist books. *How to Read Donald Duck* was a famous one. Since then, he established the Stichting Egress Foundation with all the textiles he's collected. He's always been a really interesting character, and the panoply of stuff that he's been into is fascinating.

LOB: Before we leave *Six Years*, I was curious about Carl Andre compiling the index. How did that happen?

LL: It was such a terrible index too! He just left people out he didn't like. I didn't know that. I never checked it. I just thought, Oh, that's cute that he wants to. My book had come out just before that, and I guess it was changing. It didn't have an index. I worked at the Modern's library and archives, so when Carl offered to do an index, I just thought, Okay. And then I started getting complaints from people saying, "He didn't put me in the index!" And I thought, Uh-oh, I think I know why ...

LOB: From Julia Bryan-Wilson's essay in the exhibition catalogue I learned that there are different versions of *Six Years* at the Archives of American Art?

LL: People are always asking, "Where's the first manuscript? Can we see it?" I think it's just sort of in pieces in that archive. I don't think there's anything labeled "Six Years: First Manuscript." I think it went through some other stages—I really don't remember much about it.

LOB: She also talks in her essay about how the book is not overly political. As you say, there are more undertones than overtones. Is that what you meant when you said that the politics felt weaker?

LL: That's what I was talking about before. It was the contextual content of Conceptual art compared to other art that was more political. You have to realize the incredible power [Clement] Greenberg had then. He was a real fascist. Going up against Greenberg was hard but I did it verbally—I was just young and stupid enough to do it. He went for my gut at one point. Anyway, that felt like the revolution on some level. We were all of course doing this anti-war stuff too, but it didn't really get into the art. *And babies*—the 1969 poster by the Art Workers' Coalition—was an important thing. It's the only really good poster that came out of the art world. Ron Wolin and I did a poster show in 1971 called *Collage of Indignation II* at the New York Cultural Center on 59th Street. Bob Ryman did a poster—the only political piece that he ever did. It was a white sheet and then in pencil, written in awkward handwriting, it said P-E-A-S-E. Then, Alex Katz did a portrait of my son and put the word *peace* underneath it. None were terrifically radical, right-on posters.

LOB: By 1973 or so you become even more politically active. Why?

LL: Because we had the mirage of airports and things. We weren't really affecting the world by doing this stuff. And, as I had feared—and the reason Seth left New York, I think—was that it all ended up as these scribbled little things and these misspelled texts and these little Xeroxes. In the end, it ended up making some people huge amounts of money. These books could be marketed, which really surprised us. We should have noticed that every little scribble the Dadaists did was out there too. I think that's as far as it went. The 1970s was all feminist, political stuff for me. In the 1980s, I got more into the New Left.

LOB: More direct action, too?

LL: Yeah, with PAD/D, or Political Art Documentation/Distribution, which we started in 1980. And we opened Printed Matter a little before that, in 1976—and before that we had the Art Workers' Coalition in 1968. In 1980, Mike Glier and I did a show at Franklin Furnace called *VIGILANCE*, about artists' books exploring social change, and we had a banner of Antonio Gramsci's idea—my very favorite quote in the world—"Pessimism of the intellect, optimism of the will," which everybody knows by now. Anyway, at the show everything was accessible: you could handle the books. They were just attached by strings to the legs of card tables. And each card table had a separate theme. It was great. There were many political artist books out there, especially by then.

LOB: And then you finally ended up in New Mexico, working with grassroots organizations?

LL: In New Mexico I'm on the planning committee for my village of 250 people. For sixteen years, I've done the community newsletter and worked on watershed restoration—fending off gas and oil—but it's not the stuff of my previous activism. I'm still a great believer, though, in taking responsibility for the place where you are at and working on that.

LOB: Does that relate to the initial sense of freedom you mentioned before?

LL: Whatever decisions I've made—and I actually don't make decisions, I usually wander off in a direction or whatever—they were all affected by that. People come up to me and ask: How can I be a critic like you? And I say, well, you keep your standard of living extremely low. Nobody wants to hear that.

LOB: Right, keep the standard of living low and hang on to *all* your ephemera.

LL: Yes, I've still got about sixty file drawers of junk. My partner says that my son is just going to go in and toss a match when I bite the dust, because somebody's going to have to go through it all. But they'd be crazy to do that because there's a lot of stuff that people will pay for, like silly little drawings and letters. I've mostly tossed the love letters. When you work in a library, even for a short time, you gain tremendous faith in every little scrap of paper. I was having dinner with some people the other night, and they said, you've got to scan all of that stuff. My reply was: Do you have any idea how long it would take to scan all of this?

LOB: You said in the preface that the book comes full circle with this exhibition. What did you mean by that?

LL: I'm not quite sure what I meant by that. I think probably that, every now and then, I refer to *Six Years* as a curatorial project rather than a book. It doesn't really make sense because they're not going to have half the stuff on view. One of the things I love about the book is that I could cram all this stuff in there, and of course the exhibition space isn't that big and no one wants to make a show that's so full. So, in a funny way, it's not *the* curatorial project I had in mind, but I'm kind of curious to see it. I have no idea what it's going to look like. *557,087* in 1969, the first of the number shows I curated, and 1970's *955,000*—neither were Conceptual art shows. There was a lot of stuff, physical stuff, in those shows. I don't think people realized that. At the Brooklyn Museum there's going to be Eva Hesse, Sol LeWitt, and Bob Ryman and various other people. For *955,000*, Richard Serra let me build his piece. All these people had me doing their work for them on-site—badly.

LOB: What are you working on now?

LL: I'm trying to finish a new book called *Time and Time Again* that I'm doing with a photographer, Peter Goin. He did a rephotography project of Chaco Canyon, taking historical photographs of it and placing them alongside new black-and-white images he shot. Chaco Canyon is an amazing archaeological site in northwestern New Mexico, which has always been a mystery, and people just love mysteries. Everybody left there after three hundred years and no one knows why. I always swore that I would never be caught dead writing about Chaco Canyon. Every archaeologist has messed with it, and there's all kinds of different theories floating around. Nobody knows what the social organization was—and that's the most interesting part of it. How did they build these huge beautiful things with fantastic masonry? It looks like it came out of nowhere, but it didn't.

LOB: Can we talk about why you moved to New Mexico?

LL: I was there first in 1972 with Charles Simonds and my son Ethan. We went to Pueblo ceremonies and camped out though it was December and really cold. I also went down there quite a lot in the 1980s, and I'd got interested in rock art and petroglyphs. I was living in Boulder, Colorado, five months out of the year, and I fell in with some people who just went off and camped and looked at this stuff. Anyway, I got very interested in the Galisteo Basin. It's a famous place that nobody had written about. Twenty-five years ago, Harmony Hammond, my neighbor—who is also an old, good friend—trespassed with me all over the Basin to see the ruins, and we didn't get shot. I just was interested in it; I took notes and stuff but I didn't really expect to write a book. Then the archeologists never got it together, and nobody ever wrote this book. Finally, I had enough material, so I just thought, I'm going to do it myself. And that was my book *Down Country*.

There was going to be one big book of the whole history of that area right up until now, and then I got obviously carried away with the archeology, so I have another two hundred years to go. It's the one I'm going to do on my Bob Barry money. That's going to be far more interesting and difficult.

LOB: Do the people who live in Galisteo know your history in the art world?

LL: A few art people do. Every now and then, someone will say, "We saw a show in London and there was a quote by you on the wall. Why?" I prefer it that way.

I could go on and on about this area. I wrote a book called *Mixed Blessings*, which was about cross-cultural stuff, and then I landed in New Mexico in this village—there are no native people living there at all anymore. The cross-cultural aspect of it really interested me, but it's very hard to write about. I was visiting a wonderful old woman there, who was almost 100 years old and had lived there as a child, and she picked up the phone and said, I can't talk because I have the American here. It was like it was 1848 when the Americans showed up in New Mexico! Another guy said to me: Even if someone would tell you their stories, which they won't, you'd never be able to print them. I think there's some truth to that. So, it's going to be fun and a challenge to write. Plus, I want to live there for the rest of my life, so ...

LOB: Can you imagine if you had stayed in New York?

LL: Yeah, I don't know. Boulder was different ... my father had died and my mother was in New Haven, and I had to go back and forth a lot. Not being very good at it, I needed a breather from that. I'd never taken teaching jobs, and I was offered just a one-semester thing in Boulder. I had been out there as a visiting artist, and I liked it and I saw that as an escape for a few months. My grandparents had both come from Colorado. Then I loved it out there and I realized that the New York activist community was kind of falling apart—it was '85. I had just been fired from the *Voice*, and it was a good time to do something else. Then I fell in with these people who were traveling all over the west, and I just felt crazy about the west. There's no bad way to take a road trip out there.

And then my partner, now for the last thirteen years, was raised in New Mexico and went to UNM and spent the rest of his life elsewhere and came back. So, we both have a thing about this state, which a lot of people do. The famous story of most people is that they come—they're going to California or somewhere—and they stop in New Mexico for a day and they never leave. Harmony was living in Galisteo. Before that, Judy Chicago had a place in Santa Fe. I used to go visit her and sometimes cat-sit when she was away, and got to really like the place.

I realized that Boulder was just too civilized. I didn't want to live in a place that was so university oriented.

LOB: And you never looked back? You didn't want to go back to New York?

LL: No. My mother died finally—in 1992—and I actually had some money for the first time in my life. I had been sort of staring around Galisteo, wishing I had some money, and then I did. I just walked across the creek from Harmony's and bought some land and built a house. It's a funny little house, sixteen by twenty feet. I love showing people a picture of it. I've built onto it since then and I've planted trees. It was just this little box, like a kid's drawing in mud. There were no trees or anything. I love it.

LOB: Should we talk about feminism a little bit?

LL: To everybody's horror, I've said that I've been turning down talking and writing about feminism because I don't have anything new to say. I spent a decade of my life writing about feminism. I just seem to have used myself up on the brainpower. I knew that feminism keeps going and there are all kinds of things that could be written about it now. So many of them have to do with media, and I'm so out of it: I don't have a television, and I didn't have email until a year and a half ago. I'm really a Luddite. I jump around a lot. I use up my ideas on something. I'm not a deep, deep, deep thinker that can go forever on one subject. I move on.

I mean, I'm still a feminist; it affects everything I do. I gave a talk at the Modern a couple of years ago, and someone in the audience said, "Well, we don't want to call ourselves feminists." And I said, "That hurts our feelings!" It wasn't entirely true, but it is funny. I have women friends who I meet often and we always still talk about feminist issues. In fact, we have a women's dinner right here in Maine.

LOB: That's so great.

LL: It's fun. It started out commemorating the day when women got the right to vote in August 1920. Sometimes people would come with banners across their fronts like suffragettes.

Lucy R. Lippard

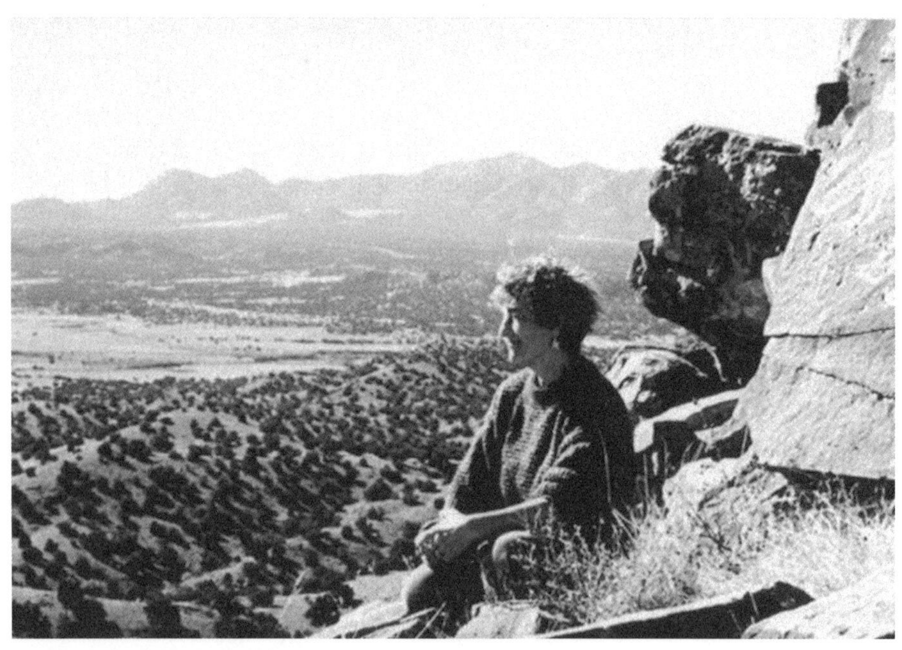

Lucy R. Lippard in the Galisteo Basin Preserve, ca. 1994, photo by Peter Woodruff.

May 12, 2014
Artforum

Lucy R. Lippard's book Undermining: A Wild Ride Through Land Use, Politics, and Art in the Changing West *(New Press, 2014) pinpoints vexing environmental issues, such as gravel pits and fracking, and contextualizes them within a spectrum of larger problems, while also considering histories of the West, photography, adobe buildings, ruins, Land art, and more.*

This book began when Tate Modern asked me to speak at a symposium on cities and I replied that I wasn't learning from cities anymore. They said, Well, talk about whatever you like. An exchange about gravel pits that I'd just had with a local developer from my community had popped into my mind, so I said, OK, gravel pits. There was a silence ...

But the talk was fairly well received, and afterward I realized there was much more there, connecting urban and rural. I published a brief piece on a local gravel pit in *New Observations* and after a while just forgot about it. Then I resurrected the idea for a related talk years later in San Antonio; Chris Taylor, from Land Arts of the American West, was there and said it would make a good book, which had been occurring to me too. One thing leads to another!

In terms of influences, J. B. Jackson is a longtime inspiration, but I didn't go back to him much in this book, which is really just a rant about what's happening right now in the West. The influences were mainly local activism: articles in *High Country News* and my local paper, and our battle in 2008 to keep oil drilling and fracking for natural gas out of the Galisteo Basin. Another influence was artists' books. I wanted to do a small book for a change—an extended essay with a lot of images, a parallel visual/verbal narrative. (I notice some readers are getting that and some aren't.) The Center for Land Use Interpretation's take on the world—and its work on gravel pits—is an ongoing influence. Native American art in the Southwest is another. A lot of younger native artists are activists around land use issues, for obvious reasons, given the way Indian lands have been trashed. They helped me tie the present to the past.

One problem is that as I was writing, and even since I saw the last proofs in December, the "facts" have been constantly changing. Corporations bought out other corporations. Lawsuits were initiated or settled or not. Statistics changed. This book shouldn't be read as a factual textbook. I just hope it raises awareness of what's going down, and encourages readers and artists to follow some of these stories on the internet, or wherever, and act on their own. For instance, since I stopped writing, the dangers of fracking—earthquakes, methane gas release, etc.—have become more widely known, and they're direr than we thought before. The mainstream media is finally, grudgingly, acknowledging them to some extent. And climate change is obviously the big one.

Right now the most pressing local issue—which came up after the book was out of my hands—is a plan to take crude oil in tanker trucks and offload them into railroad cars at Lamy, another tiny village that's five miles from Galisteo, with a dead-end road. If there were a spill, no one would be able to get in or out. And nationally, spills and pipeline leaks have wildly increased since I stopped writing. Everything is getting worse.

Obviously everything isn't local and I'm not recommending blinders. But the message of my 1997 book *The Lure of the Local* was that everybody, artists included, should take responsibility for wherever they find themselves, as long as they're living there. Once you know the local you realize how connected it is to global capitalism; its tentacles are everywhere. It's multinational corporations that are buying up local resources—just as my friend said years ago about gravel pits. CLUI tells us that the aggregate industry may be the largest in the United States. And it's all interrelated—gravel, development, water, tourism, adobe architecture, Land art, rock art, and so on. After finishing the book, I was left with a million questions—mainly about where the hell we're headed. I offered very few answers. But one of the obvious questions is the role of art in coming environmental catastrophes. Photographers, and "high" artists using photographic media, obviously have the best access to communicating information about these endless crises. For better or worse, people "believe" photographic imagery more than paintings and sculpture. Activist DIY groups are also doing their part. But it's difficult to concentrate on the causes, and the causers, because the art world doesn't like naming names. Hans Haacke is the rare artist who's more or less gotten away with it. And of course the indomitable Yes Men and their growing cadres. More power to them.

Lucy McKenzie

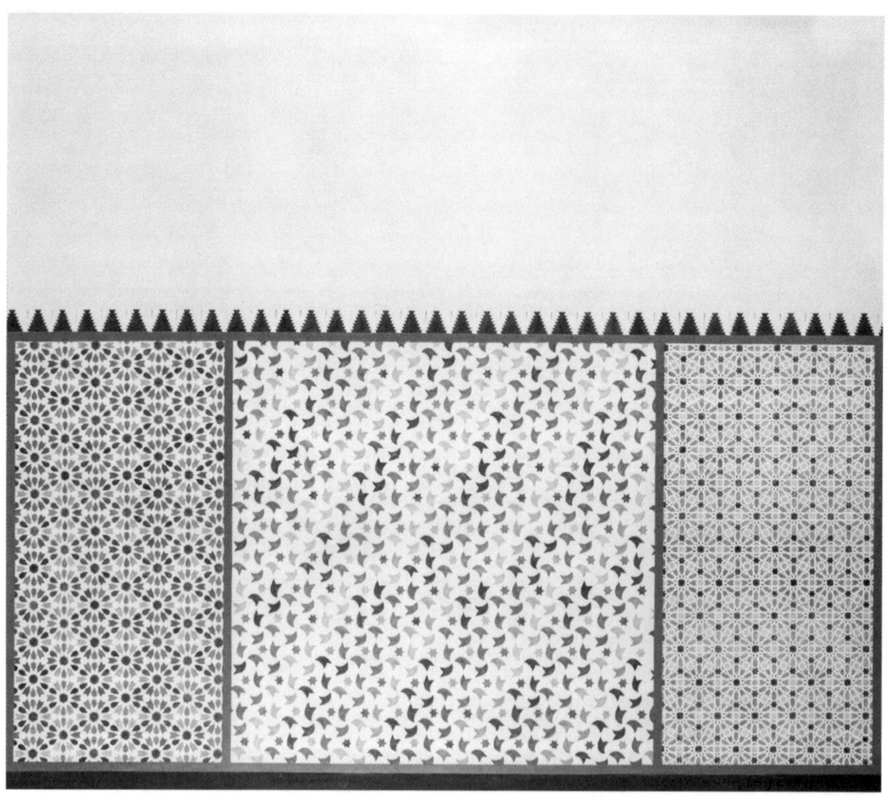

Lucy McKenzie, *Alhambra Motifs II*, 2013, oil on canvas, 133 ¾ × 157 ½ inches (340 × 400 cm).

April 22, 2013
Artforum

Lucy McKenzie is a Brussels-based Scottish artist. In 2008, with designers Beca Lipscombe and Bernie Reid, she launched Atelier E.B., a company that works on fashion and design projects with a particular emphasis on applied arts and artisan techniques. McKenzie's first exhibition in Amsterdam, at the Stedelijk Museum, took place in 2013.

The Stedelijk show began with my impressions of visiting three different sites at the end of 2012: the Alhambra Palace in Granada, Spain; Adolf Loos's Villa Müller in Prague; and an exhibition of Sol LeWitt's wall paintings at M Museum Leuven. I knew I wanted to investigate the Villa Müller and Alhambra a little more after I realized that these two places share several things in common: they're archetypal, ideal representations of perfection in interior design; they're UNESCO-protected places; and in both, women are present but also hidden from the outside world. In the Villa Müller, for instance, there's a boudoir with a small window that looks down into the main space so that the lady of the house could watch but not be seen.

I taught myself how to devise and paint some of the patterns I saw in the Alhambra. If you want to understand patterns you just have to make them, and the paintings in this show are big studies of how those patterns work. My initial interest in the Alhambra came from reading Owen Jones, one of the founders of the Victoria and Albert Museum in London. He was the first Western designer and architect to give the palace any kind of importance. He had the elaborate texts rendered on its architecture translated into English, and he realized that these are like speech bubbles. It's the building talking directly to you.

With the Villa Müller, only seven people at a time could visit, so you could feel very clearly how it would have been to live there. I created a scale model of that structure, using fake marble in a sculptural way—to explore what it is about those volumes and their spatial harmony that's so satisfying to be around, as well as go against Loos's driving principle of using only natural materials for surface decoration.

But the show is about opposing ideas, not chic architecture; there's a counterbalance of themes that are direct and personal. *Quodlibet XXVI (Self-Portrait)* deals head-on with appropriation—or, rather, a whole cycle of appropriation. In it the viewer can read that not only do I appropriate, but also that artists have tried to appropriate images of me (particularly those taken by Richard Kern). And there are mannequins on view; idealized skeletons underneath clothes. I want to show the direct connection between architectural interiors and the body, to what's always under clothing, as well as reflect on what's private and what's public, real and idealized.

The *Ost End Girls Collection* showroom will be open in May. It's like being in a very square band, touring different cities: Amsterdam, Brussels, London. We'll come to New York in the fall and we'll have a shop with the Artist's Institute on the Lower East Side. We don't do normal retail because shops put on too much markup and we want the clothes to be as cheap as possible. Also, we're interested in alternative economic models and different ways to distribute and present our designs.

Lucy Skaer

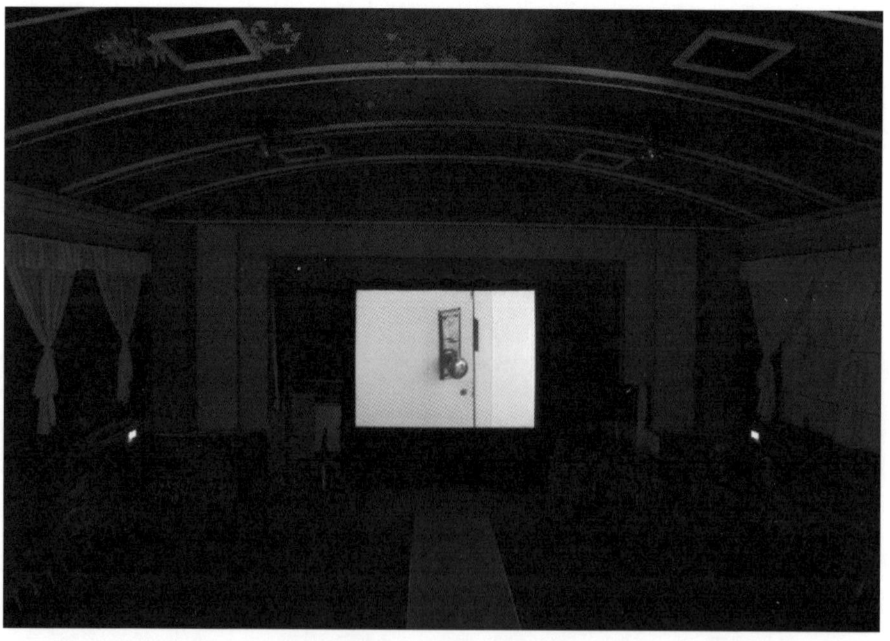

Lucy Skaer, *Film for an Abandoned Projector*, 2011, 35 mm color film (still), 20 minutes. Lyric Picture House, Leeds, England, installation view.

October 5, 2011
Artforum

A site-specific work by the Scottish artist Lucy Skaer that revives an old Kalee film projector was on view at the Lyric Picture House in Leeds, England, in fall 2011. Here, she talks about how the work "attempts to see outside of the human experience or viewpoint."

Making a work from the point of view of the projector is a way of escaping my own imagination. It's an attempt to create the memory of the machine. *Film for an Abandoned Projector* began with finding such an object, which wasn't easy. The projector didn't necessarily have to be inside a cinema; it could have been in a warehouse or in a storage room. My only parameter was that I didn't want it to be in a working cinema. Once we found it, we had to refurbish it. While that was happening I started to shoot a site-specific film that would be meaningful to the particular place in which the projector had been found.

I like thinking of a machine as a kind of "animal eye," like a cat's eye, as in my previous work *Rachel, Peter, Caitlin, John*, which attempts to see outside of the human experience or viewpoint. Perhaps it's a backward way of thinking about film, because the medium itself is made to play on any projector and intended to transport the viewer from a physical place into a new state of mind. This work walks a line between escaping into another reality and being very firmly located in the space.

The film is made up of small "episodes" that are related not by content so much as by movement or contrasting shots—pairing very shallow shots with very deep shots. Some are colored panels I filmed in the studio as they moved backward and forward, toward and away from the camera. Some of the episodes make it hard to determine what's been filmed, while others point toward a narrative. I've also been trying to connect things that happen in a frame, like a movement or a change in light, as a way to stitch the film together. I'm thinking a lot about how the projector itself will light the interior of the cinema, using either clear or color film leader so some parts will be a kind of an imageless return to the space itself.

There's a feeling of the film being made as you're watching it, because some of the shots are of the projector firing up. There are also shots of the building itself and the church group that uses it. I think this feeling of being grounded or escaping is going to be a bipolar thing that keeps working its way out as the show goes on.

People will also be able to walk into the projection booth and see it running. When we first got there, it'd been sealed up since the 1980s and there was film all over the floor—it was very romantic, dusty, and intriguing. Originally we wanted to keep it like that, but because the projectionist has to work, it's been cleared out. I want the booth to be open for people to see the mechanics of it, to get a feel for the history and for the archaic sense of the projector itself.

Lynda Benglis

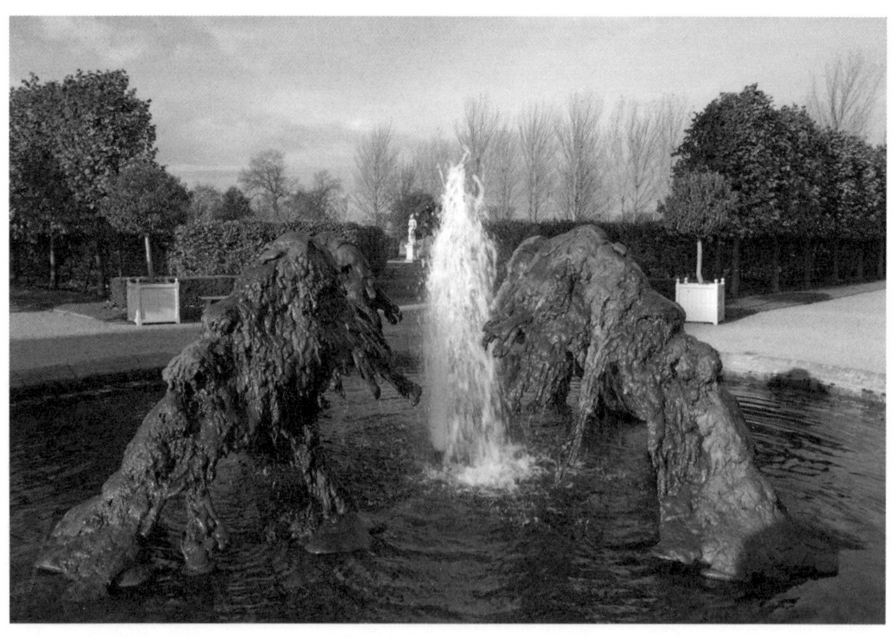

Lynda Benglis, *North South East West*, 1988/2009, bronze, 66 × 184 × 184 inches (167.6 × 467.4 × 467.4 cm).

November 15, 2009
Artforum

The singular artist Lynda Benglis is widely known for her poured-latex sculptures and fallen paintings of the 1960s, as well as her videos and gilt works. Below, she talks about a fall 2009 show at New York's Cheim & Read Gallery and her traveling retrospective at the Irish Museum of Art in Dublin.

The idea for my new works came to me about ten years ago, when I was thinking about polyurethane foam and what else it could do. I wanted to draw with this texture and let the drawing become the form. I began making sphere after sphere in the studio, casting some of the pieces in bronze. Those shapes looked like helmets or brains. Since then, I've used the foam to make hemispheres and large egg forms and free-edge works that are wave- and torso-like.

These works relate to my earlier pour pieces, when I began to affix those to the wall directly. I would take the underpinning—the wire and the plastic—away from the form, then there would be kind of a wave coming out into space. Some works, like one at the Hayden Gallery at MIT in 1971, weighed about three hundred to four hundred pounds. The structural engineers there couldn't figure out what happened—but it was cellular, and the crosshatching in the pours made the form very strong.

The exhibition at Cheim & Read is really about combining the complexity and simplicity of form. I'm interested in the gestalt; how we read surfaces through texture and form, and how the texture creates the forms, whether matte or shiny, and if the form has varied edges. Although the show is about simplification, it does open up a discussion about the illusion of matter. Conceptually, the works are about open-ended rather than closed systems, but they are deductive in terms of their materials.

I've always found my supplies through the Yellow Pages, and I made my contacts that way. In the '70s, I would walk through Chinatown and get ideas. I've looked at a variety of imagery in a variety of contexts. For instance, I'm a scuba diver, and I became interested later in the underwater coral formations in the Pacific, then the Great Barrier Reef and the Indian Ocean. Trees, darkness, light, the beach, water—all this has informed my work.

There's a connection, in a linear and textual sense, with my new work and the pieces in the retrospective. Originally, I wanted to make my own paintings and use my own format; I began with the wax. In the early to mid-'60s, I began to work in an unheated basement studio. It had electric plugs, and I used a heater and hot plate to melt my own wax and pigments. I defined works according to a human scale, and that's been one consistent element in all my work. I'm a humanist first.

Another aspect that comes out in the retrospective is that I want the viewer to move around to interact with the forms. In the past twenty-five years, I've been producing fountains. I've always wanted to do them. In 1971, after several early installation pieces all over the country (including at the Kansas State University Museum, Vassar College, the Milwaukee Art Center, the Walker Art Center, and MIT), I didn't want to make art in situ within a museum context. I felt like I couldn't wear art on my sleeve and do installations anymore that were meant to be permanent in idea and form.

For the gardens at the Irish Museum of Art, I've made *North South East West*, which has four bronze cantilevers. They come together in the center, and a geyser of shooting water creates a column for five minutes! It's like a spurting of a continuous volcanic eruption. It was amazing to see this idea that I've had since the early 1970s realized and to see the idea in motion, literally. I've always wanted to make a fountain that moves water in four different directions through the bronze elements.

The new work and the retrospective have reminded me of what it was like when I arrived in New York, at the height of the Pop movement. I remember that James Rosenquist was wearing paper suits to openings. At that time, I was interested in Frank Stella, Ralph Humphrey, and Barnett Newman, and I liked a few of the painters of my own age. Things seemed very doctrinaire, however, in terms of the way people were thinking about the "wheres" and "hows" of art. Critics were beginning to ask whether easel painting was dead, and so hundreds of people would show up at panel discussions on this issue. I can't imagine that, at this moment, there could be that kind of intensity over such issues. But that's how it was.

Lynda Benglis

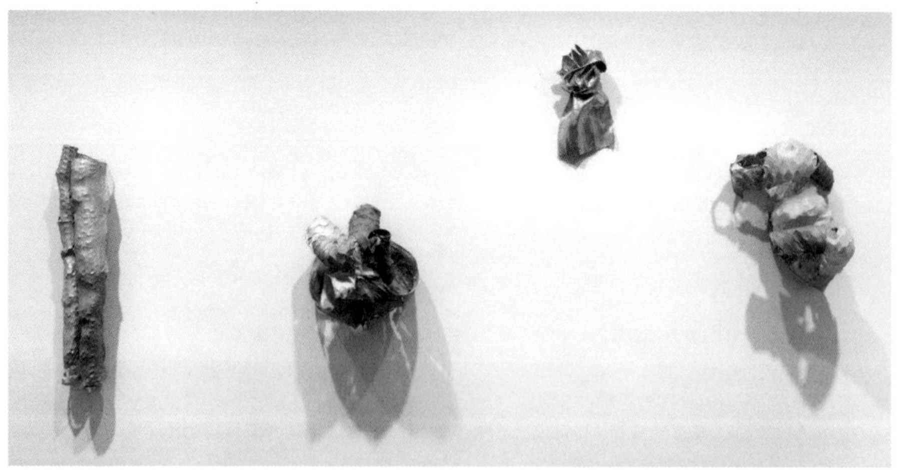

View of *Lynda Benglis*, Paula Cooper Gallery, New York, 2018.

June 8, 2018
Artforum

Lynda Benglis was born in Lake Charles, Louisiana, in 1941 and arrived in New York shortly after graduating from Newcomb College in New Orleans. Then, as now, her visceral approach to viscous materials and media is singular and timeless. Here, Benglis shares key episodes from her life.

When I moved to New York in 1964, there were race riots going on in Harlem. I attended the Brooklyn Museum Art School, and there I met a Scotsman named Gordon Hart. We both had arrived at the school at the same time, and he knew the goings-on about town. Right away the art world just opened up, and it wasn't like there were huge lines of people at the openings. There were actually few people. There was also Max's Kansas City, where we all hung out at the bar and began to talk. There were people I knew going every night, and that was where you'd hear the gossip about who was in a fight and who threw drinks on somebody—that silly stuff. I remember going there and seeing Carl Andre or Brice Marden. It felt like the only place where you could meet other artists in the evening. And usually it was the artists who closed the place down, early in the morning. The liquor flowed, and people were always drunk—they stayed so long that by the time they left they had eaten two or three meals, and they were just sober enough to get home.

I was also taking dance classes near the Park Place Gallery at that time. Paula Cooper was directing the gallery, and it was there that I saw Brice's paintings for the first time. There were so many excellent shows there. In 1968, Paula opened her own place—the first gallery in SoHo. The thrilling thing was that Paula was showing new works and knew all the artists personally, which was unusual at the time. In 1974, when I took out my scandalous advertisement in *Artforum*, Paula was incredibly supportive. The editors wanted the name of the gallery to be on the ad. So we put it there in very small print on the top of the page. It was all very shocking in terms of the inner workings of the magazine, but in the end, I think the ad received the kind of attention that it deserved.

I had previously begun working for Paula part-time and was showing my work with her as well. One day in 1970, Clement Greenberg came to my first solo show and walked around my sculpture made in situ (looking dumbfounded). I happened to be sitting behind Paula's desk watching him. He stopped and scratched his head, then left in the elevator opposite me. I was so delighted that it confounded him because it was doing everything that I had heard he was suggesting to other painters that they do, such as turn their work upside down or present it on the floor.

As for feminism, it was a wave I was riding on. And it was a big wave. It meant that I was being offered jobs at schools and universities, even on the East Coast, because they needed women. It was probably a numbers game. I benefited. But I think so many women were aware of this, and we just had fun with it. These days, I love the idea of #MeToo. First of all, it's a catchy name. But I also like that it's mocking a little bit. It's saying, "Hey, me too. Catch up."

Lynne Tillman

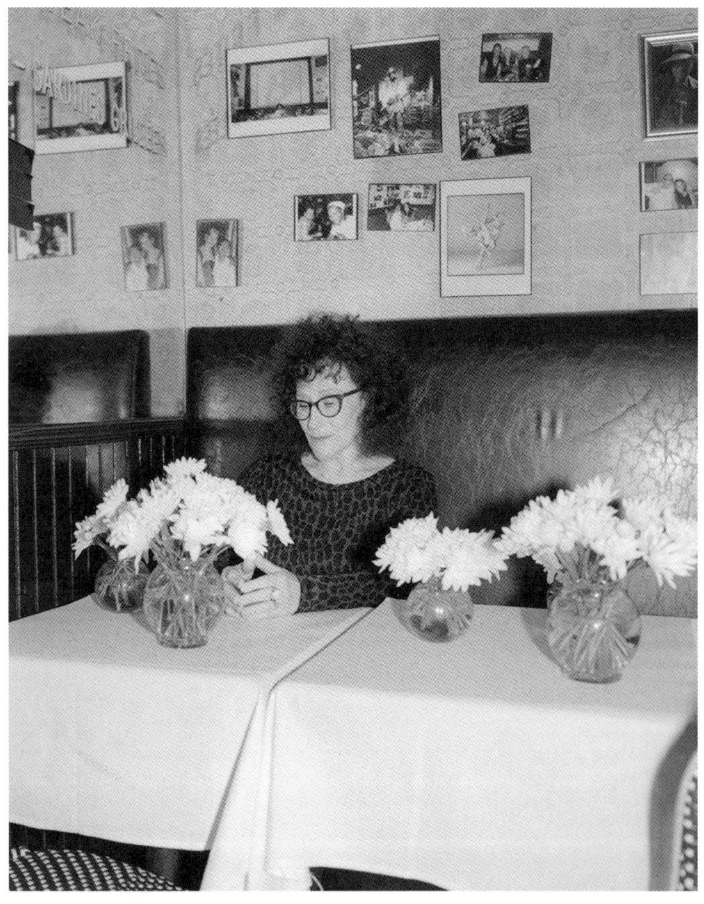

Lynne Tillman, photo by Heather Sten.

April 12, 2011
Artforum

Lynne Tillman's collection of short stories Someday This Will Be Funny *was published by the imprint Red Lemonade in 2011. The fiction editor of* Fence, *Tillman is also the author of several novels and books of short fiction.*

One of these stories was written a long time ago. "The Way We Are" was written around 1978, and it appeared without my name in a little magazine I was doing with a friend back then—*Paranoids Anonymous Newsletter*. It probably reached about three hundred people. Anyway, I decided to revise it a bit and put it in this book. There was another I fussed with more: the novella "Love Sentence" was published in the psychoanalytic journal *American Imago* in 1993. Thomas Keenan was guest editing an issue on love, and he asked me if I'd write something. At the time, I thought it would be best to start by dissecting the sentence "I love you," which led to my thinking about death sentence, the death sentence, and several other puns. In the 1980s and early '90s, there was a particular emphasis on writing with puns and other language games. Usually I let something stay as it was written, but in this case, the amount of punning unsettled me a bit. I thought that I went overboard, in unnecessary ways. Perhaps I was just being a little too tongue in cheek—I guess my tongue was outside my cheek, too.

Usually, I don't have the impulse to revise a published piece. I look at the work I've done in the past with wonder, because I couldn't do it now. And it's neither better nor worse than what I've done recently; you write in a certain moment in your life and your experiences and ideas have reached a certain point at that time. Let's just say you move on. It's not "progress"; it's something different. You don't necessarily get better as you get older. If only. You have more of a sense of what the problems and possibilities are. I believe my craft is better, and I've allowed myself more choices.

By putting these stories together I could see the different ways they're related, but there are so many differences too. This question of the "family" or the association among the characters is hard for me to answer. I do like to work with male protagonists as well as female protagonists, and in this book you might notice more male voices than in my previous short story collections. It's also been lovely to work with Richard Nash from Red Lemonade [and formerly of Soft Skull Press], because I trust him totally as an editor. He ultimately chose what should go in this book and what shouldn't. It's most important to me that the ideas go beyond the words and live off the page—that's what any writer wants, right? When I read something that I love, it haunts me for days, maybe years; sometimes it gets confusing and I find myself wondering, Was that a dream or did I read that in a book? In some ways, the kind of writing that gets embedded in your mind is a wonderful thing to strive for.

I think most writers would say that they're most involved with the book that they're writing now, or that they're trying to write now. I'm looking forward to Richard's reprints of my books, but I have no idea how people will respond. So many books go out of print right away—at least, many of mine have. In the '80s, under Reagan, I think, a law went into effect that publishers would be taxed on their inventory. Suddenly they had to get rid of all the books they had in warehouses so that they wouldn't have to pay money for them. The books were treated as income rather than as something that could potentially be income. So that really screwed things up, in the same way that under Reagan a lot of things got screwed up.

I hope most for Richard's doing well, selling a lot, with the new press, more so than with my books. I'm not really interested in sales; I can't be, though it'd be great. Most writers don't sell that well, even if their reviews are great. Now with e-books and Kindle, I think there may be a renaissance in reading, and that's really important. Loads of books can be on something portable and lightweight, and that is just so cool.

Marlene McCarty

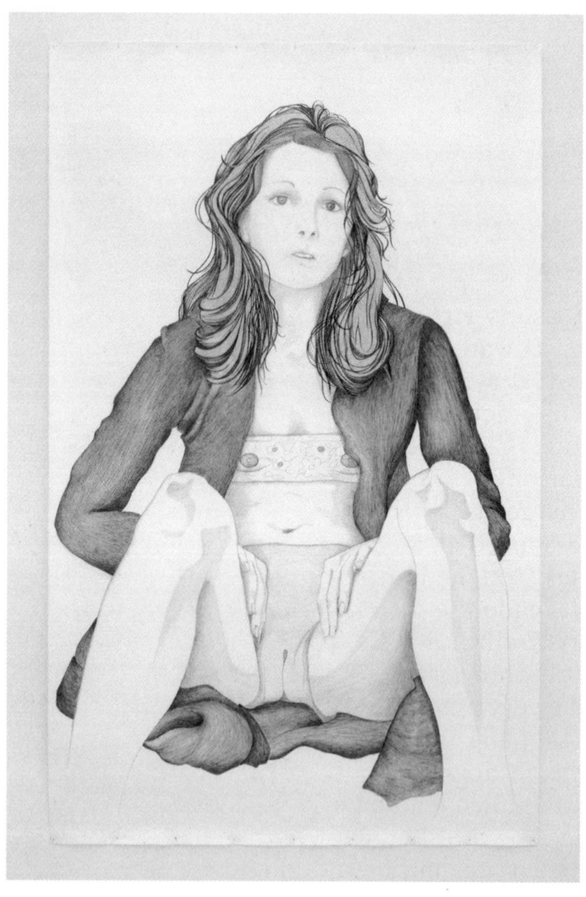

Marlene McCarty, *Patty Columbo – May 15, 1976*, 1999, graphite, ballpoint pen, and colored pencil on paper, from a set of 4 drawings, 72 × 55 inches (182.9 × 139.7 cm) each.

October 29, 2010
Artforum

Marlene McCarty has worked across various media since the 1980s. She was a member of the AIDS activist collective Gran Fury and also created the transdisciplinary design studio Bureau with Donald Moffett in 1989. McCarty is well known for her early work, including her hard-hitting text paintings. She has been recognized for graphite, ballpoint pen, and colored-pencil portraits that probe issues ranging from sexual and social formation to parricide and infanticide. The first major survey of her work opened at New York University's 80WSE Gallery in fall 2010.

One of the reasons I chose to work in an oversize scale in the mid-1990s is that I wanted the girls depicted in my drawings to be taken seriously and not to be dismissed as diminutive Barbie dolls. I wanted the interaction with the viewer to become a more immersive situation rather than a subject–object situation. The scale became a very important physical quality. My portraits of girls who killed their mothers—poltergeists, as I like to call them—bled into a long-term project. What started as a compact series, which I thought would take six months, has stretched into fifteen years. It wasn't the works' monumentality that made the project take longer, but more the way I chose to draw—I was trying to draw in a way that a teenage girl would have depicted herself or in a way that she might have found herself attractive. This required a very meticulous kind of drawing that takes a really long time. The quick, bang-it-out, mechanical-reproduction thing of my previous work wasn't doable, and that's part of the reason why my series have just slowed down enormously. The process kept going deeper and deeper and became more immersive to me as an artist. I was no longer able to just chew it up, spit it out, and move on.

When I started the *Poltergeist, Girls at Home* series, I was emerging from the late '80s and early '90s. As you know, this had been a time that was intensely concerned with identity politics. The expectations of that period were *heavy*. I was involved in Gran Fury, so I was very much a part of this concentration on identity, thinking about who speaks for whom, who assumes the dominant voice, and so forth. But I didn't feel like I could keep churning out the same things. Identity politics was a catalyst in the beginning, but it's something from which I've slowly moved on. Though saying that doesn't mean it's not there—a piece of that discussion always exists as an underlying foundation somewhere in my art.

If someone had told me at the beginning that it would go on for fifteen years, I would've been like, "No way—you're out of your mind!" And if someone had told me three years before that, "You're going to do figurative drawings," I would've been just as unlikely to believe them. You know, there have been many funny little twists and turns.

I'm often asked about the underlying violence of those works, but actually I've never been motivated by violence. Instead, I'm interested in intense bonding situations, which might be related to identity formation. Thus, my newer work about primates and religion. It's true that most of the situations I've researched and depicted have ended badly. But the violence isn't what initially attracted me to them; it's merely, oddly, a coincidence.

This exhibition has been tricky because most of my art life has been in New York, and pretty much all of my work has at some point or another been shown in New York. It was a challenge for me to figure out how to make something that would be both a survey and at the same time not too redundant. I didn't want locals to walk in and think, Oh, didn't I see that last year? In my initial conversation with Michael Cohen, we discussed organizing the show thematically, but there wasn't enough space in the galleries to do that. My drawings are so huge that I didn't have the freedom to place them just anywhere in the gallery to support a theme. The space is also kind of rambling, with lots of small rooms. In the end, the galleries' spatial organization forced me to radically edit the work. The trajectory of my work has been at times extremely varied. The small spaces have given me the possibility of placing different bodies of work in proximity to each other, thus creating a conversation between my old and new output, instead of just a chronology.

At first it felt strange that the show was being organized by NYU and not a more established art organization. But this turned out to be fairly liberating. I didn't feel the pressure that might have been implicit with some big art institution and its legacy. I've positively embraced the marginal status of this gallery.

Mary Beth Edelson

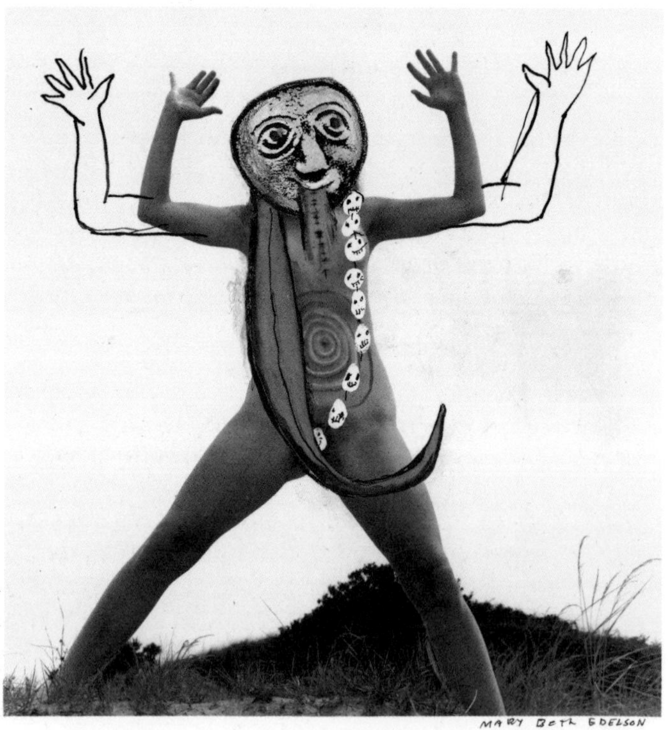

Mary Beth Edelson, *Sheela's Secret Weapon*, 1973, oil, ink, china marker, and collage on silver gelatin print, 10 × 8 inches (20.3 × 25.4 cm). From the *Woman Rising* series.

November 10, 2011
Artforum

Mary Beth Edelson was a founder of the Heresies collective and journal and an early member of A.I.R. Gallery. She was a key voice from the first generation of American artists to ground their practice in feminist issues, and her paintings, collages, installations, and photographs have been shown worldwide. Here she talks about her fall 2011 show at Balice-Hertling-Lewis in New York and Paris.

There's a feminist adage from Audre Lorde: The master's tools will never dismantle the master's house. To which I say: Let's get some other tools! Fuck his house—who goes there anyway? I've always felt that we can claim our own tools by deeply examining history, by researching the eras when women were revered in a different way—or so the myth goes. This is why I'm so interested in ancient goddess figures—for example, the enigmatic Baubo, the trickster Sheela-na-gig, an Egyptian bird goddess, and Minoan snake goddesses. All four of these figures can be reinterpreted and repurposed, and thus they show up over and over again in my collage work.

I've been making art since I was twelve years old and have saved basically everything. The first task in trying to organize these exhibitions was to sift through and narrow down this massive amount of work I've produced—since I'm really, really old. When I was in school, artists were either sculptors or painters, and for a long time I was just a painter, but I arrived at a point where I realized that I didn't need to follow such a narrow road. In the early 1970s, I was living in Washington, DC, and very involved in a Jungian seminar. I was fascinated with Jung's ideas about the collective unconscious and tried to make work that depicted that—very presumptuous of me, but to some extent it was good and became important to me as a feminist. The critique that Jung made of the symbolic world, myths, and the figures therein was liberating, and around that time I began working with fire, photography, collage, and performance. I was still painting, too! Over time, though, I began to understand that what Jung offered was still in the end a patriarchal construct, and I broadened my approach and analysis, informed by feminism.

The title of the new show references a project I made in 1994, *Combat Zone: HQ Against Domestic Violence*, a three-month-long storefront space in Times Square that was sponsored by Creative Time. The most successful thing I did there was to invent ways for women in abusive situations to use self-defense. While working on that project I also started an artist's book about Lorena Bobbitt, exploring what it meant for a woman to castrate a man, and what effect it had on culture. The book included eighty-one drawings and is the anchor for the Paris show.

My interest in Bobbitt is obviously a feminist one—I had a point of view about it immediately and wanted to examine and express that. I started thinking of her as Saint Bobbitt because she really did something for all women: she retaliated. In addition to the book, I've also created a lot of other drawings and a sculpture of a Kali figure that I made out of a mannequin. She has a number of arms and a girdle of knives around her waist as well as a bracelet of severed penises around her arm. In short, she's decorated. I first exhibited the work at Combat Zone and put this very dramatic lighting on it. It sums up my feelings about the Bobbitt situation, a situation that I feel the same way about today as when I first heard about it—I thought it was really funny. As someone once said: A hundred ten million women worldwide are survivors of genital mutilation, and then there is just John Bobbitt—one man, one name.

Mary Ellen Carroll

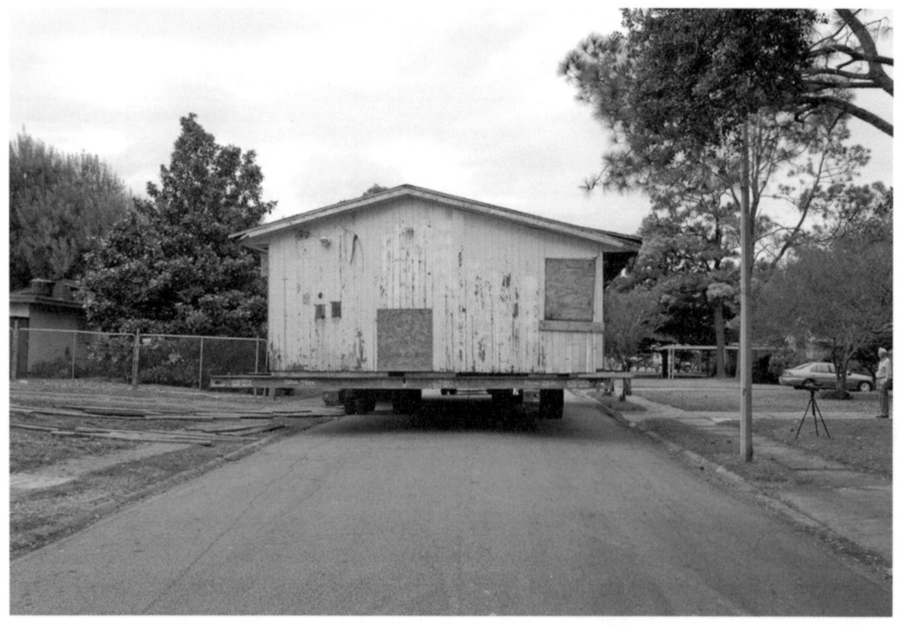

Mary Ellen Carroll, *prototype 180*, 2009–, photo by Kenny Trice.

July 27, 2009
Artforum

Mary Ellen Carroll is a conceptual artist based in New York and Houston. Below, she discusses prototype 180, *a work she created in collaboration with the Rice University Building Institute, as well as a mayoral forum on land use in Houston at the Contemporary Arts Museum Houston that she organized and moderated.*

Houston is the only metropolitan area in the United States without a formal land-use zoning code. The no-zoning policy creates conditions, both physical and atmospheric, for extending free enterprise over the city, the energy capital of the world. Density and urbanism are replacing the ideal of the West as an open, expansive territory, both economically and as a seemingly endless repository of natural resources.

Ten years ago, this urban policy condition brought me to the Gulf Coast, and the city essentially self-selected itself as the site for *prototype 180*, a work of art that will make architecture performative. It's literally a ground-shifting exercise, in that it structurally involves the rotation, back to front, of a house and its surrounding land in the development of Sharpstown. Following the rotation, it will be retrofitted and rehabilitated to become an occupied structure that will be become an institute for the study of considered urbanism.

An early condition for this work was that the surrounding context and its process not be considered as urban renewal. This necessitated a location in a relatively stable yet aging subdivision—one that's invisible in effect, not calling attention to itself either socioeconomically or typologically. The area would also ideally be a model of shifting demographics, reflecting the growth patterns and diversity of the city. Sandwiched in the path of Houston's redevelopment to the northwest and new developments to the southwest, these conditions exist and manifest themselves in the development of Sharpstown, a diverse, middle-class neighborhood.

I designed a 16-foot table/stage that replicates the dimensions and hardwood floor of the living room of *prototype 180*, which is now in the exhibition *No Zoning: Artists Engage Houston* at the Contemporary Art Museum Houston. Referencing furniture created for peace talks, treaties, and negotiations, the table functions as a site for meetings and symposia that will eventually take place in *prototype 180*.

On Thursday, July 9, I programmed the table/stage for its intended use by organizing and moderating "NOZONE, Houston's Mayoral Forum on Land Use." The forum was based on the research and a seminar I teach at Rice University's School of Architecture. I posed five questions to the mayoral candidates pertaining to land use.

All of Houston's mayoral candidates participated, and the forum lasted two and a half hours. Since then, everyone I've spoken with who attended the forum seems to now know whom he or she will vote for. To me, this indicates that the political image became the artistic image.

Mary Heilmann

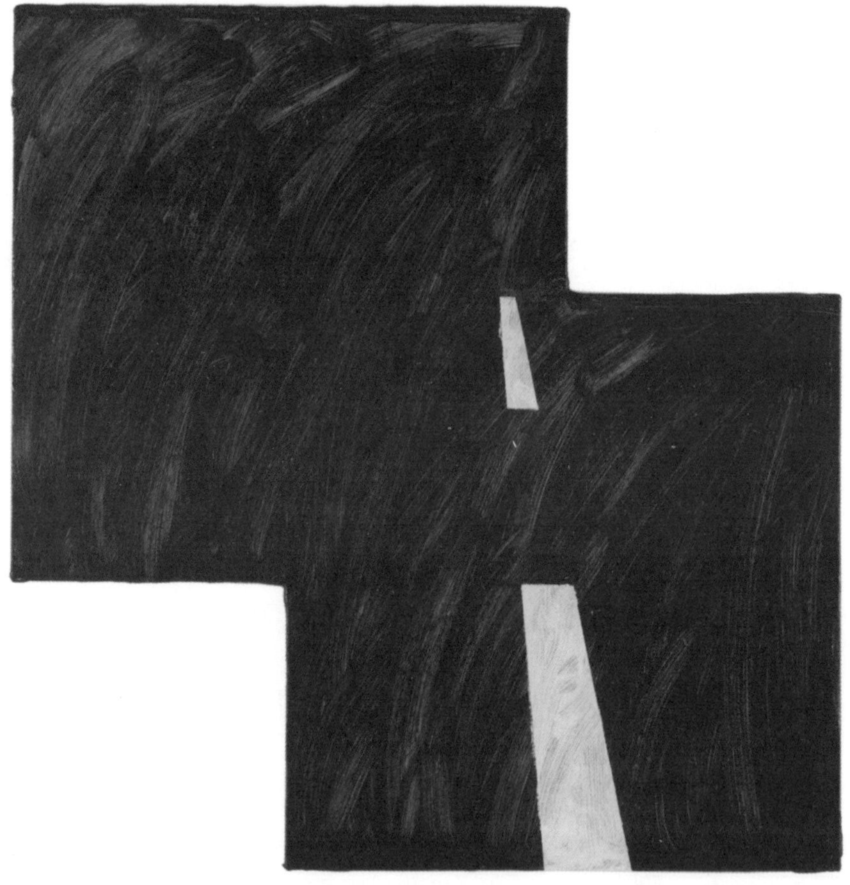

Mary Heilmann, *Road Trip*, 2010, oil on canvas, 30 × 30 (shaped) inches (76.2 × 76.2 cm).

February 20, 2012
Artforum

A painter, sculptor, and ceramicist, Mary Heilmann is perhaps best known as a consummate colorist. Her high-keyed exhibitions often blend elements of Pop and Minimalism, devotion and sociality, and are always infused with an inimitable chromatic charge. Heilmann's show Visions, Waves, and Roads *was at Hauser & Wirth, London, in spring 2012.*

The waves have always been in my life and work. My father was a body-surfer and as a kid I would join him on the beach in San Francisco. I have a very early memory of watching him in the huge, crashing, cold surf. Whenever I'm in the Bay Area, I go to the beach and check it out. California remains a big part of my life even though I've lived in New York since 1968.

I went to Santa Barbara to study literature in 1959, and I got by just fine, but I never really felt like I was there for academic reasons. The surfing scene was really cool back then. I was constantly zooming up and down the highway from Santa Barbara to Mexico, stopping at all the surf spots. One of my boy pals from school loaned me his surf-board, and I tried it, but never pursued it. I wouldn't say I ever really surfed—not too many girls did back then. But I loved to watch.

I was studying criticism and poetry, and then started making ceramics as a hobby; there was a whole crew in Santa Barbara getting really into that. I loved it so much that I ended up in Berkeley in 1963, studying with Peter Voulkos in the art department. Of course when I moved to New York I couldn't get any attention for that kind of work. So I started painting. Everyone in the city hated painting, including me!

We thought it was the lamest thing. But by 1972 I was building stretcher bars and really getting into it. I felt like I was pushing paint around in almost the same way I did for sculpture and ceramics. I was inspired by what was going on with anti-form and with the works that Eva Hesse, Richard Serra, and Barry Le Va were making. They're huge influences.

My titles are usually poetic and often refer to places or things—in this show, for instance, there are works with names like *Vanishing Point* or *Yuma Arizona* or *Renny's Right Geometry of a Wave*—so perhaps as you look a certain image might arise. The paintings have always had some connection to reality even though they're mostly abstract. I'm also totally obsessed with symbolic imagery, geometry, and Ellsworth Kelly. The waves come out of this and so does my Malevich-inspired work. I've been in a Malevich phase for a while, which has meant a lot of deep thinking about geometry and pushing geometric figures around in a sort of puzzle-making way. In *Malevich Spin*, for instance, there's a sense of movement through geometry—perhaps in your mind you rearrange it, move the pieces around.

I've been thinking about the design for this show for nearly a year. I always want my exhibitions to be read in a theatrical way; people walk in and just around the corner one of the first things they see is a two-lane highway road image. And then they become part of this set. Perhaps they sit in the chairs, which have wheels, and they move around, getting nearer to each other, or looking closer at the work. This show will have a domestic element, too, with some of my pottery, dinnerware, and a couple of tables. My shows have never encouraged a quick visit—just standing in front of one work and moving swiftly to the next and then the next. It's always been important to me that visitors be able to sit down, relax, and have a conversation in the gallery.

Mary Kelly

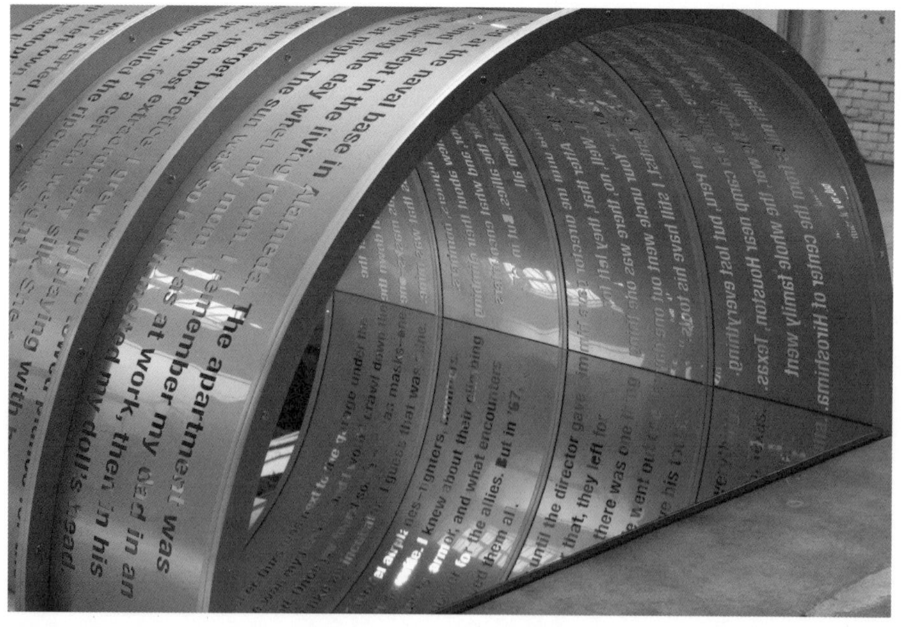

Mary Kelly and Ray Barrie, *Habitus*, 2010, laser-cut acrylic, mirror, and wood, 48 × 96 × 96 inches (121.9 × 243.8 × 243.8 cm).

February 18, 2011
Artforum

The influential American conceptual artist Mary Kelly here talks about her show at Manchester's Whitworth Art Gallery, which opened in winter 2011.

There is a way of understanding my work in relation to film, especially when you see so many of my projects together. Although I moved away from film in the early 1970s, I took many of the medium's aesthetic strategies about real time and duration into the installation context. A work like *The Ballad of Kastriot Rexhepi* requires a 360-degree pan, and that's quite satisfying for me because the viewer gets pulled in and has to walk around it. Those phenomenological aspects are also very important in my later pieces. I used to call this "narrativizing space," but now I wonder whether that's the right term to use. I've been thinking about this since "The Dialogic Imagination," a workshop we had in Stockholm last October, and perhaps the title of that workshop offers a better way of thinking about this process. I'm more interested in the way a construction of dialogic space is created in the later works through fairly anecdotal writings, which you can see in much of my art.

The Moderna exhibition was thematic, not like a retrospective or a survey, but concentrated on four works in a way that interested me. When we discussed the show at the Whitworth, I knew that I wanted to include as much complete work as I could, rather than just bits and pieces. I wanted the viewer to get a sense of the major projects over my career, and to have an idea of the questions I've been addressing over time. That's why we decided to call it *Mary Kelly Projects, 1973–2010*, and it does include nearly all of *Post-Partum Document*, which hasn't been seen in the UK for over thirty years, and several of my more recent works, such as *Vox Manet* and *Circa 1968*, which explore political activism. It also has the *Multi-Story House* from *Love Songs*, works that draw upon women's experiences. Additionally on view is *Habitus*, my latest work, an installation based on the Anderson bomb shelter that was mass-produced for domestic use during World War II. I hope that viewers gain an understanding of what I've called the "discursive site," a support for the work that's much broader than a specific medium, but something more like a location, or a community, or an oppositional discourse. For me, this discursive site began with the women's movement in Britain at the end of the '60s and the kinds of questions that emerged at that time around sexual difference and identity. Those questions carried on after *Post-Partum Document*, from the mother–child relationship to questions about masculinity, and those then evolved into the questions about war and ethics that underpin my later work.

What really excites me most is what's going on in the present moment. Even in work where I'm returning to 1968 as an image, it's not really about the past but more about how the past is appearing in the present. Quite a while ago, when I had a show at the New Museum in 1990, I began to ask if in fact this moment of feminism and psychoanalysis was really over, or if it had any meaning for people now. At the time I realized it just keeps reinventing itself in many different ways, and I think that comes out in some of the pieces. Around the same time, I began to think about generations, not anthropologically, but through the major historical events that have affected people and have cast a really wide net around them. The generations between 1965 and 1985 were very much impacted by what happened in 1968. And that made me think about the period of World War II, and wonder why the generation brought up during the Cold War was so cut off from our parents. We weren't curious because we thought we were going to change the world—we weren't going to make that same mistake again!

When I looked over all the work I also realized how important voice is to me; it's almost a found object in my practice. Although I've never published my notebooks before, it seemed important to include some pages from them in the catalogue. Over the years, I've kept conversational notes, drawings, and more theoretical notes. These are all mixed up and interconnected, but they become the material that I try to work on. So there's always the combination of the everyday experience and an attempt to grasp the big picture at the same time, but in the notebooks you can see how organic it all really is.

Mary Mattingly

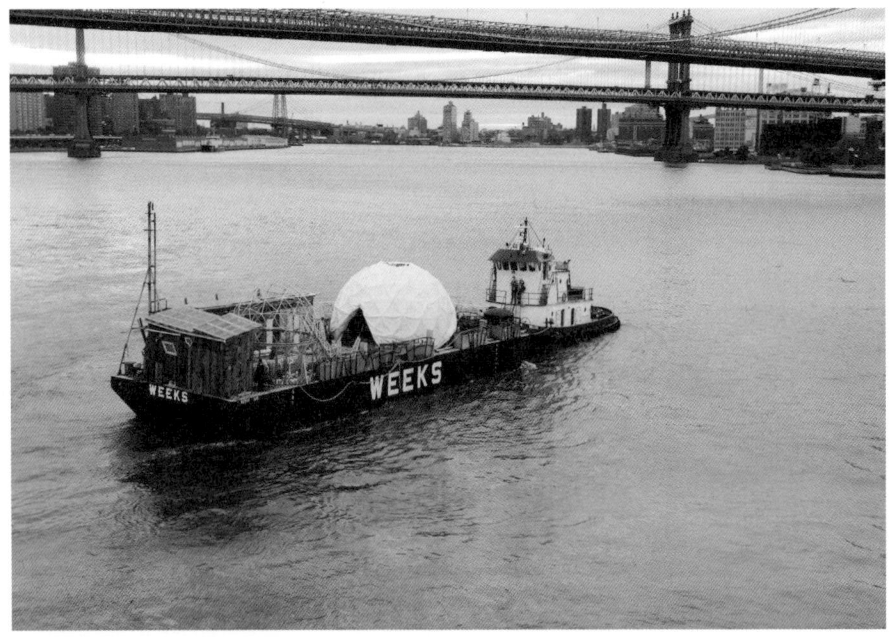

The Waterpod™, 2009, photo by Mary Mattingly.

April 1, 2009
Artforum

New York–based photographer and sculptor Mary Mattingly designed The Waterpod, a floating eco-habitat that recalls the work of Buckminster Fuller, Andrea Zittel, and Constant Nieuwenhuys. Here, she discusses the project, which launched in May 2009 in the East River.

The Waterpod is three years in the making. Prior to this project, I made wearable homes with three layers, fit for mobile people in different environmental conditions (arctic, desert/tundra, and water). I began to design these as I was traveling often and as I became increasingly worried that government and corporate agencies were largely ignoring problems caused by pollution and climate change. I wanted to respond to the growing instability of cultures and the political unrest arising from inattention to these issues.

After my first show at Robert Mann in 2006, someone asked me what I was going to do next. I responded that I wanted to create a live/work capsule in the East River, perhaps in the Newtown Creek, since, at the time, New York City was doing very little to prepare for rising sea levels. *The Waterpod* project began with preliminary sketches; it was a translucent sphere with two levels. One was a sleep and study area underwater, essentially an aquarium, a quiet and contemplative space. The top level would be for work; it would feature a garden space and would resemble a small autonomous system. An infrastructure of soil connected to a wire framework would keep the pod upright.

It was interesting to learn how to create this kind of system, one that the inhabitants wouldn't necessarily need to leave and that could exist as a mobile space. Finding sustainable solutions for living made me question the design, as well as the role of community, in the space. I thought about the relationship between individuals and utopian spaces and kept in mind future possibilities. *The Waterpod* also developed from my series of photographs of abandoned utopian spaces, entitled *The Anatomy of Melancholy*, and conversations I had with Eve K. Tremblay, a future *Waterpod* inhabitant, which forced me to consider why most attempts at utopian systems fail. I began to focus on creating a fluid space with spheres for inhabitants that draw together many different communities. I wanted it to be mutable in design, concept, integration, and autonomy.

At first, I designed it as a personal space, but as the idea evolved, it became clear that it needed community to be sustainable and to benefit from multiple inputs and interpretations. I became more interested in the benefits that could be gained from a diverse community living on and interacting with the pod. I started to form a group of people who were interested in the project, either from an artistic, infrastructural, or technological point of view. Artist Mira Hunter was one of the first people I approached. Mira was raised in a famous floating house in Vancouver designed by her father. Eventually, we formed a democratic group, a meritocracy, and developed a set of guidelines. Right now, there are five people who will be living on *The Waterpod*. One guideline is that as a resident you don't need to stay on board; but while on board and off, residents are encouraged to catalog their activities, so we can have a record of what's coming and going. Everyone will have to help out with repairs, gardening, cooking, and composting. Basically, everyone will learn how to take care of everything. I think this is really important—as the first industrial and technological age in the developed world is drawing to a close, people need to relearn how to do a lot of things.

Many elements of the project are currently underway. Derek Hunter and Alison Ward are building a modular superstructure in a warehouse in Long Island City while the barge platform is docked in Bayonne, New Jersey. We're in the process of finalizing insurance before we move to Pier 35 in Manhattan. Once that's ready, we'll have a month to build there, and we should launch and move in by the end of May. Even though this is a project that I imagined having a very long life span, here in New York it's going to be abbreviated. Due to various environmental guidelines, we need to move the pod every two weeks. We also have to secure a sufficient number of piers to be able to move it and still have a long enough time to live on board.

Engineering students are building some of the technological elements. Artist Stephanie Dedes is coordinating a barter system with local greenmarkets, while Carissa Carman has designed the onboard living system. Carissa is creating a greenhouse and an outdoor garden space, which is based on companion planting. Through open calls, groups and individuals in New York have started to grow specific vegetables on behalf of the project, and we'll transplant them to the barge's garden space in early May. People have been sending us pictures of the vertical gardens in their apartments; it's one of my favorite parts of the project right now.

As with *The Waterpod*, many of the images in *Nomadographies* are about autonomous mobile systems of living that are low-tech, ad hoc, and adaptable. *The Waterpod* embodies these ideas and responds to their present uses, while *Nomadographies* projects into the future in a performative and metaphoric way. Some of the photographs follow artist (and *Waterpod* inhabitant) Veronica Flores and me as we travel through Mexico toward Mexcaltitan, using bicycles piled high with boxes to carry our belongings. This journey forced me to reconsider notions of ownership, harsh climate conditions, scarcity of clean water, and conflicts between the state and warring cartels. While *Nomadographies* embodies future histories, *The Anatomy of Melancholy* revisits the past, and *The Waterpod* enters the present, blending fiction and autobiography with different ideologies.

Mimi Thi Nyugen

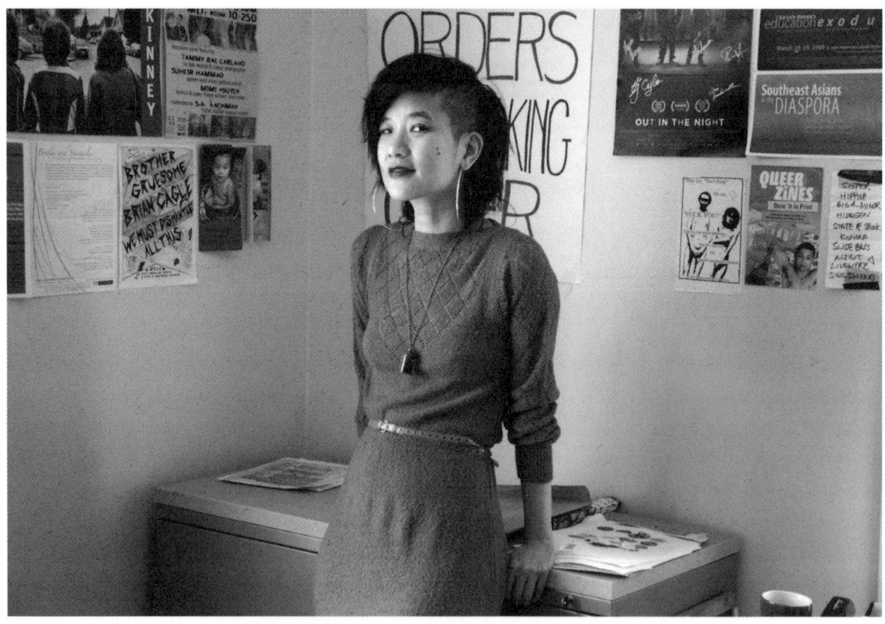

Mimi Thi Nguyen, 2020, photo by Rachel Lauren Storm.

November 5, 2020
November

Mimi Thi Nguyen is a Vietnamese American scholar, punk, and zine author. She has made zines since 1991, including Slander *(formerly known by other titles), and was a* Punk Planet *columnist and* Maximumrocknroll *contributor. She is well known for her compilation zine* Evolution of a Race Riot *(1997 and 2002), in which she and contributors of color challenged racism in the punk scene. Nguyen earned tenure in 2012 at the University of Illinois at Urbana–Champaign. She received the 2014 Outstanding Book Award in Cultural Studies from the Association of Asian American Studies for her first single-author monograph,* The Gift of Freedom: War, Debt and Other Refugee Passages (2012). *Here, we talk at length about her next project,* The Promise of Beauty. *The interview was conducted in October–November 2020.*

LOB: I was just rereading your excellent Fales Library Donation Statement with a class. For those who aren't aware: with the help of Ariana Ruiz, you donated photocopies of your original copies of zines by women of color to the Fales Library Riot Grrrl Collection in 2012. Could you tell us more about collecting the zines over the years and what it was like to write that statement?

MTN: My first encounter with punk proper—not post-punk or new wave, with which I was familiar as an alternateen in the late '80s—was through zines, specifically, the longest-publishing punk magazine *Maximumrocknroll*. I made my first zine soon after I stumbled across *Maximum*, and the zine reviews in the back of the magazine (next to the classifieds), and I have been collecting zines since then. I have bins and bins of zines, mostly by women, queers, and people of color, in my closet; after I did the compilation zine *Race Riot* to address race and racism in punk and its adjacent scenes, I collected hundreds by people of color from the 1990s and early 2000s. I've been asked multiple times what I intend to do with this collection, and I honestly don't know. I have a lot of feelings about being archived and institutionalized.

In 2012, I donated some select materials to the Riot Grrrl Collection in the Fales Library at New York University in order to "diversify" their holdings, in hurried anticipation of the publication of selected documents from the collection. I believe Lisa Darms, then curator of the collection, tweeted out a concern or a call for donations in light of the dearth of materials from women of color. The institutional record at the moment (not just at Fales, but broadly speaking) perceived women of color as outsiders or latecomers to zines and to riot grrrl, and someone reached out to me to encourage me to "correct" it with this donation. I totally understand this impulse, even as I am wary of it. As I ask elsewhere, What does it mean to make radically minor objects archivable, accessible, or legible? To what labors is the radically minor object recruited beyond what the mere facts of documentation, preservation, and circulation claim to do? Which is to say, I was worried that something else might go missing in the act of "correcting" this archival absence, namely, the conditions for that absence and also its correction. That is, how are race and racism made visible in riot grrrl or any other feminist historiographies, first as absence and second as crisis? I donated despite these misgivings, obviously, in part to see how I would feel about it (I kept my originals and sent copies). All that said, I never identified as a riot grrrl. I was always very much a punk.

LOB: Even as things are saved in the archive, things are lost—this seems somehow inevitable to me. You ask in the essay if perhaps this donation/intervention could become "*the* story to tell," and not merely an addition or supplement. I'm wondering how that thought has sat with you since you first wrote the essay. Do you think it's happened, to some extent, or not really?

MTN: Honestly, I try not to read scholarship in what is punk studies broadly, and no work that mentions me. In part because I find scholarship about something I wrote for a specific audience (other punks) to be weird, and the incorporation of "difference" into this increasingly institutionalized archive to be discomforting. But I am deeply concerned with historiography, in my own work. So one concern I have is that something I call a "minor object" might serve a particular function as a course correction that allows for a return to a status quo. In this familiar telling, a minor object is a necessary intervention in a time of crisis, but also a *temporary* intervention that thereafter restores the integrity of a movement or an institution (like the state) and returns us to a continuous history. We can discern this structure operating in stories about punk or riot grrrl, in which the "problem" of racism is contained as a chapter or episode in a longer story. So I worry about that still. But, of course, I also don't read the work that might do otherwise, because of the weirdness!

LOB: Speaking of historiography, have you been able to write or research during the pandemic? I'm curious as to what you've been working on lately, or if it's been possible.

MTN: I manage anxiety and inchoate rage with television binges and work, which is not necessarily healthy. I managed to draft two chapters of my manuscript called "The Promise of Beauty" in the last eight months while prepping for the courses I teach. Of course, our historical moment has deeply informed the writing, which considers the promise of beauty under the strain of registering the future as one disaster after another. But I have been writing about this for years now! I encountered this conceptual pairing—beauty and crisis— throughout the course of writing about refugees and regime change, through to the midst of the COVID-19 pandemic, over and over again. How might the promise of beauty engage crushing harms and exhausted signifiers, whether through an ordinary wearing down or the normalization of war and terror, slow violences or sharp terrors, in which our sense of time is disturbed, and there is no future on the horizon? How does the promise of beauty become a practical or philosophical concern?

So I have been circling this question about what a commitment or an attachment to the beautiful means for how we endure. In the face of crisis, or despair, I argue that beauty functions as a promise, a commitment to *act*, premised on the will or power to bring into being that which is missing, incomplete, or endangered in the present. Beauty is, of course, a capacious judgment and elastic property—sometimes a means (to achieve love, or democracy) or an end in itself, sometimes an obstacle or an opening to other forms or habits of being. And sometimes in narrative and aesthetic constructions of crisis, the nature of the danger is crystallized in the threat of disappearance and destruction to beautiful objects, persons, and even lifeworlds. Such constructions evoke beauty to critique the limits of a structure or practice, such as authoritarianism, or man-made climate crisis; and when such a structure or practice can't sustain beauty, these constructions can also recruit interference on beauty's behalf. These forms could be familiar, or sometimes strange; there are roses, mountains, and lovers, but one mantra in particular strikes me in this moment—and it's from John Waters's *Female Trouble*—"crime is beauty," through which lawfulness under a dehumanizing regime is not an option.

LOB: This sounds like an incredible book. As primarily an art worker/writer, I'm curious if there are any particular artworks that you consider? And a second question I'll include now: In what forms of protest, dissent, or crime do you find beauty?

MTN: The book is organized around specific crises for which beauty is imagined to promise a feeling of life being furthered (to borrow unfaithfully from Kant), so among the things I consider are Vietnamese refugee *ao dai* (the "traditional" dress) pin-up calendars, the brief life of the Beauty Without Borders NGO in post-invasion Kabul, and a pageant for landmine survivors, but also Virginia Woolf's *Mrs Dalloway*, Ocean Vuong's *On Earth We're Briefly Gorgeous*, Leonard Koren's *Wabi-Sabi for Artists, Designers, Poets, and Philosophers*, Cauleen Smith's "BLK FMNNST Loaner Library, 1989–2019," Chanel Miller's *Know My Name*, and the Nap Ministry. A *lot* of genres of beauty appear throughout the book, including beauty as an emergent truth or as the purest possibility, as a false idol or as a fascist country. Some presume the truth of beauty's nature, the content of which might bind us to a situation of plentitude or profound scarcity; some accuse it of failure, circumscribing the grounds of a given universal like beauty to narrow understandings of the species category of "the human."

What I want from beauty is the disturbance of what it means to be attached to forms of life produced by practices of death. That is, I want from beauty a political vocabulary that can capture what it is to want another life that does not yet exist—while questioning whether this life is possible under present conditions, and what conditions would make it so. A life in which we make the best of having to linger in this in-between, in which we tell each other that another world is possible, another end of the world is possible. The uprisings this summer, then, were beautiful to me. The actions shutting down eviction courts happening right now are beautiful to me. These are all beautiful to me because they disrupt that which we are told is necessary—the violence of law, the violence of private property—to say to us, "There are other ways we can live that don't depend on death."

So beauty for me is one name for how some are grasping at "what to do in crisis," and how to imagine we live after it. It's one name for new ways to care about and redress that violence, both as something specific and personal and as something general and structural; one name given to living through this visceral moment of suffering and uncertainty, in which we are presented with multiple conflicting diagnoses about the present and competing prognostications about the future. Beauty is one name we give to what we imagine or hope sustains us beyond mere survival. Saidiya Hartman writes, lovingly, about the anarchy of colored girls in a riotous manner, "Esther Brown was wild and wayward. She longed for another way of living in the world. She was hungry for enough, for otherwise, for better. She was hungry for beauty. ... What was beauty if not 'the intense sensation of being pulled toward the animating force of life'?"

LOB: I love that quote. It sounds like there's an Arendtian form of natality involved with beauty—a sense of new beginnings that makes possibility ... well, possible. Would you say that's correct? I was also thinking about Arendt earlier when you mentioned a commitment to *act*.

MTN: Absolutely, though what this commitment to act looks like depends on a lot—which is the premise of the book! But yes, if beauty designates that which is required to live through a historical conjuncture, beauty also solicits a promise—a commitment to act. Or as Toni Morrison put so well, and I cite here with all necessary ambivalence, "Beauty was not simply something to behold, it was something one could do." So rather than dispute the concept of beauty through contradiction or incommensurability, which would presume that beauty is something other than an instance or force, and that the ideal presence of beauty is calculable or predictable, beauty inhabits this book as an analytic for a historical investigation into the forms and events that constitute us as subjects of dreaming. Toward this end, I argue the significance of beauty as a politics of intervening in history (the conditions under which beauty endures) and life itself (what meaning beauty lends). This could absolutely be an Arendtian natality, but it could also be and has often been a "civilizing" social order (see beauty's invocation in the US invasion of and ongoing operations in Afghanistan).

LOB: In the latter case, when it's a "civilizing" social order, is beauty then instrumentalized or weaponized? If so, how can that be challenged or overcome?

MTN: I mean, this question gets at this line I'm walking—I'm not trying to say that beauty is one thing or another, as a horizon or a weapon. Instead, I want to say that beauty is the empty space into which we put those things that we conceive as necessary for a historical sense, a consciousness of life, and this is its crucial conceptual power—as a magnet, as a force, and an effect toward which others move, and are moved. Understood in these terms, rather than as a predictable expression of social infrastructure or transcendental universal, the concept of beauty, even when it appears in its most banal and familiar forms (for instance, as "beauty standards"), could be described more expansively as an accessible concept to make claims about our ideal relations to objects or persons in the world.

And it's hard, because I'm asked all the time, about this book, "What does this mean? What does beauty matter, against the material and solid foundation of life and death?" And I'm asked about all those moments in which beauty is a weapon, or its promise a failure. As we know, beauty is just as often an object of suspicion as it is anything else. And my response is, "How is it that beauty can be understood as inconsequential, trivial, or ornamental, but its absence or its other—ugliness—is described as devastating, dehumanizing, or violent?" So to answer your question, finally, is that the promise of beauty establishes a contingent politics for a feeling of life being furthered in a historical terrain, which can always be transformed or undone, by asking again and again: What conditions are necessary to live, what forms of life are worth living, and what actions must follow to preserve, secure, or replicate such conditions, forms, and actions to sustain such life that the beautiful promises to us? So if a law or a constitution is called beautiful (which happens, especially when and where beauty is understood as fairness or symmetry, which are received as necessary qualities but are still evaluative frames), we can say, But what is the life that can be lived under the shadow of this law? Whose life is circumscribed as outside its promise of beauty?

I hope this makes sense, because if not, this book is fucked!

LOB: It does! You said earlier that you arrived at some of this thinking from writing about refugees and regime change, about crisis and real-world concerns where beauty may seem elusive. This interview has also brought to mind equally expansive political conceptions, namely of freedom—along the lines of Angela Davis's thinking (freedom is a constant struggle). We need more formations beyond something like freedom, to show, as you said, there are other ways we can live that don't depend on death. So, I'm curious to hear more about the trajectory of this book and how some of your previous essays, for example on the politics of the hijab, may have informed your thinking.

MTN: The seed of this book began with my participation in the massive anti-war protests in 2001 and 2003, and the Transnational Feminist Practices Against War authored by some of my then mentors, in a clash with a liberal feminist agenda that gladly collaborated with imperialist powers to "free" brown women from brown men. I was in graduate school at Berkeley at the time, writing a dissertation about another war to grant to others the so-called gift of freedom, so I followed the justifications closely. First Lady Laura Bush, in a November 17, 2001, radio address to the nation, said, "the fight against terrorism is also a fight for the rights and dignity of women," against the monsters that want to "pull out women's fingernails for wearing nail polish" and "impose their world on the rest of us." Here at the onset of the forever war, the burqa specifically, and hijab generally, stood for a constellation of deviant bodies, objects, and subjectivities found at the scene of the US invasion of Afghanistan. We saw the burqa invoked by US officials and liberal feminists as an analogy or a substitute to decry all that which was presumably missing—education, freedom, democracy, and beauty.

And then I began to hear about a campaign to open a nongovernmental trade school called the Beauty School of Kabul to teach Afghan women the "art and commerce of beauty," which garnered widespread popular acclaim and industry support in its merging of feminism with empire and capital. And I was so baffled, and baffled by my own reactions, that I wanted to understand what was happening. The essay I eventually wrote about this campaign was focused on how beauty became a "deliverable" object or social good for this NGO, but I also argued for taking seriously beauty as a force. In the course of learning about the school, writing and talking about it, I would often encounter one of two reactions—either a focus on the Afghan women's resilience (in the face of fundamentalism or war), which was called beautiful, or a dismissal of the initiative for its promise of beauty, despite the thousands of other NGO or government-funded initiatives around the world that claim to bestow similarly elusive qualities such as dignity through social enterprise.

So, the book started with wanting to understand the celebratory and the condemnatory responses at once: What is promised by beauty, what does it mean to fulfill or to fail it?

There was much fanfare about the Beauty School at the time (as well as scorn) but it's all but disappeared from the archive—literally! My friend Thera Webb, who is an archivist and professional researcher, couldn't find any materials anywhere—not even at the institutions which developed the school's curriculum. So, as I revisited this essay to consider how it might figure into the book, I had to ask another set of questions about the disappearance of the promise of beauty alongside the prospect of peace from our longest war in Afghanistan.

To hold those things together, I want to argue that beauty need not be conceived of as an ornament, a supplement, or a "mere" image which power fastens to other calculations. Beauty is instead a prime motor through which certain bodies, certain gestures, certain desires, come to identify and constitute rights-bearing individuals, or sociolegal nonpersons. I mean, as late as 2017, US national security advisor H. R. McMaster used a black-and-white photograph of Afghan college women in miniskirts strolling through 1972 Kabul to convince Donald Trump that increased troop presence would encourage the return of lapsed "Western norms."

LOB: This interview has me thinking about previous *November* interviewee Nell Painter—specifically her writing on how beauty was conceived in the eighteenth and nineteenth centuries (in chapter five of *The History of White People*, "The White Beauty Ideal as Science"). She shows that the production of race as a category for oppression and violence had much to do with the fetishization of white skin— all that white marble in Ancient Greek statuary. She discusses how the so-called "father" of art history, Johann Joachim Winckelmann (1717–1768), was unaware that the original sculptures were often dark in color and typically painted. I'm curious what your thoughts are on how whiteness and beauty have been interlinked.

MTN: These two things—whiteness and beauty—have been interlinked historically, absolutely (but not inevitably). Beauty is foundational to theories of humanity and subjecthood as an effect of its presence, especially where the capacity to perceive and also embody beauty are tied to ideas about ontology and epistemology. Again, I propose beauty not as a description of a historical situation ("This person, or thing, is beautiful"), but as a distinction that produces and at times codifies knowledge about time, about history, about humanity; it's not an ontological truth, but it claims status as such.

For myself, I'm interested in those linkages between whiteness and beauty when and where they can be understood to measure humanity. Immanuel Kant, David Hume, Edmund Burke, and many others naturalized a civilizational, lawful order as scenes for aesthetic capacity. For them, human self-possession circumscribed as the consciousness to act, and to enter into covenant with others (to promise, in other words), is the property and precondition for the appreciation of beauty. The Arab, the African, and the "Oriental" are all deemed historically deficient in this aesthetic faculty; consider Kant's atlas of Chinese grotesqueries and African foolishness ("still not a single one was ever found who presented anything great in art or science or any other praiseworthy quality") in his pre-*Critique* essay "On National Characteristics So Far as They Depend upon the Distinct Feeling of the Beautiful and the Sublime."

This is significant because the capacity for political participation has long been derived from or has corresponded with aesthetic faculty, through the production of identification with a liberal vision of humanity. Adam Smith in his *Theory of Moral Sentiments* wrote that "a spirit of system" motivates the desire to perfect "a certain beautiful and orderly system," while Friedrich Schiller proposed the aesthetic of beauty as a means of joining "free" individuals, through an appeal to the "common sense" of a social arrangement, under a moral–political law. A presumably fair system is thus sensually compelling because of its aesthetic correspondences. Elaine Scarry names the second line of the US Declaration of Independence (admiring the cadence of its syllables, "We hold as self-evident ..."), or the assembly hall (with its "bowl of space" reminiscent of the equidistant proportions of a sphere), as beautiful; she names the law, when "both written and applied with consistency across all persons," as beautiful. We should want to preserve such forms, and replicate them, as a consequence, she argues, for the benefit of others to share in such beauty. And if the Declaration is beautiful, and therefore just, it follows that it's a model for others—in other words, being beautiful and therefore just qualifies it to solicit its replication from others. But this is also the historical promise-violence of colonial benevolence and tutelage, which presumes to teach the racial, colonial other how to copy their betters.

So that's what I'm interested in—how beauty bears the weight of much ideological management and pedagogy in its associations with humanity and its others. Sylvia Wynter calls those distinct categories that emerge from this divide "genres" of the human, each featuring its own aspirations and ways of relating—which, taken together, make up what Wynter calls a culture's "descriptive statement." Wynter argues that the West, through imperial expansion and colonial violence, has imposed its genre-specific truths on the world; its descriptive statement is overrepresented in the history of humanity. The promise of beauty has long shored up this overrepresented statement—but I want to believe that the promise of another beauty can also be that which helps us to imagine otherwise.

Mira Schor

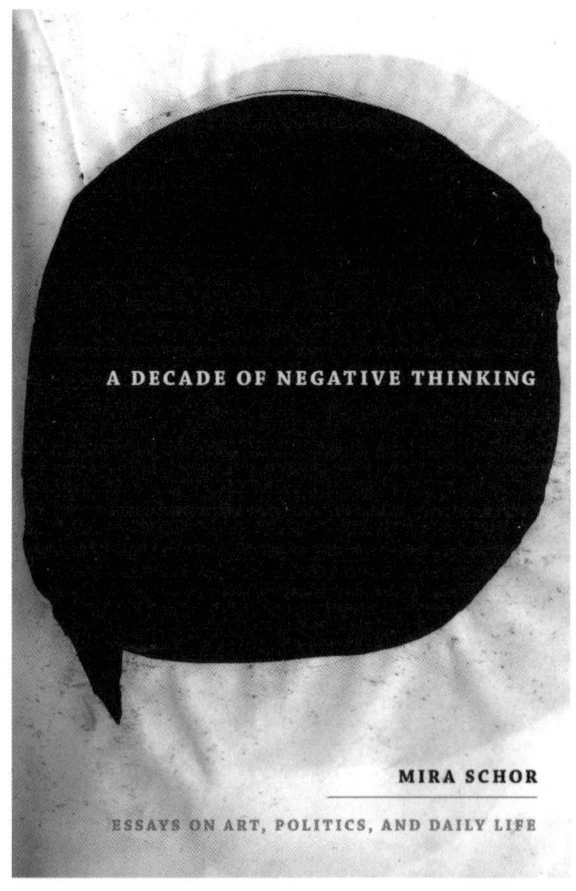

Cover of Mira Schor's *A Decade of Negative Thinking: Essays on Art, Politics, and Daily Life* (2010).

Recognized for her contributions to painting theory and to feminist art history, the painter and writer Mira Schor here discusses A Decade of Negative Thinking *(Duke University Press, 2010) and her blog,* A Year of Positive Thinking.

Am I a negative thinker, as the title of my book suggests? I don't think so, although it may seem that way because I speak out when I suspect that other people are just drinking the Kool-Aid. It's necessary to dig beneath press release culture, and not just take the promotional sound bite as gospel and let it go viral into art discourse. So I decided to give myself the test or the experiment of *A Year of Positive Thinking*. There are so many things that I love in art, film, art history, and political history, which help me to be an artist; I really want to share that part of my experience.

I've been doing a lot on Facebook, posting links to things I think are beautiful, funny, moving, inspiring, while venting on various political issues that make me angry. The blog will be a battle between the two sides of my personality, maybe like Cassandra and Pollyanna. Cassandra tells truths no one wants to hear, but it's good to keep in mind that Pollyanna actually does the same thing: she's not at all the sweet, cloying kind of character we think of when we use the name in a disparaging way; instead she's more like a realistic, grounded character in a Kurosawa movie, albeit via Disney—she confronts with a generous curiosity the repressed private griefs of the inhabitants of the little town she has come to live in, as an orphan. My father, the artist Ilya Schor, died when I was eleven. The Archives of American Art asked my mother for his papers sometime in the 1960s, when I was a teenager. My father didn't do that much writing, but they said they were interested in *everything*—the ephemera of his life, art supply bills, that kind of thing. I helped put some of the material in order. At that time they did microfiches. Later, I was an art history major in college and I studied with H. W. Janson for one semester, which was in some ways very tedious and in others very interesting and an honor. It also pretty much persuaded me not to pursue art history! One of the things it taught me is that classic art history is actually doing things like researching Donatello's laundry list—you know, his receipts, where he lived when. I decided to study art in graduate school instead of pursuing art history.

I've been an inveterate self-documenter since I was a child. For example, I preserved carbon copies and early Xeroxes of all my letters from when I was a twenty-one-year-old grad student in the Feminist Art Program at CalArts and working on Womanhouse. I read them at the F-Word conference at CalArts in 1998, and I've included some of them in *A Decade*, in a chapter titled "Miss Elizabeth Bennett Goes to Feminist Boot Camp." I'm kind of amazed at how articulate and outspoken I was as a twenty-one-year-old, and how much the character of my writing voice was already in place. It's at times highly critical, but also passionate and politically engaged.

If I don't paint over a period of time, I start to go crazy. Painting is a primary language that I need to "speak" and "hear" in order to survive at a very deep level of my existence. I love the process of drawing and painting, and I love creating images, but I can't imagine not writing—it would be like not thinking or speaking.

Monir Shahroudy Farmanfarmaian

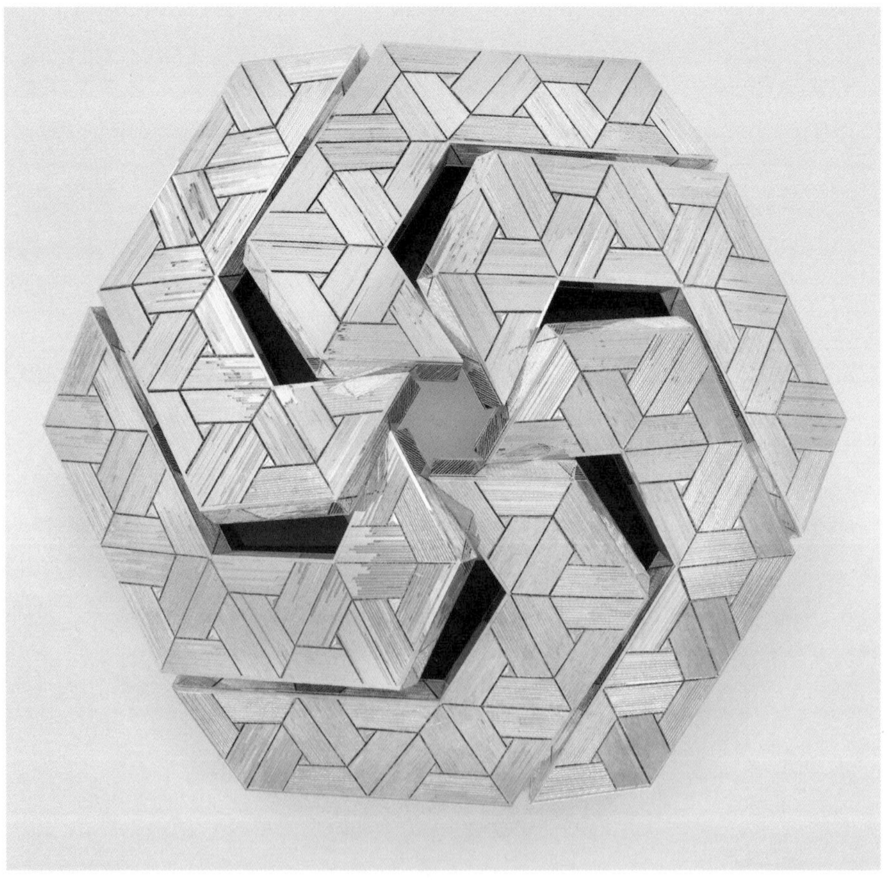

Monir Shahroudy Farmanfarmaian, *Fourth Family Hexagon*, 2013, reverse painted glass, mirrored glass, and plaster, 42 ½ × 47 ½ × 14 ½ inches (108 × 120.7 × 36.8 cm).

March 13, 2014
Artforum

Monir Shahroudy Farmanfarmaian was born in Iran in 1924 and was well known for her dazzling approach to geometric abstraction, primarily in the mirror reliefs and drawings she had been making since the 1970s that derive from ornamental elements in traditional Islamic architecture. The first museum retrospective of her work, curated by Suzanne Cotter, was on view at the Serralves Museum in Porto, Portugal, and the Solomon R. Guggenheim Museum, in 2015.

Last spring I had a survey exhibition at the Third Line in Dubai which then traveled to Doha. Suzanne Cotter had seen these shows, and she invited me to bring my drawings and sculptures from the past forty years to Porto. My work is largely based on geometry, which, as you know, always begins with a single point and can move from there into a circle. Or a point can become three leading to a triangle, or four to a square, five to a pentagon, hexagon, octagon, and so on—it's endless. I was inspired by the geometry I found in old mosques with their tile, metal, wood, and plaster work. A master metalworker that I studied with once told me, "Everything is in geometry." I then found out that with a hexagon you could do so much. And today, I still work on geometry—it's at the base of my art because it has an infinite amount of possibilities. You can create thousands and thousands of designs in textiles, metal, tiles, everything.

These recent shows have been a remarkable time in my life because for so long I was really a nobody. Little by little, I've become ... I don't know ... better known? Certainly the Guggenheim wasn't giving me a show until now. I lived in New York for almost forty years, and moved there initially in 1944 to be a student. I was friends with many poets and artists at the time: Calder, Mitchell, Avery. I used to go to a club once a month on Tenth Street; all the artists would gather there and one would give a talk. I remember Philip Johnson, de Kooning, Newman, and then after that they would all go to the Cedar Tavern. I would follow but I wouldn't drink. I had a lot of fun, though. Anyway, these days in Tehran the disco doesn't let me in!

I met Warhol a little later on. After studying at Parsons, I got a job through a classmate of mine at Bonwit Teller. I met the head of the art department, and they hired me for eighty dollars a week. I used to also do freelance work for them, drawing a bottle of perfume, slippers, or a bag. Andy was drawing his shoes. He was very friendly, and at the time we thought we were making a lot of money. We used to go on picnics for lunch. When I returned to Iran in the '60s, I knew Andy was becoming a very famous Pop artist in New York. So he came to Tehran to make a portrait of the queen. I had a big luncheon for him and his crew. My daughter arranged it. At the time we exchanged some works. I had so many great works in my collection until they were confiscated during the revolution in 1979, which also marked the beginning of my twenty-six-year exile in New York. Thankfully, many of my drawings were still in New York at Denise René's gallery, where I had a show in 1977, as well as at her Paris gallery that year.

The Serralves show is an honor for me. Suzanne was the first one to notice that my drawings are something different and deserve a special focus, particularly those that were made when I didn't have a studio following the early years of being exiled in the United States. Many of these drawings will be in Porto and New York, and they've never been exhibited before. Honest to God, I'm grateful to those who have helped me to get my work back into the world. From Chris Dercon at Tate Modern to Gary Tinterow at the Museum of Fine Arts in Houston to Hans Ulrich Obrist to Frank Stella to Suzanne, and to everyone else I might be missing.

Nan Goldin

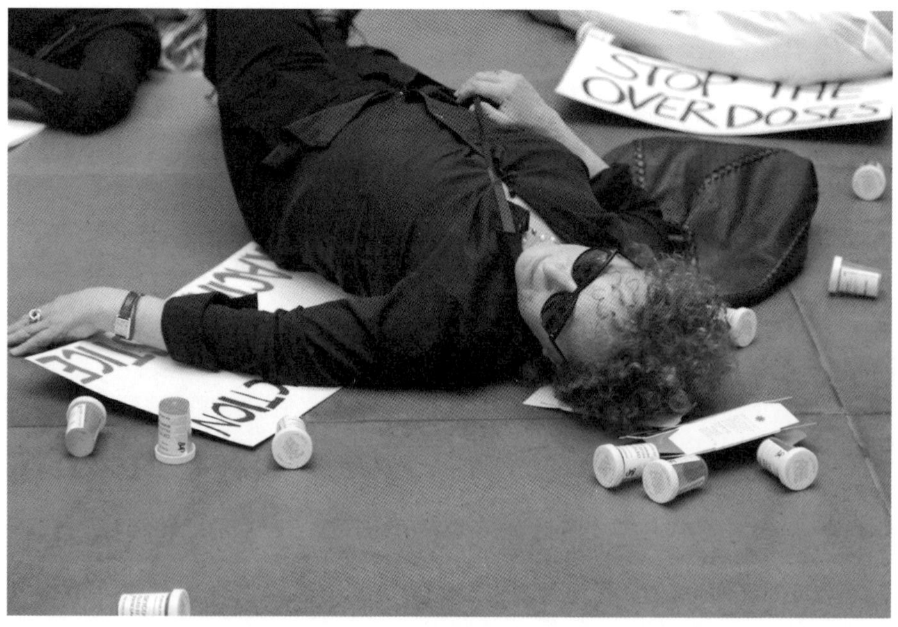

Nan Goldin in a protest at the Harvard Art Museums, Cambridge, MA, July 20, 2018.
Photo by TW Collins.

February 11, 2020
unpublished

In 2018, Nan Goldin organized the activist collective P.A.I.N. (Prescription Addiction Intervention Now), which led a series of protests in museums broadcasting the Sackler family's connections to the opioid crisis. Several of these institutions went on to reject Sackler family money. While writing an essay about photography and activism for Aperture *magazine, I spoke with Goldin about P.A.I.N., its influences, and its connection to* Witnesses: Against Our Vanishing, *the first New York exhibition about AIDS, which Goldin organized in 1989 at Artists Space.*

LOB: Do you see a connection between P.A.I.N. and *Witnesses*?

NG: In both cases they came out of my own personal concerns about what was going on, on the ground, rather than something that had already been framed or established. In the case of *Witnesses*, the show turned out to be the first one about AIDS in New York, which really surprised me at the time. P.A.I.N. began from my learning about the Sacklers' involvement with the opioid crisis through Patrick Radden Keefe's story for the *New Yorker*.

There's a lot of direct links. The opioid crisis is the epidemic of our times, like AIDS was, and it's also related to government malfunction and to the lack of medical practices and lack of prescriptions that are used to help people. They also share the same stigma, and so a lot of our work is to try to de-stigmatize addiction, and to educate people on that. Our battles are similar.

LOB: You've said that P.A.I.N. is based on ACT UP (AIDS Coalition to Unleash Power).

NG: ACT UP has been our model for P.A.I.N. because ACT UP has provided the most effective direct action in contemporary American history that I know of. They were fighting for their lives. They were very well organized. They worked well together. Whatever problems they had were discussed. They knew their targets and they went after them, sometimes by creating sexy media campaigns, as we now do. The main thing is that there was a deep truth behind them.

I watched ACT UP become huge. I wasn't really a member. I went to a few meetings and protests. But the important thing was that there was a lot of photography going on showing AIDS victims, as in Nicholas Nixon's work, which the community of people living with AIDS hated. They supported the work I was doing around the crisis. They told me that, and it was very important to me that I was working in parallel on some level.

LOB: How has working with P.A.I.N. affected your life?

NG: When I first started P.A.I.N., people said it would be dangerous—either because the Sacklers would come after me and do something like dox me, or that it was dangerous from my position in the art world. And I didn't even think about that. It seemed like it was more important that it had to be done—to speak out in this way. It has not, to my knowledge, hurt me in the art world. In fact, now there's an embrace of activism in the art world for whatever reason. I have no idea what goes on behind the scenes, whether or not I'm taken out of group shows or by museums, whatever. But P.A.I.N. has been more important to me than propelling my art career. Even if it has hurt me, it doesn't matter.

LOB: Does P.A.I.N. work with affinity groups?

NG: Yes. We work with a group called Vocal New York, which is on the ground and in the Black and brown community. They're very active and have been for I think about ten years or more. They fight against mass incarceration. They were instrumental in the new bail reform laws and the new tenants' rights. We work with them on the opioid crisis, predominantly. We also collaborate with Housing Works, which has existed since the AIDS crisis. We go to their demonstrations and they come to ours. We've gone to their offices to get Narcan training.

Our small group of twelve in P.A.I.N. has brought Big Pharma and its money into public awareness. But I've also been told that we've become ground zero for other activists' groups and campaigns to get attention. In fact, we just got off the phone with a student at Tufts, where they had scrubbed down the Sackler name from a building.

Nancy Goldring

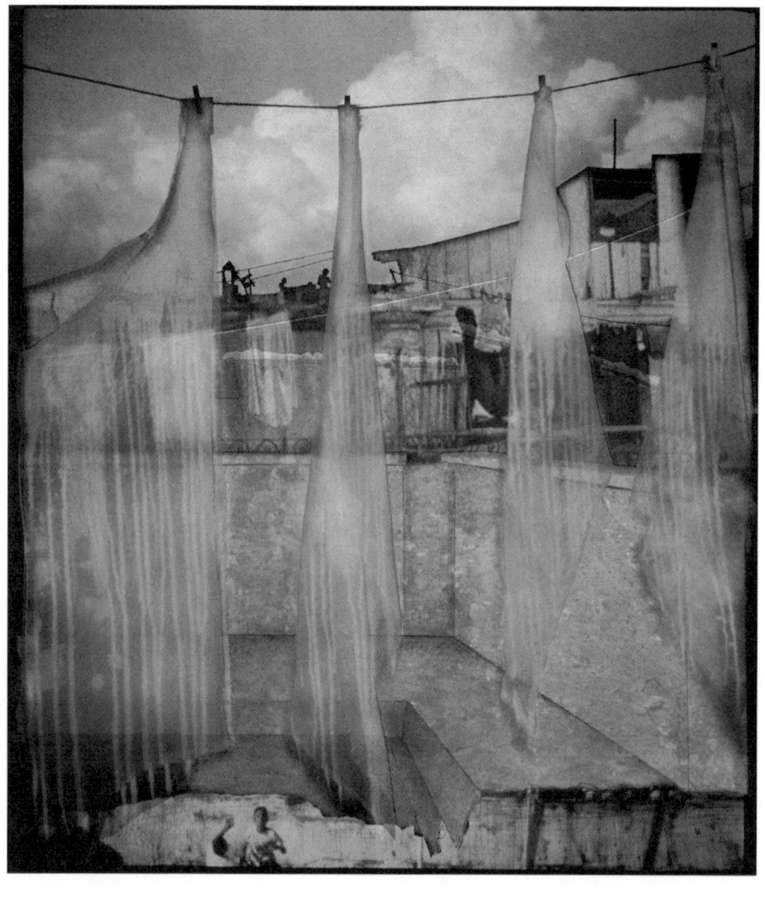

Nancy Goldring, *La Guarida*, 2011, framed Cibachrome, photographic projection, 30 × 34 inches (76.2 × 86.4 cm).

September 28, 2018
Artforum

The New York–based artist Nancy Goldring has sustained a profound inter-est in perspective and analytical representations of space. In tandem, she has fine-tuned her awareness of the ultimate fiction of both by homing in on a place and then disrupting it, via a destruction of the static, privileged monocular view. A solo show of her "foto-projections," as she calls her multifaceted work, was on view at Carrie Haddad Gallery in Hudson, New York, in fall 2018.

One of the main lines of inquiry that has driven my work for so many years concerns how to conjure place—whether a dreamscape, a town or country, somewhere you've never been, or the studio in which you spend your days. The challenge is to find a way that can encompass how you anticipate it, how you encounter it, how you remember it and store it away, and what it reminds you of. In that respect, the notion of place is open-ended, and my work is not so much about picturing a place as about finding a way to represent our experience of it in the fullest sense. Some places I've gotten to know over long periods of time, like Italy, but I have spent many years traveling around the world—from Indonesia to China to Syria to Sri Lanka to Cuba—mostly through grants, trying to understand where I was by making extensive drawings and taking photographs. These document the place and, at the same time, reveal the notion that we can never fully grasp what we see. The process then becomes an intense strug-gle to fathom what's unknown and unknowable. It sets in high relief that you can never fully understand a place, while underscoring the importance of trying.

I never intended to develop a singular technique as many photographers do. It's more like Wallace Stevens writes in "So-And-So Reclining on Her Couch," where the poem becomes a pendulum moving between the mechanism or apparition and back again to the invisible gesture that suspended it, in a condition of constant change. For some of the works, there's a general procedure from which I often deviate. There's the drawing that works out what I see and will become the model for the finished piece, essentially serving as the architecture, and meanwhile, I'm shooting lots of slides, gathering material. I then craft a relief model based on the drawings: a collage that suggests a more profound space than a flat surface could provide. After that, I take snippets of the slides by masking them out, and using three, four, or even five projectors, I meld them into a single image by projecting them simultaneously onto the model—some from the front and some from the rear—and take a picture. And then I change the slides and continue the process. The layering becomes an archaeology or history of the encounter with that place.

Besides restructuring space, I frequently play with scale. I might have taken a picture of a rock and then projected it onto a composition so it reads as a mountain. This kind of experimentation is potentially endless, and at a certain point I stop when I feel I have suggested that the possibilities are infinite. Piet Mondrian's *Pier and Ocean* series of 1917 has always been a great influence in the way it negotiates the notion of the infinite by pushing it to the edge of legibility toward abstraction, while nonetheless insisting on its meaning as place.

I have never used slides taken in one place for another piece. It's important that the images are built of actual material to make them authentic or true. I don't know exactly why that is, or why it's so important to me, but it gives some guidelines to the process. For instance, while making the series *Via dei Solitari*—which friends thought was a nod to romantic solitude but is in fact titled after the street where I lived that leads up to a monastery in Sarteano, Italy—I drew the same view for four to five hours a day. It was difficult to render because of the medieval town's structure with its winding, interconnected streets. But after about five weeks, I felt I nailed it. I find this way of drawing helps to crystallize or fix the place so indelibly that I can draw it without looking. I had also been photographing that vista and its surrounding landscape. The photographic material then reappears cropped and resituated in the "foto-projections." In this way, they suggest how we move through the town gates, carrying the landscape with us. In this series, I'm conflating time and space, past and present, into a single image that's both townscape and landscape. There are, of course, many examples of artists capturing a place as they felt it, but I'm more interested in negating the concept of a single vantage point to correspond more accurately to human experience.

I still use analog methods because digital doesn't create the kind of space I'm trying to evoke. The latter describes forms through precise edges rather than chiaroscuro modeling, which is a different system entirely. And for forms to seem to recede into the remote distance you also need to deploy atmospheric perspective—things should appear to disappear, dissolving as they approach the vantage point. Analog systems work better for creating this effect. As I project onto the model, the light creates profound shadows, heightening the sense of depth. I intend for the work to end up assuming a convincing level of realism, improbable though the views are. I've been surprised to see people interact with my installations, mistaking the illusion for reality by putting a hand through what they thought was a tunnel or field. It's fun to watch their response as they realize their credulity.

Nell Painter

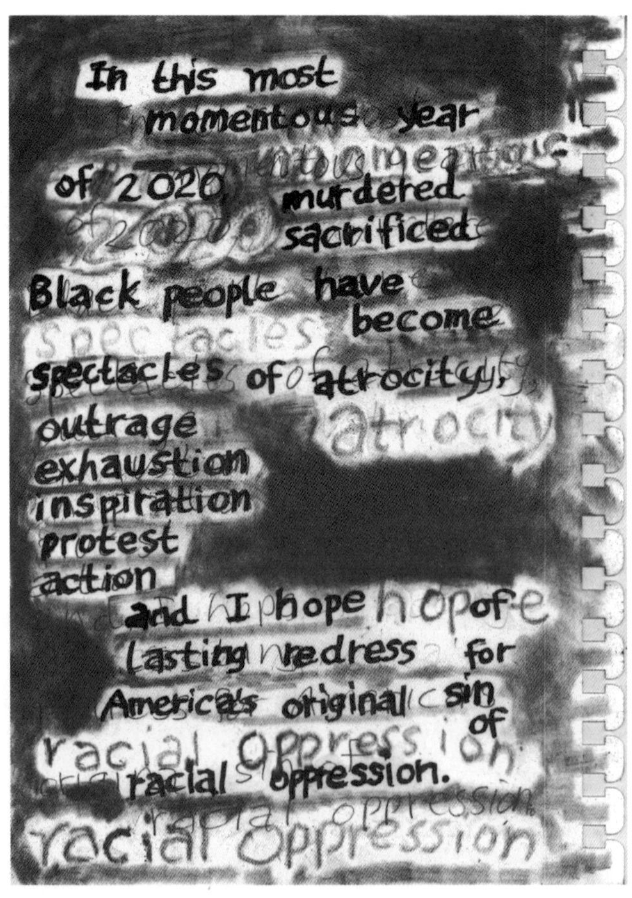

Nell Painter, *From Slavery to Freedom*, 2020, artist's book.

September 29, 2018
November

I met the Newark-based artist Nell Painter a decade ago at the Rhode Island School of Design (RISD): I was "too young" to be teaching a graduate theory and criticism seminar, and Nell was in the class, "too old" to be an art student. It didn't take long to realize that she was Nell Irvin Painter, esteemed scholar of history and race, whose best-selling book The History of White People *(2010) was just about to be published.* Old in Art School *(2018), Nell's eighth book of nonfiction, is a wonderfully frank reflection on her brave years as an art student after her decades spent as a prizewinning, tenured academic. In 2019, her solo exhibitions* Freedom from Truth: Self Portraits of Nell Painter *and* Odalisque Atlas: White History as Told through Art *were mounted at Harvard. Earlier this summer, she published a new commissioned artist's book,* From Slavery to Freedom. *Curious to hear more about this book and her recent art, I reached out to Nell after so many years. The interview was conducted in September 2020.*

LOB: You begin *From Slavery to Freedom* with a text that seems to have been written and rewritten over and over: it speaks of your "hope for a lasting redress of America's original sin of racial oppression." All of the script throughout the book has this liminal quality and I wondered if perhaps the two yous, historian/writer and artist, are collaborating?

NP: You are absolutely right about writing and rewriting and absolutely right about my "two yous" in collaboration while always contending over coherence. Historian/writer strives for discursive legibiity, so that consumer takes away what producer put in. As a scholarly historian and even as an op-ed writer, I wanted to take my readers by the hand rhetorically, and lead them down my path, the path that I had laid out for them in words.

This is not how I make art, in part because such a legible visual surface looks boring. Historian/writer wants intelligibility, but artist wants emotion, feeling, intensity of meaning that will not necessarily be viewed in the ways I was creating. Historian/writer always wants more words; artist keeps taking words out, or if not taking words away, then overwriting and obscuring them in the interest of intensity, of touching viewers first in the eye rather than in the mind.

Historian/writer named my artist's book after an iconic textbook of African American history, John Hope Franklin's enduring *From Slavery to Freedom*, first published in 1947 and now in its ninth edition. I knew Professor Franklin personally, not only as a path-breaking historian, but also as the creator of horticultural beauty. John Hope Franklin raised orchids. There's even one named after him: the Phalaenopsis *John Hope Franklin*. For me as both historian and artist, Professor Franklin wrote across the color line and cherished flowers that were not objects of racial classification.

The spirit infusing my art differs from that of Franklin's classic text, which tells you what you need to know once and for all. For me as historian as well as artist, meanings change as the times change and as the author/artist changes. My history writing now, as well as my art, insists first and last that things change. One aspect of change is varying readers/viewers, each of whom brings something different to my work and so also takes away different meanings.

There's more to my use of the terms *slavery* and *freedom* in this momentous year of 2020, when George-Floyd-Black-Lives-Matter anti-racism demonstrations pitch their struggles against police-brutality-racism-Confederate-monuments/flags-Trumpy-militias-Nazis. That's what I mean when I quote *slavery* (police-brutality-racism-Confederate-monuments/flags-Trumpy-militias-Nazis) and *freedom* (George-Floyd-Black-Lives-Matter-anti-racism demonstrations). So my artist's book begins with *slavery* as in victims of racist murders, as in the Confederate flag, the song "Dixie," and Confederate statuary.

Freedom is glimpsed in the words of "God Bless America" and further envisioned as Juneteenth, as its proclamation and its celebration, literally, of freedom. My book ends with "Lift Ev'ry Voice and Sing," what's now called the "Black National Anthem" but that I grew up with in the twentieth century as the proud "Negro National Anthem." An anthem of optimism in frightful times, which haven't yet ended. That may, in the United States, never end.

A word about the perforations running along the side of each panel: the perforated pages that come from my sketchbook turn the work away from the panels associated with precious fine art and make them into pages of a book, with its connotations of multiples and publication and wide circulation.

LOB: How did the book come about and can you talk about the process of making it?

NP: Since becoming a visual artist in 2011 I'm unable to think or write without visualization. Whenever I think of a narrative, images crowd into my mind. *From Slavery to Freedom* sprang from my engagement with the exciting, chaotic, inspiring, frightening, hopeful spring of 2020. But its form belongs to other work I've been making since last winter. In February I had an artist's residency in the Bogliasco Foundation in Liguria, Italy, where my artist's book project was *American Whiteness Since Trump.* This project picks up from my last scholarly book in 2010, *The History of White People,* a *New York Times* best seller that has only increased in interest since 2016. In February–March in Italy, I was making *American Whiteness Since Trump* but had to stop working on it when the pandemic shut everything down. So *American Whiteness Since Trump* ends in mid-March 2020, before coronavirus upended our lives and before the political events that have been making 2020 momentous. *From Slavery to Freedom* skips the pandemic but confronts the protests of the spring of 2020.

Between *American Whiteness Since Trump* and *From Slavery to Freedom,* I published a photo book on the MacDowell website of my life from escaping Italy in mid-March, refugeeing up here to the Adirondacks (where I remain now with my husband), and being laid low with coronavirus lethargy. What overcame lethargy was the protests and demonstrations that began in June, even in the Adirondacks. We joined two up here, and I wrote and drew and wrote and drew in the excitement of that time. My favorite piece from the early summer appeared in the *Paris Review,* entitled "On Horseback," pulling together my delight on seeing protesters riding horses with my own autobiography and my own art.

From Slavery to Freedom, responding to the protests of spring 2020, was actually a commission from Aferro Gallery in Newark. In terms of process, it proceeded in two steps: first, I drew and collaged the basic pages of the book; then I manipulated those pages digitally, so that the handmade cover, largely in yellow, became overwhelmingly blue after digital manipulation, with digitization emphasizing the texture of the graphite ground. The final piece exists only digitally, though the next-to-last step exists physically.

LOB: You once said, "In art, I can delve into what I can't know as a historian, imagining images that historiography can't document. That's a freedom that artist Nell Painter can exploit, but historian Nell Irvin Painter must back away from." Do you feel that's the case with this artist book?

NP: Yes, freedom from the facts of history is very much a part of *From Slavery to Freedom*, because my artist's book doesn't make the rhetorically necessary connections between, say, the song lyrics I quote, people on horseback, the names of victims of racial violence, Confederates tumbling down, and my own thoughts. My art is infinitely more personal than my scholarly history, so you can look at my art without necessarily following my train of thought. Just look. I want you to look for a while and let some images and some thoughts cross your mind's eye.

Digital manipulation inserts a crucial step between the manually produced image and the final image, a step away from what might have been historical accuracy and into something akin to abstraction. This step I deeply appreciate. For me, digitization is akin to post-studio manipulation of popular music, which produces entirely new sounds with no pretense or necessary relation to what comes out of acoustic instruments. Many of the instruments don't even exist acoustically. Computers have their own logic, in music and in image.

LOB: Have you been making art since finishing *From Slavery to Freedom*? Or mostly writing?

NP: Oh, lord! I've been writing and drawing up a storm, despite coronavirus lethargy. My website now has (or soon will have) a special section on what I made and wrote in 2020, when the George Floyd–Black Lives Matter upheaval sent editors scurrying after Black writers. So in addition to two existing commitments (an essay on the painter Alma Thomas and preparation of the second edition of my essay collection *Southern History Across the Color Line* for the University of North

Carolina Press), I contributed written essays to the *New Yorker*, *NBC Think*, *Washington Post*, and *Paris Review*, and the MacDowell website I already mentioned.

We've already spoken about *From Slavery to Freedom*, which I completed at the end of June. Right now I'm working on a piece whose shape I don't yet know but which originated in a Holocaust diary that ends with the phrase, "It is impossible to know the date of the murder of the author of this diary." I posted a couple of my new pieces on Instagram, as works in progress, as I feel my way in a narrative whose poignancy touched me deeply.

LOB: Could you talk a little bit about the shows you had at Harvard last year and specifically about your interests in self-portraiture? The exhibition *Freedom from Truth*, which featured some of these works, also seemed like a reference to your biography of Sojourner Truth, is that correct?

NP: My curator, Jonathan Square, had first approached me a few years ago about showing the *Black Sea Composite Maps* of my *Odalisque Atlas* series at NYU. That show didn't come to fruition, but Jonathan kept my work in mind, for which I'm grateful. In the fall of 2019, he mounted two shows of my work at Harvard, one of *Black Sea Composite Maps*, the other of self-portraits, loosely construed.

In conjunction with the opening of the shows, one of my former graduate students, Walter Johnson, now a professor of history at Harvard, and I had a public conversation on some of the issues you and I are talking about now. In January 2020 the *Boston Review* published our pieces on my shows.

You're quite right that *Freedom from Truth*, the title of the self-portrait show, resonates with my biography of Sojourner Truth (*Sojourner Truth: A Life, A Symbol*), so, yes, Jonathan's title and choice of pieces to show utterly delighted me. My self-portraits hew less and more closely to my personal appearance, not trying for verisimilitude. They began at Mason Gross as exercises in figurative painting, for in art school I didn't have any dark-skinned models, so I used myself as a handy model for practicing up on painting dark skin, because I knew figuration would be part of my art.

Even beyond convenience, it was freeing for me to use myself, because I didn't care if I made myself look too dark or too light, too cute or too ugly—which could have caused problems with other models on account of the politics of Black imagery being so fraught. Theorists like Deborah Willis have written whole books on "the Black body" (e.g., *The Black Female Body: A Photographic History*, 2002, and *Posing Beauty: African American Images, 1890 to the Present*, 2009) and how it's portrayed. I could avoid all that by just painting myself. So I painted and drew and digitally manipulated my own image ad infinitum. I haven't made self-portraits recently, for current events and historical politics have consumed my art. Self-portraits are bound to return, later rather than sooner, however, the way the times are going.

LOB: Were you making self-portraits when you were at RISD? I seem to remember you were.

NP: I made at least twenty-five small (12 by 12 inches on paper) self-portraits at RISD in a winter session class I deeply resented, having been forced to take it to compensate for being such a bad painter. One of my RISD painting teachers would start our every studio visit with "You can't draw, and you can't paint." Ninny that I was, I not only believed her, I thought being able to draw and paint really mattered deeply, which any perusal of art magazines or gallery tours will quickly disprove. Another of my RISD teachers assured me that I'd "never be an artist." That, thankfully, I immediately recognized and denounced as criminally bad teaching and total bullshit.

So I was being punished for being a bad painter by having to take what was basically an undergraduate painting class, in which I did, in fact, live up to expectations by painting very badly. But somehow the self-portrait assignment intrigued me, and relishing the task, I made twenty-five self-portraits. One of them served as the advertisement for a visual arts course I taught back at Princeton in 2015.

LOB: My favorite passages in *Old in Art School* are those in which you talk about recognizing the total bullshit being proffered by such bad teachers, and in crits. It's enlivening to read you on those topics—the way you rightly call out both the art world and art schools as sexist, ageist, and racist. I have noticed that over the past decade much has changed and is still changing: decolonized syllabi and a great importance placed on hiring BIPOC teachers and speakers, for instance. Do you think this bodes well for art schools? I know you recognize how deeply the problems are entrenched in most of them, despite the claims of inclusion.

NP: Turns toward inclusion certainly bode well but turns alone won't suffice for real improvement unless there's lasting change. The many kinds of consciousness raising taking place now really are encouraging, but consciousness raising is hard and, while hard, takes only a first few steps. Existing institutions may throw up their hands when they discover that they can't just turn to some neat, monolithic "Black community" for solutions. Black people aren't a monolith. Even Black arts people aren't a monolith. It'll mean engaging with relevant Black people, not just throwing up hands and quitting.

As for lazy teaching, I think inclusion will help there because so much education (of teachers, of artists, of curators, of critics) will be taking place. I happen to enjoy learning things, so I hope teachers, artists, curators, and critics would also feel rewarded as they learn about art and artists that had been ignored or obscured. I imagine the pleasure a teacher of painting might feel in exploring, say, Robert Colescott's paint handling and strategies of composition.

LOB: You said a few years ago that there's room in our culture to be interesting and female, and interesting and Black, but hardly any room in our culture to be interesting and old. Do you still feel that way? I've noticed things seem to be changing in the art world—art writers winning grants to cover women artists aged seventy and over, for instance.

NP: A few old women artists have entered the limelight recently, it's true. My favorites are two painters who have been doing exciting work for almost half a century each, Howardena Pindell and Jaune Quick to-See-Smith. But things improving for old women artists is like things improving for Black Americans. Things improve. But things stay awful. For myself, an old woman artist, I make the art I want to make, knowing it will most likely not attract a massive following. Artists' books are not an earth-shaking genre, and the subject matter that intrigues me doesn't necessarily address what American culture wants from Black artists: commentary on race in America now. Within the context of the Art World, with its obsession with youth, whether or not things improve for old women artists isn't a theme that preoccupies me.

LOB: Shifting to recent events: What are your thoughts on the Black Lives Matter (BLM) protests worldwide? Do you believe they will cause changes in US or global culture, and if so, how?

NP: Nationwide, worldwide protests against police brutality and in support of Black Lives Matter thrilled me deeply. As I said above, my husband and I participated in two actions up here in the Adirondacks, both attracting unheard-of support—about 150 people in Keene/ Keene Valley and some 500 people in Saranac Lake. The sheer magnitude of people in the streets moved me, and the heterogeneity struck me as new and crucial if ever the United States is to move past white supremacy or even make an enduring dent in it. I don't know if either positive outcome is possible. That may be asking too much of the mass of American white people. Already there's backlash, much of it mean-spirited, some of it heavily armed. And even among those who are well intentioned, it's hard to face up to ugly realities of American history and society. It's hard for many even to pronounce the words *racism* and *Black*.

I remember the Civil Rights Movement of the 1960s, which cost so many lives, literally. Backlash snuffed out promise then, as it may do again now. Nonetheless, 2020 feels different from 1968 to me, given masses of non-Black people insisting that Black Lives Matter, given two generations' worth of African American studies' accumulation of knowledge and cultural power, and given the widespread nature of attestations of intentions to diversify virtually all sectors of American life. I have all my fingers crossed and am doing what I can in the places where I have influence to ensure this future doesn't replay 1968.

LOB: Were you still living in Los Angeles in '68? Could you tell us a little more about your life then—what it was like to come back to the United States during this period of snuffed-out promise, specifically after studying at the Institute of African Studies in Ghana in 1965–66?

NP: Geez, where the hell was I in 1968? Yes, UCLA and my secret year teaching in San Jose. So much was going on in the world, in the United States, and in my life then! I had left Ghana after the coup d'état that deposed Kwame Nkruma, so Ghana was no longer looking like a hopeful beginning for African politics, and we Black American pan-Africanists (Maya Angelou included) scattered. In the United States there was the Vietnam War, during which I was among those in the streets protesting. In California I felt confused and alienated, spent a lot of time with one of my French professors of African history with whom I could speak French, and set some distance between me and USA-chaos. In San Jose I was teaching at the City College, where my colleagues and older Black students felt to me like rewards, but a few younger Black students who fancied themselves Black Panthers briefly threatened me if I didn't give them good grades they hadn't earned. The older students put that down, but the experience sent me back to graduate school, to Harvard.

LOB: Just to back us up even further, you studied at UC Berkeley in the early 1960s, which must have been incredible—I noticed you were recently quoted in a *New York Times* article about Kamala Harris's parents (who also met at Berkeley around the same time, in a Black study group). I was curious to hear more than the one line the writer quoted from you; were you involved in that group? Or any political groups at the time?

NP: Yes, I was political, but not a leader. I've always been more of a reader. I certainly picketed the Bank of America on Telegraph Avenue and attended the meetings mentioned in the *Times* piece, which I now see were laying the groundwork for African American studies. I hung out at Stiles Hall and International House and had international friends, some through my father, who worked in the College of Chemistry and mentored many graduate students. But I never really fit anywhere—I *still* don't fit anywhere. My left-leaning family was well educated, hardly wealthy, but not poor. Who could be more distinctly uncool than me, a middle-class Black woman! These were the years of Eldridge Cleaver, with his violent masculinist bravado and mean-spirited misogyny. In those days there was "the Black man," period.

LOB: Do you think the BLM protests will cause changes in the art world, and if so, how?

NP: Though limited in scope, changes in cultural leadership that began before the George Floyd protests seem to be continuing in a positive direction. While the loss of experienced leaders who may have been perpetuating exclusionary habits looks like a good thing, I hope new leaders, BIPOC leaders, will receive the support and mentoring they absolutely will need to pull institutions out of this time of pandemic-related chaos and financial need.

I hope also that arts institutions will be able to accomplish two hard tasks: first, acknowledging the racism that shaped their creation and longtime habits of doing business, when the prevailing pattern has been to cover up and pretend white supremacy did not affect how things got done in one's own institution. Princeton University seems to be doing a decent job of owning up; I have my fingers crossed for improvement. Second, the close relationship between rich people and arts institutions needs reform. Looking at the millions that museums were spending on buildings prompted my dismay years ago. Looking further at the tight relationship between private trophy collections of blue-chip artists and the entry of those collections into museums, I can't see how museums can become more publicly responsive, more racially diverse, if dependence upon very rich donors and boards continues.

The arts institutions of my city of Newark—Newark, a city of Black power, which matters deeply—have been forging ties between Newark artists and performers and the public for more than a generation by now. Newark can show the way toward more democratic art worlds in which a variety of artists and publics and institutions coexist.

LOB: Of your many books, do you have a favorite? Or is there one that you consider your most important work? And why?

NP: For years I felt *The Narrative of Hosea Hudson* was my favorite, because I enjoyed collaborating with this Southern Black communist with his firmly held opinions. He felt kind of like a grandfather to me, as my mother's father had died before my birth, and I only met my father's father once briefly when I was a girl. After Hudson and I finished our book, I took him to meet my Knopf editor, whom Hudson lectured on politics. For Hudson, a true-to-life communist, both Republicans and Democrats were the same, as opposed to communists, who were right. My editor rejected our book on account of Hudson's not "tugging at our heartstrings," which Hudson certainly didn't do—part of what I liked about him. My introduction to that book is in my essay collection, *Southern History Across the Color Line*, whose second edition comes out in April.

Now, though, I think *Old in Art School* is my favorite, for talking personally and showing my art as works in progress. I also appreciate readers' responses to my memoir, which are also personal. I feel like my memoir is doing good work in the world on a personal basis, especially for women.

LOB: Same questions as above regarding your art! Is there an essential piece or series?

NP: This also is hard, because in art as in writing, the most recent piece is the most beloved. But two pieces I made at Mason Gross as an undergraduate feel true as self-portraits and as instances of why I make art. I know *Alternator Self-Portrait,* 2008, inspired in part by Marcel Duchamp, was in the Harvard self-portrait show that Jonathan Square curated. The other, *Chapter Revised*, 2007, is not in *Old in Art School,* and I don't think was in the Harvard show. Both these pieces visualize my "two yous" as historian/writer and as visual artist.

Pauline Oliveros

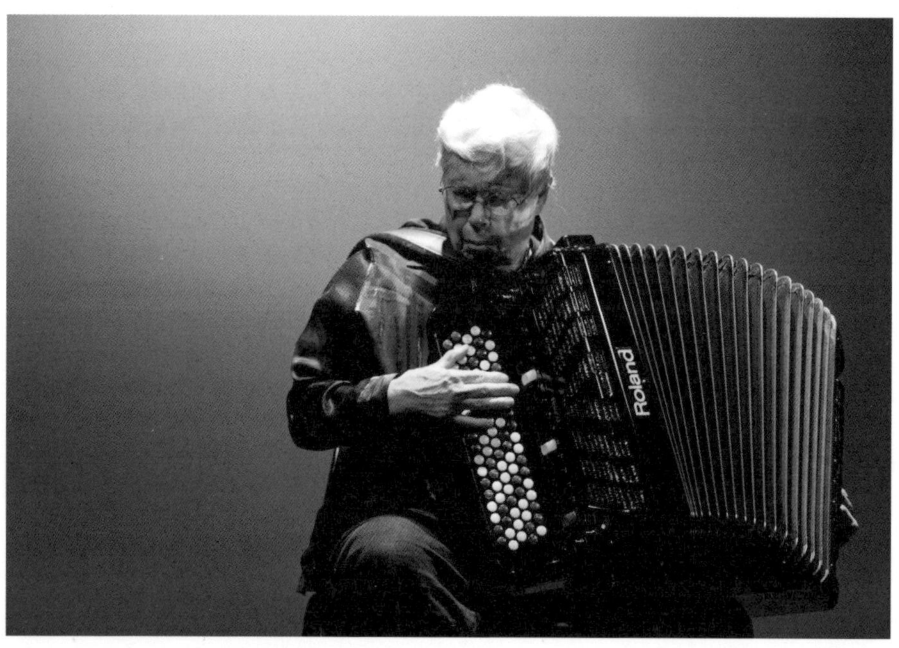

Pauline Oliveros performing at the Centre Pompidou, Paris, in January 2011, photo by Vinciane Verguethen.

April 30, 2012
Artforum

Composer and educator Pauline Oliveros was the recipient of the 2012 John Cage Award. In the same year, she presented the keynote address at the Her Noise symposium at Tate Modern, which was followed by a performance of a score from 1970 that she describes below.

Turning eighty has been fantastic. Forty years ago, people weren't so familiar with performance, and they certainly didn't know my work very well. But now esteemed groups such as the International Contemporary Ensemble play my compositions, and it's very heartening. Receiving this year's John Cage Award was a total and welcome surprise, too. I thought this would be a relaxing time in my life—a time to retire! I was wrong.

As Cage said, composing is organizing sounds in time—and you're a composer if you're organizing the way sounds manifest in duration. It certainly isn't necessary to be a schooled musician who knows how to notate pitches on a staff. Nonetheless, I've still noticed that women have had a more difficult time actually calling themselves *composers*. So many women go to school to study English or theory or musicology. Perhaps they don't enter the composition programs because they don't have enough role models who are women, and this must change. Several composers, and some former students of mine, are working toward amending that: Clara Tomaz, Maria Chavez, Jaclyn Heyen, Brenda Hutchinson, and Ellen Fullman.

In 1970, shortly after I read the *SCUM Manifesto*, I finished a piece that we'll perform at the Her Noise symposium—*To Valerie Solanas and Marilyn Monroe in Recognition of Their Desperation.* I remember that I was impressed with Solanas's politics and her structural thinking, and I began to wonder how a more equal distribution of rights in society could be manifested or paralleled in music. Monroe had died eight years earlier, and after Solanas shot Warhol in 1968, I began to see a connection between Monroe's and Solanas's lives as the growing, and very exciting, women's movement gained momentum. I titled the piece this way not because I wanted to directly comment on Solanas or Monroe, but rather to reference the women's movement in general and its various sides and the significant effects it was having on culture.

Structurally, the piece is based on Solanas's exposition about equality and overall it's nonhierarchical: each musician chooses five different pitches and one of the pitches has to be in a different dissonant relationship to the others. There are three sections to the work that correspond with lighting overhead—a yellow, red, and blue section. In a way, these changes really conduct the piece, as the players have to perceive them to understand the queue. The duration of each section depends on what's happening, on what the musicians decide to do. It could be a very long meditation, with each part lasting more than thirty minutes.

In the first section, the players can only work with one pitch, and somewhere in the middle of that a photoflash goes off and then the second part begins. Then the musicians are free to imitate the pitches the other players are using, so there's some exchange that begins to happen. They can actually modify those pitches, articulating them in very different ways, and they begin to play with different qualities of sound. In the middle section they introduce four more pitches each. In the last section they return to their first choices. Finally, there's another photoflash and after that they're back to the very first pitches they chose and they work it back toward the end of the piece. Of course, this is a *very* broad outline of the piece. We'll see how it goes in London.

Polly Apfelbaum

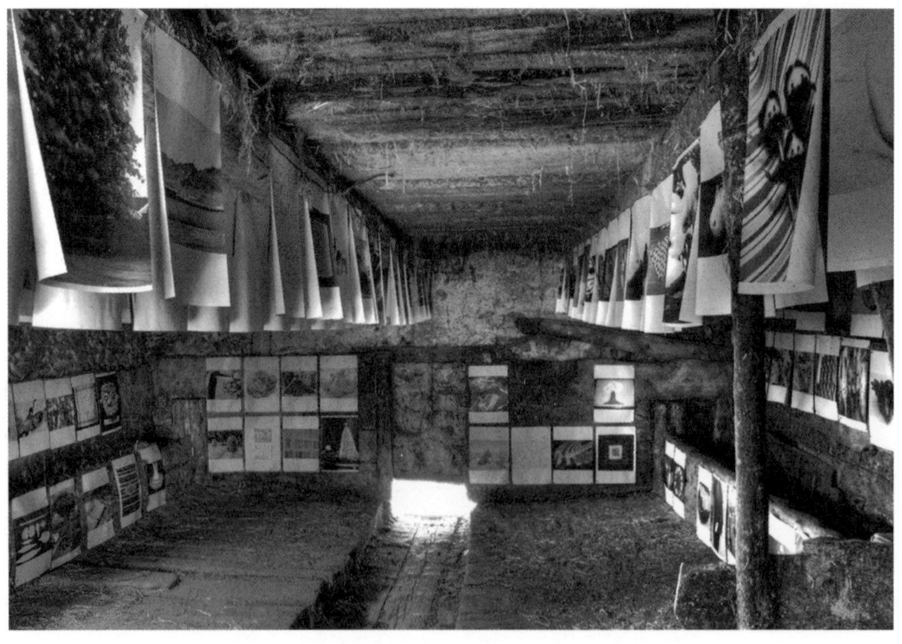

Installation view of *Haunted House*, 2011.

May 19, 2011
Artforum

Polly Apfelbaum's summer 2011 exhibition at the Atelier Amden in Switzerland featured a four-hundred-page poster book–atlas, which she discusses here.

Haunted house. That's the first thing that came to mind when I was asked to do this show, which will be installed in a tiny mountain refuge, accessible only by hiking there. No electricity, no plumbing. There's a haunted house where we go in upstate New York, and I'm sort of obsessed with it. My friend calls it a hillbilly meth lab, and it might be one of those. I've never dared to go in. I began thinking about fears—what could be in a place like that? Why are we so afraid of abandoned shacks anyway?—and for nearly six months I've found myself combing through Google, searching for images that, at least for me, conjure the feeling of a haunted house. But the idea for the show also came from actually taking a house apart. My father-in-law had lived in his house for fifty years, and as we were going through it we found so many pictures, the kind you'd see at a flea market or tag sale. These are such meaningful objects filled with memories that are sometimes just left behind. So I thought it would be interesting to use Google to make a collection of random images that seem similarly discarded. I decided to make an atlas of images for a haunted house.

It's a poster book and there are 350 images in it—pictures of old children's projects, family vacations, nature shots, and crude craft projects. It features everything from Noah's ark to piñatas, from Hong Kong to the Wild West, rainbow-colored pancakes to forget-me-nots. There will be one unbound copy so that visitors can choose an image to take.

It's the first time I've distributed my art that way—although people have been known to walk off with random parts of my work. But there will also be some moonshine they're welcome to take too. I wanted to bring the hillbilly to this pristine alpine location in Switzerland.

I do think often about how places have memories and how those can be just floating around in the air. With all of the images on the Internet, it's like they're floating around there too. I wanted to materialize these images because I think we're losing something without the concrete object. I mean, does anyone print out family photos now? I still love having them, even if that's very strange. But I've begun to embrace Google too, especially the randomness of what it means when you search for "haunted house" and you get a picture of somebody's dog.

To me, this new work seems very abstract, even if the pictures are representations of people, places, or things. All of this falls in line with the rest of my art. I'm either trying to get to abstraction or beginning with it. There has always been a tension between those elements in my work. In the past few years, I've changed the way I work in my studio. I spend more time thinking about how to make the work and how to play with elements of chance. So when I discovered the massive amount of images on Google and realized that I could even take them as I wanted, I was like a very bad kid in a very big candy store.

Rachel Foullon

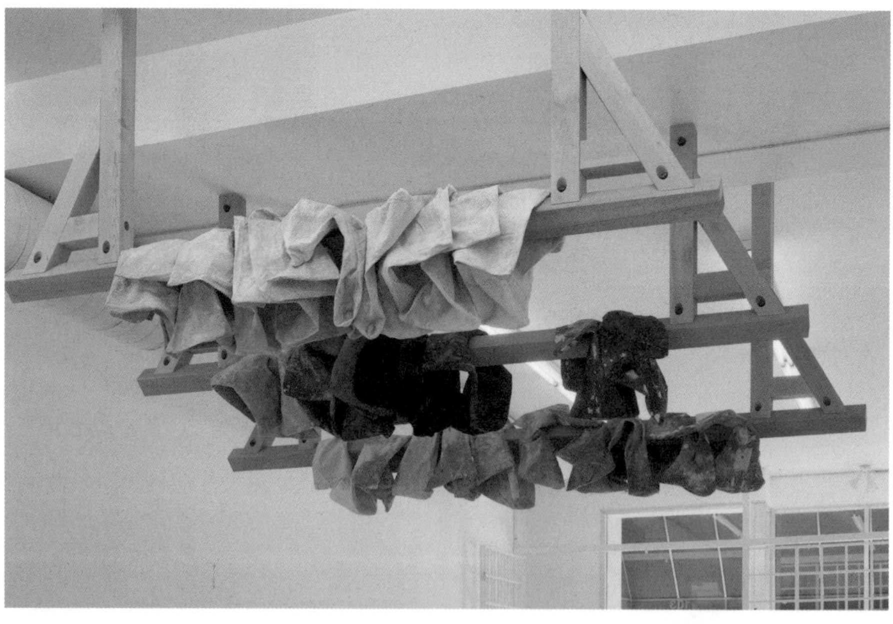

Rachel Foullon, *The Abacus*, 2010, canvas, Western red cedar, dye, stain, and hardware, 56 × 114 × 96 inches (142.2 × 289.6 × 243.8 cm), installation view.

March 9, 2010
Artforum

The Los Angeles–based artist Rachel Foullon has exhibited her work widely and was a founding member of the curatorial initiative Public Holiday Projects. Here, she talks about her first solo exhibition in Los Angeles, at ltd, held during spring 2010.

This exhibition is entitled *An Accounting*, and the twofold definition (with references to economics and narrative) applies. At ltd, a sizable new gallery founded by Los Angeles collector Shirley Morales, I'll be showing my largest sculptures to date. The scale will provide an atmospheric contrast to my show last fall in New York at Nicelle Beauchene Gallery, where I maximized the use of a smaller space by creating a dense, workshoplike environment that fostered an appropriate sense of intimacy. My work of the past couple of years has referenced specific types of barns and rural dwellings wherein living quarters for humans, livestock, and work animals are all combined under one roof that also houses tools and food storage: it's an original live-work scenario of potentially the most grueling and imagery-rich kind. I'm dealing with the same thematic locale in this show, but it's almost as if we step outside the barn (there's a little more fresh air out here, no?) and begin to refer to a few more of the players on this landscape of self-reliance.

The centerpiece of the show is a ceiling-mounted sculpture called *The Abacus*. Built from Western red cedar four-by-fours, the piece is milled, finished, and assembled with a sensibility akin to furniture making. The abacus's familiar horizontal bars are oriented in relation to the ceiling, so the viewer passes underneath it like a short-lived arcade. Its structure is derived from the *Hallenhaus*—Saxon farmhouses that conjoined the house and barn functions in one and made their way to North America in the 1600s. These barns share the same architectural origins as churches. In the abacus's design, the supporting diagonal braces have been turned outward, like a ballet plié, making room for the traditional counting beads.

The beads are cut and sewn from canvas, each as a Möbius strip with a hole in its center. I came on the Möbius strip lurking within functional design in England in 2005, when I purchased a bundle of household rags from an agricultural fair. They were made from rectangular pieces of fabric that, when given a half twist and folded before being seamed together, created an endless surface with an enigmatic sense of volume, excellent for cleaning, as well as for accessing ideas of infinity. This form's usage in *The Abacus* relates to the cyclical passage of seasons, harvests, generations, and an iteration of time as a stretchable shape. It's like Mark Twain's axiom, "History doesn't repeat itself, but it rhymes," or a dog chasing its own tail.

Each bead is individually dyed using cold-process fiber-reactive dyes and a low-water immersion technique, which yields a random marbling effect. As the viewer passes beneath the abacus, the color progression of the beads is like that of pale flesh being slowly cooked, browning and then burning black, then bursting open as something red is exposed, revealed and visually intense. The rawness subsides and scars pink. This color event is an abstract idea, but it serves as a methodology to create an experience that's visually explosive and saturated in relation to ideas of something graphic and full of life, desirable albeit painful. Such is the seduction and intensity of living close to animals and the land. I'm interested in a contemporary relationship to that desire, as well as the parallel of the farm to an artist's studio. While this room-size abacus isn't interactive (it doesn't hang low enough for a viewer to "use"), the experience is one that's definitely bodily.

The Abacus is an accounting device that tells the story of how something sustains or survives. Its economy belongs to collective cultural memory. An abacus doesn't record or store historical data like a computer can, but counts and takes stock of the present moment. Much like the all-in-one space of the *Hallenhaus* barn, it looks both backward and forward and, in this way, is a reckoning of past, present, and future time.

Rachel Mason

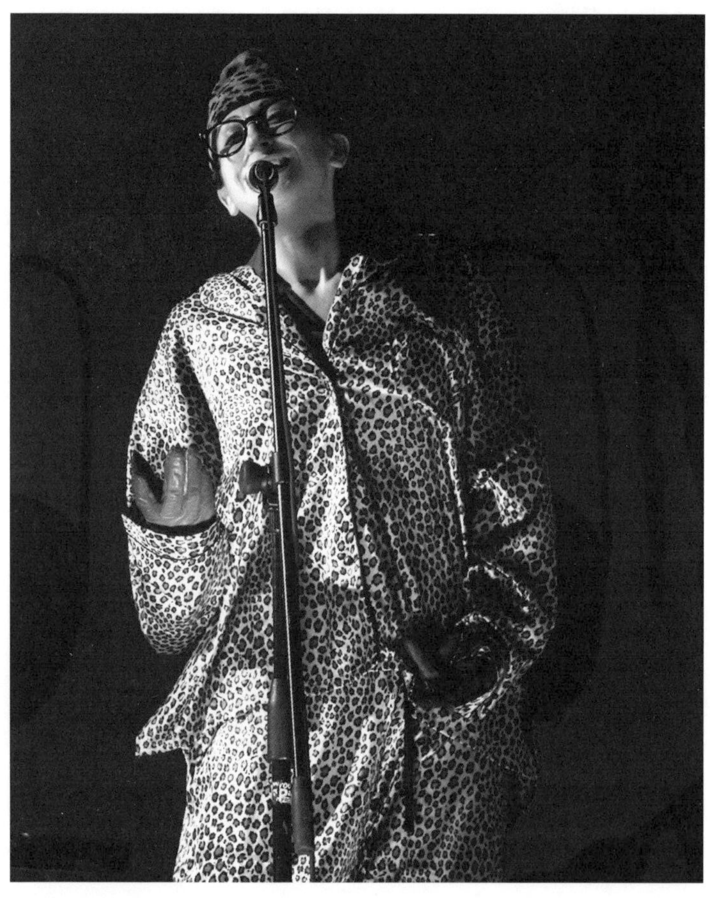

Rachel Mason, *Mobutu Sese Seko* from *The Songs of the Ambassadors*, 2004, performance view, NADA Art Fair, Miami, 2007.

February 7, 2011
Artforum

The artist and songwriter Rachel Mason here talks about The Songs of the Ambassadors, *a work involving miniature porcelain busts of political figures, self-portraits, and her music.*

The Songs of the Ambassadors began in the winter of 2004, when I saw a TV news report about the death toll in Iraq. I waited to see more, but the newscast ended abruptly. Suddenly a huge throng of people were cheering at the two warring teams facing off on an arena floor—a football game. I switched channels to try to hear more about the war but the game was on every one. I wondered: How many were dead? Three thousand? I couldn't remember. I tried to recall when the war started. What was I doing to prevent it? I went to some protests, but this was just one war. What about the others? How many wars happened in my lifetime?

Then I began to really think a lot about President Bush. What must be going through his mind? What was his world like? How was he deciding what he was deciding? What could I do about anything? And later, I started to fantasize that I could play with all of these world leaders like dolls. If they were small enough for me to hold in my hands, maybe I could have a better sense of who they were and what had happened during my lifetime. I love collectible sets, like the plates of all the presidents. If I had a special edition set, I would have porcelain busts of the leaders of countries at war and I would play the part of an ambassador to each conflict. I would wear their costumes so that I could sit with them and be an ambassador.

From 2005 to 2009, I sculpted my life in wars. I chose conflicts big and small for each year of my life, and I began writing and recording songs to go along with them. The first album was a collaborative effort with fourteen friends whose lyrics I set to music. The artist Michael Queenland wrote a two-part song about the president of Burkina Faso. Jennifer Herrema of the band RTX wrote about Guy Phillipe, the rebel leader of Haiti who tried to depose Aristide. The writer Emory Holmes II, whose poem about Mobutu Sese Seko is on the first album, once remarked, "In fiction you can express more reality than in nonfiction." His words really prophesied what would happen with this project.

In March 2007, I wrote to Manuel Noriega and sent him a picture of the bust I had made of him, and he wrote me back from his prison cell telling me to read his book. While reading his book, my ear became infected and I wrote the song "*Se infecto mi canal*" (My Canal Is Infected). We exchanged another letter just before he was transferred to France.

I made a video in 2008 for *My Chechen Wolves*, a song in which Dzhokhar Dudayev, the fearless fighter of the small nation of Chechnya, challenges the Russian army. I used footage from YouTube, and when I put it back on that site it went viral in the Caucasus and I became involved in the cause. I attended a rally last December where I sang the song for a protest in Times Square against recent racial attacks on the people of the Caucasus.

A friend suggested I call Ramsey Clark, former attorney general and Saddam Hussein's lawyer. He answered the phone and invited me to his house, where I showed him the busts. He knew each figure personally. He asked me if I wanted to have a copy of his final defense. I did. The defense statement inspired a script I wrote and performed at the Emigrant Savings Bank on the Lower East Side with artists Shana Moulton, Tyler Coburn, and Frank Benson playing characters from *Zabibah and the King*, Hussein's novel, and I played Hussein as he hung from the noose singing his last written words, a poem called "Unbind It."

Rebecca Solnit

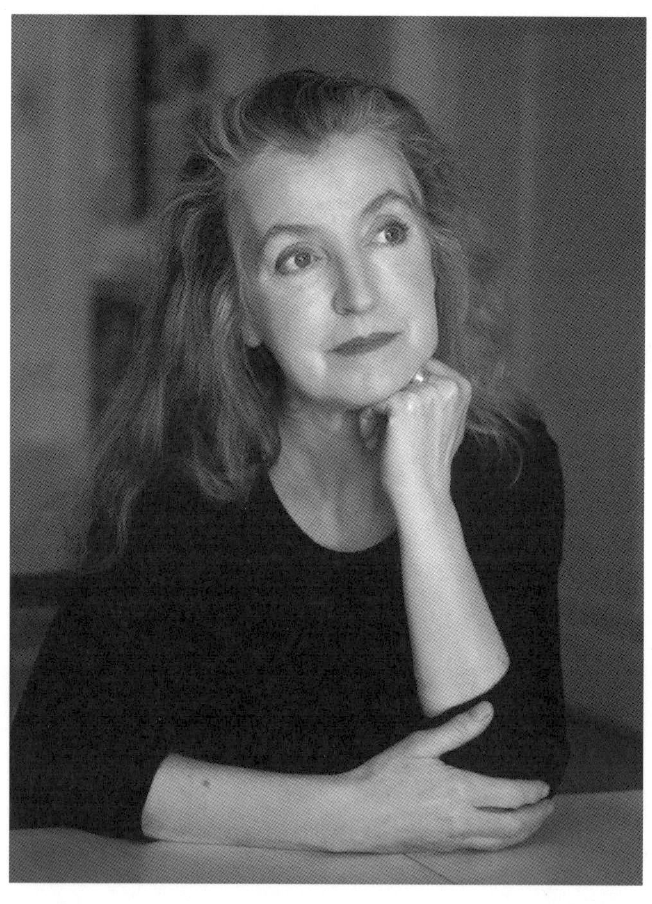

Rebecca Solnit, photo by Adrian Mendoza.

August 14, 2009
Artforum

Rebecca Solnit is the author of Savage Dreams: A Journey into the Landscape Wars of the American West *(1994),* Wanderlust: A History of Walking *(2000), and* River of Shadows: Eadweard Muybridge and the Technological Wild West *(2003), which won the National Book Critics Circle Award and the Mark Lynton History Prize. Here she talks about her 2009 book* A Paradise Built in Hell: The Extraordinary Communities That Arise in Disaster.

The 1989 Loma Prieta earthquake in California was an extraordinary event for me: I remember noticing that people appeared to be having a relatively positive experience. I also observed that my own emotional tenor shifted radically; even my sense of time and place shifted. After 9/11, I found that people were having what I couldn't possibly describe as a good time, but what you might call a "deep" time. If one of the problems besetting American internal life is shallowness, suddenly people found some satisfaction, purposefulness, and unity, and, for a couple of weeks, an openness to rethinking everything about our role in the world.

I was invited to give the Raymond Williams Memorial Lecture at Jesus College of Cambridge University in 2004, and I thought—in honor of Williams—that I should start something new, so I decided to do a lecture on the subject of disaster. This wasn't long after the publication of my book *Hope in the Dark* [2004], but for at least a decade before, I had been writing about the personal and emotional sides of public and historic events.

I didn't necessarily expect the subversive positivity of disasters to play such a large role in my research, but I became interested in the ways that such events have been misrepresented by the media and the film industry, as well as the studies of disaster sociologists—who, for the past sixty years, have done extraordinary work documenting the constructive and imaginative responses to catastrophes. It's as though I thought I was opening a door to a room, and the door opened to a huge landscape that I then felt compelled to explore.

After the talk, I published a piece in *Harper's*, which went to press the day Katrina hit. This immediately involved me in trying to interpret Katrina and provide a counter to all the (untrue) narratives of marauding barbarians and savagery that the media, pundits, and a lot of elected officials were creating. I hesitated a bit after Katrina, as I wasn't sure if this was the material that I wanted to commit myself to for the next few years, but it felt so important and so divergent from the ways that people are given to imagine what happens during disaster that I felt I had to do it.

One crucial discovery during my research was the writing of Charles Fritz. Disaster scholars seem to revere him, though they would also say he's a little too perfectly sunny. He writes, with inspired clarity and precision, that everyday life can itself be a kind of a disaster in which we're alienated and suffering from a sense of purposelessness. He argues that disaster can amend all those things, which is why it can be a tremendously positive experience. He also points out that illness, suffering, and death go on all the time—that it's not as though these things only happen during disasters. It's similar to what William James says about the 1906 earthquake in what may be an ur-essay for disaster studies: that we're not alone. James says it so beautifully: "Surely the cutting edge of all our usual misfortunes comes from the character of their loneliness."

I also drew on the research of J. K. Gibson-Graham, two women economists who write as one voice and who discuss existing counters to capitalism. Their work made me see more clearly what I had talked about in other ways in *Hope in the Dark*: that our society is purportedly capitalist but sustained by a host of unaccounted-for gestures of altruism, generosity, barter sharing, and other forces that keep the official system from entirely destroying us. And even though the rhetoric is always, How can we start from scratch to find something good?, while writing the book, my rhetoric instead became: How can we work with the good that is already there to make it more pervasive, more available, and, most important, more visible?

I wanted to incorporate that last question into another: What are the altruistic, improvisational, and sociable responses that disasters provide us with? For one, they give us a sense of the depth and intensity of our desire to be members of civil society, to belong and connect and do meaningful work. The task is not simply to respond better to disasters (which are intermittent) but to rethink who we are and what's possible every day. It's very much a prescriptive and a utopian book in that sense.

Rebecca Warren

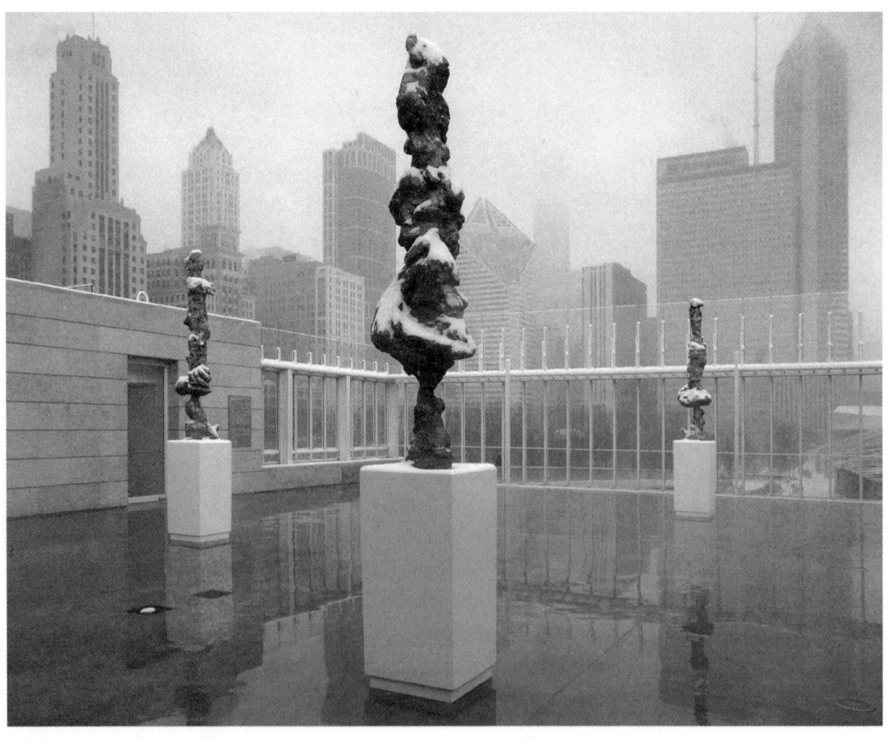

Rebecca Warren, *The Main Feeling*, *Bow*, and *There's No Other Way* in the snow, Art Institute of Chicago, 2010.

September 28, 2010
Artforum

The London-based artist Rebecca Warren is well known for her clay and bronze sculptures, which she has said initially drew on the output of a range of artists, including Auguste Rodin, Edgar Degas, Willem de Kooning, and cartoonist Robert Crumb, in order to find and develop the core of her own work. A pair of solo shows featured her works at the Renaissance Society and the Art Institute of Chicago in fall 2010.

The bronzes that will be exhibited at the Art Institute—*The Main Feeling, Bow*, and *There's No Other Way*—are cast from actual size hand-worked clay models rather than enlarged from maquettes, giving them an immediate, real scale. This has a subtle and important influence on what you're looking at: the sculptures are big, slabby, twisted, and built up with wet malleable material under gravity, and it's actually that which has been fixed in bronze. All the works have pale pink plinths, the heights of which are in part determined by the heights of the glass parapets on the building. I wanted the sculptures to peek over the lower parapet but to be shorter than the highest. That way they serve as the binding force for the differing levels. It also means the feet of the sculptures are around face height. They're awkward to look at, or to look up at, so you have to make that bit of effort, bending your neck, adjusting your eyes to the sky.

The sculptures are also visible from vantage points outside the terrace. They act in some part as a response to Chicago's famous modernist architecture, inasmuch as they evoke maximalism or the extra-rational. But the sculptures face inward toward each other, giving themselves a solidarity separate from any context. It's this triangulation of their own dynamic that allows them to not necessarily have to adapt or assimilate to the city. And yet the surfaces aren't harsh or reflective, so the sculptures can still roll with the city, with anything.

For the show at the Renaissance Society, I've made mainly new work—a combination of pieces in clay, steel, and bronze. I wanted areas of intense color concentration in the space. They are, in a way, an extension of similar, earlier sculptures that were smoother and sweeter. These new ones are uglier and more awkward, like chewed-up Meissen ware. For the earlier pieces, I had thought of Otto Dix and depictions of Weimar corruption and excess. For these, I kept thinking of an imagined modern Weimar—like *The Hills*. There's also a backward sequencing for a few of the sculptures. *The Other Brother 2* and *A Culture* look like family, with one seeming older, rustier, and more provisional than the other, although the one that appears to be the original was, in fact, made later and perversely is covered with a Perspex case. I've also made four steel sculptures. I like that the size of one of them, *Large Male*, was partly determined by the size of the lift—I had to shorten it by a couple of inches at a late stage in its development, so in a way the lift's height restriction became a deciding aesthetic factor.

The Renaissance Society is a bit baroque, which helped me to develop an idea of what could work in there. Similar to *Feelings* at Matthew Marks Gallery and my Serpentine exhibition last year, I wanted this show to work a bit like one of my vitrines, where the separate items energize certain elements in one another. I also wanted the arrangement to enact those preparatory states that are a hallmark of such shows: where, afterward, everything gets dispersed or housed in splinter groups. In this show, I wanted to make visible the moment when the relationships between the physical objects become like the relationships between the ideas being worked on. You can see families of memes and motifs in the work. The various materials curiously start off seeming to contrast along lines of durability, brittleness, rectilinearity, and crumbliness. But these qualities are never stable or definitive for long, and they start to invade one another in ways that I find interesting.

Renée Green

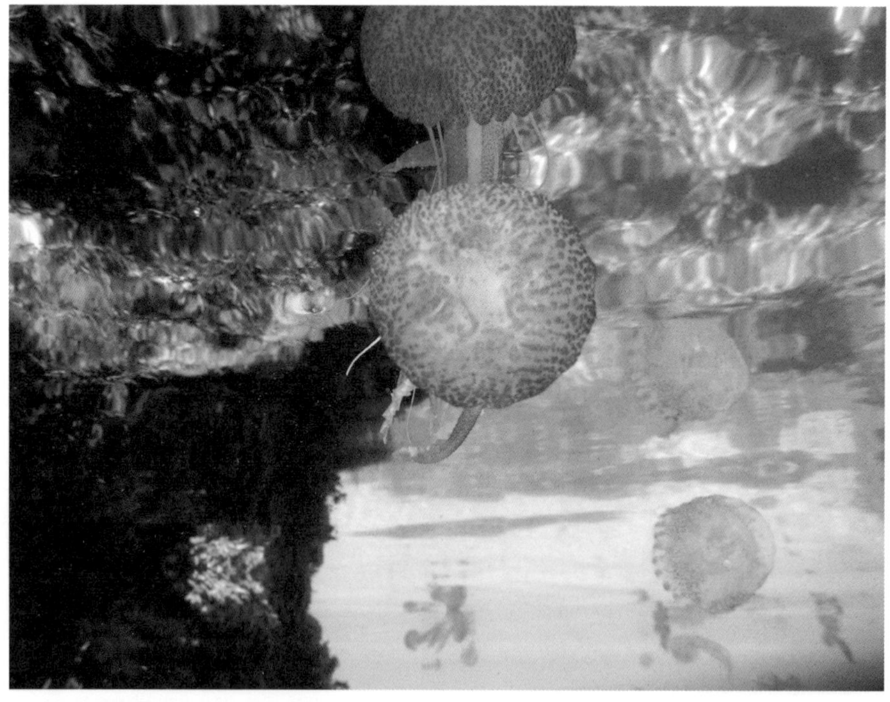

Renée Green, *Begin Again, Begin Again*, 2015, HD video projection (color, sound, 40 minutes).

November 28, 2014
Artforum

The artist Renée Green is well known for working with a wide array of media, which often converge in layered installations. Here, Green shares "doubly transmuted" pieces from the introductory essay in her new book Other Planes of There: Selected Writings *(2014), which surveys her writings between 1981 and 2010 and was published by Duke University Press.*

As a prelude to *Other Planes of There*, I offer these recently written and doubly transmuted excerpts from the book as one way of telling a story, titled, for example, as "Other Planes, Different Phases, My Geometry, Times, Movements: Becomings Ongoing."

When I look at the many shelves of books in my library and focus on the section of books and catalogues in which my work resides, the titles and covers all look interesting in their own way, yet I continue to search. I don't find what I'm looking for, it hasn't been made, yet I can imagine something other than what I'm finding. I return to the manuscript of this book you now read. I think about the vast breadth and varying depths of the events and encounters throughout my life as an artist and as a writer as I select what to give you at this time. I don't think of this as the definitive book of my work, as I'm still alive, writing and working, "wondering as I wander," yet there are some combinations and words I'd like you to be able to read, which I haven't yet read elsewhere. For that reason I feel compelled to give you these words.

A note to myself: "A certain boredom with 'artist's books' and 'artist's writings.' What about writing? What about one's perspective as it is informed by living and thinking and feeling and enacting? In this case, to enact living and thinking and feeling as an artist. Can I think of examples? And beyond. Ongoing becomings. Limiting classifications challenged. More paradoxes of democracy. Letters of all kinds."

When reading particularly about art, sometimes it seems that the twentieth century ended in the 1960s. In terms of any hopes and dreams. Afterward everything that followed became post- or neo-. Strange to be born in and grow up in a time that appears to be an extension of something perceived to have been authentic.

If one carefully reads what was published during the years even from one's birth to the present, what can be discovered can astonish, as well as satisfy nagging curiosity, temporarily. The ah-ha! effect. Speculative puzzle parts click into place, for a moment.

The story I have to tell is an artist's story. This becomes the story of many people through time. It is a growing seed. There remain things to know and to acknowledge that are still difficult to calmly discuss, as Jimmie Durham says; or difficult to more broadly recognize, such as a claim to multiple histories and a willingness to accept the range of participants in shaping these, despite the immensity of words circulating and despite the passages of time.

Other Planes of There contains writings that provide intimations to my works, written works that include essays, fiction, film, and audio scripts, and those that exceed a category, as well as writings that approach the works of others. The book is divided into five sections: Genealogies, Circuits of Exchange, Encounters, Positions, and Operations. Each section contains writings that span stretches of time and locations, yet share a relation. This is not a memoir meant to describe a life, but is, rather, a selection of primarily published writings, written in different parts of the world at different times during my life as an artist between the years 1981 and 2010, in relation to different works—considered in an expansive sense of the word—made by myself or made by others.

Rhonda Lieberman

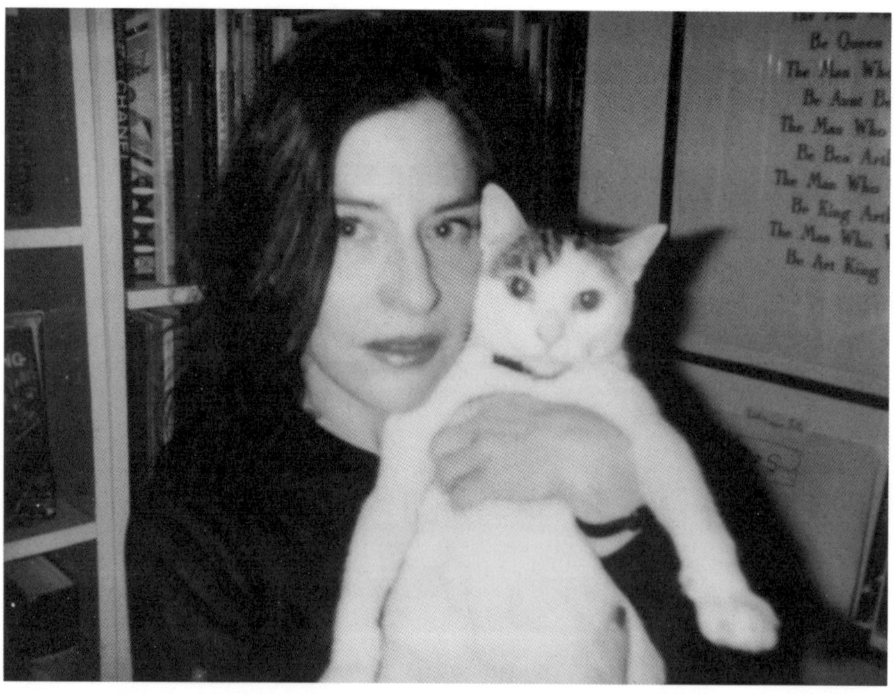

Rhonda Lieberman with Yingy, New York, ca. 2003.

June 11, 2013
Artforum

"Cats and Art Together at Last at White Columns" proclaimed the press release for The Cat Show, *an exhibition curated by writer and artist Rhonda Lieberman and developed in partnership with New York's Social Tees Animal Rescue. Here, Lieberman discusses the origins of the project and the "Cats-in-Residence Program," where cats were offered for adoption in the gallery in summer 2013.*

Back in the mid-'90s, I lived in a loft in Long Island City and started tending an outdoor cat colony in an empty lot on my street. I wasn't even a cat person when I moved in, but LIC had tons of street cats and they pulled me in. The cat party started at dusk when we arrived with the cans. It was my favorite art installation at the time! The cats evaded discourse; they didn't buy some discursive, blathering response! Going to this Zen kitty garden cleared a lot of the mishigas in my head.

High-rises were about to go up on the lot, displacing the cats my neighbors and I had grown fond of. We placed some and approached some rescue groups—all overflowing with adoptable pets—and that's when I got a crash course on the overextended rescue situation in NYC. These groups go to animal control to take the animals from death row. Bringing them more from the street was just adding to the overflow.

I thought it would be amazing to help the rescue groups by creating an un-depressing space where the public could meet the cats, a place where strays would be appreciated as the gorgeous creatures they are and not wretches in a cage-lined facility! For animal lovers, it's very depressing to encounter the broken system that treats strays as throwaways. I thought the cat area itself was a great installation and this project would use the art context to actually facilitate adoption—as well as being an aesthetic, meditative space.

Around that time, at MoMA PS1, I went to James Turrell's *Meeting*, a bench-lined room whose ceiling opens up to the sky. Nothing but presence—like the cat area. "This piece could only be improved by cats," I said to myself. My original idea for the show was for it to be like *Meeting*—a place for pussies to meet the public—with stuff for the cats to use, because they like to climb, to scratch. No tableaux or tchotchkes—just interactive pieces where cats and people would hang out. In the show's current form at White Columns, the cats do their "purrformance piece" in a kitty playground set within a salon-style kitty kunsthalle of cat-inspired—and sometimes cat-assisted—art and objets. Work by more than fifty artists and a zine with lots of personal pieces express our mysterious and intimate bond with cats through an array of sensibilities: the pieces are moving, sad, beautiful, comic.

Back in 1999 (!), the artists and designers I approached got the project instantly. But finding a space that would host rescue kitties—and the funding—was a challenge. This project integrates art and animal rescue, so it kind of fell between the cracks, grant-wise. A space whose name I won't mention agreed in 2003 to do it but kept dropping the ball when it came to development. That was an arduous and disappointing saga—so the project took a catnap there for a few years. But it was always a dream project of mine—one that had nearly happened. People would say, "What about that cat project?" Rather mortifying.

To my relief and gratitude, White Columns, the purrfect partner, stepped up and ended this purrgatory. This is the right time for the project. There's so much relational art—it was there in the '90s, too, and part of my mental framework for the project. And the Internet Cat Video Film Fest at the Walker Art Center last summer was a big hit. I've always been passionate about animal rescue, and this was one way I thought I could use my "skills" to help more cats than I could on a one-by-one basis. Plus there's something magical about hanging out with cats anywhere. They're aesthetic and fun, so an art space is a perfect fit.

The point of this show is to use art as a lever to transvalue how we see and treat strays. I propose this as a prototype to show that this kind of thing is possible, hopefully on a sustainable basis at some point. The centerpiece is the cat habitat/kitty playground: an enclosure with a tubular cat tree designed by architects Freecell (John Hartmann and Lauren Crahan) and Gia Wolff. It will swerve around seven other interactive sculptures for the cats to use, and seating so people can visit. Michelle Handelman is doing on-site video documentation and installing a multichannel video of the cats in the space for when they are not "in residence." Social Tees Animal Rescue, a partner for the project, is providing our ten cats-in-residence: Meowrina Abramovic, Bruce Meowman, Jeff Maine Coons, Claws Oldenburg, Alex Katz, and Frida Kahlico, among others. The purr-formers will have artist bios in the zine we are producing for the show, and most of all, we hope they'll all gain purrmanent homes during the two two-day adoption events that open and close the show.

Postscript: After White Columns, there were three later iterations of "The Cats-in-Residence Program": 356 Mission, Los Angeles (December 2014); Real Art Ways, Hartford, CT (Fall 2014); and Worcester Art Museum, Worcester, MA (Summer 2016). A grand total of seventy-seven cats were adopted through the piece.

Rita McBride and Kim Schoenstadt

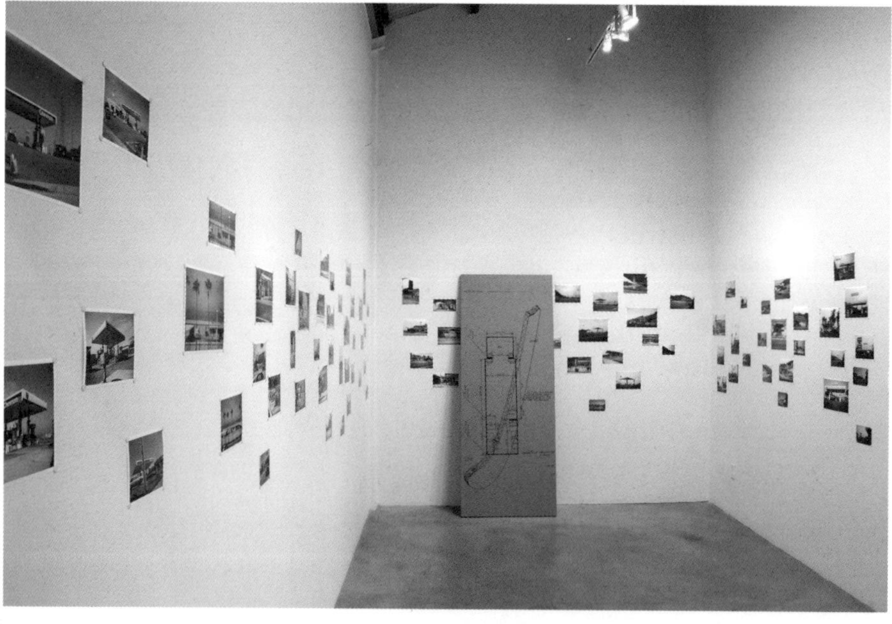

Tell Me Something Good: A Collaboration between Kim Schoenstadt and Rita McBride, 2009, photographs, record, record player, and drawing on door blank, dimensions variable, Santa Monica Museum of Art, Santa Monica, CA.

September 7, 2009
Artforum

Tell Me Something Good, *a collaboration between Rita McBride and Kim Schoenstadt, is loosely based on* Art by Telephone, *an exhibition the Museum of Contemporary Art, Chicago, organized in 1969. Departing from the conceptual premise of that show, McBride and Schoenstadt made works from instructions they had exchanged over the phone. The project premiered at Alexander and Bonin Gallery in May 2009.*

This collaboration began with a misunderstanding. Thankfully, there were more to come. In early 2008, I had a few curators from the Santa Monica Museum over to my studio to see a new project (just released from customs) that I had made for the Van Abbemuseum. At some point, the curators asked what else I'd been working on. At the time, I was still toying with the idea for *Tell Me Something Good*, so it was all pretty vague and based more on a telephone game. Whereas *Art by Telephone* had artists phone in to an institution for installers to make their works via instructions, I wanted this collaboration to include artists calling in their directions directly to each other and asserting their own aesthetic choices. It was the sort of half-baked idea one brings up in idle chitchat, but, the next thing I knew, the museum was interested in doing that show.

After several meetings, it seemed that the scope was too large, and I decided to narrow it down to a single collaboration. I suggested Rita because she's a sculptor based in Düsseldorf, and it seemed better to combine artists with geographic distance and different modes of working.

When I called to ask her about working together, she had just returned to Germany from LA to find that all the pictures she had taken for a publication due the following week had been inexplicably compromised. Since I was pitching this "phone-in" concept, she indeed felt like I was telling her something good, as I could retake her photographs (in this case, of all the service stations from Point Dome to LAX). However, with an extended deadline, she ended up retaking her own pictures the following month.

For our first show at Alexander and Bonin, I instructed Rita to execute a new piece in my ongoing *Fax Drawing* series. These works originated when I unintentionally loaded my fax machine with a recycled drawing while receiving floor plans from a gallery. The resultant combination of the drawing and floor plan created a hybrid, which I ultimately installed as a wall drawing in the gallery that had sent me the fax. So Rita made a piece that combined one of her drawings for a sculpture and the floor plan of the gallery. For our new exhibition, she's using the same wall drawing, but she instructed the museum to create the work with black glossy lines on a prefabricated door that's painted hot pink. I installed her service station photographs along the gallery walls, and she leaned the door against some of the photos, thereby obscuring the view.

We decided to make our works based on instructions given to each other during a single phone call—like the original MCA show—and to record the calls to vinyl as the museum did in 1969. Since our exhibition will be much smaller in scope, we thought it would be appropriate to create a 45 rpm single rather than a full 12-inch album.

The logic of *Tell Me Something Good* relies heavily on chance, miscommunication, and phone lines, and so conceptually it fell together nicely. One part I like best about the collaboration is the question: Who made it? I'm still not sure whether either of us can claim to be the single creator for either piece. Perhaps the project gains strength by putting itself in that area between misunderstandings.

Ruby Sky Stiler

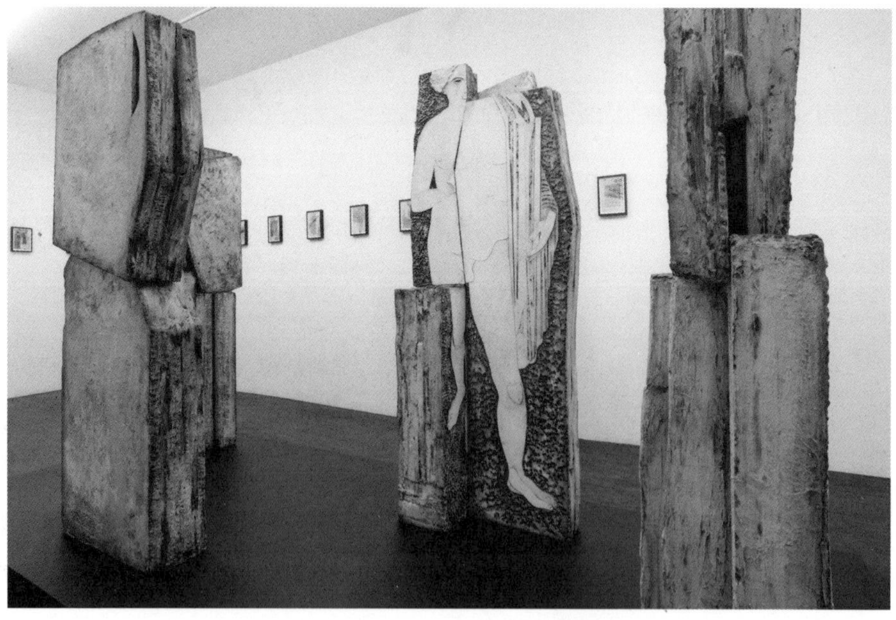

View of *Inherited and Borrowed Types*, 2010, Nicelle Beauchene Gallery, New York.

August 31, 2010
Artforum

Ruby Sky Stiler's handsome yet disorderly foamcore sculptures, which often reference classical antiquity, were featured in her solo project for TBA:10 in Portland, Oregon, in fall 2010.

I've been developing the work in this show for the past year. Kristan Kennedy, a curator at the Portland Institute for Contemporary Art, encountered two of the initial sculptures in my studio, and the undertaking moved forward from there, with a steady dialogue between us and the site in mind. The project consists of three "figurative" works, each slightly larger than life, and a group of twenty-two collages. I've created a corresponding artist's book that includes the collages and shares the title of my installation: *Inherited and Borrowed Types*. Though the pieces themselves are independent, I'm excited to see how the formal, academic aspects of Washington High School create a different context to support them, and I've worked with the space to tease a distinct mood from the classroom/gallery.

The reference to classical iconography popped up in my work a few years ago. I was in Naples for a brief visit with friends, and we visited Pompeii, the formerly ash-buried Roman town–cum–tourist attraction. A controversy involving the colors of the frescoes captured our attention during our time there. Apparently "Pompeii Red," which is synonymous with our collective sense of this historical time and place—and a standard paint-chip color—*may* have been an archaeological mistake. Reports stated that the original color could have been oxidized through the heat of the fire and mutated to appear red. Meanwhile, the entire site has been restored with this color in mind, which is nuts. I love this subject, which exists primarily through the lens of contemporary historians and is therefore a constantly evolving and engaging fiction. The sculptures in this show play with authenticity and with how that quality is perceived, creates value, and can prompt an atmosphere of authority surrounding the object.

My basic process for this work is to jam together disparate parts to make a whole. I think of this as a hopeful, loving gesture: finding solutions (or a suitable repair) that will bring the figure to life out of crumbling, incomplete appendages. The sculptures are made to be viewed in the round: from one side, a classical figure is seen, while the opposite section gives off an abstract modernist vibe. The resulting sensation is that these works are referencing both ancient art history and sculpture of the twentieth century. My incorporation of shifting perspectives, varied art historical references, gender combinations, and juxtapositions in scale encourages a sense of *striving* to make something work, even when one doesn't have all the appropriate resources at one's disposal. This activity feels like a metaphor for daily life.

The shifting line between common kitsch and singular originality is an element that interests me. On first glance, these ancient-seeming figures appear to be chiseled from marble. Looking closer, it's clear that they are constructed from contemporary art supplies and conflate iconography that spans different centuries and societies. On the one hand, elements of these works copy from recognized ideals of art history, and in this sense, they are tacky imitations. On the other hand, however, I aim to make the sculptures' presence feel elegant, convincing, and originally expressive.

Sakiko Sugawa

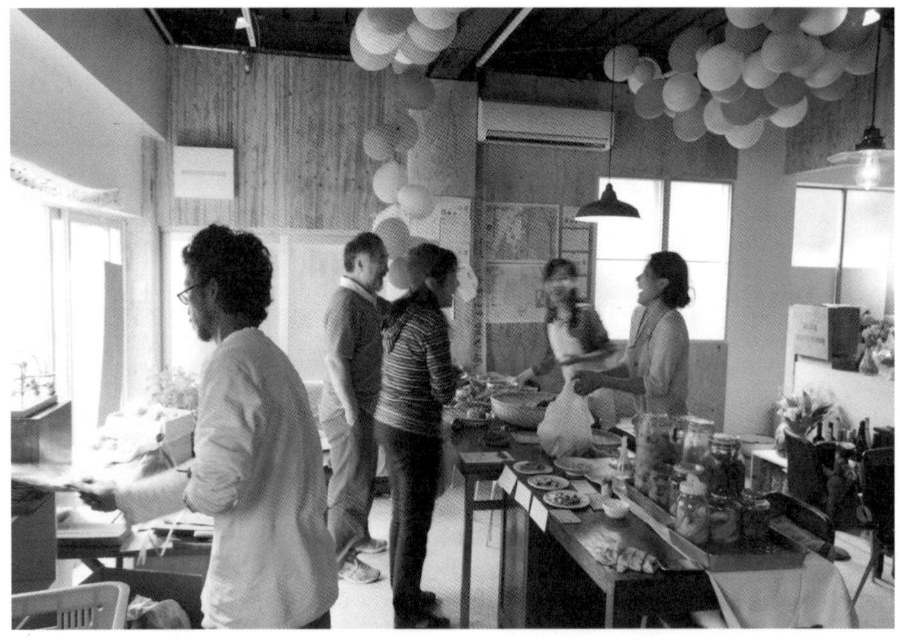

A Social Kitchen event.

August 21, 2013
Artforum

Social Kitchen is a small but industrious social and cultural center in Kyoto. Founded in September 2010, the center has initiated a variety of participatory projects, often involving local communities—from supporting emerging artists to selling rice, and from engaging citizens to participate in a mayoral election and raising awareness about nuclear energy to reading books on relational art. Here Social Kitchen cofounder Sakiko Sugawa talks about the origins of the project and some of its work.

Social Kitchen began after five successful years of working on the project Kissahanare, a weekly underground café that we held on Monday nights at my home in Kyoto. Kissahanare was a social project rooted in sharing our everyday experiences, and after we felt that we achieved our goals—for example, to initiate a network of people across broad walks of life—we realized that we needed to tackle more universal issues. Social Kitchen is a place where people bring their own ideas to the table, and it differs from cultural institutions because there's no fixed relationship between those who organize/curate programs and those who participate in them. The results have all been pretty organic, and perhaps that's because when a project starts, one person takes the initiative and other people simply back them up. Leaders change, depending on the project.

We were, and still are, very frustrated with the lack of a public sphere in Japan in which individuals can come together to freely identify and talk about social problems and, in turn, create political action. Some Japanese people argue that the idea of a "public sphere" is merely a Western concept, and that Japanese society is better off without this direct, confrontational attitude. They say that Japanese culture has a different way of bringing individual, personal concerns to a political level. Perhaps this argument comes from an illusion or nostalgia for the formerly tight-knit communities that could be seen in Japan, even in urban cities. Today, in rural areas, this type of community still exists and "Japanese ways" of doing things could work. But in an urban environment like Kyoto, we don't have that kind of community anymore; all we have are fragmented, isolated individuals, just like in any other globalized city. So, despite a wide range of criticism toward our somewhat utopian concept of public sphere, we still thought creating a public space was urgent and necessary in Kyoto. In this sense there's nothing unique about Social Kitchen as a public place. The ambitions behind its origins are very fundamental as well as traditional.

The activities of "Working Group 1: Earthquake and Nuclear Power Plant" in 2011 were really inspiring. But again, while Social Kitchen's organizers made an open call to gather participants, the beautiful and complex results—the success of the project—should be credited to each member, and not to us. In the wake of the 2011 Great East Japan earthquake and Fukushima nuclear disaster, a loose collective of citizens gathered at Social Kitchen to form the first "working group." Participating members proposed and discussed ideas and put actions into practice over a one-year period. They have carried out activities with refugees from the Tohoku region and volunteered at restaurants in the disaster area, among other things. They discussed, tried, failed, and succeeded with help from Social Kitchen staff members.

These activities eventually led to Working Group 1's February 2012 exhibition about the Kyoto mayoral election, which conveyed critical issues including voters' concerns about nuclear energy and set up opportunities to discuss how citizens are involved in the making of the city, and the meaning of democracy itself. While this leap from helping evacuees to organizing an exhibition on the city's mayoral elections seems to be big, it made perfect sense to the group. With the help of a graphic designer, Takuya Matsumi, they gathered information in more critical detail than any Kyoto-based journalist, learned election-related laws, and created informational graphics, which presented important information to voters.

This is not a success story, but a story of the social and cultural center struggling very hard to exist and serve people in this world.

Sara Greenberger Rafferty

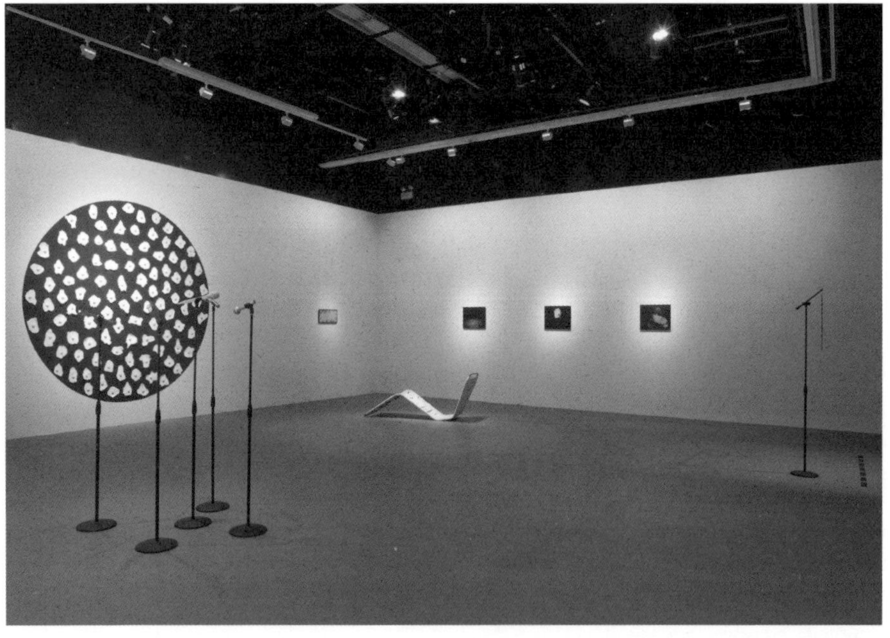

View of *Bananas*, 2008, The Kitchen, New York.

December 23, 2008
Artforum

The New York–based artist Sara Greenberger Rafferty has exhibited widely since 2001. Her exhibition Bananas—*exploring humor, performance, and everyday life—was on view in the winter of 2008–9 at the Kitchen in New York.*

I've always thought of my work in the context of performance, so I was thrilled when the Kitchen, a long-standing nonprofit performance venue, proposed this exhibition. Even though I don't make "performance art" as such, my work engages with that medium via more static forms. The exhibition space at the Kitchen is quite large, which has forced me to consider scale in this show more than in other contexts. There are several small pieces and other works that have parts that fit into a larger whole. Rather than an "installation," it's a show of discrete objects and images. As opposed to a novel, I thought of the show as a collection of short stories.

The imagery refers to cooking, women, and stand-up comedy—subjects I've been working with for a while. But the works were primarily born out of simple color studies. I had previously made a lot of monochrome works based on black-and-white photography from the 1950s and '60s, and I wanted to reincorporate color. But I had pared down the color vocabulary in my work so much that the process felt a little like coping with a broken leg. In trying to teach myself how to walk again, I began to do color studies and look at Josef Albers's pedagogy. I read historical and contemporary texts on color theory and examined a few New Age texts on color therapy. I wanted to try to use colors conceptually to explore cultural connotations and associations.

For instance, with the color yellow, I began to incorporate the theme of the egg. It seemed very related to motifs and objects I had previously used in my work, such as cream pies and other foods that could be thrown at someone's face. And of course, it's gendered as female. In this show, there are a series of silk-screen prints that were made with egg whites; they're like bootleg albumen prints. For these, I worked with Forth Estate Editions, an enterprise that publishes prints by mostly young artists. Like other works I've made, these are prints of drawings based on photographs, but they're silk-screened with egg whites over the top, which forms a latent or invisible image.

In addition to bringing color back into my work, I've been trying to make the work *actually* funny rather than simply *about* funny. Previously, I was invested in tropes of comedy and imagery involving jokes, but now I'm interested in works themselves operating more as comedians. Something seemed a little off with making work about comedy while never garnering any laughs. Typically, my work tends to be on the scale of just one person. I'm not interested in being a master of something; I want my work to look physically underwhelming. That's basically the idea of the stand-up comic anyway—it's not a Broadway production but a single person on a stage. It's just one body in front of a microphone with a stool and a glass of water. I like the idea of that solitary presence that functions like an artwork, with its back against the wall. As I was making the work over the past year, there were ups and downs in the world as well as in my own life, so in the end there are some funny works and there are some melancholy pieces; but these are, after all, just two sides of the same depreciated coin.

Sarah Crowner

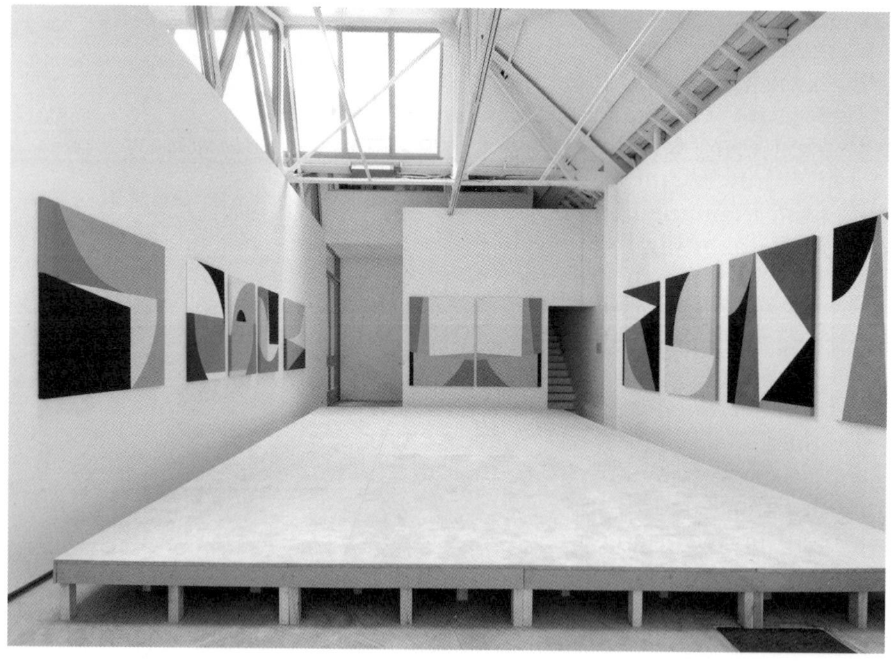

View of *Ballet Plastique*, 2011, Galerie Catherine Bastide, Brussels.

September 5, 2011
Artforum

Sarah Crowner is a Brooklyn-based artist whose vibrant sewn paintings have been based on specific compositions from the past, such as early works by Victor Vasarely and Lygia Clark. In two concurrent shows in fall 2011, at Nicelle Beauchene Gallery in New York and Galerie Catherine Bastide in Brussels, Crowner presented her work.

For several years, I painted with a certain impatience about painting. Its flatness, its weight and slowness, irritated me somehow. So I turned my back on it for a time and started to explore ceramic sculpture. As it happened, there was something about using my hands and manipulating clay that led me back to painting, but in a different way. I realized that I wasn't interested in the conventional fixity of these media; I didn't want to wait for a line of paint or some clay to dry. I wanted more immediacy and spontaneity, and I realized that I could just treat a painting like a collage: cut up forms, arrange them on the ground, rearrange them, and sew them up again. The physicality of this approach, using paint, canvas, and a stretcher, as if to make an object rather than a picture, made sense to me.

I've been occupied with making sewn and shaped geometric canvases since then. Each new work contributes to this project. An encounter with one piece—a symmetrical diptych with bright, sharp, red triangles on either side—led to the new bodies of work I'm showing this fall. Between the red triangles there's an exposed center of raw linen, an unfolding square of white paint, and, below this, black rectangles. It struck me as theatrical curtains opening onto an empty stage—a proscenium painting. The image of the stage was the result of the collaging process, and my interest—in this case—to play with symmetry. I spent time looking at the work alone, and with people standing in front of it, yet still couldn't shake the idea that it was a backdrop with an open curtain.

I'm curious about the impact of time on our experience of painting: What does time do to an abstract collection of static forms? If you walk into a gallery or museum you might experience a painting for as little as one minute—but what if that same painting is hanging in your living (or work) space for thirty-five years? Or what if you were seated in an auditorium "watching" that painting—perhaps with dancers moving in front of it—for, say, forty-five minutes? What is that experience? How can its quality and contours change inside the frame of a minute, forty-five minutes, or thirty-five years? These hypothetical propositions are compelling to me as I manipulate the materials that come together in my work. I hope that somehow they translate, such that the exhibitions *could* be read as proposals to choreographers and theater directors.

The paintings thus materialize as backdrops, or proposals for backdrops, for an undefined performance or theatrical event. In Brussels, I'm showing a series of paintings on three walls. Hung tightly together, they will appear as one continual painting with various compositions and forms colliding. I'm building a stage in the gallery, a simple low plywood platform. To encounter the paintings, viewers will have to step up onto the stage and assume the position of performers.

In New York, a similarly tight row of canvases will cover the walls like a frieze. To accompany the paintings, I'm working on a group of small wooden sculptures, about thirty inches tall, with flat geometric-shaped fronts and curved and linear backings. I see these as tabletop maquettes for stage props. Together, they recast my questions around painting; they offer the idea that a painting or a sculpture might function as a proposal for something else. If a painting can suddenly read as a huge backdrop, could a small sculpture be a model for something larger than life? Rather than qualifying the status of painting or sculpture, they retool these forms, giving them a new feeling and a new function in space, one that invites movement—interaction, even.

I'm always using art history as a medium, cutting it up and trying to reengage it. In these new bodies of work I'm thinking about moments in the early twentieth century when the avant-gardes were collaborating freely and cross-pollinating from music to theater to painting to poetry (think of Hannah Höch's Dada dolls, Sophie Taeuber-Arp's sculptural puppets and set decorations, Maria Jarema's abstract theatrical backdrops, or Oskar Schlemmer's Bauhaus theater workshop). This is a departure from my previous work employing specific compositions, and this wider conceptual field has also added a new dimension, perhaps somehow historicizing the physicality and material immediacy that has entered my process. The meditation on "medium" has expanded the sense of that word, for me. If wood or clay or paint acts as one kind of medium, supporting and *materializing* thought at the level of intimate engagement, then the scale and dynamics of performance and the metaphysics of stagecraft might conduct another kind of channeling.

Shannon Ebner

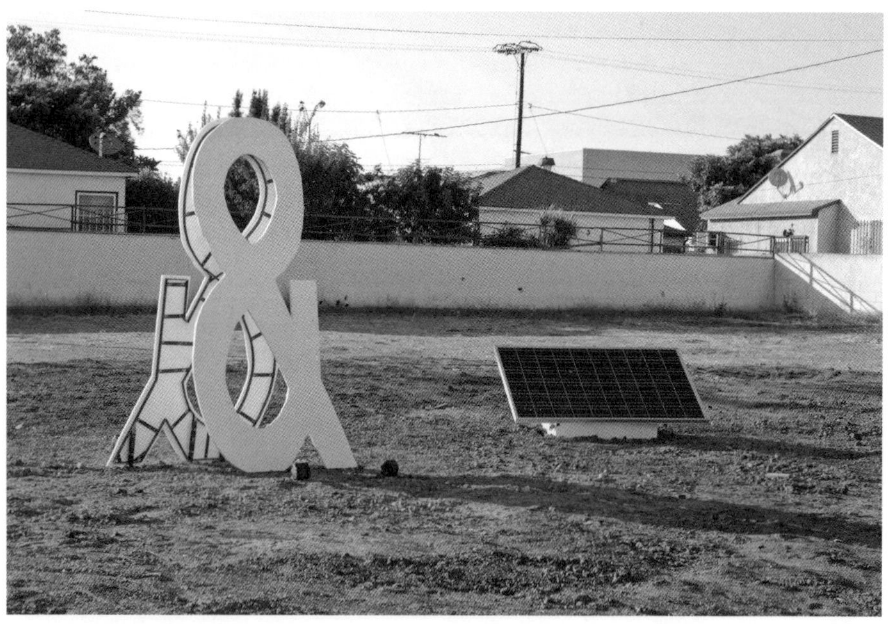

Shannon Ebner, *and, per se and*, 2011, painted wood, steel, aluminum, light-emitting diodes, photovoltaic solar cells, and marine battery, 96 × 48 × 33 inches (243.8 × 121.9 × 83.8 cm).

October 4, 2011
The Paris Review Daily

Shannon Ebner is an artist known for using handmade letters, symbols, signs, and other means of representation to call attention to the limits and loopholes of language. Photographs and sculptures from Ebner's project The Electric Comma *were featured in the 54th Venice Biennale and in a solo show at the Hammer Museum in Los Angeles. Two public sculptures, both titled* and, per se and, *accompanied these shows and were installed, respectively, on the Grand Canal in Venice and in Culver City, California.*

LOB: In the essay she wrote to accompany your exhibition at the Hammer, curator Anne Ellegood describes your work as "manifestly American." How does American identity relate to your recent pictures, and how does landscape figure in?

SE: That makes me think of how Robert Smithson once asked if Passaic, New Jersey, had replaced Rome as the eternal city, with buildings that rise into ruin rather than fall. My interest in landscape, materials, and the indeterminacy in photography is concerned with the opposite: falling while rising. Some of my early landscape images were literally of felled trees. I suppose it's the medium that acts as a medium and can make things rise from the dead.

LOB: How does the idea of the monument influence you? For instance, do you consider *and, per se and* a monument? And if so, to what?

SE: I don't consider *and, per se and* to be a monument. If anything, I would say it is more of an anti-monument, in the sense that it is fundamentally about incompleteness and requires the viewer to do some work to fill in the blanks. It exists in two different states—during the day, one can see the solar panel but not understand, or see, that it's storing energy so that the sculpture can be illuminated intermittently at night, like a signal. I had a number of other ideas about how the sculpture relates to photography and the sun, funny coincidental things like how the person who invented photovoltaic technology—a Frenchman named Alexandre-Edmond Becquerel—did so the same year that photography was invented, in 1839. But more than anything, what interests me about the sculpture is that it is never dormant and can exist in the continuous present, because it is either drawing energy from the sun or releasing that energy. And while I suppose one could have a monument that is living, as opposed to dead, I always think of monuments as being really super-dead.

LOB: And then we have the strange history of the word *ampersand*. It was originally a phrase students recited at the end of the alphabet—"X, Y, Z, and per se and." In Latin, *per se* means "by itself." And in your sculpture, we have the symbol both by itself and continually renewing itself. But what about a photograph? Can it exist in the continuous present?

SE: The *Oxford English Dictionary* says that the ampersand is a "corruption of '*and* per se—*and*,' the old way of spelling and naming the character &; i.e. '& by itself = and.'" When I worked with the translator Jen Hofer on making a bilingual handout for the Culver City piece, she translated the title of the sculpture in Spanish to "*y, per se y. el signo &*," which I thought was quite beautiful.

As it turned out there is no term for *ampersand* in Spanish or, rather, the term used is "*el signo &*" (the sign &), meaning that the & becomes part of the term for *ampersand*.

And as for your question about a photograph and whether it can exist in the continuous present, maybe it can't, but I'm trying to figure it out regardless. I guess what I like about photographs of symbols is that they can redirect an image or create uncertainty and indeterminacy and suggest that one thing is two things or one thing is an incomplete thing, an incomplete picture. My hope is that the activity of thinking about a photograph or a word or an isolated symbol—literally, the time it takes one to think—places a person in the continuous present.

Sophie Calle

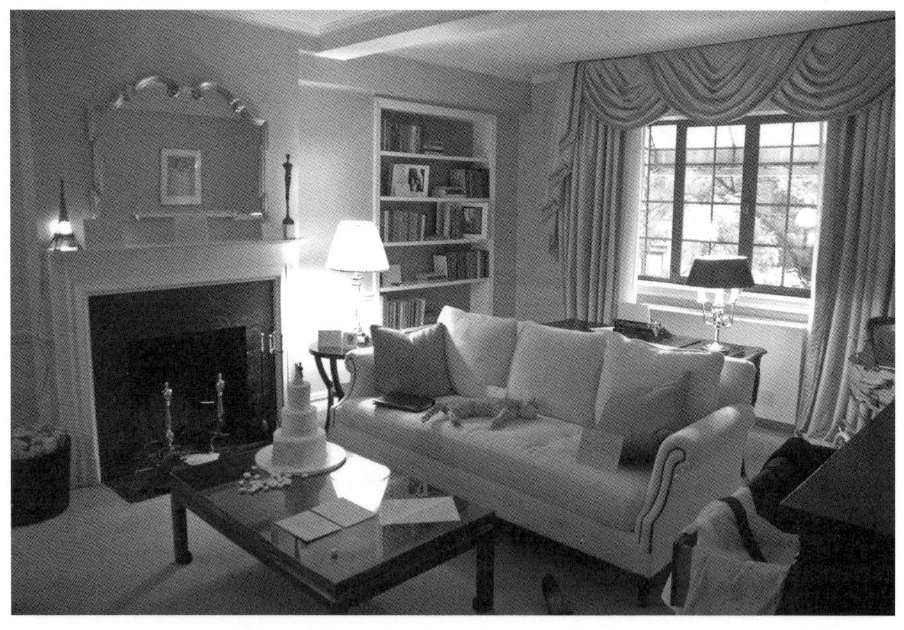

Installation view of Sophie Calle's *Room*, The Lowell Hotel, New York, October 13–16, 2011.

October 10, 2011
Artforum

For the 2011 Crossing the Line festival, presented by the French Institute Alliance Française, Sophie Calle presented Room, *an installation of autobiographical work in the Lowell Hotel on New York's Upper East Side.*

The hotel room will have forty or so objects, all from my *True Stories* project, which is an ongoing work about important events in my life. Parts of this project have been previously published in two books. Depending on the story, visitors will see either the actual object in the hotel room—for instance, my wedding dress—or something that could be evoked from the story, such as a coffee cup.

This project can be exhibited anywhere. It's been shown before at the Pompidou and the Freud Museum, among other places. But this is the first time I've installed it in a hotel. It's not a specific hotel, but I think that speaks to the way the work can adapt to any setting and how, perhaps, it's not quite a show or a performance but something in between. It's more like a roving installation. More like life.

I recently added a new story. It's about the view from my house in the south of France, a vista I've looked at for the past thirty years but one that I only just decided to write about. In the hotel room there will be a text by a window in which I describe the view from my house, but there won't be an accompanying object, since I'm just speaking about a landscape.

It's very hard to know how many people will visit. In 2003, when I spent the night in a room set up for me at the top of the Eiffel Tower, for

Room with a View, I thought at most one hundred people would come, to tell me a story and to keep me awake. But something like sixteen thousand visited. So suddenly the project was very different than what I imagined. But since this hotel room will be open to the public twenty-four hours a day for three days, and since it's also free, it will be interesting to see what happens. Yes, Christian Marclay's *The Clock* was visited all night, but it's a masterpiece and the result of three years' work. This "room" is not as ambitious! Personally, I would wait ten hours to watch that work, but probably not to see my *Room*!

This is a long-term project with no definite end. So many of the stories have just popped into my mind after being lost for many years. I'll keep adding stories until I have nothing left to say, or nothing left to remember.

Sturtevant

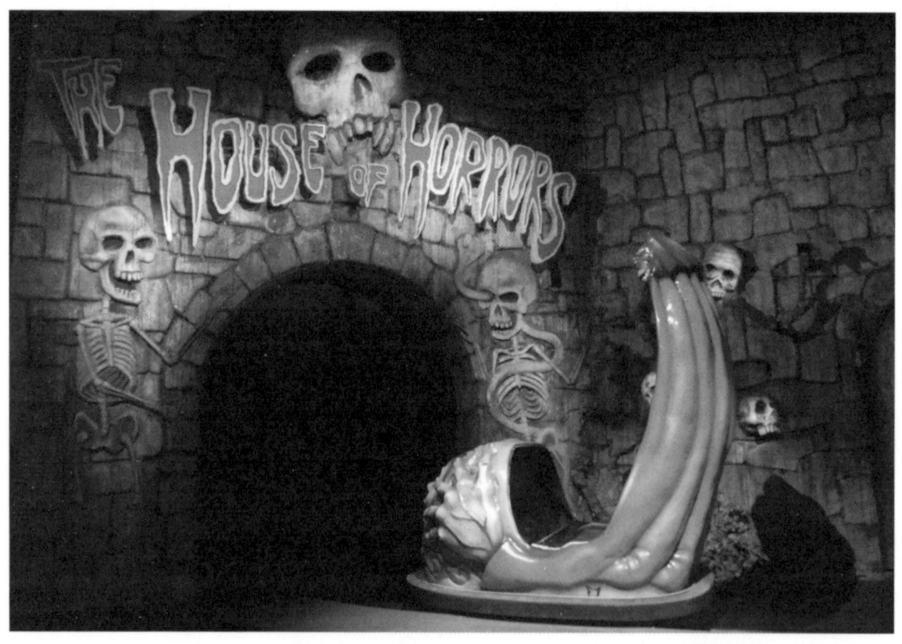

Sturtevant, intallation view of *House of Horrors* (detail), 2010, mixed media, dimensions variable.

February 26, 2010
Artforum

The renowned Paris-based American artist Sturtevant defied expectations for over forty years, mostly through works that push the limits of the copy and the counterfeit through repetition. The Razzle Dazzle of Thinking, *her exhibition at the Musée d'Art Moderne de la Ville in Paris, was on view in spring 2010.*

There are two sections to this show. One is called "Wild to Wild" and contains works from the 1970s to the present, including *Duchamp 1200 Coal Bags* [1972], *González-Torres Untitled (America)* [2004], *Vertical Monad* [2008], and *Finite Infinite* [2010]. *Finite Infinite* is projected on a 141-foot curved wall. The other part of the show, which is also a new work, is the *House of Horrors*. It's in complete opposition to "Wild to Wild."

The house is a classical carnival design, a ghost train. It was fabricated by JES Studio in France. The entrance has gray stones with skeletons and other scary things. When you enter it's all dark, and you hear screaming, banging, and flying bats. You'll be scared, and that's fun. The carts in the work come from an original house of horror. They're very beautiful, incredible. JES Studio made the automated pieces like the Frankenstein who rises up from his gurney to the sound of great organ music, a dead head that moans and groans, a skeleton that jumps out almost into your cart, and, of course, the wonderful Divine with her doggy in the window. The studio knew other studios that then did the makeup, clothes, sound, lights, and engineering.

When you go into the museum, you turn and there are very beautiful steps that lead up to the famous Dufy Room, which I concealed with another new work, *Elastic Tango*, a nine-monitor video. It's intrusive, big, and visual. The monitors are shaped in an inverted pyramid and the videos are devised as a three-act play in a very formal sense: presentation of problem, escalation of conflict, and then resolution without narrative. The resolution is, obviously, simulacrum.

The dynamic force is the razzle-dazzle of thinking.

That's what I did, and that's what it does.

Voilà!

Sue Coe

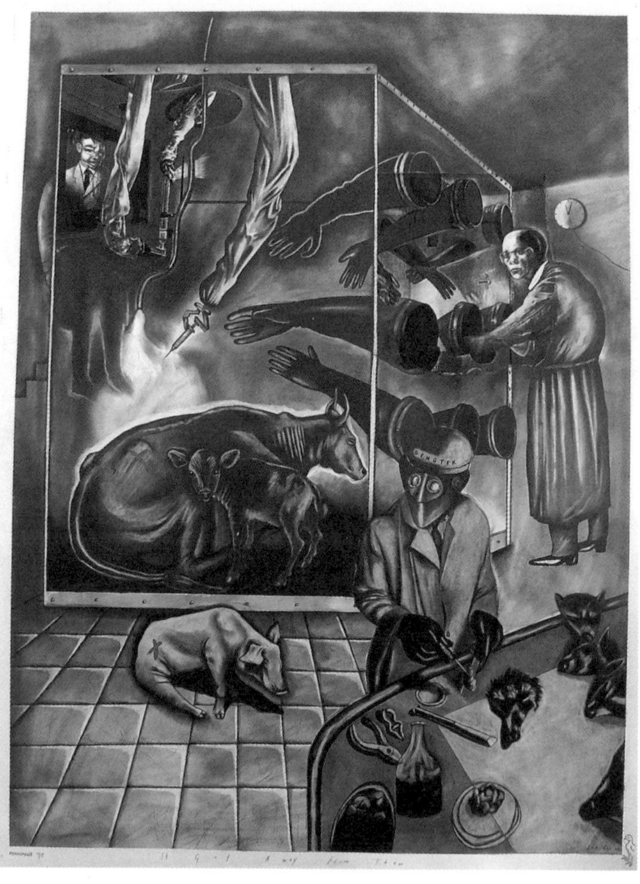

Sue Coe, *It Got Away from Them*, 1990, graphite, watercolor, and gouache on white Bristol Strathmore board, 40 ⅛ × 30 inches (101.9 × 76.2 cm).

August 21, 2018
Artforum

Sue Coe's anti-career career, as someone "double-parked on the highway of life," as she puts it, has been one of nonstop art as activism. Graphic Resistance, *a survey of fifty works from the past forty years, was on view at MoMA PS1 in summer 2018.*

I make art for people on the front lines. That's my family: a community of activists who aren't artists but who want to use art as a weapon. That's who tells me if something is working and how I can make my art more effective. Some of my work is direct propaganda; some of it is visual journalism. I was an editorial artist for many decades—that's what I'm supposed to be. At sixteen, I began doing work for newspapers and never looked back. But at some point that changed into doing my own research and books, as opposed to illustrating somebody else's words.

Usually an artist is known for only one body of work, but I'm lucky that I'm known for two: the ongoing project about animal rights and the rape painting, which is now at MoMA PS1. The former work continues, and I'm always learning. As I see it, animals liberate themselves. They need our help, but it's not Lord and Lady Bountiful saving them. I'm aghast at how animal rights today have become all about the human diet—about being gluten-free. Animal liberation is a social justice issue, and I've always promoted the abolitionist approach: eradication of all use. But now animal rights have been twisted into the market, where the meat industry disrupts itself by buying up vegan food producers.

Art always has to go beyond human health, human drama, and human issues. It has to be about social justice for all animals, including us. I initially made that connection as a kid in England after World War II, growing up around bombed-out ruins and living next door to a slaughterhouse. As a child, I was forced to see the correlation between war, violence, and fascism, and animal cruelty and abuse. Once I figured that connection out, so early on, I realized that the Other is always at risk.

When I was a vegan back in the late 1970s, there were like ten of us. Now it's like half the student body at places where I teach. Food animals are raped every time they're inseminated and are molested almost constantly. It's only within this animal rights movement that you can have "rape-free Mondays" and "child molestation–free Tuesdays." Would saying "I feel like raping a child right now" be acceptable in any other social justice movement? No. The mistake of taking "baby steps" toward progress has happened in nearly every social justice movement, and animal liberation is no different. Yet, there can't be any baby steps in this movement because there are no baby steps for an animal going into a slaughterhouse. They are *babies*, and they're being slaughtered.

For me, there's no difference between someone who works in the slaughterhouse and someone buying animal products from Whole Foods. They are morally exactly the same. Except one is usually poorer—the professional life span of a meatpacker is six months. Oh, and meatpacking places are called "harvesting centers" now. It's beyond Orwellian how the language changes.

What should be a rights movement has become a welfare movement. We need to understand how welfarism is keeping the system going. Welfare is always said to be a panacea that supposedly will make things better in the long term, but it doesn't. That's why my message carries an element of hopelessness. But there's something else: a dignity in struggle. There's a dignity in having comradeship. There's a dignity in not having our brains so destroyed that we think any problem has to be solved by a market solution. Unlike in the 1980s, people don't believe the market is going to provide the solution anymore. So that's changed.

As for feminism, the first review I ever had in the *New York Times* said I was a feminist artist. It's always been difficult for me to be in two bodies. People ask, "How does it feel to be a woman artist?" I mean, how does it feel to not be? But the more serious answer to the question about feminist content in my work is that I've always seen that as a bourgeois movement controlled by the dominant classes in America. If Hillary Clinton breaks a glass ceiling, does that really change anything? I'm much more focused on what I'm working on now: Dump Trump. I could just do it in my sleep.

Suzanne Lacy

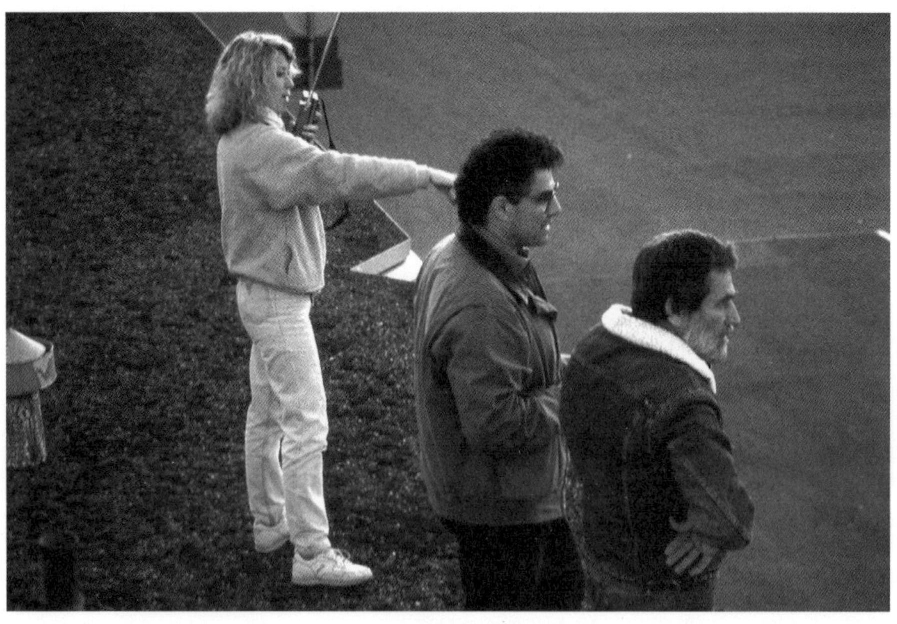

Suzanne Lacy and Allan Kaprow in a planning meeting for *Road of Poems and Borders*, 1989–90, photo by Tuula Tavi.

September 17, 2010
Artforum

In Leaving Art: Writings on Performance, Politics, and Publics 1974–2007 *(Duke University Press, 2010), the renowned artist Suzanne Lacy considers the changing politics of public space. Lacy resides in Los Angeles, where she is founding chair of the graduate public practice program at Otis College of Art and Design.*

Leaving Art seemed like an ironic, maybe humorous title for this collection of essays stretching over thirty years. Throughout my career there have been people who have left the art world to continue a trajectory of ideas and concerns within other disciplines. Today, some of the earlier aesthetic investigations are becoming more interesting again. The notion of actually leaving the art world, or metaphorically leaving through a break with conventional art markets and media, was established in the 1970s. The permeability between "art" and "life" is one of a series of concerns resurfacing now.

In one early work, for example, I practiced carpentry as art. I actually was a carpenter, and I decided to frame that "making" process as a performative artwork. People came by and watched me build walls. The actual product of the activity wasn't important; rather, we focused on the fabric of the relationships among the artist, activity, and (in this case occasional) audience. One could say that a significant project of the '70s was to rethink "audience," or "participant."

While politically America suffers from historical amnesia, it's not unusual for artists to revisit past working strategies as a result of perhaps similar social conditions. The Iraq war has some parallels to

Vietnam. Now is an interesting time to reconsider the aesthetic and ethical concerns of the '70s because, to put it plainly, the "horses' mouths" are still around. My students are interested in public artistic practices from that era, and many of these artists are still alive, and working, although sadly people like Allan Kaprow (to whom this book is dedicated) are no longer with us.

People seem to have problems categorizing my work and writing. Having been trained during the rise of performance and Conceptual art, I have a diverse output, and the essays in this book, which were originally published between 1974 and 2007, are also quite varied. It seemed useful to organize the book according to decades, although some do fall out of sequence. A project that I'm working on with the Reina Sofía museum and the Spanish Ministry of Equality, for example, echoes the subject of violence against women, one central to my work in the '70s. How that project is like, and different from, earlier works is an interesting problem within the artwork itself. How it responds to other contemporary projects on this and different subjects is of great interest to me as a conceptually oriented artist as well as a writer.

I address changing conventions of critique in *Leaving Art*. When I was an art student, the art world and the performance scene were very small. Relationships were crucial to our practice and there weren't so many people to know. Most of us traveled internationally, and our knowledge of one another's work was achieved directly. Now the art world is larger, and the marketplace dominates. Before, art historians would investigate and report dutifully on the artist's works and concerns, but now the critic-historian inserts him or herself more centrally into the writing. There are blurrings between curatorial and artistic practices where before lines were more clearly drawn.

One of my contributions to the upcoming Getty-sponsored series of exhibitions *Pacific Standard Time: Art in LA 1945–1980* is an essay I'm writing with Jennifer Flores Sternad for the exhibition *Los Angeles Goes Live*, sponsored by Los Angeles Contemporary Exhibitions. We worked with scholars and students to interview about fifty Southern California performance artists to examine linkages among various groups between 1970 and 1982—including feminists, Marxists, and African American and Chicano artists. We asked each artist to sketch a map of influences during the emergence of his or her performance work. From these we will construct webs of relationality. Unknown artists are going to emerge through this naming; surprising new influences might also appear as a result of an interrogation of that vastly interdisciplinary moment.

Tauba Auerbach

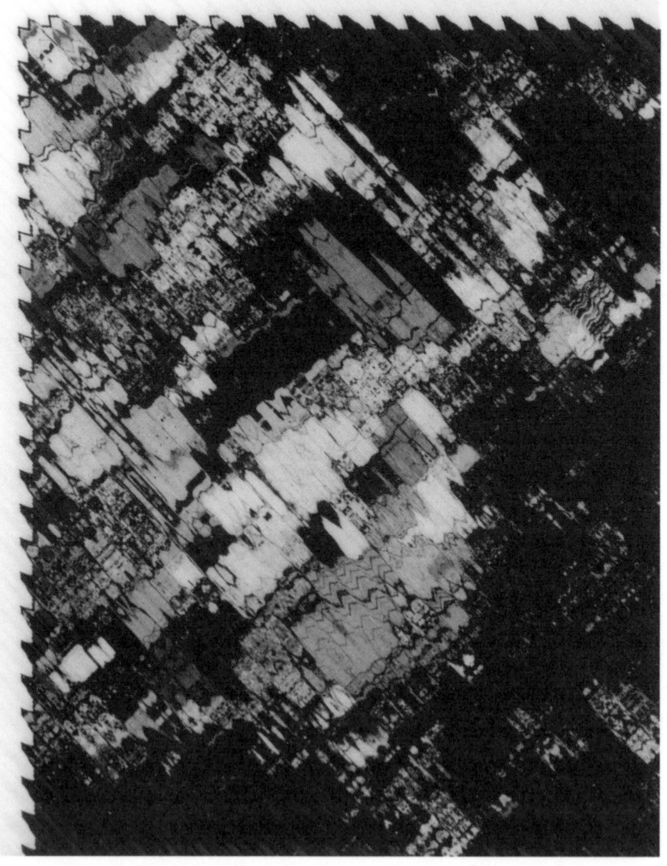

Tauba Auerbach, *Prism Scan II (Cross Polarized Mesosiderite)*, 2014, C-print, 55 × 44 inches (139.7 × 111.8 cm). Edition of 2, 1 AP. Photo by Steven Probert.

April 28, 2014
Artforum

Tauba Auerbach is a New York–based artist whose debut solo exhibition in the UK was at the Institute of Contemporary Arts in London in spring 2014. The show extended her interests in chirality and topology and took Martin Gardner's book The New Ambidextrous Universe: Symmetry and Asymmetry from Mirror Reflection to Superstrings *(2005) as a source for both the work on view and the exhibition's title.*

One of the concepts that confounded me in Gardner's *The New Ambidextrous Universe* is how, on a molecular level, asymmetry is a distinguishing feature of life. An asymmetric carbon compound, for instance, can be assembled from its constituent atoms in two ways which are mirror images of each other. Nearly all of the asymmetric compounds in living things appear as just one of their two mirror image configurations, while the exact same compounds in nonliving material are made up of 50 percent of each configuration. How baffling is it that these materials are essentially the same, but the living matter is chiral and the nonliving matter is not?

Louis Pasteur—who passed polarized light through racemic and tartaric acids—discovered this fact. Light is polarized by passing it through a grating, the structure of which is present in a slatted wall I had built to separate the exhibition space from a neighboring corridor. You could also imagine that a grating or comblike structure would have sliced the wood sculptures on the floor into their strips.

To make these pieces, I drew an irregular line on my computer tablet, which I copied, pasted, and water-jet cut across a 4-by-8-foot sheet of plywood. I laid the strips on the floor in reverse order, which yielded a rough mirror reflection of the original piece. The grain looks sort of continuous but jagged, and the overall shape of the wood is distorted by twice the amplitude of the original undulations in the wavy line. In order to create the mirror image of an asymmetrical, physical 3-D object (like this piece of wood with its asymmetrical grain), one would have to flip it over in four-dimensional space. To think about that more easily, you can go a dimension down and imagine a 2-D asymmetrical shape lying on a table.

In order to turn it into its mirror image, you would have to pick it up off the 2-D table and flip it over in 3-D space. These wood pieces take a stab at circumventing the impossibility of turning a 3-D object into its mirror image without passing it through 4-D space. My hope is that there's something ghostly about this puddle of wood on the floor, like it left our universe, went into another space, and came back.

I've been thinking so much about four and more dimensions, and I guess that working in 3-D gets me a little closer to that than working flat, so I produced mainly sculptures for this show. Most of my paintings for the last few years have been weavings, so I've been doing a lot of textile research too. There's a sculpture based on the structure of a knit stitch and one on a hook-and-eye clasp. They each have different symmetry relationships that cause them to interlock.

In the show there's also one photograph, *Prism Scan II (Cross Polarized Mesosiderite)*. This is an image from a book titled *Color Atlas of Meteorites in Thin Section*, of a piece of meteorite that was photographed with polarized light—such as Pasteur used—which I scanned through a piece of corrugated glass. The halftone of the source image is spread out and compressed periodically according to waves in the glass, and the orientation of the image flips backward and forward in each period of the wave.

I keep trying to train myself to be more ambidextrous. I'm right handed, and I've been using my computer's mouse with my left hand. I've brushed my teeth with my left hand for the last few years. Sometimes I do a meditation on symmetry, and all kinds of other little things. There's an option on the iPhone where you can invert the colors, and though it's not really a left/right reversal, it falls into the same category of "exercise" for me: to use a familiar object in a flipped way. All of this has made me realize how handed the world is, how nonambidextrous it is—the more I try to engage with the world in a symmetrical way, the more I run up against its asymmetry.

Virginia Dwan

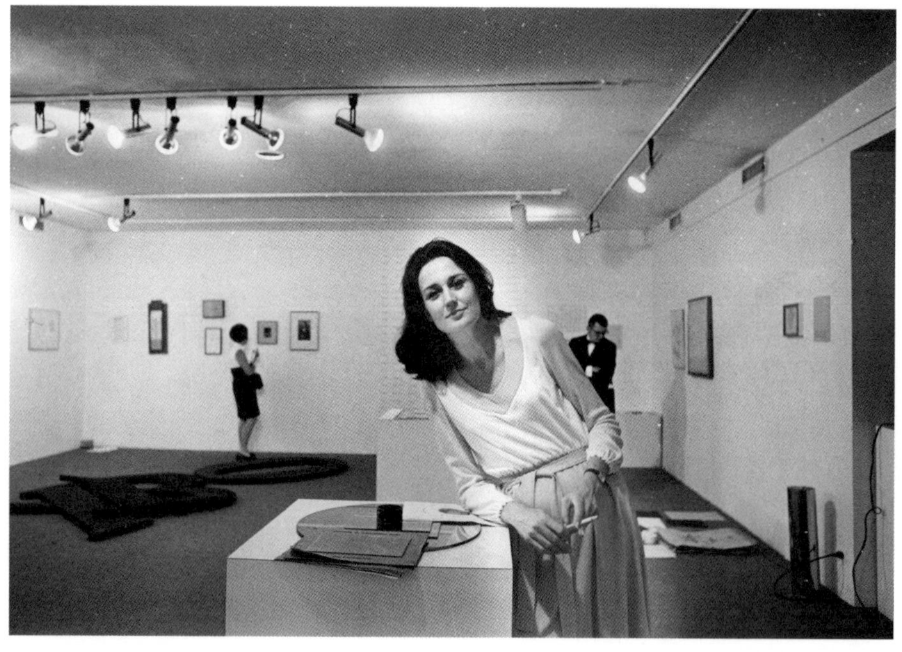

Virginia Dwan at Dwan Gallery, New York, 1969, photo by Roger Prigent.

February 11 and 14, 2014
Artforum

Virginia Dwan's philanthropy was of another art world. In 1969, she financed Michael Heizer's Double Negative *and provided funding for the publication of Carl Andre's* Seven Books of Poetry *to publisher and dealer Seth Siegelaub. A year later, she sponsored Robert Smithson's* Spiral Jetty. *Also well known in the 1960s as a dealer, Dwan opened her first Los Angeles gallery in 1959, giving Yves Klein his debut West Coast solo show in 1961. In 1965, she opened a new space in New York with Ed Kienholz's installation* Barney's Beanery *and produced landmark Minimal, Conceptual, and Land art shows. After closing her gallery in 1971, Dwan assumed another social role and began to make films with and about artists, including Sturtevant, John Cage, Mark di Suvero, Andre, and Heizer. In fall 2013, the National Gallery of Art in Washington, DC, announced Dwan's bequest of 250 works—paintings, prints, drawings, photographs, films, and artists' books—to the museum. Selected pieces were featured in* From Los Angeles to New York: The Dwan Gallery 1959–1971, *an exhibition curated by James Meyer, which opened in 2016.*

By 1959, I had wanted to have a gallery for some time, though I didn't know anything about it, really. I just went ahead and did it anyway the *Innocents Abroad* sort of thing. A few years later, when I was no longer "innocent," I built another space in Los Angeles that was much larger and had wonderful walls, lighting, floors, everything. Unfortunately, that building has been torn down now, but you entered into it through a tunnel. I loved the idea that people could cool down their eyes before seeing a show.

In that era, there weren't many precedents for women to own galleries, and feminism was only just beginning in the United States. I wasn't so concerned about that, but I do remember telling my husband that he shouldn't go to parties or dinners with me, as people always assumed it was his gallery. Of course, I wanted people to know that it was *mine*—and he was very understanding about that. But history can be cruel: art historians and critics have tended to compare and contrast me with "female dealers." Betty Parsons had a wonderful gallery, but it was a completely different time and place.

Yves Klein and Ad Reinhardt had perhaps the strongest influences on me. Yves came for his first show in Los Angeles and made new works there. My husband and I met Yves one summer in Nice, France, and he introduced me to many artists there: Arman, Niki de Saint Phalle, and Jean Tinguely. I learned back in the United States that there was a strong reaction against showing Europeans. For instance, the first exhibition I produced with Yves Klein didn't receive much press.

Reinhardt would always visit from New York when we had his openings, too. When I selected my second gallery, which was in the Westwood area of Los Angeles, I did it with him in mind: I wanted to make sure that the ceilings would be high and that his paintings would fit, as at the time they were very tall. I had an area of white marble along the floor, in front of the hanging area—to keep the viewer at a distance so one couldn't touch his surfaces. But then he showed up with the "ultimate" paintings, which are sixty inches square. On November 22, 1963, two days before that show was to open, John F. Kennedy was assassinated and we decided not to have an opening party. Then later on people came and said, "Oh, what good taste, to show only black!"

In New York, I became very interested in and involved with Minimalism and gave solo shows to Sol LeWitt and Carl Andre, and later Robert Smithson. When I moved the gallery to West Fifty-Seventh Street, I didn't have enough space for them to do very large works, so I kept the gallery in Los Angeles with my assistant John Weber still working there, and I sent the artists out there to put up their shows. A favorite memory was when Merce Cunningham, John Cage, David Tudor, and Robert Rauschenberg drove from New York in a Volkswagen bus for one of Robert's shows. They parked it in front of my house in Malibu and out of this bus came *nine* people. It was like a circus bus with endless people emerging. They had all driven from New York to Los Angeles and stopped along the way giving performances. I didn't know how they all fit, yet there they all were in the bus. In New York, many artists started reaching out to me; several were making interesting, contemplative, and quiet works. I thought that so many of these artists were wonderful, but I couldn't show them all. I hated visiting studios and seeing people's work for that reason. Still, I realized that I could help artists in different ways. In 1969, Robert Smithson told me that he wanted to do something at the airport in Fort Worth, Texas, and that he was involved with some engineers who were going to be working there. He had asked Carl Andre and Sol LeWitt and Robert Morris to also propose works for the airport site but then the project fell through. Nevertheless, Smithson, Nancy Holt, and I began to look at sites around New York and New Jersey and further south into Virginia. We ended up taking a number of trips together in search of land on which to make works. In 1968, when we couldn't find land that was available, we were inspired to organize the *Earth Works* show in the gallery. In 1969 we traveled together again, to the Yucatán, where Smithson produced his series of mirror works known as the *Nine Mirror Displacements*. When Smithson told me he was going to make *Spiral Jetty*, I wanted to make funds available for him to do so. And I wanted to be there for it.

Earth Works was a beautiful and important show, and there were all kinds of effective works. Smithson presented a few of his non-sites, and Robert Morris worked with a pile of dirt, wire, and gasoline oil, which he had collected from right around the corner from the gallery on Fifty-Seventh Street, where a building was being constructed. Michael Heizer showed big transparencies of work he'd already done, which was considerable.

From March to April of 1969, Walter De Maria showed his *Bed of Spikes* in the gallery—five steel panels on the ground with different numbers of spikes projecting from them. The show was essentially a herald for his *Lightning Field*. Because the works were very sharp, each one essentially a bed of nails, we drafted a release that visitors would sign as they entered that would absolve the gallery of responsibility if they were injured. People laughed about that, but the spikes were actually dangerous. Later, in 1974, Walter installed the first *Lightning Field* on the property of Burton and Emily Tremaine near Flagstaff, Arizona. It was made of thirty-five stainless steel poles. But when we weren't able to sell it, I ended up with these gorgeous, twenty-foot stainless steel poles in my storage space. Eventually I gave them to the Dia Foundation.

Agnes Martin was the primary artist I really wanted to work with but didn't. It was bad timing. I showed one of her works in *Ten*, in 1966, but then she left New York, saying to Robert Elkon that she was never going to paint again. And I should know now that when people say things like that, they don't really mean it! Duchamp is a case in point.

<u>PART TWO:</u>

The question of why I closed the gallery always comes up. I just ran out of energy to do it. I call it burnout. I liked having a gallery, though: I enjoyed producing shows, coming up with the advertising, and things like that. I certainly loved being with the artists. But the business of art dealing was something I was never good at. I came to realize it was really hard work for me. I suppose I would have enjoyed being a curator, but I would have had to have a free hand, which you typically do with a gallery, but not with a museum.

Many artists were leaving New York by 1971. I'd heard that some said they were fed up with the art world and wanted to get away from it, though no one ever said that directly to me. But I do know many wanted a bigger canvas. They wanted more space to work with. Particularly most of the artists I was involved with—Michael Heizer and Robert Smithson, especially.

I knew all along that I would give most of the major works I'd collected to a museum, and I found the offer that James Meyer and Harry Cooper were making from the National Gallery very compelling. In essence, they wanted to open a newly renovated building with a major show and catalogue about the gallery. On top of that, I learned that the National Gallery can never deaccession works. I couldn't refuse.

There's the idea that things could sit in storage for many years to come, and not be out in the world where people can see them and be moved by them. It depresses me. I've previously given works to museums: Heizer's *Double Negative*, for instance, to the Museum of Contemporary Art, Los Angeles, as well as six of his large-scale projected photographs (*Actual Size: Munich Rotary*, 1970) to the Whitney Museum. I've given works to the Museum of Modern Art, the Art Institute of Chicago, and the Walker Art Center, among others. But I've always felt that I wanted the collection to have the widest possible viewership—perhaps for some it will even be an introduction to Minimalism. The idea is really that people should *feel* something from the collection. When the works are finally shown at the National Gallery, the opportunity will be there for the public to linger, to absorb.

History should be constantly rewritten, and I hope that happens for the gallery. I shared many important feelings about art and artmaking with the artists I've worked with. I cared deeply about them, and part of my way to express this concern was by presenting their work. Of course the artists were always primary, absolutely. But I was never a disinterested bystander.

429

W.A.G.E.

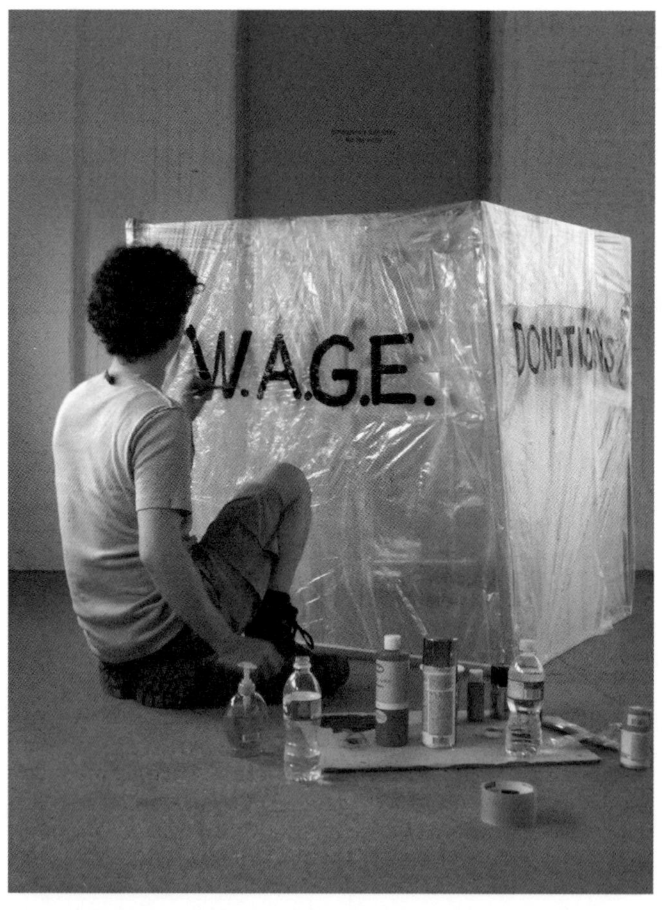

Dean Daderko preparing a complaint, suggestions, and donation box for W.A.G.E.'s booth at *No Soul for Sale: A Festival of Independents*, X Initiative, New York, June 22, 2009.

November 23, 2011
Artforum

W.A.G.E., or Working Artists in the Greater Economy, is a group of cultural workers advocating for the implementation of fee schedules within cultural institutions that contract their work. Here they discuss their first certification project at the New Museum and their work in fall 2011 at Artists Space in New York.

The project with Artists Space will be very different from our first certification at the New Museum primarily because we're now focused on certifying institutions rather than single exhibitions. Last fall, curator Lauren Cornell invited us to participate in the group show *Free* at the New Museum, but because we're not an art-making collective but rather an arts advocacy group, our participation involved negotiating artist fees for everyone in the exhibition. W.A.G.E. also submitted several other requests—some were met and others weren't. Achieving the most important component—the payment of artist fees—made it clear that this was possible *if* mandated by the curator, and this became our first experimental platform for W.A.G.E. Certification. However, the museum administration refused to meet with us regarding the inclusion of artist fees in their budget as standard practice, and they still have no policy on this matter.

Our latest collaboration began with a discussion initiated in March by Artists Space's director Stefan Kalmár and curator Richard Birkett about the payment of artist fees, among other hot button issues. Once we started talking, it became clear that paying fees and providing production support is very much a priority for Artists Space. We decided to work toward W.A.G.E. Certifying them but didn't know what that would mean in practice: How much would a minimum artist fee be? Would it be different for solo and group exhibitions? Would it be relative to the size of the institution's budget? Would fees be mandated by funders or by the organization's board? Would there be oversight? Clearly, answering these questions was going to take time, investigation, and discussion, so W.A.G.E. proposed a temporary partnership with Artists Space to help us in that process.

In January, we'll begin the first in a series of public forums and think tanks at Artists Space involving artists, activists, grant makers, arts administrators, curators, sociologists, and the public in an extended conversation about the economic practices of arts organizations. Each event is designed around a specific set of concerns relevant to W.A.G.E. Certification—and to the economic health of the community as a whole—in service of our goal of having fully established the tenets of W.A.G.E. Certification at the conclusion of the partnership. And if compliant, Artists Space will become the first organization to receive Institutional W.A.G.E. Certification.

Artists Space and W.A.G.E. will host and participate in this critical dialogue, but the equal participation and feedback of the community is also essential. How the discussion takes place is still a question that we're going to answer with the help of the exponentially expanding arts activist community coming out of Occupy Wall Street.

But we can tell you about a few of the subjects: the first event, a presentation by artist and economist Hans Abbing, author of *Why Are Artists Poor: The Exceptional Economy of the Arts*, will take place at Artists Space on January 6 at 7:00 p.m. "Unionizing and Other Models" will bring together international artist-activist groups to look at ways of organizing art workers around alternative economic models; "Funders Talk" will be a discussion between key government and foundation funders about the viability of establishing a verification process to ensure that funds are indeed being redistributed to artists in the form of fees and other support, essentially creating a system of accountability between nonprofits and their funders; and "Profit Sharing" will be a discussion about the problems of support and exploitation between commercial galleries and nonprofit organizations in the commissioning and production of artworks.

We'll organize and facilitate viable and productive activism among statistical researchers of artist communities, legal advisers, institutional directors, alternative economy activists, artists, performers, independent curators, and union organizers. Artists Space is being very transparent with their budget and institutional structure, which helps us to enter into dialogue with their staff and board members to develop strategies that will increase pressure on—and implement necessary change within—the arts community.

We're also going to release the 2010 W.A.G.E. Artist Survey results as part of our work with Artists Space. An important hard fact is that 58 percent of the 577 survey respondents who exhibited at a nonprofit organization or museum in New York's five boroughs between 2005 and 2010 didn't receive any form of payment, compensation, or reimbursement—including the coverage of any expenses. These conditions are unacceptable to us.

Yoko Ono

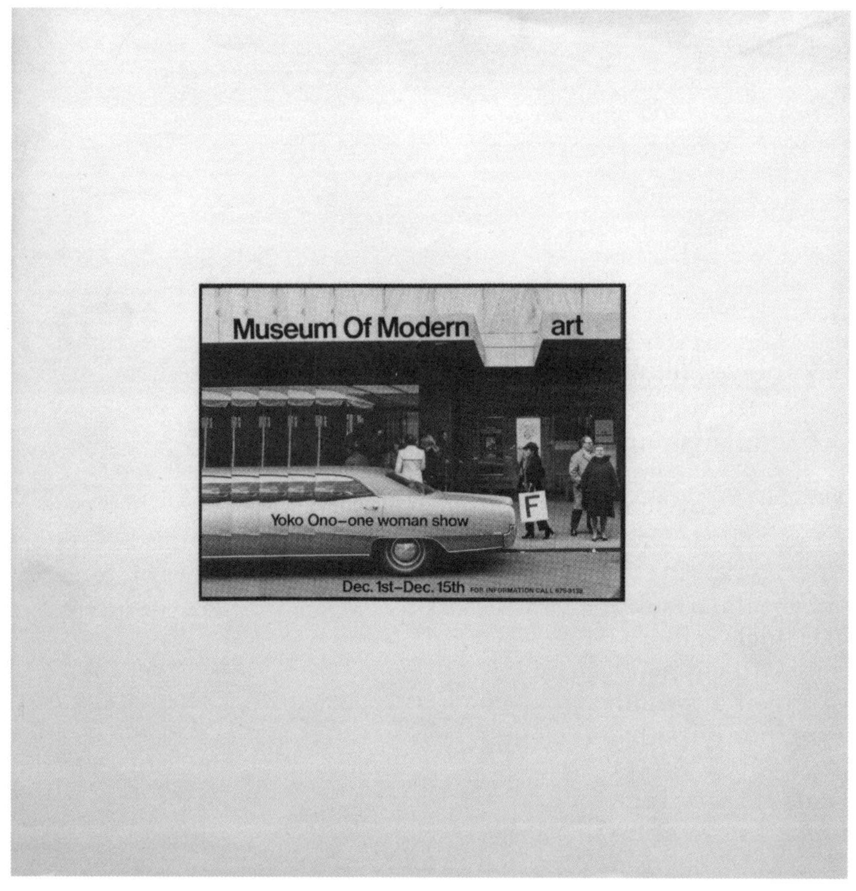

Yoko Ono, *Museum of Modern (F)art*, 1971, artist's book, offset.
The Museum of Modern Art Library, New York.

May 13, 2015
Artforum

In December 1971, Yoko Ono famously announced that she was to have a solo exhibition at the Museum of Modern Art in New York. The supposed exhibition was, in fact, a conceptual artwork, executed without the participation of the museum itself. In May 2015, Ono opened a solo show at MoMA, which featured her early works on paper, paintings, installations, performances, and audio and instruction pieces.

What I did between 1960 and '71 seems to have influenced more people than any other periods of my work. But I really don't know how I survived. Whenever an idea for an artwork came to me, I would act on it. I would get so excited and make the work, and, at the time, it seemed nobody wanted to know. So, I always thought, OK, on to the next idea. I've gone through life like that; there was never any time to commit suicide or anything.

To drop out of school in 1960 was sort of an unusual thing to do, but for me, college was too much and so I left and went to New York City. It was an exciting time. I already knew a few people in the music world. Many of them had far-out ideas about art; they couldn't just do a show in an ordinary gallery. Most were composers who didn't fit in at Carnegie Hall. At the time it seemed there was no good venue to present work. I decided I would get a place and begin doing concerts there. I remember I first had this thought while walking on Broadway, around Ninety-Sixth Street. I noticed the second floor of a building, where you could see everything that was going on—ballet dancers were exercising. So I went up there, and perhaps witlessly, asked, "Is this place for rent?" They were very polite about it and said, "No, we're using it." Not deterred, I thought there must be a location like that, and finally a friend of mine told me to go downtown and check out the "lofts." In those days people didn't really think about lofts as places to live or work—they just thought they were dangerous. But I got a loft and it was really great.

Many people came to see the concerts, probably because there were no other loft concerts going on. Also, I think the fact that John Cage, Peggy Guggenheim, David Tudor, and others came to the very first show, right after a very heavy snow, was important. But every event was very exciting. I eventually did my stuff too, though I didn't want to be the first one. I also ended up sleeping there. I felt that it was important. I don't know why. I collected about six orange crates and put them together as my bed. It was right underneath the skylight. It was beautiful.

The incredible thing about this MoMA show is that in '71 I staged my "first" show at MoMA from December 1st to the 15th. In those days the museum hardly presented women or Asian artists. Nobody thought much about it. I put an advertisement in the *Village Voice* for my "one woman show" at the museum. I also printed a catalogue titled the *Museum of Modern (F)art*. And I posted a sign on the museum's entrance that said I had released flies in the museum, and that everyone was invited to find them throughout the city. What was great was that MoMA came to me recently and said they were interested in "my show" that I did there in '71. They said they wanted to do it now, as a real exhibition. And I thought, Well, that's pretty hip, OK.

Again, this was something I'd mostly forgotten about, so I was glad when the curators said that we could transform the idea. People always say to me, "Yoko, you know we're never going to have world peace, right?" And I think, Yes, we're going to have it if you believe in it. So even from that point of view I can say, this happened and then forty years later it became a reality. It's not going to be a reality the next day. But what you're thinking of, what you're envisioning now, *is* going to be a reality—so just be careful.

From the feminist point of view, it was important to me to be open about my experiences. There was a time, about five years ago, when people started to not want to talk about feminism—as if it was a dirty word or something. I think that some people successfully made sure that we became intimidated. But, logically, feminism should go on. It's not natural to keep women down. For one thing, it's essential to have women's energy, and without it, there's an incredible imbalance in the world. That's why we have all this illness, violence, and war. It's really basic, if you just think about it. It doesn't have to be so complicated; things can be simpler than that.

Acknowledgments

Thank you first and foremost to all the wonderful people speaking their brilliant minds in this book and to those who provided valuable feedback as I put it together: Nancy Goldring, Adam Putnam, Katy Siegel, Brian Sholis, and Lisa Tan. Huge thanks to Karma (to Brendan Dugan for taking this project on, to Miles Champion, Amelia Farley, Paige Hanserd, and David Schoerner for their design and editing expertise), to my *November* comrades, to the publications for permitting reprints, and to all the eagle-eyed editors and copy editors who worked with me over the years—you know who you are. I'm forever grateful to Adrian Piper for granting us the cover image and for always being game to chat. Finally, my deepest gratitude goes to Arthur Ou.

Image Credits

Cover
From the portfolio *10: Artist as Catalyst*, 1992. Published by the Alternative Museum, New York. Collection of the Museum of Modern Art, New York © Adrian Piper Research Archive Foundation Berlin.

p. 14.
Adrian Piper, from the suite *Food for the Spirit*, 1971. Collection of the Museum of Modern Art, New York. © Adrian Piper Research Archive Foundation Berlin.

p. 26.
Private Collection. © Adrian Piper Research Archive Foundation Berlin.

p. 36.
Agnès Varda, © succession varda.

p. 40.
Aki Sasamoto, photo by Arturo Vidich, courtesy of the artist.

p. 44.
Alex Bag, courtesy of the artist.

p. 60.
Anohni, photo by Colin Whitaker.

p. 64.
Aura Rosenberg, courtesy of the artist and Martos Gallery.

p. 68.
Beryl Korot, courtesy of bitforms gallery, New York, photo by John Berens.

p. 72.
Beverly Semmes, photo by Jason Mandella. Collection of the Frances Young Tang Teaching Museum and Art Gallery at Skidmore College, Saratoga Springs, NY, courtesy of Susan Inglett Gallery, New York.

p. 76.
© Carol Bove and David Zwirner Gallery.

p. 80
Carolee Schneemann, photo by Terry Schutte.

p. 86.
Catherine Christer Hennix, *Traversée du Fantasme,* Stedelijk Museum Amsterdam, 2018, photo by Gert Jan van Rooij.

p. 90.
Claudia Rankine, © Toyin Ojih Odutola. Courtesy of the artist and Jack Shainman Gallery, New York.

p. 96.
Constance DeJong, photo by Bureau, New York.

p. 100.
Dianna Molzan, photo by Brian Forrest.

p. 104.
Donna Haraway, still from *Donna Haraway: Story Telling for Earthly Survival,* directed by Fabrizio Terranova.

p. 108.
© Dorothea Rockburne / Artists Rights Society (ARS), New York, gift of Jeanne Lang Mathews.

p. 112.
© Ebony G. Patterson.

p. 116.
Elaine Reichek, courtesy of the artist and Marinaro, New York. Photo by Paul Kennedy.

p. 120.
Eleanor Antin, courtesy of the artist.

p. 126.
Ellie Ga, courtesy of the artist and Bureau, New York.

p. 130.
fierce pussy, courtesy of the artist. www.fiercepussy.com.

p. 138.
Frances Stark, Portikus, Frankfurt, photo by Katrin Schilling.

p. 142.
Georgia Sagri, Documenta 14, Athens and Kassel; photo by Panos Kokkinias; photo copyright: Georgia Sagri; courtesy of the artist and The Breeder, Athens.

p. 146.
Hong-Kai Wang, *Music While We Work*, The Heard & the Unheard—Soundscape Taiwan, Taiwan Pavilion, 54th Venice Biennale, Yunlin, Taiwan, 2011, photo by Chen You-Wei.

p. 150.
Howardena Pindell, courtesy of the artist and Garth Greenan Gallery, New York.

p. 158.
Iman Issi, courtesy of the artist and Rodeo London/ Piraeus.

p. 162.
Jeanine Oleson, *Hear,
Here*, experimental opera
at the New Museum, June
13–14, 2014. Writer-director:
Jeanine Oleson; composers:
Rainy Orteca and Kelly Pratt
(aurihorn solos); performers:
Beth Griffith, David Gould,
Lisa Reynolds, Sister, Diwa
Tamrong, Tony Torn, and
nyx zierhut; musicians:
Rainy Orteca, Kelly Pratt,
and John Michael Swartz;
costumes: Kim Charles
Kay; lighting design: Derek
Wright. Photo by Marina
Ancona.

p. 166.
Jennifer West, commissioned
by Tate Modern, London.
Made as part of live performance for Tate's Turbine Hall
for Long Weekend 2009. Curated by Stuart Comer, photo
by David Thain.

p. 170.
Jessamyn Fiore, photo by
Tim Nighswander.

p. 174.
Jesse Jones, *The Struggle
Against Ourselves*, 2011.

p. 178.
Jo Baer, photo by Ralph
Goertz © IKS-Medienarchiv.

p. 186.
© 2021 Joan Jonas / Artists
Rights Society (ARS), New
York

p. 190.
Joan Semmel, courtesy of
Alexander Gray Associates,
New York, photo by Taylor
Miller.

p. 198.
Judy Chicago, © 2021 Judy
Chicago / Artists Rights Soci-
ety (ARS), New York.

p. 206.
Julia Bryan-Wilson, photo on
book cover by Robert Morris,
installing *Untitled [Concrete,
Timbers, Steel]*, Whitney
Museum of American Art,
New York, 1970. © 2021 The
Estate of Robert Morris /
Artists Rights Society (ARS),
New York.

p. 210.
Karla Black, courtesy of
the artist and Modern Art,
London.

p. 214.
Kathryn Andrews, courtesy of
David Kordansky Gallery, Los
Angeles, photo by
Andreas Cortellini.

p. 222.
Lisa Tan, courtesy of the
artist and Galleri Riis, Oslo,
photo by Lisa Tan.

p. 226.
Lisi Raskin, image courtesy
of the artist.

p. 230.
Liz Deschenes, photo by Jorit
Aust.

p. 234.
Lorraine O'Grady, image
courtesy of the Savannah
College of Art and Design.

p. 238.
Lorrie Moore,
Christopher Berkey/The New
York Times/Redux.

p. 244.
Lucy Dodd, courtesy of the
artist and David Lewis.

p. 248.
Lucy R. Lippard, Gramsci
banner by Mike Glier.

p. 260.
Lucy R. Lippard, photo by
Peter Woodruff, ca. 1994,
courtesy of Lucy R. Lippard.

p. 264.
Lucy McKenzie, courtesy of
the artist and Galerie Buch-
holz, Berlin/Cologne/New
York.

p. 268.
Lucy Skaer, courtesy of the
artist and Peter Freeman, Inc.

p. 272.
Lynda Benglis, *Lynda Benglis*,
Irish Museum of Modern
Art, Kilmainham, Dublin,
November 4, 2009–January
24, 2010.

p. 276.
© Lynda Benglis / VAGA at
Artists Rights Society (ARS),
New York, photo by
Denis Mortell Photography.

p. 280.
Lynne Tillman, photo by
Heather Sten.

p. 284.
© Marlene McCarty, courte-
sy of the artist and Sikkema
Jenkins & Co., New York.

p. 288.
Mary Beth Edelson, courtesy
of David Lewis and the
Estate of Mary Beth Edelson.

p. 292.
Mary Ellen Carroll, © 2010
Mary Ellen Carroll / MEC,
studios prototype 180, photo
by Kenny Trice.

p. 296.
© Mary Heilmann, photo by
Stefan Altenburger Photography Zurich, courtesy of the
artist, 303 Gallery, New York,
and Hauser & Wirth.

p. 300.
Mary Kelly, installation view of *Mary Kelly: Four Works in Dialogue*, at Moderna Museet, Stockholm, 2010. © Mary Kelly; courtesy of the artist, Mitchell-Innes & Nash, New York, and Vielmetter, Los Angeles.

p. 304.
Mary Mattingly, *Waterpod in the East River*, 2009, courtesy of the artist.

p. 308.
Mimi Thi Nguyen, photo by Rachel Lauren Storm.

p. 318.
Monir Shahroudy Farmanfarmaian, courtesy of The Estate of Monir Shahroudy Farmanfarmaian and James Cohan, New York, photo by Phoebe d'Heurle.

p. 320.
Mira Schor, *Black Thought Bubble*, notebook page, 2007, ink on paper, 7 ½ × 4 ½ inches, cover of *A Decade of Negative Thinking: Essays on Art, Politics, and Daily Life* (Duke University Press, 2009).

p. 328.
Nan Goldin, photo by TW Collins.

p. 336.
Nell Painter, courtesy of the artist and Aferro Gallery.

p. 352.
Polly Apfelbaum, courtesy of the artist, Galerie Nächst St Stephen, Vienna, and Frith Street Gallery, London.

p. 356.
Rachel Foullon, courtesy of Rachel Foullon, photo by Robert Wedemeyer.

p. 360.
Rachel Mason, performance from *The Ambassadors* series, 2004.

p. 364.
Rebecca Solnit, photo by Adrian Mendoza.

p. 368.
© Rebecca Warren, courtesy of Matthew Marks Gallery, photo by the Art Institute of Chicago.

p. 372.
Renée Green, *Begin Again, Begin Again*, 2015, film still. Courtesy of the artist, Free Agent Media, and Bortolami Gallery, New York.

p. 376.
Rhonda Lieberman, photo by Dana Byerly.

p. 384.
Ruby Sky Stiler, courtesy of the artist and Nicelle Beauchene Gallery.

p. 388.
Sakiko Sugawa, courtesy of Social Kitchen.

p. 392.
Sara Greenberger Rafferty, installation view, *Bananas*, The Kitchen, January 9– March 7, 2009, curated by Matthew Lyons, photo by Adam Reich, courtesy of the artist.

p. 396.
Sarah Crowner, courtesy of the artist.

p. 400.
Shannon Ebner, organized by LA><ART, Los Angeles, and the Hammer Museum, Los Angeles; installation view, Culver City, CA. Courtesy of the artist, Altman Siegel Gallery, San Francisco, kaufmann repetto, Milan/New York, and Sadie Coles HQ, London.

p. 404.
Sophie Calle, © 2021 Sophie Calle / Artists Rights Society (ARS), New York / ADAGP, Paris. Courtesy of the artist and Paula Cooper Gallery, New York, photo by Damien Saadtjian.

p. 412.
Sue Coe, *It Got Away*, © 1990 Sue Coe, courtesy of Galerie St. Etienne, New York.

p. 416.
Suzanne Lacy, Suzanne Lacy and Allan Kaprow in a planning meeting for *Road of Poems and Borders*, 1989–90. Photo courtesy of Suzanne Lacy Studio.

p. 420.
Tauba Auerbach, courtesy of Tauba Auerbach, photo by Steven Probert.

p. 424.
Virginia Dwan, courtesy of Dwan Gallery Archive.

p. 430.
Image courtesy of W.A.G.E.

p. 434.
Yoko Ono, *The Museum of Modern (F)art*, 1971, artist's book, published by the artist for a fictional exhibition at MoMA, New York, *YOKO ONO – ONE WOMAN SHOW*, December 1–15, 1971 © Yoko Ono.

Lauren O'Neill-Butler
Let's Have a Talk:
Conversations with Women
on Art and Culture

Published by
Karma Books, New York

Edition of 2,000

Publication © 2021
Lauren O'Neill-Butler and
Karma Books, New York

Texts © Lauren O'Neill-Butler

Artwork © the artists

Cover:
Adrian Piper
Let's Talk, 1992
serigraph
26 × 26 inches

ISBN: 978-1-949172-53-9